Flexible Authoritarianism

RECENT TITLES IN

OXFORD STUDIES IN CULTURE AND POLITICS
Clifford Bob and James M. Jasper, General Editors

Base Towns
Local Contestation of Global U.S. Military Presence in Korea and Japan
Claudia Junghyun Kim

The Return of the Native
Can Liberalism Safeguard Us Against Nativism?
Jan Willem Duyvendak and Josip Kešić with Timothy Stacy

Rally 'round the Flag
The Search for National Honor and Respect in Times of Crisis
Yuval Feinstein

Gains and Losses
How Protestors Win and Lose
James M. Jasper, Luke Elliott-Negri, Isaac Jabola-Carolus, Marc Kagan, Jessica Mahlbacher, Manès Weisskircher, and Anna Zhelnina

The Silk Road
Connecting Histories and Futures
Tim Winter

Unconventional Combat
Intersectional Action in the Veterans' Peace Movement
Michael A. Messner

Discursive Turns and Critical Junctures
Debating Citizenship after the Charlie Hebdo Attacks
Donatella della Porta, Pietro Castelli Gattinara, Konstantinos Eleftheriadis, and Andrea Felicetti

Democracy Reloaded
Inside Spain's Political Laboratory from 15-M to Podemos
Cristina Flesher Fominaya

Public Characters
The Politics of Reputation and Blame
James M. Jasper, Michael P. Young, and Elke Zuern

Empire's Legacy
Roots of a Far-Right Affinity in Contemporary France
John W.P. Veugelers

Situational Breakdowns
Understanding Protest Violence and other Surprising Outcomes
Anne Nassauer

Democratic Practice
Origins of the Iberian Divide in Political Inclusion
Robert M. Fishman

Contentious Rituals
Parading the Nation in Northern Ireland
Jonathan S. Blake

Contradictions of Democracy
Vigilantism and Rights in Post-Apartheid South Africa
Nicholas Rush Smith

Plausible Legality
Legal Culture and Political Imperative in the Global War on Terror
Rebecca Sanders

Legacies and Memories in Movements
Justice and Democracy in Southern Europe
Donatella della Porta, Massimiliano Andretta, Tiago Fernandes, Eduardo Romanos, and Markos Vogiatzoglou

Taking Root
Human Rights and Public Opinion in the Global South
James Ron, Shannon Golden, David Crow, and Archana Pandya

Curated Stories
The Uses and Misuses of Storytelling
Sujatha Fernandes

The Human Right to Dominate
Nicola Perugini and Neve Gordon

Some Men
Feminist Allies and the Movement to End Violence Against Women
Michael A. Messner, Max A. Greenberg, and Tal Peretz

Flexible Authoritarianism: Cultivating Ambition and Loyalty in Russia
Anna Schwenck

Flexible Authoritarianism

Cultivating Ambition and Loyalty in Russia

ANNA SCHWENCK

OXFORD
UNIVERSITY PRESS

Oxford University Press is a department of the University of Oxford. It furthers
the University's objective of excellence in research, scholarship, and education
by publishing worldwide. Oxford is a registered trade mark of Oxford University
Press in the UK and certain other countries.

Published in the United States of America by Oxford University Press
198 Madison Avenue, New York, NY 10016, United States of America.

© Oxford University Press 2024

All rights reserved. No part of this publication may be reproduced, stored in
a retrieval system, or transmitted, in any form or by any means, without the
prior permission in writing of Oxford University Press, or as expressly permitted
by law, by license, or under terms agreed with the appropriate reproduction
rights organization. Inquiries concerning reproduction outside the scope of the
above should be sent to the Rights Department, Oxford University Press, at the
address above.

You must not circulate this work in any other form
and you must impose this same condition on any acquirer.

Library of Congress Cataloging-in-Publication Data
Names: Schwenck, Anna, author.
Title: Flexible authoritarianism : cultivating ambition and
loyalty in Russia / Anna Schwenck.
Description: United States of America : Oxford University Press, [2024] |
Series: Oxford studies in culture and politics |
Includes bibliographical references and index.
Identifiers: LCCN 2023033919 | ISBN 9780197751589 (hardback) |
ISBN 9780197751596 (paperback) | ISBN 9780197751619 (epub)
Subjects: LCSH: Authoritarianism—Social aspects—Russia (Federation) |
Neoliberalism—Social aspects—Russia (Federation) | Russia (Federation)—
Politics and government. | Russia (Federation)—Social life and customs.
Classification: LCC JN6695 .S33 2024 | DDC 320.530947—dc23/eng/20230926
LC record available at https://lccn.loc.gov/2023033919

DOI: 10.1093/oso/9780197751589.001.0001

Contents

Preface ix

1. Introduction: Flexible Authoritarianism, Loyalty, and Quests for Change — 1
2. Interlude: Entrepreneurial Start-Up Culture Meets Soviet-Style Suspicions: Reflections on Two Russian Youth-Leadership Camps — 28
3. Soviet Traditions in Service of Flexible Authoritarianism — 41
4. How Flexible Authoritarianism Looks and Feels — 69
5. Loyal Youths' Individualist Quests for Change: Self-Development for the Good of All — 110
6. Professionalizing Patriots: The Branding and Staging of Heroic Masculinity — 159
7. Conclusion — 188

Appendix I: Methodological Approach and Description of Empirical Research — 197
Appendix II: Overview of Youth-Leadership Summer Camps in Russia — 217
Notes — 225
Bibliography — 275
Index — 307

Preface

In 2013, when I began the research that forms the basis of this book, international news headlines were filled with hope for a democratizing wave in Russia following persistent country-wide protests against fraudulent elections. Ten years later, Russia's cruel war in Ukraine and the Putin government's severe punishment of dissenters prompt observers to ask how Russian citizens, and young people in particular, relate to these events. While my initial inquiry preceded these developments, the book that has resulted may nevertheless reveal some of the reasons why ambitious young citizens in Russia's provinces have supported the broad narratives legitimating the government's actions, even as they criticize the country's rampant corruption, favoritism, and infrastructural decay. The book may also engender debates about the two decades of Putinist rule leading up to the current war—a period whose sociopolitical significance exceeds a narrow focus on Putinism and, at times, even on Russia as a polity. Though the war may have raised public interest in Russia as a society, my intention with this research was always to uncover more general trends, such as the interweaving of authoritarian practices and neoliberal techniques that are neither Russia-specific nor exclusive to states widely regarded as authoritarian.

This book draws largely on my PhD research, which I pursued within the framework of the European Doctoral Program in the Berlin Graduate School of Social Sciences at the Humboldt-Universität zu Berlin, Germany. It would not have been possible without funding from various institutions. Besides the scholarship pertaining to my position as a researcher in the graduate school, which included a budget for research-related travel, my work was facilitated and funded through an Erasmus Mundus Action 2, Strand 1 grant in the European Community Mobility Program called "Aurora— Towards Modern and Innovative Higher Education." Granted to cover a period of twenty-four months, this support entailed a provision that the Russian Research University for the Humanities in Moscow would host me as a visiting researcher during my stays in Russia. The European Community Mobility Program was administered by the University of Turku, Finland. I was also granted a six-month dissertation-completion scholarship by the

Centre for East European and International Studies (*ZOiS*). I was able to finance the professional transcription of Russian-language interviews through an Equal Opportunities Fund (*Frauenfördermittel*) from the Department of Social Sciences at Humboldt-Universität.

I am very grateful to my dissertation committee—sociologist Klaus Eder and political scientists Silvia von Steinsdorff and Valerie Sperling—for their valuable guidance, critique, and intellectual exchange during the various stages of my PhD-related research and writing process. Nicole Doerr not only forwarded the advertisement for the PhD position and urged me to apply for it, but also motivated me to send a book proposal to Oxford University Press. From the very start of this project, Mischa Gabowitsch provided me most generously with contacts, advice, and multiple opportunities to participate in relevant intellectual debates, such as the roundtable conference "Societal Transformation in Russia since 1980" at the Potsdam Einstein Forum in 2016. There I met, among others, Aleksandr Bikbov, who supported me, as did Valerie Sperling, Nicole Doerr, Antony Pattathu, Anna Fruhstorfer, and Félix Krawatzek, in turning the dissertation into a book. Another important forum of intellectual exchange was the Berlin Study Group on the Soviet and Post-Soviet Self, including among others Mischa Gabowitsch and Polina Aronson. The research for this book was considerably shaped by ideas and debates that I became acquainted with through university seminars led by Olga Malinova, Alexei Yurchak, Kristin Luker, Klaus Eder, Grit Straßenberger, Matthias Rothe, Gert Pickel, Susan Morrissey, Alena Ledeneva, Sean Hanley, Philipp Ther, Stefanie Diekmann, Detlef Pollack, and Reinhard Blänkner, several of which I attended as a visiting student.

At Humboldt-Universität I was supported from the very start by various people who participated, like myself, in Silvia von Steinsdorff's research colloquium, which was characterized by its exceptionally constructive criticism and benevolent intellectual exchange. I am especially grateful to Nargiza Abdullaeva, Ilya Levin, Maryna Shevtsova, Nadja Douglas, and Anna Fruhstorfer. When the youth organization that I had planned to research was dissolved in 2013, Professor Steinsdorff and the colloquium's encouragement motivated me nevertheless to stick with my initial research questions and embark on an even more explorative project. Through the Berlin Graduate School of Social Sciences, I met Nino Khelaia and Guilia Borri with whom I share to date an interest in neoliberalism and Mihály Gyimesi who, like me, researches authoritarian forms of stimulating bottom-up support.

I am grateful to Sevil Yakhyayeva for polishing my Russian and drafting my applications to various youth-leadership summer camps.

In Russia, I was supported by several local scholars, above all Sergei Margaril, Olga Malinova, Ivan Klimov, Oleg Oberemko, and Elena Omelchenko. During the project's field research phases I benefited enormously from discussions with and practical support from Safura Zavaree, Olesya Shayduk-Immerman, Aleksandr Bikbov, Andreas Meister, Laia Vicens, Daria Krivonos, Lena Govorina, Ellie Mack, Darina, Dasha, Natasha, Katia, Asia, Iulia, Ilgis, and Vadim. Olga Reznikova in particular was a wonderful conversation partner during and after my time in Russia; she supported me in identifying frameworks that allowed me to tie my findings to existing academic debates that exceeded the literature on Russian national identity and patriotism. Sima, Baatr, Ulla Pape, and Christian Fröhlich helped me to frame interview questions in Russian and prepare interviews. The Zakharov family invited me into their intellectual home and provided me with warm clothes when my passport was stuck at the visa office. Conversations with Anna Poltavtseva, Ksenia Meshkova, Tatiana Golova, and Ina Schröder were most helpful during various phases of data analysis. I am also grateful to Heiko Pleines and Regina Elsner, for invitations to discussion groups and conferences, as well as for helpful comments on my research. I thank Robert Fine, Ricca Edmondson, Elan Reisner, Katharina Buck, and Dasha Che for their constructive criticism and endorsement.

The final phase of the PhD would have been much more difficult without the support of researchers in a collectively-run office in Berlin, especially Jochen Lingelbach, Doris Liebscher, Sophie Schmäing, and Kevin Stützel. I will not forget our uplifting conversations over the meals that we enjoyed at Türkiyem and Gözleme restaurants. Hannah Fitsch's tremendous help enabled me to finally get my PhD over the line by making a plan and sticking to it.

I am thankful for the intriguing debates that I had on the role of popular culture in strengthening authoritarianism with all members of the transnational project "Popular Music and the Rise of Populism in Europe"—in particular, Emília Barna and Ágnes Patakfalvi-Czirják who, along with Mihály Gyimesi, shared with me many insights into Hungarian politics and popular culture. Not least, I am grateful to my current employer, sociologist Katharina Inhetveen, for hiring me on a temporarily part-time basis until fall 2021, so that I could work on completing the manuscript.

I thank Sima and Elena Renje for their wonderful help with updating the research on Russian summer camps and checking transliterations and Russian entries in the bibliography. I thank Sebastian Zahn for support with downloading video clips from various platforms before they were deleted, Aleksej Tikhonov for advice on formulations and putting me in touch with Elena, and Dion Malcolm Eaby-Lomas and Simon Ferdinand for double checking endnotes and help with the bibliography. Lebogang Mokwena, Ulriche Jantjes, Duane Jethro, Lebohang Banda, and Liz Gunner cheered me up during a phase of final revisions that coincided with a research stay in South Africa.

I thank the co-editors of the Oxford Studies in Culture and Politics Series, Clifford Bob and James Jasper, for their support. The book's anonymous reviewers and a delegate of the press strongly encouraged me to reflect upon my results in light of the Russo-Ukrainian war, foreground my ethnographic observations, and strengthen my argument's footing in cultural analysis. I am grateful to James Cook at Oxford University Press for his most helpful comments and professional yet heartening communication. Likewise, it was a pleasure collaborating with Sarah Ebel, the project editor at Oxford University Press; Nirenjena Joseph, project manager at Newgen Knowledge Works; and the copy editor Joe Edwardes-Evans. Lucy Duggan was invaluable in assisting me with translating Russian quotes into English and in language editing the first drafts of Chapters 4 and 5. This book would not have been possible—neither conceptually nor language-wise—without the support, guidance, and meticulous work of Sarah Rabkin.

I had initially planned to include photographs of Russian youth-leadership camps, summer camps for children, and pictures of Russian vigilante-entrepreneurs' merchandise on online platforms—but, in the end, seeking publication permissions from Russian authorities in the midst of a war that they frame as being waged against Western domination struck me as a vain pursuit.

The war's repercussions also affect the way in which I thank those whose support and guidance have been pivotal for the intellectual debates and research on which I draw in this book. As a person who did not grow up in a Russian-speaking country and whose first language is not Russian, I am deeply indebted to numerous people who, to date, live in Russia and Belarus. As much as I would wish to mention their full names, I have decided to use only first names to avoid drawing any harmful attention to them. I hope that at some point another version of this preface can be published that gives them the full acknowledgment that they deserve.

Friends are a crucial part of my life, and I am happy for my close connections with many, old and new, despite my being on the road as a commuter and researcher for many years. In particular, exchanges with my close friends and colleagues Olga Reznikova, Emeline Fourment, Iwona Janicka, and Katharina Lux have shaped my thinking and a healthy attitude toward intellectual work.

A special thanks goes to Jenya, the friend who introduced me to so many things, including the memoirs of Nadezhda Yakovlevna Mandelstam, the art of Louise Bourgeois, all of Zemfira's albums, and the benefits of Cognac after a day spent in the cold. My happiest times in Russia were with Jenya and her circle of friends. My other special thanks goes to my love and companion, Georg, who has kept reminding me of the beautiful and daunting fact that our experience of time is not linear. His encouragement, usually in the form of a reminder that living through difficulties is a necessary part of (research) adventures, also comforted me when given from afar.

This book is dedicated to Galina Arkadevna, who began teaching me Russian when I was a nineteen-year-old volunteer arriving in Belarus with only a few basic phrases in my repertoire. The research that informs this book would not have been possible without her warmth and intellectual charm, which enlivened our biweekly evening lessons in her Minsk apartment.

Flexible Authoritarianism: Cultivating Ambition and Loyalty in Russia

Permissions

An earlier version of Chapter 5 was published as "Russia's Vigilante YouTube Stars. Digital Entrepreneurship and Heroic Masculinity in the Service of Flexible Authoritarianism," in *Europe-Asia Studies*, Volume 74, Issue 7 (2022): 1166–89. I thank the publisher for their permission to use that material here.

I submitted an earlier version of Chapter 5 as well as several sections of Chapters 2, 3, and 4 as part of my PhD thesis, "Legitimacy in an Authoritarian Polity: Government-Sponsored Summer Camps and Youth Participation in Russia," to Humboldt University Berlin in 2018. Copies of the thesis are stored on microfiche in the university library. The university grants all rights to former PhD students to use thesis chapters for later publications.

Note on Transliteration

All Russian terms and names are transliterated according to the ALA-LC (Library of Congress) Romanization without Diacritics. In ALA-LC the Cyrillic soft sign is transliterated with a single quotation mark (ь: '), and the hard sign with a double quotation mark (ъ: "). Examples: Русский язык: *Russkii iazyk*; Культурность: Kul'turnost'

I do not use this transliteration for the names of well-known politicians, public figures, and institutions. For instance, former Russian president Boris Yeltsin is not spelled according to the transliteration (which would be *Boris El'tsin*). Likewise, my spelling of the Federal Youth Agency *Rosmolodezh* conforms with other English-language academic titles, but departs from the correct transliteration (which would be *Rosmolodezh'*). Equally, the names of researchers working in Russia, who have either published in English or have English web profiles, appear as they do in these publications and profiles. Only when their names have been transliterated differently in cited English-language publications do their names appear in this form in the references and bibliography. In these rare cases, I chose to use the more common transliteration in the main text so that other texts by the same author can be more easily found by readers.

Note on Translations

All translations are my own unless otherwise stated. While I have tried to avoid using the masculine as a generic in the text, it does feature in quotations from interviews, reflecting my interviewees' usage.

1

Introduction

Flexible Authoritarianism, Loyalty, and Quests for Change

"We, today's youth, we are the new generation. And it's our task to improve the situation, so that we live better." So spoke 25-year-old Maksim, a Russian citizen of Sakha nationality (*natsional'nost'*) who runs a farm in the remote Russian region of Sakha. The Republic of Sakha (Yakutia) is mainly inhabited by the Sakha people, who became Soviet citizens after the October Revolution and Russian citizens after the demise of the Soviet Union. The republic is huge, five times bigger than France. Its capital, Yakutsk, is located 3,000 miles east of Moscow and 1,500 miles north of Seoul. Maksim's eagerness to change life for the better in his municipality, in the region, and across all of Russia more broadly stemmed from his dissatisfaction with his country's current economic and political workings. "We all fully depend on a few people: on the president, on his inner circle,"[1] he said during my interview with him at a local youth-leadership summer camp sponsored by the Russian authorities. The camp was designed to spur local development as well as engender loyalty to the government and the regime—that is, the normative order underlying political life in Russia.

Maksim's attitude was representative of that held by most of the ambitious young adults I met at these idiosyncratic establishments, which combine elements from leadership and start-up business seminars with activities traditionally conducted at Soviet summer camps for leisure. The nature of these leadership camps, which have sprung up in all of Russia's federal districts over the past fifteen years, had made me curious about how ambitious young people from provincial Russia squared their quests for change with loyalty to the existing authoritarian political order.

During group and one-on-one interviews, Maksim and the other young campers I spoke with asserted that favoritism was the biggest problem in their country. Indeed, many felt strongly that it was endemic to federal politics and big business. Several offered remarks such as "in Russia, the problem is that knowing the right people is much more important for your career than your skills and knowledge."[2] One of their primary motivations for participating in the leadership camps was to improve life in their municipality or region.

Such comments on the shortcomings of Putin's strongman rule and on favoritism as an endemic defect of the country's current politico-economic system led me to assume that the campers understood the systemic nature of these serious problems besetting Russian politics and society. Yet it turned out during our conversations that they believed the individual act of changing their own lives would resonate with fellow citizens and eventually bring about much-desired improvements to their quality of life.

Representative of this widespread belief, Maksim claimed that if every Russian citizen strove for self-development and to overcome laziness—which he saw as an essential ingredient of the Russian national character—things would improve. "We have to get rid of laziness," he told me. "Laziness is our curse, which always stops us! . . . All depends on laziness. When one person stops being lazy, when everyone stops being lazy, then the situation will improve." When I asked him for a concrete example, he looked around: "Well, that our children will not dump this garbage [he points to a candy wrapper] just somewhere along the street but carry it to the waste bin! To be a personal example, to change ourselves."[3] Like Maksim, most of my interviewees considered change to be possible through such minor deeds as picking up garbage, or small projects enhancing citizens' entrepreneurial spirit and decency. The young campers' individualist quests for change demonstrated their tendency to attribute the systemic nature of Russia's reform deadlock to the individual shortcomings of their fellow citizens.

The campers' belief that the individual is the driver of change—that it is not politics as a collective endeavor but rather a person's enthusiasm for self-development (*samorazvitie*) and taste for hard work that will shape the world—is widely shared across an ambitious younger generation not only in Russia, but globally. Political theorists such as Wendy Brown posit that there is a global loss of faith in the power of collective social action under the conditions of what they call a neoliberal governing rationality.[4] This mindset evaluates human actions primarily on the basis of their potential use for economic, capitalist ends and the advancement of individual success. There is a widespread disbelief that joining forces "with others to set the terms by which we live together"[5] is capable of producing positive outcomes, and this outlook resonates with what most people witness under neoliberal capitalism: that those who do well in life do so because they believed strongly in an individually set goal and have adjusted their lifestyle to the demands of the market or their employer. While many sociological studies show that not everyone has the same access to career opportunities, the myth that "life is what you make it" is reproduced in much popular culture, telling and retelling "life-stories of self-change, redemption and personal triumph."[6]

Unquestioned popular beliefs about the benefits of an entrepreneurial mindset and common recipes for individual success increasingly shape politics in authoritarian states. They allow authoritarian leaders such as Vladimir Putin to stabilize their rule by deflecting criticism from systemic ills, showcasing instead the apparent moral deficiencies of ordinary citizens: they cultivate a belief that it is not political procedures or economic policies in need of profound change, but popular attitudes.

By legitimation I mean the processes through which political rule becomes tolerated, accepted, or supported by different groups of people, which can result, temporarily, in what Max Weber called political legitimacy: the shared belief that socioeconomic arrangements and political rule are righteous and appropriate.[7] The study of legitimacy presupposes that political authority and power are not the sole possession of political leaders.[8] All forms of modern political rule, with the exception of some military dictatorships and places where civil war makes governing impossible, require a social basis, a foothold in the governed population.[9] In order for government to be possible, a given minimum of citizens must either tolerate, accept, or positively identify with a polity's authorities, institutions, and socioeconomic arrangements.

Certainly, dictators in particular use the considerable symbolic and material resources at their disposal to enforce their will, and regularly resort to violence to crush public protests. In 2020, people around the world saw images of thousands of individuals being beaten and detained by security officers in Belarus for protesting against Aleksandr Lukashenko's fraudulent reelection.[10] Yet even for dictators, the use of coercion and violence is costly and often leads to further social unrest.[11] Indeed, such violence often breeds violent resistance; the desire to impede social unrest is a powerful incentive for enduring authoritarian rule with the halo of legitimate authority.[12] It is not possible to conclusively determine the extent to which ruling politicians themselves believe in the alternative realities that they promote to justify their case. It is, however, productive to assume that their very notion of what is instrumental in a particular context is shaped by cultural understandings that they share with larger parts of their constituency.[13]

I argue that in what I call flexible authoritarian states, where innovation-based economic growth is encouraged, governments are even more reliant upon citizens' basic approval and their participation in public matters. Many authoritarian rulers have, while expanding their states' coercive apparatus, invested considerably in alternative realities in which—contrary to actual policies—the well-being of citizens *appears* central to their policymaking. At the same time, they have expanded opportunities for citizens' participation in public matters. Social scientists often describe these escalating participatory gestures as a form of authoritarian cooptation, the "intentional extension of benefits to challengers to the regime in exchange for their loyalty."[14]

My politico-economic perspective accepts but also goes beyond an understanding of this participatory turn as a form of cooptation intended to prevent regime change—by which I mean a change of the underlying order of political and economic life in a polity.[15] I argue that the expansion of participatory opportunities also reflects the degree to which authoritarian elites in countries with less powerful economies seek to spur those organizational and technological innovations that they see as a key factor for national economic development. What economists call catch-up experiences—states' efforts "to escape the low development trap and raise their standards of living toward developed country levels"[16]—are increasingly associated with a change of developmental strategy. The aim is to move "from a passive role of implementing imported technology, to a more active role of introducing incremental improvements," allowing developing countries to venture "into the forefront of innovation-based competition in the industry."[17]

To some degree, such excitement about entrepreneurialism has changed how contemporary authoritarianism looks and feels. Spicing up youth political programs with entrepreneurial techniques for self-improvement, novel forms of participation in local politics, and design features deemed contemporary convey the impression that life under flexible authoritarianism can offer the same possibilities as liberal democracies. The slogan "Russia—Country of Possibilities" (*Rossiia—strana vozmozhnostei*), echoing the characterization of the United States as a country of unlimited possibilities, is a case in point. The slogan designates, to date, a pro-government NGO created in 2018 through an order by Vladimir Putin[18] and a new online platform that makes it easier for ambitious young adults to obtain information about how to attain public grants, engage in charity work, build their careers, or apply for youth-leadership summer camps.[19]

In a similar vein, many authoritarian societies take a great interest in up-and-coming young people as their national economy's "human capital," regarded as a unique asset in the international race for marketable innovations. Particularly in societies where upward social mobility is complicated by informal rules, authorities need to convince promising young people—those potential strategic elites who could become "responsible for the realization of major social goals and for the continuity of the social order"[20]—to stay.

One strategy is to invoke the patriotism of the well-educated so as to induce them to put their skills to use for the motherland, resulting in a novel understanding of patriotism. Patriotism is no longer crafted primarily through military duty and personal sacrifice via the army. Love for the motherland is increasingly portrayed, rather, in terms of loyalty to a national economy that experiences hardships—a change that is easily discernible in today's Russia. Putin's launch of a full-scale war on Ukraine[21] caused hundreds of thousands of young and well-educated Russian citizens to leave the country.[22] People working in the IT sector and up-and-coming young adults were especially represented among those who left during the first months of war, while many more followed when the government announced the partial mobilization of all those deemed fit for military service in late 2022. Their stigmatization as "scum" or "traitors" by Vladimir Putin and the Kremlin's spokespeople signaled not only the increased repression of dissent, but also an appeal to "true patriots" to stay in the country even "in such difficult times."[23]

Putin's decision to invade Ukraine[24]—long advocated by only the most hardline nationalists with little interest in innovation-based economic growth and whose voices had been marginal to high-level decisions[25]—perplexed many observers, because it seemed to contradict the two decades of serious investment in neoliberal modernization and brain-drain prevention that had accompanied the Kremlin's steady criminalization of dissent. A war economy, capitalizing on neo-imperial territorial gains,[26] has not fully replaced the ideals of neoliberal modernization from previous decades. The ongoing relevance of this earlier neoliberal modernization lineage is evidenced by the founding in 2021–2022 of eight new youth-leadership summer camps, organized and sponsored by state organs; the Federal Youth Agency *Rosmolodezh* classified six of these under "federal-level status" in 2022. One of these camps, called "Young South" (*Iug molodoi*), took place for the first time in 2022 in Ukraine's Zaporizhzhia oblast. This shows how several flexible authoritarian aims have continued to shape Russian government politics during the emergence of a war economy.[27] These aims are to convince promising youths to stay in Russia, prepare them for the job market, and use them as an entrepreneurially minded vanguard to spread the government's official narrative—not least in the occupied Ukrainian territories.

The significance of promising young adults to the authoritarian state's economic competitiveness makes their support central to both its fiscal survival and its political legitimacy. As such, their doubts, hopes, and ambiguities are crucial to a better understanding of present-day authoritarianism. I would go as far as to claim that investigating the dreams of self-fulfillment and hopes for local and national development of potential strategic elites, as well as their understanding of what being a patriot means, is as pivotal for assessing the possible political trajectory of authoritarian states as understanding the plans developed by ruling dictators and their cronies.

Based on these observations and assumptions, this book discusses some key questions: Which traits render flexible authoritarianism a compelling agenda that is accepted or tolerated beyond the small circles of ruling elites? How do acts of meaning-making and practiced cultural forms stabilize flexible authoritarian orders? How do often-unquestioned beliefs about the economy and social life influence the expectations of promising youth—toward themselves, their fellow citizens, and the state? To what degree do potential strategic elites perceive the government and the regime, the underlying order of political and economic life, as legitimate? If they do not actively support the regime, but merely tolerate it, how can we assess their loyalty—that is, their willingness to make personal sacrifices in order to conform to the regime's general goals and norms?[28]

Flexible Authoritarianism and Strategic Elites in Russia and Beyond

The pattern of beliefs and values held by Maksim and his peers at Russia's state-sponsored youth-leadership summer camps is crucial to making sense of what I call flexible authoritarianism: a form of government marked by the interplay of neoliberal and authoritarian practices. Flexible authoritarian regimes such as those of Russia, China, and Hungary[29] incentivize individual personal growth while expanding their coercive apparatus. They combine neoliberal appeals to citizens to take responsibility for their individual success with classic authoritarian practices such as the systematic suppression of dissent. This form of authoritarian government is more flexible than classic authoritarianism: coercive practices, seeking to create obedience to state authority by force, are combined with techniques such as branding that were heretofore used to inspire loyalty to products, not to states. I argue that flexible authoritarianism is, however, more than merely a novel device in the toolkit of authoritarian rulers. It is shaped by the global economic imperative of *flexibility*. That is, in today's neoliberal capitalism, not only companies and labor markets, but also states and their citizens, are required to adjust quickly to changes in market conditions if they wish to remain competitive.[30] At the same time, this form of authoritarian government is not just a passive response to neoliberal capitalism's imperative of flexibility. Flexible authoritarian styles of government skillfully deploy the aesthetics, promises, and techniques of cool start-up capitalism[31] to create loyalty among potential strategic elites.

It is important to note that by strategic elites I do not mean the small entourages of powerful people surrounding authoritarian leaders such as Vladimir Putin or Viktor Orbán, but those people whose contributions may promote "economic growth, political stability, or scientific advance"[32]—that is, those goals most national economies strive for. Loyal strategic elites strengthen authoritarian governments' transnational economic and political power. Moreover, their support for the political regime—the underlying order of political life—is especially crucial, because they serve as public examples of how to succeed under current conditions. In turn, their sense of legitimacy is more consequential for upholding the political and economic order than that of ordinary people.[33]

My identification of what I call a flexible authoritarian style of government, meaning the incorporation of neoliberal techniques into authoritarian government, questions the popular thesis that the recent rise of authoritarianism can be understood as a backlash against neoliberal capitalism.[34] It casts into doubt the claim made by authoritarian powers such as Russia or China that they would provide alternatives to neoliberal capitalism. The example of Hungary provides an especially clear reason to question interpretations that see the rise of strongman rule as primarily a backlash against neoliberalism.[35] While it is widely agreed that Viktor Orbán's ascent to prime minister was conditioned by an election campaign that condemned previous governments' neoliberal policies as having served foreign business interests, announcing a new national era,[36] neoliberal policies have in fact remained a mainstay of Orbán's rule. To date, Hungary is home to the lowest corporate tax level and the most flexible labor policies in the European Union (some of which are dubbed "slave laws").[37] State-sponsored programs to promote popular culture in Hungary are of a neoliberal register and evaluated according to their economic revenues.[38]

For its part, and from an economy-centric perspective, Putinist Russia is certainly not an example par excellence of the implementation of neoliberal economic and monetary principles. However, since the early 2000s Russian citizens have increasingly been called upon to individually provide for their own professional futures, health care, and old age.[39] They are encouraged to voluntarily support the state in the provision of collective and individual security, good infrastructure, and cleaner cities.[40] The state approaches them thus as the architects of both their own fortunes and that of their country. As Richard Sakwa, a preeminent scholar on Russian politics and society, notes, neoliberal social policies are a crucial element of Putinism:

> There has been no attempt to restore even a basic level of Soviet-style equality, and instead Russia remains one of the most unequal countries in the world. Putinism is a distinctive synthesis of authoritarian managerial practices and democratic proceduralism, neo-liberal social policies and neo-Soviet paternalism.[41]

While the Russian government has issued various anti-democratic decrees over the past decade, culminating in the 2022 criminalization of referring to the country's war in Ukraine by its name (the official label is "special military operation"), such measures are still portrayed by the authorities as being necessary to "manage," rather than abolish, pluralism.[42]

Soviet curtailments of freedoms such as the rights to free movement and occupational choice have not been reintroduced by any of the pro-Putin governments—a reluctance that has been posited as a major factor for young adults' acceptance of Putinist politics.[43] The enormous increase in repression against dissenters since rumors of a possible Russian military offensive first emerged in late fall 2021 has led many observers to draw parallels to Stalinism. One should, however, remember that when Vladimir Putin came to power, large parts of the populace did not wish to return to communist doctrines and a uniform ideology.[44] The language of liberal freedom—the ability to choose one's occupation, to travel freely, and to forge one's own destiny—may thus remain relevant in the government's attempts to legitimate its course, even when actual freedoms are curtailed to a post-Soviet minimum.

Flexibility as Mindset and Technique

Richard Sennett describes the neoliberal transformation of global capitalism over recent decades as being accompanied by the praise of flexibility in corporate praxis, labor policies, and individual self-control. According to him, flexibility can be understood as "the willingness to let the shifting demands of the outside world determine the inside structure of institutions."[45] This willingness to adapt to the changing demands of the market is increasingly identifiable among those who wish to find pleasure and fulfillment in their work, exemplified by attendees of the Russian youth-leadership summer camps. Like many of their contemporaries in other parts of the world, campers such as Maksim adopted the sort of flexible mindset that is commonly called neoliberal. They sought to achieve personal fulfillment through self-development and carefully planned investments in themselves. They believed that engaging in such continuous self-development would make it easier to find, or create, a job, thereby allowing them to make the most of their talents and gain inspiration (*vdokhnovenie*). Indeed, most of the campers that I interviewed had been drawn to the camps for what they offered in terms of career-advancement. This ranged from project-development training to personal-development coaching to networking opportunities with influential politicians, NGO leaders, and businesspeople. The assumption that *anyone* can be a successful entrepreneur, artist or NGO director—a belief that is almost globally reproduced in all kinds of advertising, marketing, and popular self-help literature today[46]—seemed to imply for many young campers that a person's lack of success and happiness was attributable to their lack of willpower and flexibility.

This popular reasoning among the campers was even more astonishing considering recent Russian history. Russia's ambitious youth have long experienced and continue to face bleak prospects for upward mobility and personal fulfillment through work in their home regions. Indeed, post-Soviet Russian youth who are not from the metropolises of St. Petersburg or Moscow have been pressed for decades to find work that promises intellectual or creative pleasure *and* economic survival outside of their home region.

When Russian youth politics and regional economic development politics started to promote the development of marketable innovations among young people around 2009, the state began to address promising youth in novel ways—as the potential entrepreneurs and innovators of tomorrow, who could bring economic and social change.[47] Certainly, this political shift served the Russian government's aim to unite the country through what was framed as a joint modernization effort after a thorny election campaign and a major crackdown on oppositional protesters. It was also, however, a response to the advice of development economists from international financial institutions, whose recommendations are that emerging economies develop their human capital and foster marketable innovations to ensure long-term economic growth.[48]

This policy shift put promising youth in a new situation. Government discourse now promoted an alternative to emigration for those seeking inspiring and challenging jobs. State-sponsored offers to advance young people's careers now echoed the transnational self-help and business literature that became popular in Russia in the second half of the 2000s, and that influenced TV shows as well as private extracurricular education.[49] Staying in one's region no longer meant being regarded as unambitious and passive. On the contrary, those who stayed to develop their surroundings could now be perceived as "cheerful, upbeat, passionate, entrepreneurial [...] constantly vigilant in regard for opportunities for projects,"[50] just like those promising youth who had left to find their vocation in London, Moscow, Seoul, Berlin, or San Francisco.

Around the same time, some state organs started to promote a new version of heroic patriotism in Russia, one that had little in common with the so-called hooray-patriotism (*ura-patriotizm*) that most campers, alongside the summer camps' trainers and youth political staff, condemned as superficial and meaningless. Rather, this novel heroic patriotism characterized the entrepreneur as exceptional, as described by the Austrian economist Joseph Schumpeter at the beginning of the 20th century:

> Then there is the will to conquer: the impulse to fight, to prove oneself superior to others, to succeed for the sake, not of the fruits of success, but of success itself. From this aspect, economic action becomes akin to sport—there are financial races, or rather boxing-matches. [...] Finally, there is the joy of creating, of getting things done, or simply of exercising one's energy and ingenuity. [...] Our type seeks out difficulties, changes in order to change, delights in ventures.[51]

The entrepreneurial qualities described by Schumpeter—willpower, drive, and the pursuit of ventures and change—were highly valued by the campers that I interviewed as traits of what they called "active" people, adapting the Soviet notion of an active disposition toward life (*aktivnaia zhiznennaia pozitsiia*) to the neoliberal capitalist challenges faced by young people today.[52] The qualities that they attributed to an ideal active person echoed the exhortations of famous sportspeople to never stop believing in yourself even if the odds are against you. The young campers seemed to trust that people with such an active ethos would avoid turning to a criticism of everyone and everything in order to justify their inability or unwillingness to take life into their own hands. The campers invested their hopes in the possibility of transforming themselves and the people around them in what I call a new heroic entrepreneurial type. They believed that this novel type of person would be capable of inducing development and positivity in their immediate surroundings, initiating a domino effect of positive changes.

Thus, when campers such as Maksim talked about prospects for social change, they predicted how their individualist quests for betterment would lead more and more people to become active, caring for themselves and their surroundings. Notably, during these parts of our conversations, the young campers' criticism of the systemic flaws in Russian politics and business, including favoritism and the sabotage of procedures that ensure political accountability, seemed to fade into insignificance. Instead, they appeared to join in those neoliberal narratives that, rooted in an economic understanding of human beings as subjects of "competition and human capital enhancement,"[53] attribute people's poverty or professional failure to their alleged lack of willpower. The only other narrative genre that equally appeared to dismiss or belittle the systemic flaws in Russian society were stories of Russia's—often the Soviet Union's—former wars and the country's novel opposition to the West after the annexation of Crimea by the Putin government in 2014. Because many highly valuable accounts exist of the significance of memory politics and the reactivation of enemy images for the Putin government's attempts at legitimation,[54] I focus more on those narratives that justify severe social inequality and help to blunt the intense and widespread criticism of favoritism and corruption among Russian citizens. What is more, I found that the campers were much more motivated by goals such as self-fulfillment and the desire to live a life that inspires them (*vdokhnovenie*) than by great power ambitions[55] or attitudes that are typically subsumed under patriotism, such as unconditional love for the motherland or admiration for the country's president.

Legitimation and Cultural Understandings

I have so far argued that authoritarian rulers integrate neoliberal and authoritarian strategies in response to globally operating economic pressures, and as a means to legitimate their goals in order to increase political and economic power. However, support for, or mere tolerance of, a regime can only partially be explained by the legitimation strategies of dictators and their crafting of alternative political realities.[56] Going beyond such an instrumental perspective has become more urgent in light of the rise of narrow, Putin-centric explanations of authoritarianism since the launch of a full-scale war on Ukraine.[57]

There is no doubt that Russia has for many years been home to a set of institutionalized authoritarian practices—"sabotaging accountability to people over whom a political actor exerts control,"[58] to use Marlies Glasius' pioneering definition of authoritarianism. The sabotaging of accountability, meaning the substantive and repetitive breaking of rules and formal procedures that guarantee that elected politicians take responsibility for their doings vis-à-vis those they govern, is, according to Glasius, the most significant criterion for determining "the authoritarianness" of states. Given that most authoritarian states have institutions of supposed accountability such as parliaments, and, in the case of Russia, even citizen councils, the phenomenon of accountability sabotage is central to defining them as authoritarian.[59]

Expanding on Glasius' work, I define authoritarian states as polities that systematically undermine accountability, meaning that their authoritarian practices are firmly institutionalized and shape daily politics. In Russia, some institutions of accountability have emerged partially in response to the neoliberal imperative of flexibility. These do increase citizens' participation in public consultation bodies and their enterprising spirit, but not their influence on political outcomes.[60] Authoritarian states' experimentation with new forms of citizen participation, and programs aimed at motivating promising youth to work both for their own careers and for the well-being of the nation, make it even more important to analyze how authoritarian values and practices are reproduced not only through governmental instruments, but also through processes of meaning-making among, for instance, ambitious youth.

Marlies Glasius argues, along similar lines, that in order to better understand the transnational rise of authoritarian practices, we must engage in greater detail with the collective processes that lead people to tolerate, accept, or even support authoritarian practices in specific contexts:

> People do not obey an isolated dictator out of pure fear, or collaborate with him out of pure greed or hunger for power. They develop common understandings of how things are done within their social context, whether they are true believers in the government's legitimation narratives, or just pragmatists, or somewhere in between.[61]

I also expand on what Samuel A. Greene and Graeme B. Robertson have called, with regard to contemporary Russia, the need to study how a "social consensus around the inevitability and righteousness of Putin's rule"[62] is reproduced beyond the circles of ruling elites. Yet unlike these authors' analyses, which center on the reception of parliamentary politics and Putinist rule, I am more concerned with how unquestioned beliefs and cultural understandings that are taken for granted may reproduce such a consensus at concrete sites,[63] such as youth-leadership camps, and in specific situations, such as group interviews. As with Valerie Sperling's endeavor to unpack how unquestioned beliefs about gender norms subtly stabilize authoritarianism beyond the ruling class, I uncover how acceptance of the benevolence of flexibility and self-development legitimates authoritarian practices.[64]

Thus, I conceptualize legitimation as a process that—even in autocracies—takes place in societal arenas that are not political in the narrow sense of the term.[65] People's sense of the most pressing problems of the day as well as their assumptions about possible solutions are arguably no more shaped by official speeches and media reports than they are by received wisdom that comes from popular culture; practiced cultural forms, such as the summer camp tradition that I discuss in Chapter 3; and storytelling situations at family gatherings, workplaces, educational institutions, or summer camps.[66] In all these situations, cultural understandings are crucial for communication and meaning-making.[67] Thus, I consider cultural understandings and persisting cultural forms as relevant sources of legitimation and delegitimation.[68]

As seen in the creative methods used by numerous Russian citizens to protest their country's war on Ukraine, such as the laying of flowers at memorial sites or the encoding of anti-war messages in posters, cultural understandings are not fully controllable by authoritarian rulers and remain dynamic.[69] Processes of meaning-making are unruly. Dictators will always lack control over the social and symbolic.

The same processes of meaning-making that help to understand what destabilizes a regime, by which I mean the order underlying political and economic life,[70] also need to be explored for a better understanding of what upholds regimes symbolically and socially beyond the interests of a small circle of ruling profiteers. These processes can be analytically distinguished from widespread fears of repression. Though my analysis centers on cultural understandings as sources of legitimation, I do not aim to explain the survival of authoritarian regimes in terms of legitimation processes alone. Techniques of coercion and intimidation, as well as international political and economic networks, are crucial factors for regime stability.[71] Rarely is a change in popular will the single major force that brings a dictator down. I thus regard cultural understandings as only one among several factors that are crucial for regime legitimation. Students of authoritarianism have pointed to elite unity, political ideology, the forestalling of opposition action, and socioeconomic performance as crucial for sustaining or producing legitimacy.[72] Expanding on their insights, I use the concept of culture—understood as an analytic category that is fundamental to society and social relations, *not* as a description of a bounded collective's innate character—to stress that processes of meaning-making are fundamental to explaining what constitutes elite unity, how political ideologies are communicated, and how assumptions form about economic growth as a guarantor of socioeconomic stability.

My exploration of ambitious youths' loyalty to the regime suggests that a critical stance against the government can go hand in hand with support for, or at least tolerance of, the regime's goals. David Easton's classic differentiation between popular support for a government on the one hand, and support for a regime on the other,[73] helps to make sense of young people's tendency to criticize the regime's shortcomings while simultaneously approving of the grand narratives on which the current authoritarian order rests.

To explore this coexistence of critique and toleration, I differentiate between legitimacy and loyalty. Unlike the subjective belief in the legitimacy of political rule, loyalty does not presuppose a deep commitment. While loyalty may accompany the belief that a government is legitimate, it may also remain when this sense of righteousness vanishes.[74] Even when promising youth criticize concrete political practices, they can remain loyal to the regime. Even if they are primarily drawn to youth-leadership summer camps for their entrepreneurial and start-up culture features, they may accept an authoritarian pedagogical style (*Erziehungsstil*)[75] at camp as something that is not worth picking a fight over.

Globally Circulating Images of Success and Economic Growth

Popular beliefs about how social well-being depends on economic growth and how the latter must be ensured through engagement in the competition for marketable innovations are global. As Philip Cerny notes, this near-universally assumed connection is undergirded by the powerful notion of a society populated by entrepreneurial individuals:

> The ideal of a neoliberal society and economy populated by entrepreneurial men (and women), whether out of human nature or imposed by a strong regulatory competition state, is a myth, but it is a myth that has a deep hold on economic actors, policymakers and, indeed, the public at large, not only in the developed world but in the developing world too.[76]

As he further highlights, the myth of neoliberalism as an ideal mode of modernization informs what counts as contemporary, what promises to be sold and exported widely. All those evaluations are not determined on a national basis. Neoliberalism as both a bundle of socioeconomic policy reforms and a governing rationality calls for a reflection on how a *transnational* expert, management, and business culture has shaped cultural understandings in most parts of the world.[77]

Globally circulating images of success, contemporariness, and development shape the ways in which both ruling and strategic elites envision a good society. Such images are easily evoked when conversations turn to topics such as "contemporary lifestyle," "self-care," "successful business start-ups," "innovation," and, increasingly, "happiness."[78] Young people in particular are influenced by transnational flows of popular culture through new media. Young adults in Russia, for example, are well versed in trendy forms of speech, dress, design, and social-media communication, even when they reject them for various reasons.[79] As we will see in the following chapters, authoritarian incumbents refer to those globally circulating images in order to be perceived as moving with the times and connected with Russia's younger generations.

Contrary to much of the literature on authoritarianism that still tacitly assumes the nation-state as the primary context within which to study authoritarian legitimation,[80] my politico-economic perspective requires an exploration of cultural understandings as rooted in transnational flows. This premise responds to analyses such as Cerny's, and equally to persistent stereotypes about an immutable "Russian culture" that haunt research on this geographical area, especially when the concepts of authoritarianism and culture are combined. The alarming ways in which culturalist arguments have been used to explain Russian and Soviet authoritarian government—including in social research—merit discussion.

For instance, during the 1940s the psychologist Geoffrey Gorer, alongside the renowned anthropologist Margaret Mead, attempted to find out more about an alleged "Great Russian national character" that would explain which personality traits are prone to developing among a majority of Soviet citizens. Gorer, who had never visited the region and did not speak Russian, identified the Soviet and Russian practice of swaddling infants as the single most outstanding feature of such a collective character and claimed the practice itself to be the major cause of Soviet citizens' tendency to develop authoritarian personality traits.[81] Though the study damaged Gorer's scientific reputation in the US, and even more that of Mead, who was participating in its research design and sponsorship in the framework of her global Culture and Personality project, it shaped US foreign policy both at the time and for years to come, and put flesh on the bones of long-standing stereotypes.[82]

This particular research, also known pejoratively as "diaperology," is an extreme example of how stereotypes of an alleged Russian national character shaped social research on the Soviet Union and Russia, especially during the Cold War era. Its explanations are cultural-determinist, conceiving of culture as something that is immutable and inextricably bound to place and origin. Cultural determinism is at play when a phenomenon such as loyalty to an authoritarian government is not seen as the outcome of a complex process, but rather "explained" in terms of an unchanging national or tribal culture. As the historian Dietrich Geyer argued in the mid-1980s, both widespread Russophobia and Russophilia have often impeded thorough scientific analysis on developments in this region. As Geyer wrote: "The tendency remained to observe Russia or the Soviet Union through old glasses, to see there only what one has believed to see from time immemorial: that ever-same, never-changing Russianness, packaged in low-maintenance clichés that are always already confirmed through history."[83] To be sure, not only Russia, but the whole region of Eastern Europe, has suffered from characterizations as a "hotbed of ethnic nationalisms," to the extent that socioeconomic processes have been neglected in social scientific analyses.[84]

Against this backdrop, it is of little surprise that several anthropologists specializing in the region eschew using the concept of culture, due to its inaccurate popular association with an integrated, bounded whole and its misuse as an explanatory container.[85] Vladimir Gel'man, a renowned researcher of authoritarian politics in Russia, rejects analyses that bring culture into the picture altogether, independent of the widely differing conceptualizations and operationalizations of culture between social researchers.[86]

The subdiscipline of cultural sociology developed a couple of core assumptions to differentiate its signature concept from essentializing uses of the notion of "culture" that are politically and socially dangerous. It is widely accepted among sociologists employing the concept that "culture is contingent, context dependent, and not fixed either in time or in space" and "is manifested in practice—the things that people do together from speaking the same language to common behaviors and repertoires of evaluation."[87]

Building on this definition of culture, I want to expound some assumptions guiding my analysis. The two main ideals around which flexible authoritarianism revolves in Russia, that of neoliberal modernization and that of neotraditionalism, are not country-specific. I use the term "ideal" in the sense of a goal toward which society ought to strive, a standard worth striving for.[88] The first of these ideals enshrines being modern, contemporary, and economically competitive; the second highlights neotraditionalism—protecting and preserving what is romanticized as a national society's cultural traditions to legitimate the pursuit of a conservative future.[89] Both are also highly relevant to the legitimation of flexible authoritarianism in places outside Russia. For instance, they form the basis of what has been described in the Mexican case as managing the tension between an economic liberalism—considered a necessary precondition for sustaining the nation's economic viability through global competitiveness—and maintaining cultural uniqueness in light of globalizing politico-economic reforms.[90] In today's Russia, as well as in Hungary and China, neoliberal restructuring is combined with a protectionist gesture toward preserving alleged national uniqueness vis-à-vis the globalizing forces of capitalist development. Likewise, in Poland neoliberal economic reasoning and policies were not rolled back, but combined with a patriotic and nationalist agenda.[91]

The rather abstract transnational notions of neoliberal modernization and neotraditional ideals take on specific meanings and forms in different contexts, varying with the polity and its history. Locally specific stories, images, and myths convey what makes a country and its inhabitants unique, how they should be, and, accordingly, which political path should be taken in the future. For instance, today's dominant conception of Russia's political community draws eclectically on myths from three distinct historical periods. There is, first, the imperial myth of Russia as a "distinct civilization" that would have developed at the crossroads of East and West.[92] Then, there is the adoption of the Soviet idiosyncratic approach to national identity that assumes a multinational constitutive people, bound together by the supranational aim of progress and the historical fight against fascism.[93] Not least, there is the appreciation of the revolution of the 1990s, whose leading protagonists wanted to end what they regarded as Russia's twentieth-century adoption of communism's "deviant oriental economic system," and who aimed to bring Russia back onto a "normal path of civilization."[94] The goal of building a normal nation-state that is integrated in the capitalist world order is taken from this period.[95]

Upon closer inspection, it becomes clear that even those cultural understandings one might call Russia-specific grew out of exchanges and conflicts with communities and peoples who became part of the Russian empire during colonization and conquest or who were residing at its borders.[96] Likewise, seemingly Russia-specific cultural understandings evolved historically in close conversation with intellectual questions discussed in Western and Central Europe. For instance, what some social scientists came to identify as an "indigenous" Russian version of the civil-society concept grew out of the reflections of Russian intellectuals on nineteenth-century debates about the public sphere in Western and Central Europe.[97] This history of exchange forms the roots of a number of concepts central to present-day debates over Russian identity, such as civilization, space, organicism, sovereignty, spirit, and wholeness. The reception and debate of both nineteenth-century philosophical romanticism, forming as a countermovement to Hegelian idealism at the time,[98] and the twentieth-century culturalist-civilizational approaches put forward by Heidegger, Spengler, Toynbee, Huntington, and others,[99] were key to the formation of these allegedly Russia-specific beliefs. What appears as a locally specific cultural understanding was thus either formed through encounters between ethnicities and nationalities of a polity, or rooted in a transnational history of intellectual exchange. The diffusion of nationalist ideas across borders in the nineteenth century might be the most illustrative example of such exchange.

The preceding examples show that cultural understandings cannot be grouped solely on the basis of their geographical or national origin. Yet the everyday salience of geographical and national attributions such as "Russian," "indigenous," "national," "autochthonous," "Western," or "Oriental," and the actual significance of territoriality and political space for our understanding of social life,[100] make resorting to such terms impossible to avoid. It follows that, while "Russia-specific" and "transnational" are makeshift terms and can serve only as rough indications, it is necessary to use them—if only to challenge dominant national or geographical attributions.

Neoliberalism and the State

Though neoliberalism has been primarily promoted by people who saw themselves as anti-state-minded globalists, neoliberal reforms have often been pushed through with considerable help from states' coercive apparatuses.[101] Given that Russia is not a textbook example of neoliberalism, there is a need to clarify how I conceptualize neoliberalism here.

The popular differentiation between economy-centric approaches to neoliberalism and neo-Foucauldian ones used in sociology and political theory is an apt starting point.[102] Broadly speaking, neoliberalism is regarded in the former as merely an economic project, demanding the creation of lean, minimally equipped states and praising the self-regulating powers of the market.[103] Rightly, neo-Foucauldian approaches criticize these standard accounts that focus on the economy for obscuring the reality that in most cases, states and markets do not exist in an adversarial relationship—as if more powerful markets, meaning the empowerment of those with capital, would mean less government intervention.[104]

On the contrary, and as I show, states are also invested in creating the ideational conditions that allow neoliberal capitalism to succeed in their territory and under their jurisdiction. Political economists studying policy regimes—that is, how economic ideas not only find their way into policies but alter the institutional setup of polities—argue that states institutionalize competition in all kinds of sectors, meaning that the ideals of neoliberal modernization are by no means confined to economic matters.[105] Neo-Foucauldians have shown that neoliberalism has evolved from an economic theory into a mindset, which operates often in the form of unquestioned beliefs. Principles that are dominant in markets, such as competition and entrepreneurship, are increasingly transferred to spheres of social life that have been formerly organized according to a different mindset.[106] The profound changes made to public education in the Euro-American world over the past decades provide a key example. Humanistic notions, which often center on the abstraction of a citizen-subject who is, thanks to a well-rounded education, capable of self-determination and self-rule (largely ignoring the ways in which class, gender, and ethnicity control access to education), have been increasingly replaced by neoliberal ones. Since the late 1990s, the belief that education should enhance human capital, meaning that young people should learn things that heighten their chances of employment and entrepreneurial success, has risen sharply around the globe.[107] Thus, neo-Foucauldian approaches emphasize that politics, social life, and public education are increasingly organized according to an economic logic—a neoliberal cognitive framework—in most parts of the world today. Moreover, they contend that these changes affect the ways in which people experience themselves in relation to their careers, their fellow citizens, and the state.

One drawback of the neo-Foucauldian approach, especially when put into practice in anthropological and sociological case studies, is that it risks treating neoliberalism merely as another example of "engineering the soul," as Johanna Bockman has aptly put it.[108] Often, such case studies skip the task of showing how particular techniques called neoliberal relate to a neoliberal capitalist project. Thus, all kinds of strategies for self-improvement and quests for self-fulfillment could be regarded as being shaped by the apparently invisible hand of neoliberalism. This tendency is especially evident when researchers, finding neoliberalism to be so complex and multifaceted, resort to concepts such as assemblage.[109] As social psychologist Margaret Wetherell argues, analyses based on the notion of assemblage—that is, a varying collection of biological, social, and technical relations—risk providing explanations in which "human labour and its history disappear, almost by sleight of hand."[110] What is more, quests for self-fulfillment like those of the young campers I met appear as mere epiphenomena of an apparently unbounded neoliberal governmentality.

Thus, although I side with the neo-Foucauldians in defining neoliberalism as a mindset that operates as a set of unquestioned beliefs, I see it as being firmly tied to capitalist production. As such, a neoliberal mindset basically prescribes that people and governments should self-improve in a way that keeps them competitive as individuals and for the market, but that ultimately serves the well-being of capitalism (economic growth) and its preservation (private ownership of the means of production and of large-scale profits). As sociologist Ulrich Bröckling puts it, the neoliberal ideal is to mobilize all social relations according to the fiction of neoliberal capitalist development.[111]

At the same time, I follow economy-centric approaches to trace how neoliberalism, as "the dominant mode of economic thinking of our time,"[112] operates through concrete government policies and is fostered by think tanks, foundations, and networks involving businesspeople and politicians.[113] While many of the institutions promoting flexibility are international in nature, leading several scholars to equate neoliberalism with a kind of economic imperialism, I do not see neoliberal reforms as being adopted solely because they are forced from the outside onto less powerful national economies and states.[114]

Several studies take issue with the widespread notion that neoliberalism is mainly a force from outside that would destroy local livelihoods.[115] State officials wanting their countries to succeed in the international economic race become invested not only in introducing neoliberal reforms, but also in signaling their willingness to establish favorable conditions for investors.[116] In this regard, in a gesture of preemptive obedience, several emerging economies have pushed through more radical neoliberal reforms than international financial institutions advised them to adopt.[117] Here again, Hungary appears to be a case in point.[118] Moreover, in Russia, neoliberal government techniques have not been forced upon Russian society solely via Western-led assistance programs.[119] While international organizations undoubtedly linked loan approvals and the prospect of membership with demands such as further privatization and open markets,[120] their influence on national governments only partly explains the gradual introduction of neoliberal principles in various policy fields. Of the Russian case, Aleksandr Bikbov has argued that the proliferation of neoliberal reforms and reasoning in Russia was also accelerated through managers who acquired influential positions in regional and federal politics. (In Chapter 3, I substantiate this argument through the example of Krasnoyarsk youth politics.) Neoliberal principles have been appropriated in different ways by a variety of actors in the Russian context—through international assistance for NGOs, managers in private sector firms becoming government officials, the educational decisions of concerned parents, or the popularity of makeover TV shows and self-help literature.[121]

The ways in which definitions of neoliberalism as an import—built on the notion that external, international marketizing forces would oppose internal, nation-state policies to spur development—may legitimate authoritarian practices is felicitously analyzed by political economist Hae-Yung Song in her work on South Korea.[122] Her analysis points to a further-reaching problematic regarding the "zero-sum" constructions of "global interests at the expense of national ones," or "market at the expense of state." Studies based on such "zero-sum" constructions fail to problematize states' intrinsic role in the reproduction of global capitalism and neglect to take issue with states' historical and current complicities in upholding exploitative labor relations.[123] Given the revival of currents of geopolitical thought that posit authoritarian states' politics as mere reactions to Western politics—a figure of thought that also underlies justifications for Russia's war on Ukraine—more refined understandings of neoliberalism are crucial to avoid popularizing portrayals of authoritarian state practices as acts of resistance against a Western domination of the world that is, misleadingly, conceptualized as ubiquitous.

As this book's title phrase "flexible authoritarianism" suggests, my analysis is as much about authoritarianism as it is about neoliberalism. In this regard I do not subordinate authoritarianism to neoliberalism. Unlike analyses inspired by the concept of authoritarian neoliberalism,[124] I interrogate the role of neoliberal capitalism in both shaping contemporary authoritarian government and altering the modes of its popular acceptance. Moreover, while my approach often converges with case studies discussing how neoliberal techniques are wedded with authoritarian practices in emerging economies,[125] it differs from such studies in its more profound analysis of authoritarianism as the systematic breaking of rules and procedures designed to share political power among various institutions and constituencies within a state.[126] I examine how contemporary authoritarianism is shaped by the neoliberal imperative of flexibility; how authoritarian states promote both neoliberal and neotraditional values to expand their politico-economic power in today's global capitalism; and how flexible authoritarian policies resonate with potential strategic elites.

Neoliberalism's Authoritarian and Democratic Borrowings and Effects

The historian Quinn Slobodian, most notably, has posited that a great number of influential businessmen and politicians have historically tolerated or even welcomed authoritarian politics in order to safeguard the market and a traditional order of society.[127] Neoliberal calls for the market were often tied to a strengthening of states' coercive apparatuses, which were needed to suppress the demands of workers and the poor for redistribution and rights to equal political participation.[128]

As the economist Ralf Ptak, among others, has successfully shown in the German case, a great many economists whose work would become influential for neoliberalism emphatically rejected any expansion of democracy in the Weimar Republic, especially after the 1929 economic crisis.[129] They found that democratic demands for political inclusion and material concessions as well as the questioning of long-standing conservative traditions threatened the kind of state autonomy and authority that would be, in their view, necessary for a healthy economic order.[130] It was not only material interests guiding these economists' rejection of democracy, however: a strong contempt for both the masses and bureaucratization, as well as the assumption that there was a natural order—upheld by elite institutions such as the academy, the church, and an elite-governed state—were equally important moral coordinates that led them to demand a state that would curtail, if need be, common people's democratic rights.[131] Because they perceived democracy—especially the representation of what they called the masses' material interests—to threaten the economic order, they advocated that authoritarian values, such as obedience to existing authorities and unquestioned respect for established hierarchies, should be enforced by the state. As Alexander Rüstow put it in 1932, less than a year before Adolf Hitler was nominated by the Weimar Republic's president as *Reichskanzler*, a plural society would threaten the state, making it "incapable of defending against the united onslaught of interest crowds. The state is pulled to pieces by avaricious interests."[132] Similar fears of a deepening of democracy can be found in the work of Friedrich von Hayek, one of the most influential neoliberal thinkers.[133]

The economic theories of the Austrian economist Joseph Schumpeter are also formed by this bourgeois, conservative mentality. Though Schumpeter is commonly not counted within the small circles of economists regarded as the main architects of neoliberal thought (thus, his anti-democratic views are seldom discussed by scholars of neoliberalism), his popular accounts of entrepreneurship and disruptive innovation are central for forming unquestioned beliefs regarding the ideal character traits of successful entrepreneurs.[134] Schumpeter, most interested in obtaining outstanding achievements and economic development by all means necessary, conceptualized entrepreneurs as exceptional geniuses, guided by willpower rather than by economic calculations.[135] He held a very negative view of a *democratic* capitalist society, because he believed that equal rights for all would weaken workers' obedience to authority. This led him at one point, astonishingly, to praise a socialist order. He did so not because he advocated a deepening of democracy. Far from that, he speculated that socialism would make possible a more totalizing social order, one that could reinstill a kind of labor discipline like the authoritarian one of the past that he held dear. As Schumpeter asserted, "whenever needed, authoritarian enforcement of discipline will prove an easier task"[136] under socialism. To him, discipline was a lubricant of economic development:

> It is not only that discipline improves the quality and, if required, the quantity of the labor hours. Irrespective of this, discipline is an economizing factor of the first order. It lubricates the wheels of the economic engine and greatly reduces waste and total effort per unit of performance. The efficiency of planning as well as of current management in particular may be raised to a level far above anything that is feasible under present conditions.[137]

Schumpeter shared the antidemocratic, bourgeois sensitivities of his neoliberal colleagues: their contempt for the masses and for state bureaucracy.[138] Democracy to him meant that the extraordinary contributions of elite entrepreneurs would vanish, along with authoritarian discipline enforcing the obedience of workers. He saw "the workman's readiness to obey orders" as being "inculcated by the feudal predecessor of his bourgeois master" and threatened by "accepting equality in the political sphere, by teaching the laborers that they were just as valuable citizens as anyone else."[139] Unlike excellent entrepreneurs, who he believed need and deserve creative freedoms, he contended that all those who are employed in dull jobs, who carry out the routine tasks that actually bring about the visions of outstanding entrepreneurs, need to be forced with strict disciplinary mechanisms to carry out this kind of work. Like that of his neoliberal contemporaries,

Schumpeter's vision of the world was clearly a hierarchical one, in which authoritarian values were central to the functioning of the economy.

All of the above suggests that neoliberalism leads to a more authoritarian society. Yet, much as capitalist development had unintended democratic consequences,[140] neoliberal arrangements could also produce more democratic outcomes—not because of the interests of neoliberal politicians-cum-businessmen, but *in spite of* them. States seeking to become internationally competitive in innovation-based economics[141] tend to foster behaviors that are widely perceived as boosting innovations, such as thinking outside the box, constructive criticism, experimentation, and cooperation.[142] Such behaviors have been associated at least since the 1930s with democratic group atmospheres and a democratic organizational and pedagogical style (*Erziehungsstil*).[143] When a governing elite wishes to raise its national economy's competitiveness through innovation, it has an incentive to loosen authoritarian work environments that, while promising a high level of control, tend to dissuade people from contradicting their superiors, engaging in experimentation, or cooperating with peers.

Moreover, neoliberal appeals make use of motivational theories, empowerment tactics, and self-care approaches that are conceptually anchored in Enlightenment ideals of self-determination.[144] While these are primarily used today to increase efficiency and reduce the costs of imposing direct disciplining mechanisms on employees and citizens, such as hiring overseers and financing penal apparatuses, they nevertheless also carry some of these ideals of self-determination. Richard Sennett emphasized that the ideals of neoliberal modernization do indeed draw subtly on the humanistic notion of a *homo faber*, man as his own maker.[145] As such, they communicate that ordinary people can shape their own lives—and might not need a national leader to guide the way.

Without a doubt, neoliberal techniques are promoted through Russian youth politics to instill in promising youth a sense of mission for the country's economic and political well-being and a sense of loyalty to its underlying order of political and economic life. In adopting the language of self-improvement, however, such inculcations do not necessarily contradict up-and-coming youths' aspirations for personal fulfillment. Crucially, my interviews show how striving to be true to oneself is not only a moral ideal that has been imposed by the Russian government upon the young people that I spoke with. Rather, it seems that these youths share in what Charles Taylor has characterized as the quest for self-fulfillment in modern times:

> Like other facets of modern individualism—for instance, that which calls on us to work out our own opinions and beliefs for ourselves—authenticity points us towards a more self-responsible form of life. It allows us to live (potentially) a fuller and more differentiated life, because more fully appropriated as our own.[146]

While Taylor is critical of the self-indulgence and the growing dependence on "self-appointed experts and guides, shrouded with the expertise of science or some exotic spirituality"[147] that quests for self-fulfillment may yield, he nevertheless emphasizes that the desire to become oneself is a moral force in our time that must be analyzed as kindred to other forms of individualism and freedom.[148]

In Chapter 4, I argue that it is precisely the pedigree of this humanistic, democratic lineage of self-fulfillment and self-realization that makes neoliberal self-techniques so attractive to young, ambitious people in today's Russia—together with the promises that applying these techniques to one's own life can lead to success and happiness.

To be sure, this pedigree of neoliberal techniques is by no means a sufficient condition to induce democratic social change in authoritarian states. As I show in Chapter 6, even to the contrary, neoliberal techniques can be successfully combined with traditional gender norms, a combination that can legitimate flexible authoritarianism. Nevertheless, the fact that humanistic and democratic ideals remain latent within neoliberal techniques that circulate globally bears the possibility that they will persist even when authoritarianism strengthens.

Thus, it might be that inculcating an entrepreneurial, can-do spirit in promising youth may lead those young people to demand a greater say in political decisions in the long run. When authoritarian rulers feed people's can-do spirit, they risk sowing the seeds of popular demands for a more just allocation of profits and greater participation in political decision-making.[149] Particularly when the teaching of neoliberal modernization ideals appears to meet potential strategic elites' desires for self-fulfillment, constrained by the firm limits felt in an authoritarian society with little chances of upward mobility, it might destabilize a dictator's standing.

It is essential to analyze this democratic pedigree of neoliberal thinking so as to understand why young people are inclined toward neoliberal arrangements beyond possible careerist, profit-maximizing motivations, or their purported inability to locate their actual material interest. Nevertheless, this appealing side of the ideals of neoliberal modernization may help, as I show in the following chapters, to legitimate the rather inert authoritarian state and its in-built resistance to reform processes in the eyes of young people.

What is more, the capacity of unquestioned neoliberal beliefs to hollow out the hope that human beings can "gestate and guide a decent and sustainable order,"[150] to act truly democratically, appears to be aided by what Olga Shevchenko, in her analysis of 1990s Russia, calls a "metalanguage of deconstruction and hidden interest."[151] Beyond as well as within Russia, the conviction that actual power will inevitably be wielded by small circles of influential people and the belief that behind every popular protest a financial tycoon may be hiding are increasingly accepted as axioms of political life.[152] These assumptions can make the prospect of mobilizing for a sharing of economic profits, greater participation in democratic processes, or stronger environmental protections seem nil.

Also in this regard, developments in Russia appear to be a forerunner of a global authoritarian Right gaining wide popularity.[153] As debates over Russia's war on Ukraine impressively illustrate, a variety of conservative and New-Right actors in Euro-American societies positively identify with Putin's rule and its ideological axioms. Such sympathies are not new; their proponents range from US-American conservatives who praise Putin's pro-Orthodox Church and homophobic stance as well as his hypermasculine self-fashioning,[154] to Viktor Orbán and his party *Fidesz*, who treat Putinism as a model for conservative and authoritarian change in Hungary,[155] to transnational conservative elite networks.[156] Such examples make a strong argument for the importance of viewing global authoritarian shifts from a Russian perspective.

2

Interlude

Entrepreneurial Start-Up Culture Meets Soviet-Style Suspicions: Reflections on Two Russian Youth-Leadership Camps

The vast majority of campers at the youth-leadership camps in Russia's Siberian and Far Eastern Federal Districts that I visited in 2013 were Russian citizens. Both the camper application process and life at the camp sites were tailored to young adults who knew Russian well and were familiar with standard administrative procedures such as submitting various health certificates—*spravki*—upon registration. In both regions, the camp organizers emphatically welcomed the application from a Western European PhD researcher keen to participate just as ordinary campers would, and who was only a few years older than the average participant. In one case, the organizers, or people close to them, even offered me a seat on a charter flight to Yakutsk to heighten the chances that I would attend camp that summer. While Appendix I covers the organizational, ethical, and methodological aspects of this and other aspects of my participation in detail, the following first-hand story, as I call it, provides a subjective description of my divergent experiences as a participating outsider at the two camps.

Unlike a standard academic text, a story is meant to be open to interpretation. It tolerates ambiguity. Calling the following narrative a first-hand *story* emphasizes that the situation in which the first-person narrator finds herself—part of a camp in the National Republic of Sakha (Yakutia), standing alone in front of her tent and experiencing a stream of thoughts—is constructed. The qualifier *first-hand* points to the fact that the reflections offered in the form of a story are, however, based on my actual experiences as a participant in the "Territory of Youth Taking Initiative *Biriusa*" camp in Central Siberia and the "*SakhaSeliger*" camp in Russia's Far Eastern District in 2013, the year before Russia annexed the Ukrainian peninsula of Crimea.

* * *

"*Podioooom*"—"get uuuuup!" The morning call woke me at 7:30 a.m. I unzipped the green one-person tent and peeked out onto a vast, flat land. It was a sunny day in July 2013, but still cold due to the permafrost ground on which we were camping here in the Sakha Republic, in Russia's Far Eastern Federal District. Most of my peers in the working group *Politika* ("Politics") at the *SakhaSeliger* youth-leadership camp, including the group of young women who had taken me under their wing, had already left their tents to wash up in preparation for the day.

I had arrived a few days earlier at *SakhaSeliger*, which was taking place that year at *Usad'ba Buluus*, a so-called tourist base that is typical of post-Soviet Russia,[1] located about three hours south of Yakutsk. Getting here from Krasnoyarsk, where I had participated in the "Territory of Youth Taking Initiative *Biriusa*" youth-leadership summer camp, had required a five-hour flight from Central Siberia westward to Moscow, followed by a seven-hour flight back toward the east from Moscow to Yakutsk's *Tuimaada* airport—which is located about 1,500 miles north of Korea. Because the date of my flight, organized by the Sakha Ministry for Youth and Family Policy, had been deferred by the ministry for unknown reasons, I did not reach Yakutsk until the second day of camp. The other campers having left by bus on the day before my arrival, I was met at the airport by a ministry staff member, who told me that they had arranged a driver to take me to the camp.[2] Another two hours by SUV and a ferry ride across the river Lena got me to the tourist base.

I learned from the driver, Stanislav Alekseevich, that such long car rides and ferry crossings are common in the Sakha Republic. Although it was 2:00 a.m. Moscow time when we started the trip, I felt wide awake, unsure about how to behave in this unfamiliar situation and impressed by the scenery of this landscape not far from the Arctic Circle, where trees are small and apples outside of greenhouses grow only to the size of large apricots. Little herds of Yakut ponies (*Sakha ata*)—a breed adapted to this region's extreme cold in winter and a valued source of meat—were dotted around the flat green land all along the lonely road leading to *Usad'ba Buluus*.

When I realized that Stanislav was happy to share stories about his two daughters and point out the region's cultural and climatic peculiarities, I started to enjoy the ride through these sparsely inhabited areas. The Sakha Republic is not only the largest administrative division of the Russian Federation, but also the least populated. Its area amounts to seven times that of California, but its population density, with an average of 0.31 people per square kilometer, is 700 times lower than Germany's. As one of Russia's national republics—a remnant of Soviet nationality politics—it is to date inhabited primarily by the Sakha and other people of non-Russian nationality such as the Eveni and the Evenki, but also by ethnic Russians. The Sakha Republic is also known for its extreme climate: winters are very cold, with temperatures falling to below minus sixty degrees Celsius. Although summers are hot, the ice several meters below the ground remains year-round (though global climate change is now causing this permafrost to thaw).[3]

While waiting for the ferry, Stanislav and I drank an instant coffee next to the landing. He told me that the promise of a bridge over the Lena close to Yakutsk—one promise of several, the first of which had been made during the Soviet period—was still unfulfilled. This meant that during the thaw, crossings were accessible only to those who could afford a plane or helicopter ride. Due to the very cold winters, though, it was possible to drive over the ice, even with trucks, as he assured me.

When we arrived, I found that the *Usad'ba Buluus* tourist base resembled a typical Soviet-type children's leisure camp, many of which continued to operate after the demise of the Soviet Union, hosting minors during their summer holidays.[4] Besides being located in rural areas, such leisure camps are often close to sites of general interest, as was the case here. The camp was near *Buluus*, a year-round glacier (*buluus* being the Sakha term for glacier), so that groups such as ours could engage in snowball fights in shorts and t-shirts during summer.[5] Next to the children's camp's red-roofed static wooden houses, the *SakhaSeliger* organizers had erected about eighty green two-person tents. This sight certainly differed from that of typical pioneer and children's leisure camps, which since the 1960s had replaced economical sleeping tents, reminiscent of a scout camp, with permanent sleeping quarters.[6] Probably to conform with the federal, high-profile *Seliger* camp's signature feature—which, unlike *SakhaSeliger*, was regularly visited by Vladimir Putin as well as his economic and political allies—local organizers sheltered campers in a temporary "tent city" (*palatochnyi gorodok*).

Right after I got out of the SUV, I was welcomed by one of our working group's team leaders. He made sure that I received the *SakhaSeliger* ID badge, a t-shirt with the logo of my *Politika* working group, and my own tent close to those inhabited by other members of the group. In stark contrast to my time at the previous camp, I found myself the center of attention the minute we left the office where I had to formally register as a camper. When we made our way to my tent, the camp's media group wanted an interview, as did a local radio station and a local newspaper. There was no possibility of "sitting around on the edges, not making a big deal of being there"[7]—the textbook advice for participant observers I had copied into my researcher's diary as a reminder. Rather, spending any time alone on the site was almost impossible, because fellow campers kept approaching me with welcoming words, many eager to ask what had brought me here, followed by inquiries about Germany and Europe. Given that I was one of only a few white campers, slightly older than the average and clothed a bit differently, I could be easily identified as the guest from Germany. As I discovered on the second day of my stay, the camp staff had gone as far as to announce my visit on the camp's social media page, even though my formal status was that of a normal camper. So, I reasoned, maybe everyone here thought of me as of an officially invited visitor— an inference that would have been supported by my late arrival.

Taking in the sunshine in front of my tent at *SakhaSeliger*, I pondered my very different earlier experience at *Biriusa*. I had reached *Biriusa*'s camp site together with other campers attending the themed session on "Civic Society and Volunteering" (*Grazhdanskoe obshchestvo i dobrovol'chestvo*). After a ride in a bus with bunting decorating the windshield, we had boarded a ferry to reach the *Biriusa* site. This camp took place on the shores of the Krasnoyarsk Sea, or Reservoir: a large artificial lake on an arm of the Yenisei River, which runs mainly along the border between Eastern and Western Siberia. We passed by the reservoir's huge hydroelectric dam, called *GES*, which was built during the Soviet period and is depicted on the ten-ruble banknote. In contrast to my energetic welcome at *SakhaSeliger*, fellow *Biriusa* campers on that ferry trip were rather reluctant to engage in conversations with me. After we arrived at the camp, I continued to notice a certain reticence toward me among some fellow *Biriusintsy* (as campers were commonly called), especially in our twelve-person-tent. One of the first *Biriusa* entries in my researcher's diary noted similarities between the atmosphere in our tent and the social dynamics that I recalled from school trips, when talking too much with outsiders could threaten one's chances of hanging out with the "cool" people.

This reticence contrasted with the open, colorful design of the camp site and the upbeat atmosphere of commonality that the daily program was intended to create. When we reached the site after the boat ride across the Krasnoyarsk Sea, it was immediately clear that it had been especially designed to host *Biriusa*. The organizers had taken the designation "Territory of Youth Taking Initiative" literally. It featured installations that encouraged us to see ourselves as part of a community of *Biriusintsy* striving for positive change in the region. For instance, a mime artist dressed as the Goddess of Justice invited us upon arrival to deposit colorful translucent stones on one of the two pans of her scale. We could pick one of the shiny stones that, as we were told, symbolized "good deeds" and put them on the pan representing positive change. Through this allegory, one could experience how our own positive contribution could add up to make a real difference when it took place conjointly with the engagement of like-minded *Biriusintsy*. Likewise, a huge painting of a "tree of life," which we were asked to brighten by adding leaves with finger paint before entering the site, encouraged the feeling of belonging to a community destined to do good.

The camp site was well equipped with media technology and enormous canopies where larger groups could meet. There was a coffee bar with bean-bag seating; a chill-out room with décor that appeared to have been taken from the latest catalog of a certain Scandinavian furniture corporation; a main stage, with an enormous screen and a PA, where general assemblies took place during the day and concerts or dance performances were staged almost every night. The last night even featured a foam party, a signature feature of *Biriusa*, as I learned from a tent mate who was participating for the second time. My fellow *Biriusintsy* seemed to really enjoy the education program. Though compulsory, it largely comprised project-management training sessions and exercises meant to boost our self-confidence that differed markedly from typical university lectures. They equally went for the facilitators' animation program and morning fitness exercises, which reminded me of the program at all-inclusive holiday resorts. And of course, sharing photographs and videos of one's camp experience on social media was very popular.[8]

Only one camper, Lev, whom I met in town after camp, prided himself on being immune to all of the "we are all in it together" spirit and what he called "NLP-moments," referring to the neuro-linguistic programming techniques used by trainers to increase campers' belief in their can-do spirit. All of this had the air of co-working environments and neoliberal self-improvement culture mixed with tourist offers for affluent young adults. In particular, the foam party on *Biriusa*'s last evening evoked the sexualized party atmosphere advertised by tourist companies to attract youthful customers.

Given this overall atmosphere, I had put the fairly cool reception from my *Biriusa* tent mates down to my older age and clumsy use of the smartphone that I had borrowed from a friend for the trip; to the possibility that

I had taken the textbook advice for participant observers of sitting around at the edges too literally; to the fact that I wrote in a diary in the evenings (though we all were advised to do so by the teaching staff to reflect upon our learning goals); and to my observation that, unlike me, most other *Biriusintsy* had apparently arrived in groups with friends or peers from the university and seldom talked freely to people in other working groups. But there was another possible reason for the wariness that I encountered from the *Biriusintsy*—one I learned of on the night before I left Krasnoyarsk for Moscow. That evening I met with Vadim, a fellow camper at *Biriusa* and an aspiring teacher, for a walk around the city's sights. After the walk, as we sat close to the museum of local history and exchanged thoughts about camp, Vadim announced that, because of his concern for "the good relations between Russia and Germany," he needed to tell me something. He went on to say that he did not want me to leave with negative impressions of his country. When my curious expression revealed that I was having trouble making sense of his words, he said that he did not want me to misunderstand the behavior of some of our fellow campers: "Don't think that their standoffishness had anything to do with you being German or the like; it was not about your nationality. Many just assumed that you are a spy."[9]

I was really taken aback. At first, being a fan of spy movies, I tried to see Vadim's revelation as a compliment, but quickly the unease returned. While I had indeed sensed a tense atmosphere between me and some fellow campers, I had never imagined that people in their early twenties might see me as a potential spy, especially since all the official organizers had been so glad that another foreigner, in addition to a group from Italy visiting for two days, was participating in the event.

In fact, Vadim was not the first person to have brought up the notion of me as a possible secret agent. Before camp, the quiz master at the Krasnoyarsk Irish Pub, which I visited with my couch-surfing host, had introduced my Bingo guess on the microphone with the words, "and now: our German spy!" I had been unsure whether to write this off as a singular instance, to understand it as a common joke about tourists visiting local bars in Siberia, or to read it as a sign of a growing general suspicion toward foreigners, fueled by the recently introduced foreign-agent law. This law, echoing the language used by Stalinist officials against dissenters of all stripes, thrives on the authoritarian notion that the state is constantly threatened from outside.

In the context of *Biriusa*, the spy rumor seemed not only anachronistic, as if a Soviet plot had been transplanted by a sci-fi director to a Silicon Valley setting; it also was at odds with how local youth politics self-fashioned themselves. Before boarding the buses, we had all gathered early in the morning at *Sporteks* (the Center for Extreme Sports)—until recently the only large-scale indoor skatepark in Siberia and one of the first projects realized by *Biriusintsy*—to register for camp. Centrally located on Krasnoyarsk's Island of Leisure, the Center also hosted the offices of the Krasnoyarsk youth political staff. Because I was to meet an organizer at her office, I encountered a quote in large silver Cyrillic letters that embellished the hallway leading to the offices:

> *Est' tol'ko odin sposob prodelat' bol'shuiu rabotu—poliubit' ee.*
> *Interesnoe delo vam podskazhet vashe serdtse.*
> Stiv Dzhobs
> The only way to do great work is to love what you do.
> Your heart will show you the interesting work.
> Steve Jobs[10]

I was greatly surprised by this display, because it contrasted sharply with common knowledge about Russian state youth politics, and especially with the manifestation of those politics at the well-known *Seliger* summer camp. This discovery, preceding my surprise about the camp site's design with its hallmarks of start-up business culture, suggested that *Biriusa* was fundamentally different from the federal *Seliger*. The latter was primarily known as having been established in 2005 by government officials in response to the anti-Putinist, pro-democratic Orange Revolution in Ukraine. In a preemptive gesture, flexing the regime's youthful muscles to intimidate local dissenters and international observers alike, *Seliger* was stylized as a pro-Putin elite camp, visited primarily by members of the government-sponsored youth group *Nashi* ("Those [Fighting] on Our Side"). Seemingly created overnight, this group made its way equally swiftly into (international) media headlines. Its recycling of Soviet-era parlance symbolized the Russian leadership's uncompromising stance toward international support for those young Ukrainians who protested to oust the Soviet-era nomenclature in their country.[11] This could be seen in the choice of the name *Nashi*; in the designation "commissar" for group members in leadership positions; in the group's invention of the URL "nashi.su," as in "Soviet Union," and in its staging of aesthetically impressive mass actions, such as its celebration of the Soviet victory over Nazi Germany, increasingly cast as a *Russian* national achievement under Putin. In this spirit, footage from the first *Seliger* camp included scenes of young activists apparently fully devoted to the incumbent president. For example, campers dressed in different colors stood in formation to depict the *Nashi* flag: a white cross on red ground in the midst of which a large campfire burned.[12] Later developments, commonly dated to have started after the 2008 presidential elections, indicated that *Nashi* shifted toward an entrepreneurial agenda, intended to educate economically trained leaders who were to create a Russian replication of the dot-com bubble.[13] However, when large-scale anti-Putin protests emerged in response to fraudulent elections all over Russia between 2011 and 2013, *Nashi*'s apparent inability to stop such actions led to rumors that *Nashi* was superfluous.

Given the pronouncedly nationalistic and authoritarian atmosphere of the original *Seliger* camp, I rather expected the youth political offices at *Sporteks* to display quotations from, say, a national figure such as Mikhail Lomonosov (the eighteenth-century polymath), or a local of exceptional merit such as Leonid Kirensky (cofounder of the Krasnoyarsk Institute for Physics, a renowned Soviet physicist of Sakha nationality). Yet instead I encountered a Steve Jobs quote, mirrored by another from the US-American philosopher and psychologist William James—the latter reminding visitors that a project's success depended on one's firm *belief* in success.[14] More incentives to boost our self-discipline and project-management skills were awaiting us at camp, which—as we were assured—was fully equipped with mobile internet access. As an interview with a long-standing youth political organizer revealed, in contrast to the federal youth political trajectory, fostering self-improvement and innovative projects had been founding principles of the region's revival of youth politics in 2006 and 2007. At a time when *Nashi*'s federal agenda was to support Putin's staying in power, Krasnoyarsk youth politics sought to spur local economic development, increase the employability of young adults, and use their ideas to modernize urban spaces.

As I looked for my toothbrush in my tent at *SakhaSeliger*, I tried to make sense of the apparent contradiction between, on the one hand, *Biriusintsys*' seemingly open-minded enthusiasm about thinking outside the box—to develop projects which would ideally increase quality of life—and, on the other hand, Vadim's revelations regarding their suspicions about me as a foreign participant. To me, the idea of putting one's creativity and passions into all kinds of projects that are then to be administered by a more optimal version of oneself was very familiar. The self-improvement training offered at *Biriusa* struck me as similar to popular advice I had received on how to heighten my employability as a humanities student; they appeared to be informed by the same assumptions that underlay the soft-skill courses that I had been offered through scholarship programs. In contrast, rumors insinuating that a fellow camper worked for a foreign secret service struck me as a relic from the Cold War, an impulse that one would find primarily in screenplays and fiction today.

Maybe, I thought, the campers had taken me for a spy simply because the camp organizers at *Biriusa* had not officially announced my visit. In contrast to my experience at *SakhaSeliger*, where I had been received as an official guest, I was treated like a normal camper at *Biriusa*, but still remained a stranger. Certainly, I had properly introduced myself to the *Biriusintsy* that I spoke to: as a young researcher from Germany who had become interested in young adult activism in Russia. I usually went on to explain that in the course of my research I had, by chance, discovered the existence of local versions of the federal *Seliger* camp and decided to apply for them: a unique chance to meet young and engaged people in Russia's far-flung regions. Yet, for sure, this introduction was still very different from an announcement on social media introducing me to campers as both a special guest and an additional camp attraction enlivening the *SakhaSeliger* experience.

I also thought that my status here might differ from the way in which I had been seen at *Biriusa* in part because, at *SakhaSeliger*, my foreign accent was not a cause for surprise. Unlike the members of the non-profit association Arci,[15] visiting *Biriusa* from Italy, I was not accompanied by a translator and spoke Russian fluently, an unusual and thus perhaps potentially suspicious situation in the context of *Biriusa*. Most campers here at *SakhaSeliger* often used Sakha terms when speaking Russian, and seemed to switch freely between the two languages. Knowing several languages struck them as normal. So, whereas among the *Biriusintsy* my particular kind of foreignness could have evoked suspicions that I might be a spy, here it did not seem to arouse any wariness.

My thoughts went to events and developments that would make it more likely for young adults to develop such a suspicion. For sure, the Putin administration had re-introduced the Soviet terminology of the foreign agent and, through the very act of creating legislation to thwart the work of such alleged agents, sown suspicion about foreigners among those who believed that Putin's policies addressed existing realities. This act certainly facilitated speculations about whether foreigners were involved in a plot against the country.[16] On top of that, the Edward Snowden whistleblower affair, with

Snowden having found a temporary refuge from US authorities in Moscow's Sheremetyevo airport, might fuel fears of secret services amassing information on quite ordinary people. The Kremlin's decision to criticize Snowden, but refusing to extradite him to the US, probably lent further credibility to the popular expectation that relations with the West would deteriorate because Russia would no longer dance to the West's tune.

Another instance of this new national self-awareness vis-à-vis an allegedly dominating West was the novel law criminalizing public talk and visibility of intimate, nonheterosexual relationships in the presence of minors.[17] A Dutch filmmaking team, for example, had been accused of speaking publicly about homosexuality when minors were present in the audience. The Western response to this Russian law was something both campers and people I met by chance wanted to discuss with me. Two fellow campers at *Biriusa* had asked me many questions about gender and sexual orientation in Europe while we were sitting on the lawn during a break. They wanted to know whether there was truth to the rumor that it would soon be forbidden in Europe to say "mother" and "father," terms now—according to media reports they had read—seen as overly heteronormative under conditions of Western ultrapolitical correctness. They wanted to know why so many people in the West supported the Pussy Riot performance—a punk prayer staged by masked Russian feminists in a Moscow landmark, an enormous Orthodox Christian cathedral symbolizing the return of (the) patriarchy and conservatism in Russia alongside the spread of authoritarian practices in government and public institutions. Like two young men that I met in the Krasnoyarsk Irish Pub with my couch-surfing host, these *Biriusintsy* were also highly curious about what people in Germany thought of same-sex marriage. (Because they were both in their early twenties, and thus clearly adults, it had felt safe to engage with them in a conversation about same-sex relationships; the fate of the Dutch filmmaking team was not something I wished to replicate.) They had been split over the issue of queer sexuality: Vania believed that homosexuality was normal, having existed since ancient history, while Vadim visibly struggled to accept that what he deemed deviant behavior was acknowledged, and even publicly displayed, in Western Europe. All of these instances of an intensifying nationalism and neotraditionalism tied into the bigger picture of an apparent emergence of a new Cold War, with past hostilities and spy-practices resurfacing.

Certainly, it seemed to me that besides the Snowden affair, the rights of LGBTQI people were the talk of the town that summer. At *SakhaSeliger*,

38 FLEXIBLE AUTHORITARIANISM

I had noticed in passing a heated discussion about whether being gay was normal—which I did not feel entitled to listen to and did not fully comprehend. What I did understand well enough, though, was a related statement by the Sakha Republic's former Minister of Education. He had been invited to meet us members of the *Politika* working group at the "campfire talk," a format facilitating networking with VIP guests. He declared that he had left Russia's oppositional Green Party (*Yabloko*) for the ruling party United Russia when the former had become "too preoccupied with gays," a preoccupation he considered to be a Western import.

It was also interesting to me that the setup here at *SakhaSeliger* was much simpler and more rustic than the one at *Biriusa*. In lieu of individual flushing toilets for campers, we used only an outhouse with three pit latrines. A wooden shed with three cold-water taps served as the communal shower for female campers. At *Biriusa*, meanwhile, tents could be heated with a stove, and it was even possible to shower with hot water. As a longtime *Biriusa* organizer asserted, the site there was even more modern than that of the federal *Seliger*. While the spirit at *SakhaSeliger* was equally upbeat and enterprising, this camp's accoutrements hardly called to mind a Berlin start-up hub. Only some posters and the tent city bespoke the format of a government-sponsored youth-leadership summer camp à la *Seliger*. The reason may have been that *SakhaSeliger*'s initial co-funding from the federal youth agency *Rosmolodezh* had been severely cut now that the camp was taking place for a second time, as one of the campers who had also attended the first *SakhaSeliger* told me. The difference in equipment might very well follow from the different budgets available for youth politics. The Krasnoyarsk Region's youth political expenditures were among the top five in Russia, and had been so since about 2007. As I learned after camp, a number of the modern-looking features embellishing the city center had indeed started as project ideas presented by *Biriusintsy* at camp. Besides *Sporteks*, Krasnoyarsk featured *Kamenka*, a refurbished Soviet palace of culture with space for cultural events, showrooms for start-ups, and co-working offices; a riverside art walk with changing installations; and a free book exchange in an English phone booth on the city's central boulevard bordered by palm trees in flowerpots. Projects like these could be realized when *Biriusintsy* won public grant money or managed to find sponsors among local businesspeople.

Taking in the open landscape and the many small green tents around me at *SakhaSeliger*, I thought how relaxing it was to be spared the jingles to signal the start of meals or lectures that reverberated from the main stage's

PA at *Biriusa*. (However, from several comments about how impressively equipped the federal *Seliger* was, I gathered that most of my fellow campers at *SakhaSeliger* would probably have preferred the more party-like atmosphere and contemporary equipment.) I also found myself thinking that despite having so little time for myself, I enjoyed the sociability here, especially with my working-group peers. This was perhaps supported by the time and effort we ourselves invested in the entertainment program. Probably to save funds, no facilitators were on hand to animate us, and no professional artists were hired for concerts and performances. Instead, we would participate almost every evening in singing and dancing contests, with a jury that often included that day's VIP guest deciding upon which of the working groups performed best. As early as the day of my arrival, my working group staged a performance consisting of different dances symbolizing the history of the United States, starting with dances deemed to have been performed by Native Americans prior to the 16th century and ending with breakdance. Although I had arrived late, I was quickly integrated into the making of costumes and participating in the choreography.[18] The jury awarded our group the first prize that evening. The rehearsals, the shared nervousness before our performance, and the tension when prizes were announced had created a temporary bond among several of us. It had not mattered that I was kind of different from the others; at least, I had not sensed that it did.

For some reason, there were also fewer security controls here, maybe because the security service was made up of campers. At *Biriusa* I had often been reminded by security guards, who had apparently been hired by the organizers, to display the Biriusa identity badge more visibly, so that they could see my photograph and working-group affiliation. I mused that perhaps it was these security precautions that had created an atmosphere of suspicion. Or perhaps it was the case at *Biriusa* that spies were simply expected to be lurking around every corner. Luba, a fellow camper at *Biriusa*, told me that she had applied for an IT job at the local office of the FSB (Russia's Federal Security Service). When I expressed my surprise that they had offices in such small towns as hers, she replied, "Oh, they have offices everywhere."

"*Aaana, davai*," my tent neighbors called to me as they returned from the washroom, seeing me still standing with my toothbrush. I needed to hurry up; it would make a bad impression among the camp organizers if not all of our working group showed up on time for the calisthenics. But I was still jetlagged, and preoccupied by the memory of Vadim's revelation that I had been mistaken for a spy at *Biriusa*. As I rushed to join my fellow campers,

I tried to assuage my worries that my own potentially misleading behavior might have caused the rumor. In all popular movies a spy, I reminded myself, has all the possible means of substantiating her fake identity. Once the trope of possible espionage takes root, it gives rise to a shared suspicion that is often impossible to counter with deeds or words.

3
Soviet Traditions in Service of Flexible Authoritarianism

Flexible authoritarianism is a regime type that depends on the loyalty of the ambitious and well educated. How to win their acceptance for a regime that limits political freedoms, but promises a brighter future in terms of socioeconomic well-being? While it is commonplace to define a political regime by closely studying its underlying ideology and government discourse, a fuller understanding of its workings requires analyzing those tropes, images, and cultural forms through which it is legitimated more or less tacitly. What are the unquestioned beliefs and conventions that a summer camp tradition, as I call it, may reproduce, largely unnoticed?

Political economist Cornel Ban has convincingly argued that too little is known about local actors' reasons for introducing neoliberal politics.[1] Expanding on his research agenda, I ask in this chapter which local actors in the Putin-era Russian context that I examine promoted neoliberal forms of youth education, and why they found those forms suitable to current conditions. Such a focus on domestic actors reveals how Soviet socialist cultural forms and practices of instigating volunteer activism, incentivizing work performance and intending to create loyalty to the politico-economic regime, have been reinvigorated in the twenty-first century to spur entrepreneurship and economic development in some of Russia's remotest regions.

The youth-leadership summer camps that I describe in this and the following chapter are officially called "Youth Educational Forums" (*molodezhnye obrazovatel'nye forumy*), invoking associations with economic leadership events such as the World Economic Forum. These camps merge neoliberal elements specific to young leaders' summits and entrepreneurial start-up culture with traits of what I call a Soviet summer camp tradition. I provide background on the cultural form of the summer camp and outline Soviet summer camps' cultural history, highlighting the interplay of internationally circulating practices at camp with Soviet specificities. The summer camp tradition is certainly used as a tool of legitimation in today's Russia;

yet it is also a popular topos in movies and novels in the post-Soviet space. As a widely known cultural form, summer camps for leisure, and especially the famous *Artek* summer camp on the Crimean peninsula, invoke the "imaginary geography of the happy Soviet childhood," to use historian Monica Rüther's expression.[2]

Thus, I use the designation "summer camps" to allude to the repurposing of Soviet forms of youth engagement, including a Soviet summer camp tradition, for flexible authoritarian ends. By "tradition," I mean here a framework for action, or a template of how to organize a certain type of event that can go largely unquestioned because it is widely shared and has an established history.

The Soviet summer camp tradition lends itself to a neoliberal repurposing, because well before the 1990s transition to capitalism, the organization of Soviet leisure was designed to engender individual initiative and self-discipline to facilitate Soviet citizens' self-realization.[3] The aim then was to create the New Soviet Person, who would, among other things, be individually motivated and, at the same time, naturally inclined toward group aims. As historian Jochen Hellbeck's account of Soviet diarists suggests, Soviet citizens did indeed strive to harmonize their individual desires with the goals of Soviet communism.[4] Ideologically, these goals were anchored in humanistic ideals such as self-realization, even though actual politics during the Soviet period often diverged from or even opposed such ideals. During Perestroika especially, there were attempts to restore a communism that was founded on the "free self-realisation of the individual,"[5] especially because the ideal of self-fulfillment through work was far from the truth for most workers in the Soviet Union.[6] In the 1980s, social philosopher Jon Elster called Marxism's "conception of the good life as one of active self-realization."[7] Marxism-Leninism as official Soviet state ideology retained traces of this conception and translated it into a set of practices, some of which came to shape Soviet leisure organization.

To distinguish between such humanistic appeals and flexible authoritarian instrumentalizations of them, I reserve the terms self-fulfillment and self-realization for the Hegelian idea of "*Bei-sich-selbst-seyn*—to be at home, not to be impinged upon by what is not one's own, by alien obstacles to self-realisation whether on the part of individuals or civilisations."[8] In contrast, I use the term self-improvement when describing attempts to instrumentalize this desire for neoliberal and authoritarian ends. Young campers themselves mostly used the term self-development (*samo-razvitie*) in their narratives, highlighting their desire to contribute through their own personal development to the development of their region. Whenever I attend to campers' own desires and expectations, I will use the terms self-develop or self-development. This choice reflects my assumption that while they are inspired by desires for self-fulfillment, they are also shaped by transnational and state appeals to self-improve so as to align their self-understandings with the demands of capitalist markets and the state.

Focusing on the repurposing of Soviet traditions for flexible authoritarian ends at the local level implies assigning the widely known *Seliger* camp and its connection with the pro-Putin youth organization *Nashi*—which translates as "Those [Fighting] on Our Side"—a less prominent role for the evolution of Putinist state youth politics than in the standard academic narrative.[9] Initially designed to prevent a possible change of government in Russia, *Nashi* was initiated by government officials in 2005 and liquidated in 2013.[10] In the early 2000s, the so-called color revolutions, whose poster children were young people in Ukraine, Georgia, and Kirgizia, ousted many politicians with ties to the former Soviet nomenklatura across the post-Soviet space.[11] By that time, almost twenty years before the Russian military fully invaded neighboring Ukraine, the Kremlin was already blaming Ukraine's so-called Orange Revolution on Western interference in Ukrainian and Russian politics and portraying it as an assault on Russia's sphere of influence.[12] The Kremlin used the portrayal of an Orange Threat to Vladimir Putin's power position, which allegedly guaranteed stability in Russia after the rocky 1990s, to curtail democratic freedoms, such as the rights to assembly and to form non-governmental associations.[13] The Orange Threat also served to justify the foundation of *Nashi*, whose youthful members gathered once a year at the *Seliger* summer camp.[14] Internationally, *Seliger* became widely known for its stagings of public support for Putin.[15] *Nashi*'s initiation—or that of its predecessor organization, "Walking Together" (*Idushchie Vmeste*)—forms the starting point of the dominant narrative of how state youth politics evolved under Vladimir Putin.[16] Without a doubt, the federal-level *Seliger* camp and the Federal Youth Agency *Rosmolodezh*, largely shaped by *Nashi* cadres,[17] have been central for the spread of the summer camp format across the country. In 2022, more than forty youth-leadership summer camps took place, most of which were at least co-sponsored by *Rosmolodezh* (for an overview of youth-leadership summer camps across Russia, see Appendix II).[18]

The alternative story that I tell about the evolution of Putinist state youth politics does not refute the significant influence of federal institutions in spreading them across the country. However, it traces the neoliberal emphasis within such a politics to the Krasnoyarsk Region of Central Siberia, where, starting in 2003, Aleksandr Khloponin, a successful manager-turned-governor, reinvigorated Soviet models of youth participation to engage young people in work regarded as socially useful. Khloponin's career trajectory testifies to the dual strengthening of both economic development and authoritarian restructuring. He was widely known before he turned to politics as manager of Norilsk Nickel—"one of Russia's economic crown jewels," as the multi-million-dollar corporation was once characterized in the *New York Times*.[19]

Before I turn to the history and salient features of the Soviet summer camp tradition and Khloponin's investment in local youth politics, I discuss neoliberalism and authoritarianism as political ideologies with a subjective side. While my discussion of these concepts in Chapter 1 revolved largely around their influence on global politico-economic processes, the micro-analytical scope of this chapter and of those that follow engages with them as ideologies that affect people in their daily lives, their interactions with others, and their relationship to themselves.

The Subjective Sides of Neoliberalism and Authoritarianism

Neoliberalism's subjective side is often described as part of a larger process of replacing top-down forms of rule with new management techniques, such as incentives, that are designed to make people act in a specific way.[20] A useful example of this kind of incentive is tipping: a waiter's dependence on gratuities to make ends meet makes for a powerful incentive scheme. Besides questions of material rewards, neoliberal incentive schemes have much to do with cultural values, as Angela McRobbie's research suggests. She argues that a romantic view of creativity, of self-expression through and in work, and of freeing oneself from routine labor drives young people's seemingly individual aim to self-improve in order to continue engaging in creative work.[21] According to her, such cultural values are fueled by orchestrated state and business incentives.

Such subjective readings of neoliberalism go back to the writings of philosopher Michel Foucault. According to Foucault, neoliberal subjects have internalized the threat of punishment. As he describes in his classic *Discipline and Punish*, disciplinary measures historically employed by sovereigns to rule others, and often characterized by the use of excessive force, became increasingly internalized by individuals to discipline and rule themselves in a gesture of preemptive obedience.[22] This self-disciplining of what Foucault calls "docile bodies" is, according to him, central for the smooth functioning of the (neoliberal) economy and the modern state. Present-day examples of this kind of neoliberal impact on subjects include the notion that jobs are supposed to be fun, the tendency for people to feel bad about themselves when theirs is not, and the propensity to regard leisure as an opportunity to improve one's employability.[23]

Unlike analyses of neoliberalism, the study of authoritarianism's subjective side has long been neglected in favor of explanations of anti-democratic politics that center on a nation-state's political system.[24] Only recently has the study of authoritarian personality—understood as an abstract combination of personal characteristics—undergone a revival.[25] Ever larger numbers of researchers are re-evaluating the Authoritarian Personality study that emerged from a close collaboration between social scientists and critical theorists in the 1940s as a valuable tool to analyze the identification of quite ordinary people with authoritarian values.[26] In line with this trend, I use the study's identification of several authoritarian values to analyze the summer camps' educational content and their dominant "organizational and pedagogical style" (*Erziehungsstil*).

This concept stems from another strand of inquiry relevant to the subjective side of authoritarianism: social psychologist Kurt Lewin's examination of the effects that ideal-typical organizational and pedagogical styles have on group atmospheres.[27] Lewin differentiated between authoritarian, democratic, and laissez-faire styles. He found that an authoritarian *Erziehungsstil* creates group atmospheres that are characterized by unconstructive criticism, mutual distrust, scapegoating, hostility, and a high degree of dependence on the group's leader for cohesion.

The Soviet Summer Camp Tradition

Summer camps as a form of education for young people are certainly not a Soviet or Russian invention. Rather, they (and some of the practices associated with them) spread from the Anglo-American world to Tsarist Russia.

They came into being during the late nineteenth and early twentieth century, when European and US-American pedagogues turned to nature as a principle frame of reference for so-called reform pedagogy.[28] As historian Abigail van Slyck has pointed out, the establishment of summer camps responded to hopes that untouched wilderness could bring "physical and spiritual rejuvenation" to urban citizens and allay anxieties about the disappearance of nature.[29] Rural recreation was intended to alleviate the negative consequences of modern, urban ways of life on young people. Early camp advocates often took an anti-modernist stance, culminating in their "revisioning of nature as a sanctuary from the artificial, mechanized world of the city."[30]

Though early twentieth-century summer camps vastly differed in their political and religious perspective, many shared a common concern over the feminization of white middle-class male adolescents.[31] Engaging in physical activity in the outdoors was thought to strengthen male adolescents' character and instill in them values such as cleanliness, obedience, and discipline.[32] The Boy Scouts is probably the organization that had the largest influence on nature-related recreation and education initiatives aimed at young people.[33] It was founded in the 1910s by the British General Baden-Powell, who was appalled at the military incompetence he encountered during the Boer War in what is now South Africa.[34] The Boy Scouts and its militaristic educational measures spread not only to the US, where it was among the first to offer middle-class white boys a summer-camp experience, but also to other parts of the world, including Tsarist Russia and the early Soviet Union.[35]

In Tsarist Russia, the Scout Movement was inspired by the Boy Scouts. There, it provided a more civilian alternative to so-called Play Regiments that promoted recruitment into the army and, soon to become co-educational, was promoted as part of liberal education reforms.[36] According to historian Catriona Kelly, this reform described the Scouts as a "means of disseminating physical education, and of propounding moral education 'under conditions that are attractive to boys and girls—close contact to the world of nature.'"[37] By 1916 the Scout Movement—*skauty*—was well established in Tsarist Russia: its members spread across 143 Russian cities, and related organizations such as the *gerly-skauty* for girls had been founded. In Russian-language scouting guides, the ideal Scout was presented as morally upright, socially committed, and stoic.[38]

The Soviet Young Pioneers, Summer Camps, and Culturedness

The *skauty* had a considerable influence on the Young Pioneers, a Soviet youth organization, which was founded in the 1920s—slightly later than the Communist Youth League (*Komsomol*).[39] As Catriona Kelly argues, the Young Pioneers had taken inspiration from the Boy Scouts, borrowing "its oath and laws, its slogan of 'Be Prepared,' its militaristic symbolism, its structure (with 'patrols' renamed as 'troops'—*otriady*, and 'sixes' as 'links'—*zven'ya*)."[40] Likewise, many of the Pioneer activities were designed to encourage young people's interest in nature: sports, trips to the countryside, and stays at summer camps.[41] And the Pioneers even promoted similar values, such as cleanliness and discipline. However, unlike their Anglo-American counterparts, their activities were co-educational from the beginning, in accordance with the Bolsheviks' attitude to gender equality. They were also undoubtedly intended to elevate the children of workers, and not the children of those who enjoyed a superior status in the prerevolutionary social hierarchy. The Young Pioneer organization was conceptualized as a firm rejection of the antimodernism that characterized several of the back-to-nature practices at summer camps in capitalist countries.[42] Likewise, pioneers were expected to renounce religion and any form of individualism, and instead cherish collectivist attitudes. They were to bear the essential characteristics of the New Soviet Person that the Bolsheviks hoped to nurture and educate.[43]

Subjugating one's own narrow interests to the larger aims of the collective was central to a novel understanding of culturedness (*kul'turnost'*). From the 1920s onward, the Soviet authorities established a general canon of good behavior, the promotion of which involved fostering workers' and peasants' appreciation of high culture[44] as well as of "hygienic habits, refined manners, and proper comportment."[45] Large-scale campaigns against alcohol, tobacco, and "sexual dissoluteness" were informed by a moral imaginary of the New Soviet Person as much as by overlapping concerns about Soviet citizens' health and their capacity to work.[46]

The sphere of leisure was as key to promoting culturedness as those of work and education. Pioneer camps were equally intended to offer edifying and educating leisure activities to children and young people. Early Soviet advocates of federal tourism promoted a purposeful vacation that would benefit tourists' health, their sense of collectivity, and their appreciation of cultural sites.[47] In addition, their aim was to instill a love for the Soviet Union in those tourists, which entailed being knowledgeable about and appreciative of the Union's many ethno-cultural groups (*natsional'nosti*).[48] Especially relevant to the question of repurposing Soviet traditions for neoliberal ends is the pioneer camps' expectation that vacations should also improve what today would be called "soft skills." Staff at tourist resorts were tasked with fostering self-initiative among the guests; amateur evenings featuring self-organized dances, concerts, and skits were a key element of purposeful vacation. These evenings were intended to cultivate the guests' capacity for group performance and team spirit, but also their public speaking skills.[49]

Overall, Soviet vacations were designed to engage Soviet citizens in types of activities that would enhance their individual initiative, self-discipline, and self-organization—traits and skills read today as pertaining to a neoliberal work ethic.[50] This was fully in line with the Bolsheviks' vision of future socialists as proficient in self-mastery and self-activation.[51]

A precise ordering of the day was thought to be of particular importance for developing a personality that was proficient in self-mastery and self-activation.[52] The renowned Soviet pedagogue Anton Makarenko emphasized discipline, structure, and punctuality as key priorities of a healthy upbringing: "From the very earliest age children should be trained to keep exact time and clearly defined bounds of conduct. [...] Punctuality means being in reach of discipline and parental authority."[53] Accordingly, state leisure institutions promoted a strict daily regime, dividing the day into units for physical exercise, rest, and cultural activities.

Such precise scheduling was especially influential for the organization of pioneer camps. As early as 1924, pioneer camps featured a strict daily routine: the morning roll call was usually followed by gymnastics and work assignments, which lasted until lunch. After an obligatory rest, the afternoon was reserved for community service, whereas games and competitions were scheduled for the evening. Conversations around the bonfire, film screenings, or self-organized performances by the campers brought the pioneer camp day to a close.[54] The 1935 poster "Pioneer Camp—Base of a cultured and healthy vacation" features such a timetable, captioned with this explanation: "The approximate daily regime for mass pioneer camps (confirmed by the central committee of the VLKSM)," and a slogan, emphasizing the purposefulness of such vacations: "The correct leisure in camp is the best preparation for the new school year."[55]

A hollowing-out of the decidedly political character of early pioneer camps coincided with changes in access to this kind of vacation.[56] Up to the 1950s, taking part in a pioneer camp was reserved for a thin stratum of Soviet youth; for a long time becoming a Young Pioneer was a badge of honor.[57] It was only by the end of the 1960s that nonmembership in the pioneer organization became a sign of social deviance and that most Soviet youth could—forty years after the first pioneer camps were established—enjoy some kind of state-organized health break during the summer. Still not all children and young people could visit a proper pioneer camp, however. Nonetheless, the mass participation in camp meant that certain experiences were becoming widely shared.[58]

Within the mundane reality of everyday life in late Soviet society, the summer camps took on a symbolic significance as sites widely associated with childhood memories, often positive.[59] Positive references to camp experiences were facilitated when, from the late 1950s, camping expeditions, football matches, concerts, and competitions replaced "socially useful work" and political rallies. Political education and agitation increasingly gave way to leisure activities, meaning that talks with renowned visitors around the bonfire and the singing of patriotic songs were among the few activities that retained an outright political character.[60] The extent to which camp experience was seen to lie in the various competitions between different troops that competed against each other was expressed by camp counselors in the 1970s: "What kind of camp experience would it be if children did not compete in sports, music festivals, and funny quiz show and sketch comedy sessions?!"[61]

The formation of a summer camp tradition was also furthered by the special position that the camps occupied in Soviet propaganda. As meeting places for young people, who uniquely embodied the future of the socialist cause, their symbolic significance for the state was considerable.[62] And as such they were ideal material for filmmakers aiming to parody Soviet life.

The Dominant *Erziehungsstil* at Soviet Pioneer Camps and at Post-Soviet Children's Camps

The satirical comedy *Welcome, or No Trespassing* (*Dobro pozhalovat', ili postoronnim vkhod vospreshchen*) provides a highly valuable source to consider the formal characteristics of Soviet summer and pioneer camps.[63] The pedagogue Aleksei Kudryashev regards the movie as "an artistic symbol of the dialectical contradictions within pioneer summer camps"[64] oscillating between, as he calls it, romanticism and regimen. The comedy was directed by Elem Klimov, who is known outside Russia primarily for his war drama *Come and See*. *Welcome, or No Trespassing*, which aired in 1964, became a classic of Soviet cinema.[65] As the anecdote goes, Nikita Khrushchev himself found the movie so hilarious that he approved of the release after it had been shelved for some time by *Mosfilm* studio administrators.[66] The comedy is set in Southern Russia, not far from the pioneer camp *Orlenok*. Its humorous critique of Soviet concerns for cultured behavior is reminiscent of Czech New Wave productions such as Jiří Menzel's 1969 *Larks on a String*. While *Welcome, or No Trespassing* is usually analyzed as a persiflage on Soviet society under Khrushchev, I focus on those elements that parody Soviet pioneer camps' authoritarian *Erziehungsstil*: the abundance of rules, the deep concern for discipline, comprehensive precautions concerning children's health, and the organization of a competitive relationship between hierarchically-structured troops (*otriady*) and their leaders (*vozhatye*).

The comedy's plot revolves around the adventures of the young pioneer Kostia Inochkin. Kostia is the antithesis of Soviet author Arkadi Gaidar's widely-known teenage character Timur. Gaidar's *Timur and His Squad*, published in 1940 in the children's newspaper *Pionerskaia Pravda*, became a classic. In 2013, the title was added to a "100 books for pupils" list and recommended by the Russian Ministry for Education.[67] Unlike Timur, whose behavior is exemplary in terms of patriotism, culturedness, and self-initiative, Kostia does not engage in socially useful work. He neither serves the motherland, exhibits obedience to patriarchal authority, or starts (like Timur) an initiative in the service of war veterans.[68] His character and behavior necessarily clash with pioneer camp director Dynin's zero-tolerance policy.

The plot is straightforward. Kostia leaves the designated swimming area (*liagushatnik*, literally "frog pond"), despite close supervision of the swimmers by the pioneer camp's doctor and two lifeguards. This transgression results in his expulsion from the pioneer camp. Because Kostia fears shocking his grandmother with this news, he clandestinely returns to the—gated and disinfected (!)—camp site, where his fellow third-troop campers increasingly support his hidden existence. Even some of the camp staff start acting in solidarity with Kostia, breaking with their previous submission to authority that camp director Dynin and the camp site's organization symbolize.

Such discipline is also supposed to be upheld by the competitive relationship among troops. When Dynin publicly expels Kostia from the camp and his fellow third-troop members start to murmur objections, Dynin publicly reprimands the troop by pointing to the exemplary behavior of the second troop. The whole second troop instantly salutes when he mentions it.

When the third troop's leader, Valia, learns about Kostia's illegal return to camp, she does not report him, but collaborates with rank-and-file troop members to help him. This has repercussions for her own standing. A key scene, alluding to both troop leaders' responsibility for the rank and file and the medical supervision of campers, is set in the pioneer camp doctor's office. Dynin checks the troops' average weight gains, displayed on a board titled "Diagram of weight gain per troop" (*Grafik privesa po otriadam*).[69] Dynin is aggravated by the collective weight loss of the third troop, who secretly share their meals with Kostia. When Valia enters, Dynin vents his anger about the weight loss and the undisciplined troop behavior for which he holds her responsible:

> You should rather be taking care of what happens in your troop. All the others have gained weight, but the third troop is not making headway. [...] Do you know why? Can you see they are playing cards? They play cards in *your* [he points a finger at her!] troop. And not only the boys—the girls, too! [...] They take the meatballs somewhere! They could be preparing to escape, or even worse.[70]

This and other scenes testify to an authoritarian *Erziehungsstil*—exemplified, for instance, by the fact that camp goals, policies, and work assignments are all determined by the organization's leader, whose sole prerogative is to criticize or praise subordinates. As the film depicts it, everything about the camp fosters obedience to authority and submissiveness to discipline.[71] At the same time, such camps encourage competition between groups and an appreciation of self-initiative—as long as it does not question the regime's consensus—with rewards for outstanding individual pioneers. Ironically, by feeding Kostia and hiding him from the authorities, the third troop demonstrates an exemplary capacity for self-organization—though for a purpose that was not approved by Dynin.

As a comedy, the movie certainly exaggerates certain features; yet posts on internet forums for pensioners and on blogs about childhood memories testify that the *Erziehungsstil* lampooned in the film is remembered today as characteristic of summer camp experiences.[72] One woman who grew up close to several summer camps, but did not officially attend them, writes critically about the over-regulation that she witnessed:

> It seemed to us that it would be unbearable to march neatly in a row, to bathe according to the whistle and only in the *liagushatnik* [*kupat'sia po svistku i tol'ko v liagushatnike*], to go to bed at 9 pm, and to take the dreadful afternoon nap. [. . .] The administrations of all pioneer camps at the coast did not like our company [. . .]. They often confused us with children from the camp site at the beach and rudely demanded that we state our surname and the number of our troop.[73]

Another pensioner accentuates the competitive relationship among the troops at the pioneer camps. Inter-troop competition was meant to incentivize the young campers to maintain order and obey the rules, but also to build a team spirit within each troop and motivate them to fully apply themselves. To her, these rules belong to an overall positive memory about a happy childhood, and she does not find the authoritarian style of conduct problematic:

> All pioneer camps in the USSR were enlivened by the spirit of competition. Always the best troops, the best links [subgroups], were rewarded and, of course, the most deserving pioneers. The best were encouraged and rewarded. [. . .] We marched neatly in a row [*khodit' stroem*] and lived according to the schedule. They gave us orders, and we did not think about whether we should obey them. But does this mean that we were not lucky?[74]

As the letters of other former pioneers testify, campers were indeed threatened with expulsion for swimming in undesignated places; they were only allowed to enter the forest when accompanied by a counselor, and "menacing posters about how infections are spread and the danger of catching the common cold were posted up everywhere."[75]

Thus, the authoritarian *Erziehungsstil* characteristic of pioneer camps survived as a topos. To date, what I call a summer camp tradition has been widely shared through cultural productions such as Klimov's, as well as collective stories about camp experiences. Moreover, many younger Russians that I met throughout my research trips, who were born in the 1980s and 1990s, were hardly surprised by my description of the strict rules at youth-leadership summer camps. In fact, they found many of these rules reminiscent of the children's camps (*detskie lageria*) that they had attended themselves or heard of through stories shared by friends and family.

Several of the conditions and styles of conduct that characterized Soviet pioneer camps persist today in summer camps for children in Russia. Many sites of Soviet summer and pioneer camps survived the demise of the Soviet Union. Even though a large number of camps closed their doors during the early 1990s, more than 2 million Russian children still visited summer camps in 1999. There is evidence that between 2000 and 2010, six million children and young people between seven and fifteen years old, that is, one third of the age cohort, visited children's leisure camps in Russia.[76] After all, the problem of organizing childcare during the long summer vacations did not disappear; some summer camps managed to survive by addressing this need, while others were reinvigorated as sites of tourism for minors, sometimes subsidized by the state.[77]

Since the 1990s, such tourism sites have offered a variety of supervised summer holidays for children. Several of them clearly sought to counter the Soviet summer camp tradition by letting children practice autonomy and find their own way of doing things.[78] Some emerged from the Perestroika critique of the dominant "command-authoritarian style" [*komandno-avtoritarnyi stil' rukovodstva*] in Soviet youth education.[79] During that period, pedagogues began to stress individual autonomy as central for encouraging initiative among young people. As Galina Sukhoveiko stated in the summary of her dissertation, which was defended at the Higher Komsomol School in 1990:

> *Perestroika* allowed us to reconsider the education of the Soviet person. Today, a new kind of person is needed in society: not the conformist, obeying orders from above, but a person who is competent in his profession, who is autonomous, courageous, who takes initiative, acts decisively and considers the consequences of his actions, a person who works creatively and responsibly.[80]

Such developments notwithstanding, most summer camps for children (*ozdorovitel'nye detskie lageria*) have held onto the authoritarian features of the *Erziehungsstil* described above.

Through personal encounters during my research trips, I became aware of the unquestioned status of a summer camp tradition as a cultural and organizational form. In the absence of literature on this persistent set of norms, an acquaintance suggested that I visit the summer camp where she had worked for several summers as a troop leader (*vozhataia*) while she was a student of pedagogy. In June 2014, we took a commuter train from Moscow to the summerhouse region of Kratovo. Besides the children's camp, operated by the union of Russian railway workers, Kratovo is known for its Soviet pioneer railways, today called "children's railways" [*detskie zheleznye dorogi*]. Operating since 1936, these are meant to heighten children's interest in railway professions.[81]

As I entered the camp site, a row of posters immediately attracted my attention. They featured empowering slogans such as "We are the rails which lead to the future!" [*Dorogi budushchego—eto my!*], as well as photographs of smiling children and youth wearing either neckerchiefs and bonnets or the Russian Railways uniform.

In the permanent sleeping quarters, posters drawn by the troop leaders outlined the daily routine, including morning sports and curfew. The schedule largely coincided with the one depicted on the poster from 1935 mentioned above. Printouts of weekly plans featured evening programs reminiscent of those during Soviet times, ranging from movie nights, concerts and comedy competitions (inspired by the TV show *Club of the Merry and the Sharp-Witted—Klub veselykh i nakhodchivykh*, or *KVN* for short) to rehearsals for Parents' Day—when campers would perform plays and songs for the visiting parents, displaying the results of their creative endeavors at camp.

My acquaintance underlined several times that troop leaders were expected above all to care about disciplined behavior among the children in their troop, the designation "troop" (*otriad*) still being in use. Troop leaders were responsible for their troops arriving on time for meals and other events; punctuality was supported not only through their reprimanding of campers, but also through loudspeakers that signaled the start of morning sports and curfew. Such discipline was also encouraged by incentives: at the end of the session, not only were prizes awarded to those campers who had won one of the many competitions (e.g. comedy, dancing, sport games), but also those who had demonstrated the greatest care for cleanliness and order. Troop leaders assigned grades for these tasks, on the basis of which the "most active camper" of the session was selected as the winner.

My acquaintance's descriptions of her experience as troop leader were substantiated by a contemporary Russian summer camp wiki, especially designed for troop leaders like her. Under the entry "discipline," the wiki states that maintaining discipline is a key task: "Discipline in the troop is very important. If there is no discipline, nothing will work: Neither atmosphere, nor creativity. Without discipline in the troop, you cannot even guarantee the security of the children (their life and health)—and this is your main duty!"[82] In fact, the related wiki entry "disciplinary principles" features a film still depicting camp director Dynin and a quote from Klimov's comedy. Dynin is quoted saying "Children, you are the masters of the camp. You! And what is demanded from you . . . ?" In response to Dynin's stern coaching, the campers answer in chorus, "Dis-ci-pline!"

Security precautions and disciplinary measures often tend to blur, and this is the case in contemporary summer camps for children in Russia. The official homepage of the Kratovo camp that we visited, for instance, prominently lists safety features, such as the fact that the camp is fully gated and guarded by a special security agency.[83] Moreover, parents are asked to sign a form stating that they have informed their children about the rules of the camp site—including that they should actively participate in the program; leave neither the site nor their troop without permission; not smoke, drink alcohol, or take any form of narcotics; and treat the staff with respect. Furthermore, long before the Covid-19 pandemic, campers were required to submit several medical certificates, guaranteeing that they were not suffering from any infection, had been vaccinated, and were in good condition to swim.[84] Such tight provisions are designed in part to secure campers' safety; they also reveal the notions of order and discipline and a certain unquestioned security standard that underlie the organization of such camps.

As we will see in the following chapter, several features of this Soviet summer camp tradition, including an authoritarian *Erziehungsstil*, disease prevention, and safety measures, inform the youth-leadership summer camps that I visited. What is more, today's youth-leadership summer camps repurpose the competitive character associated with camp, along with the Soviet appeals to engage in "work on the self" and show individual initiative (then in a collectivist spirit!), for flexible authoritarian ends. As I show in Chapters 4 and 5, it is those aspects of youth-leadership camps in particular that resonate with young people from remote areas.

Entrepreneurial Spirit and Soviet-style Youth Engagement in Siberia

Such a repurposing of Soviet forms of youth engagement for neoliberal ends, aimed at promoting individual initiative, self-confidence, and self-discipline, was key to the revival of youth politics in the Central Siberian region of Krasnoyarsk at the beginning of the 2000s. Unlike their federal counterpart at the time, Krasnoyarsk youth politics were designed to strengthen an entrepreneurial spirit among young people. Alongside the aim to ready regional youth for the challenges of flexible job markets, individual politicians' quests for power certainly played a formative role in youth politics. Yet garnering support for ruling authorities was much less pronounced in Krasnoyarsk youth politics than in the metropoles of Western Russia, where ensuring Vladimir Putin's position was the major concern for youth politics in the run-up to the 2008 elections.

Managers Becoming Governors and a New Post-Soviet Youth Politics

The reinvigoration of youth politics in the Krasnoyarsk Region was inextricably connected to the career of Aleksandr Khloponin, who was general manager of the giant mining company Norilsk Nickel before becoming the region's governor in 2002. Khloponin is part of a generation of managers whose biographical trajectories from business to politics bespeak the introduction of neoliberal reforms in Russia.[85] The Russian business weekly *Ekspert*, which named Khloponin person of the year in 2002, put it this way:

> A new generation of people enters big politics whose life experience and career took place in the new, post-Soviet Russia. Many await a significant renewal in connection with this—an orientation towards long-term goals regarding regional and national development [...], more professionalism and greater up-to-dateness.[86]

Like others in this new generation of managers, Khloponin understood his profession in an entrepreneurial manner, in the sense of creating "a new business or a radically new image/brand (*imidzh/brend*) for an existing business."[87] This understanding broke with an earlier one, which centered on the administration of state property by so-called Red Directors—those people who managed enterprises in the late Soviet period and often became their owners in the early 1990s. The Red Directors' management style was perceived as dry and routine, lacking the glamour of creativity and putative radical change usually associated with capitalist entrepreneurialism.[88]

Already in 1998, the Russian magazine *Career* (*Kar'era*) presented Khloponin as an ideal example of this acclaimed new type of manager.[89] As he himself, then CEO of Norilsk Nickel, stated in an interview that same year, echoing Schumpeter: "A true careerist lives for a Super-idea (*sverkhideia*). In this sense he is more of an idealist than a materialist . . . to create, to produce something out of nothing—these are the goals for a person."[90] Khloponin's references to personal ideals and his definition of success as "producing something out of nothing" encapsulate the notion that good management should arise from an enthusiasm for being creative, not from investing in workers' education or the modernization of factory organization.

Khloponin's career at Norilsk Nickel occurred at a time when more provincial communities where suffering from large-scale impoverishment due to the sudden market competition for articles of daily use in combination with radical privatization. To be sure, Moscow and St. Petersburg had become integrated into international business exchanges by the late 1990s, but the rest of the country was left behind, a situation sociologist Michael Burawoy vividly described at the beginning of the 2000s:

> As the center is integrating in the most advanced circuits of the global information society, the hinterland is hurtling in the other direction towards a neo-feudalism [. . .]. Their local economies are organized through extra-economic force, the racketeering mafias, connected to the local patrimonial state. On the ground, the working classes turn increasingly to subsistence production, small-scale trade, and familial exchange while relying on a cash economy for basic goods that they cannot produce.[91]

Young people in particular left what Burawoy calls the hinterland, that is, all places outside the big cities in Western Russia, in huge numbers.[92] As the authors of the government report "Youth of Russia 2000–2025" would put it, regional youth politics were designed to counteract those "serious losses for the human capital of the country."[93]

It would be misleading to portray Khloponin as a political reformer with few self interests. While, for instance, the Sakha Republic's *ALROSA*, one of the world's biggest diamond mining companies (whose name stands for *Almazy Rossii-Sakha*: "Diamonds Russia-Sakha") became the "single main contributor to the republican economy during the 1990s"[94] and continued to provide jobs for many employees during the economic turmoil of the 1990s, Norilsk Nickel was privatized and came to be owned primarily by Vladimir Potanin and Mikhail Prokhorov by the mid 1990s. The privatization was forced upon the federal government after it failed to pay back a loan. Both owners received most of the company shares as collateral for a loan that they had provided to the Yeltsin government—although the loan had been much smaller than the value of the shares. This so-called loan-for-shares scheme was central to their rise into the top ten of Russia's richest oligarchs—and to Khloponin's career as Norilsk Nickel's manager. He was the one who had introduced Potanin and Prokhorov, both friends of his, to each other in the Moscow of the late 1980s.[95]

Khloponin's turn to politics is widely perceived as being closely connected to securing big business interests.[96] For the Krasnoyarsk Region and its adjunct areas alone, he was one of three top Russian business managers to be elected governor, with several more managers competing in the ballots.[97] The background to these sudden changes of career was the strengthening of the central state vis-à-vis oligarchs during Putin's first term.[98] In this changing political climate, oligarchs attempted to safeguard their business interests through at least indirect representation in legislative bodies.[99] After stepping back from the CEO position at Norilsk Nickel, Khloponin was first elected governor of the small Taimyr Autonomous District in 2001, and—after the sudden death of Krasnoyarsk's governor, Aleksandr Lebed—successfully campaigned for the latter's post the following year.[100] When Putin abolished the governors' elections in 2004, Khloponin had already signaled his loyalty to the new president's politics: before openly supporting the abolition of those regional elections that had brought him to political power, he had joined not only the Putin-supportive United Russia party but even its Supreme Council.[101]

Given these gestures of loyalty to the Putin government, Khloponin's reinvigoration of Krasnoyarsk state youth politics could be read as simply another sign of his support for Putinism. However, his remaking of Soviet-style student brigades in 2005, which many regard as the initiation of a new youth politics in the region, differs in kind from the *Nashi* youth project that was initiated that same year at the federal level to thwart anti-Putin mobilizations. *Nashi* became quickly known for its staging of young patriotic mass support, such as on May 15, 2005, when 50,000 young people gathered on a central street in Moscow to honor the veterans of the Great Patriotic War.[102] In contrast, the reinvigoration of the Soviet tradition of student brigades in the Krasnoyarsk area was driven far more by concerns about the economy and a lack of entrepreneurialism among local youth. It also connected to a shared feeling that the end of the Soviet Union had left a cultural void regarding public leisure for teenagers and young adults.

Reinvigorating Soviet-Style Youth Engagement

Student brigades, *studencheskie stroitel'nye/trudovye otriady*, are a form of student summer break internship involving activities such as working on collective farms or assisting in the construction of large infrastructure projects such as railroads. This work was already monetarily compensated during the Soviet period. As historian Olga Gerasimova suggests, the comparatively good salary and the romance of travel drove students to become "labor fighters" in various student brigades.[103] That these brigades were resurrected as a kind of (paid!) internship program on Khloponin's initiative testifies to his managerial agenda. As Khloponin stated on July 1, 2005, at the opening parade of the new Krasnoyarsk Region's Student Brigades (*Krasnoyarskie Kraevye Stroitel'nye Otryady*), all the managers he knew had participated in student brigades, while he himself had participated in as many as five.[104] This connection to "the olden days" was further underlined when, in 2006, the local government invested more than 70,000 USD to provide the young fighters of the *KKSO* (as the movement was commonly referred to) with Soviet-style uniforms, badges, and a logo.[105]

Their retro style notwithstanding, from the outset the newly founded brigades had the clear focus of connecting students with the region's major companies, such as Norilsk Nickel, RUSAL (the world's second-largest aluminum manufacturer), and the freezer producer Biriusa, as well as with local construction and agricultural firms.[106] These paid "summer holidays" (*letnii otdykh*), as youth political organizers framed the internships, promised to provide young people with skills needed for managerial and societal tasks.[107] According to Daria Ivanovna Glazkova, a long-standing figure in regional youth politics, Khloponin had criticized young people's lack of entrepreneurial skills and initiative early on.[108] At a 2006 conference on youth and government politics, he defined what he meant by initiative in neoliberal management parlance: "I am least interested in the factor called 'work experience.' The primary thing for me is a young person's initiative, the skill to effectively generate ideas and realize them up to their final stage."[109] His words echo the downplaying of work experience and the emphasis on initiative that is so characteristic of flexible capitalism.[110]

As Daria Glazkova affirmed in our interview, the local revival of Soviet forms of extracurricular education such as the student brigades in the early 2000s was designed to cultivate soft skills such as time management (*taim-menedzhment*), fundraising, and self-management among young people.[111] As she interpreted it, organizations such as the Young Pioneers or the Soviet Youth League, which vanished in the 1990s, had been good schools of general organizational competences and of skills much sought-after by employers today:

> After 1991, after the demise of the Soviet Union, the system of extracurricular education broke down—which was strongly felt by the CEOs of the largest companies in 2003. Accordingly, around the end of the 1990s, at the beginning of the 2000s, the state started to pay close attention to youth politics [. . .] We had this system—Octobrists, Pioneers, *Komsomol*. And when a young person graduated, he did not only possess professional skills and competences, but also general competences of cultured behavior (*obshchekul'turnye kompetentsii*): How to talk with people, how to negotiate, how to organize other people. These skills were then [at the beginning of the 2000s] very much needed in enterprises and organizations.[112]

Thus, Soviet traditions such as the student brigades were deliberately repurposed in the Krasnoyarsk Region for educating a work force that would be ready for the needs of the flexible capitalist organization of business and state.

This thesis was also substantiated in an interview with Aleksandr Aleksandrovich Abramovich, a leading regional youth politician, who summarized the aim of youth politics more generally as the use of young people's potential for the sake of the region and the Russian state. Employing phrases from neoliberal management parlance such as "innovator-person" and "non-standard thinking," he highlighted in particular the idea that innovative young people are key to local and national development and the global race for economic competitiveness:

The innovator-person (*chelovek-innovator*) and the person with non-standard thinking are of utmost importance to us. [. . .] Without those people any kind of development, any kind of innovation are impossible. Today our country needs to actively participate in the race for technology, competitiveness, effectiveness [. . .] We do not want to lose. We want to be on the same/standard level [*my khotim byt' na urovne*], we want our economy and our manufacturing to thrive, we want our products to be bought abroad, and to live well and with dignity (*zhit' khorosho, dostoino*).[113]

Why did the Krasnoyarsk authorities not only seek to reinvigorate the spirit of self-activism and initiative, but also invest in creating a style—the uniforms, the badges, the language—that romanticized images of the Soviet past? This question is all the more relevant given that new forms of management discourse largely centered on the need to break with notions of routine and work experience that were closely associated with Soviet organization. As in postcommunist China, socialist planning was widely regarded by manager-politicians such as Khloponin as inefficient, irrational, and wasteful.[114]

Daria Glazkova's answer to this question testifies to the normalcy that she assigns to those acts, that is, reinvigorating Soviet traditions for market purposes: "Everything new is really the old which has been forgotten. Why should one abandon forms which are useful for both youth and the state?"[115] Similarly, Aleksandr Abramovich found that those Soviet forms which could further development in the present should be used freely: "I think that all the good things that existed in the Soviet Union should be revived, certainly taking into consideration today's state-of-the-art, the contemporary world, and the market character of our economy."[116]

While these interviews can only offer a glimpse into the motivations of local actors, they point to the importance of the partial rehabilitation of the Soviet past that came with Putin's ascent to power in 2000. Already in December 2000, the new president expressed his discontent with what he considered to have been a one-sided presentation of "the dark sides of Russian history" during the rule of his predecessor Boris Yeltsin:

And is it possible that during the Soviet period of the existence of our country we have nothing to remember besides Stalinist camps and repressions? Where do we place then [Jewish film composer] Isaak Dunayevsky, Sholokhov [winner of the 1965 Nobel Prize in Literature], Shostakovich [internationally acclaimed composer], Korolev [chief designer of the Soviet space program] and the achievements in the sphere of cosmos? Where do we place the flight of Yuri Gagarin? And equally, where to place the glorious victory of Russian weapons during the times of Rumiantsev, Suvorov and Kutuzov? And where the victory of spring 1945?[117]

The speech announced a sharp break with the post-Soviet memory politics under Boris Yeltsin, which portrayed its strongly anti-totalitarian and antisocialist stance as Russia's only route back to an allegedly "normal" Western form of development.[118] In 1991, two bills were passed under Yeltsin with the aim of forming a special commission to rehabilitate the victims of Soviet repression.[119] In contrast, between 2000 and 2014, when Putin served as either president or prime minister, political repressions during the Soviet period were remembered in only one governmental commemorative speech, given by Dmitry Medvedev.[120] This Putinist "normalization of Soviet history," in the sense of a selective appropriation of the Soviet past as both a Russian historical legacy and a distinctly Russian way of life, was a precondition for using Soviet cultural forms as a resource in service of flexible authoritarianism.[121] These cultural forms were detached from Soviet socialist ideology and nationalized under Putin: the years of Soviet rule became inscribed as part of the novel construction of a "thousand year" Russian national history.[122] To deprive these forms of the Soviet socialist ideology in which they were once rooted and transform them into elements of a Russian national identity meant that they were "no longer associated with the communist party, its leadership or totalitarian propaganda, but with an idealized imaginary of 'the entire people.'"[123]

To be clear, this official shift in memory politics was not the only reason for a revival of Soviet forms of youth engagement. When those Soviet institutions mainly responsible for organizing youth leisure vanished in the 1990s, there were local attempts to keep some forms of previous youth engagement and adjust them. This was sometimes owed to the fact that the demise of the Soviet Union simply left a vacuum in public offerings for young people. As early as the late Yeltsin government, attempts were made to revitalize the "movement of student brigades" at the federal level.[124] In 1994, long before Khloponin ordered the reintroduction of student brigades as a youth political project, the Krasnoyarsk Region witnessed the revival of *KVN* groups.[125] *KVN* groups perform comedy sketches and compete in leagues—inspired by the highly popular Soviet TV show "Club of the Merry and the Sharp-Witted" (*Klub veselykh i nakhodchivykh*).[126]

Konstantin Gureev, a longstanding youth political organizer in Krasnoyarsk, was the driving force behind the return of the local *KVN* groups. Around 2006, he became head of a novel agency devoted to the "realization of youth projects." While using neoliberal parlance to affirm the novel youth politics ("investments in young and active people are very profitable [*vygodnyi*]"[127]), his motivation appears equally driven by an emphatic affirmation of empowerment through involving ordinary citizens in civil-society organizations and giving them prospects for self-realization. As a 2007 press interview makes clear, he identifies support for local initiatives and project ideas—through providing grants and guidance—as a major step toward the gradual formation of a civil society in the region that would, ideally, compete with state institutions for power.

> It is not only important to watch how civic initiatives evolve, but also to support them so that they can establish themselves in real life, to compete with governmental and state institutions. As we hoped from the very beginning, youth do not let us down in this regard. Very many initiatives are indeed developed by young people.[128]

In this regard, Gureev and some of his colleagues were in tune with the Council of Europe's youth political goals in the 2000s. The latter set youth participation as a priority, and pursued it through policy tools such as the Young Active Citizens Award. The Council, however, saw youth politics aligned with state interests, seeking to create a "unique partnership between the representatives of youth organizations and governments."[129]

Supporting young people to realize their own ideas appears to remain a driving force for Gureev, as a 2020 press interview suggests. Here he emphasizes how, in 2006 and 2007, the new youth politics led to the novelty that "money from the state budget was given to realize ideas of 'some subcultural youth [*kakikh-to neformaly*]' in a non-state context."[130] The decision to build *Sporteks*, one of Siberia's largest indoor skate parks, was supported at the time by Khloponin, who emphasized that this move, which cost an estimated 3.7 million USD, would be important to give the extreme sports movement a "civilized appearance."[131] That the resulting establishment was to become the region's showpiece of youthful contemporariness and a central organizational hub for local youth politics, but sidelined the interests of those "*neformaly*" who had envisioned the complex in the first place as somewhere to meet for professionalizing fans of extreme sports—not as a center for local youth political organization[132]—points to the ambivalent nature of collaboration between grassroots youth projects and state or business authorities. As a matter of fact, such forms of cooptation are not specific to the Russian context, but also discussed in democratic contexts regarding the strategic use of "subcultural youth culture" for economic ends—for instance, to heighten a location's competitiveness.[133]

This mixed understanding of projects developed by young adults as both a strategic resource for local development and a tool to align young people's self-image and abilities with those deemed necessary for economic growth was formative for the founding of the "Territory of Youth Taking Initiative [*Territoriia initsiativnoi molodezhi*] *Biriusa*" summer camp in 2007. The idea for *Biriusa*, often regarded as Khloponin's brainchild,[134] apparently originated in 2006, when several local student brigades met for a couple of days outside of Krasnoyarsk. Youth political organizers anticipated that a multiday meeting in nature would be ideal to unite the city's and region's most active youth initiatives—the student brigades, *KVN* groups, and fans of extreme sports.[135] Again, as in the case of youth politics in general, *Biriusa* had from its outset a much less patriotic and party-political quality than the first meetings at *Seliger*. Kommersant journalist Ekaterina Savina described the 2006 *Seliger* as "resembling a Soviet pioneer camp with waking-up to the national anthem and political information about 'the ideology of President Putin.'"[136] Meanwhile, *Biriusa* was designed to activate young people's powers of self-motivation. It had little in common with *Nashi*'s staging of patriotic unity and idiosyncratic anti-Western, military-style installations ridiculing opposition members and human-rights activists.[137]

Even so, *Biriusa* was, from its very beginning, a highly official establishment, with close ties to the federal government. In 2007, Aleksandr Zhukov, then vice president of the Russian government, was one of several VIP guests.[138] Apparently, Vladimir Putin planned to visit *Biriusa* in 2008, though he did not end up doing so.[139] In 2006, a branch of the Young Guard of United Russia formed as a subsection of the *KKSO*, the local Student Brigades movement, and regularly participated as a team (*druzhina*) at *Biriusa*. Youth political organizers, though never failing to emphasize the bipartisan character of the event, admitted that political organizations such as the Young Guard of United Russia were regularly present. In the words of Daria Glazkova:

> *Biriusa* was not invented as a political project, but as a project that aimed at developing youth movements. Because before *Biriusa* started, the number

of active movements could be counted on the fingers of one hand. [...] This is why *Biriusa* was invented as a space to develop youth politics. [...] It was certainly not a project under the aegis of the Young Guard of United Russia. Yes, their activists have been there, because it is also a relatively big societal organization, which exists alongside other societal organizations.[140]

To prove *Biriusa*'s bipartisanship, youth political organizers pointed to the regular participation in the camp of local members of Russia's communist party (*KPRF*). It is commonly held, however, that at least at the federal level the *KPRF* in effect ceased to oppose the government in the 2000s, and now forms part of what is called the systemic opposition—parties officially portrayed as being opposed to the government, but actually supporting its rule.[141]

Certainly, determining the "politicalness" of the camp depends on whether Russian state institutions are defined by organizers and campers as an arbiter between competing parties or—as most political scientists would contend—as privileging an authoritarian one-party rule in a multi-party system.[142] The 2011 organization of an "*Anti-Biriusa*," dubbed "Territory of Civic Activists" (*Territoria grazhdanskikh aktivistov*) by local oppositional youth groups and human-rights organizations, testifies that *Biriusa* is certainly perceived by government-critical actors as both pro-state and pro-government. These crucial differences notwithstanding, *Biriusa* was never solely a meeting place of pro-government youth organizations, but rather a career springboard for the ambitious and a cheap leisure option for local youth that, as we will see in Chapter 4, many campers found inspiring.

This is why youth political organizers characterize *Biriusa* as a "laboratory for youth initiatives," an empowering and creative space where active youth—such as the local student brigades—meet.[143] Douglas Blum's apt description of post-Soviet state youth politics as manifesting the "imperative to foster 'desirable' qualities such as personal responsibility and entrepreneurial creativity, thus furthering the state's developmental and efficiency-seeking orientation"[144] is a defining feature of *Biriusa* and similar regional youth-leadership summer camps.

Instrumentalizing the Soviet Summer-Camp Tradition

When *Seliger* opened its doors to "all Russian youth" in 2008 and transformed itself into a "a giant innovation forum" under the motto "Commodify your talent" in 2009,[145] it came to equal *Biriusa*'s hitherto unique business start-up focus and innovation-hub style. Unlike *Biriusa*, in 2009 the *Seliger* camp site still featured large posters of the president and prime minister and banners with patriotic slogans. It had also retained the Great Patriotic War memorial of the "grave of the unknown soldier," with its symbol of a guarded flame.[146]

Did the Krasnoyarsk-based reinvigoration of youth politics and its successes inspire federal state youth politics? A young youth political organizer from the Krasnoyarsk region claimed in our interview that this was indeed the case: "The heads of *Rosmolodezh* [the Federal Youth Agency] already said twice that the Krasnoyarsk model [of youth politics] is the best in Russia—out of 86 subjects! And Krasnoyarsk is often referred to as an example in this regard, which is pleasant to hear and is a cause for pride."[147]

It might well be the case that Krasnoyarsk youth politics served as an inspiration for federal state youth politics. In 2009, during an organizational meeting for Russia's so-called Year of Youth at which Vladimir Putin was present, Khloponin praised *Biriusa* as an important platform for furthering youth projects and as an example of how federal youth politics could be organized to value the significance of youth as the "main reserve of the economy."[148] That same year, Vladislav Surkov, then Chief of the Presidential Administration, made a statement in which he claimed that Russia's main resource was not oil and gas, but young people, echoing Khloponin.[149] That Khloponin's youth-political ideas were well received is further proven by his promotion. In 2010 he was appointed by then-president Medvedev as special envoy to Russia's Northern Caucasus Federal District to create new jobs in the conflict-ridden region.[150] In his new function, he once again underlined the importance of youth projects for reviving small businesses and, while visiting the Northern Caucasus' newly organized youth-leadership summer camp *Mashuk*, announced a tenfold increase in grants for youth projects.[151]

The creation of the pro-government NGO "Russia—Country of Possibilities" (*Rossiia—strana vozmozhnostei*) through an order by Vladimir Putin in 2018 indicates the extent to which the ideas promoted by business managers such as Khloponin in the early 2000s came to influence Russian youth politics at the federal level—an influence that has had a lasting effect, even at times of severely tightened authoritarian measures.[152] The foundation of this NGO coincided with considerable state investment in volunteering: a program called "Social Activity" (*sotsial'naia aktivnost'*)—comprising investments of 420 million USD between 2019 and 2023—was launched that includes the founding of more than 300 volunteer centers.[153]

While assessing the degree of local influence on federal outcomes requires additional research, the story of Khloponin's resurrection of local youth politics shifts attention toward local drivers of neoliberal restructuring. It exemplifies how local preferences coalesce with global managerial scripts. Not least, it shows how changes in memory politics—what I have called the "normalization of the Soviet past"—created a political situation in which socialist organizational forms could be recycled and put into the service of flexible authoritarian modernization agendas. The disconnection of the latter from their *socialist* Soviet meaning was a precondition for their repurposing in the Russian national economy in the 2000s: to align citizens' self-understandings and abilities with the demands of capitalist markets and individualized social security arrangements.[154]

Besides tracing this alternative story of the evolution of Putinist state youth politics, I have also invoked the notion of a Soviet summer camp tradition as an example of how a locally specific cultural form can legitimate, albeit tacitly, an authoritarian *Erziehungsstil*. This *Erziehungsstil* was not only characteristic of summer camps for leisure during the Soviet period; it also permeates summer camp organization in present-day Russia. As we will see in the following chapter, an authoritarian *Erziehungsstil* coexists at these establishments with a dialogical teaching atmosphere and business start-up culture. At today's youth-leadership summer camps, this well-known tradition serves as a powerful motivational and organizational device. It shapes participants' expectations of the camps as sites of fun and summer leisure activities as much as their anticipation that these establishments are home to idiosyncratic arrangements such as compulsory calisthenics and a tight control of campers' whereabouts.

In early 2023, the malleability of this cultural form in the hands of Putinist Russian authorities made international news when a detailed report was published about Ukrainian children between the ages of six and sixteen being forcibly kept against their will and that of their parents for weeks and months, at summer camps for leisure in Russia.[155] After the full-scale invasion of Ukraine, Russia's presidential administration both motivated and forced governors of wealthier Russian regions to "adopt" a district in the occupied parts of the country, meaning that those regions would pay for young Ukrainians to attend Russian summer camps for leisure.[156] As a journalist for *The Guardian* reported, many Ukrainian children and young people wanted to attend summer camps, even those that were far away, because they wanted to follow their peers and liked the idea of spending a summer holiday by the sea or in the countryside. According to the *Guardian* report, the conditions that these young people experience at camp vary according to how they present their attitude toward the war, and whether they are willing to give up their identification with Ukrainian culture and statehood.[157] Besides being an attempt to indoctrinate the Ukrainian campers to believe the official Russian narrative which accuses the Ukrainian government of fascism, the summer camp initiative is also a propagandistic effort meant to portray Russia's alleged well-meaning ambitions for Ukrainians. Russian TV broadcasts a vision of the experiences of Ukrainian campers as being in line with the Soviet summer camp tradition, what Rüthers calls the "imaginary geography of the happy Soviet childhood": joyful participation in skits, songs, and sporting events.[158] These images might be directed just as much at Ukrainian parents as at local audiences. As the report and earlier media articles confirm, most of the Ukrainian parents whose children did not return from summer camps on Russian (occupied) territory consented in writing to their children's attendance.[159] The circumstances of giving consent—during an ongoing war and as residents of occupied territory—make it impossible to consider those consents voluntary. Nevertheless, at least some parents seem to have been partially persuaded by Russian authorities' invocation of the Soviet summer camp tradition and its popular connections with a happy childhood.[160]

In a very different register to that of the youth-leadership camps, these attempts to indoctrinate young Ukrainians—so that they believe in the Russian state's narrative of a benevolent Russia fighting against a fascist Ukrainian army—reflect Russian authorities' persistence in wanting to mold the cultural form of the summer camp to promote their politico-economic ideals. At the same time, many mundane decisions regarding the organization of the youth-leadership camps, and campers' expectations, appear to be shaped by a largely unquestioned and widely shared understanding of what being at camp traditionally entails.

4
How Flexible Authoritarianism Looks and Feels

How does flexible authoritarianism look and feel to those whom governing politicians deem most relevant for the regime's survival? Addressing this question aids our understanding of the ways in which flexible authoritarianism is legitimated, symbolically and emotionally, beyond the circles of ruling elites, and how it is endued with emotional appeal. This chapter's detailed analysis of two youth-leadership summer camps as political spectacles—enterprises that stage flexible authoritarianism and make it tangible—turns our attention to matters of style, emotion, and sociality that can be as important for creating loyalty to a regime as ideological debate.

Youth-leadership summer camps aim to cultivate both a can-do spirit and a positive attitude toward the country's future among potential strategic elites. They are idiosyncratic establishments: jointly organized by regional and federal government bodies, but also sponsored by local businesses, they mix rules and routines widely remembered as having been characteristic of Soviet summer camps for children and young people with popular elements from the world of business start-up training. Visits by international guests and VIPs from the spheres of business, politics, and non-governmental organizations (NGOs) are important for staging the summer camps as high-profile events. Prominent features of their curriculum are personal development, project management, grant writing, and soft-skill training sessions, and the teaching style privileges participatory learning formats. Some lectures, especially those on Russia's geopolitical position, employ authoritarian forms of inculcation.

Conceptualizing these government-sponsored events as political spectacles means applying a particular analytical lens, one that brings into focus the ways in which youthful support for the regime is staged and highlights the government's attempts to elicit such support by providing memorable experiences. Making otherwise abstract ideals promoted by the government—such as modernization or neotraditionalism—emotionally tangible requires connecting them with affective practices. Understanding youth-leadership summer camps as political spectacles requires us to scrutinize how the formal aspects of these events contribute to their symbolic message. What is the significance, for example, of the camp sites' design and symbolic scenery, including the carefully chosen street names and the design of tents? What are the political implications of a set daily camp routine and strict rules of behavior?

I address such questions using concrete examples of the camps' symbolism, their educational offering, and evening entertainment. Their formal characteristics—such as the symbolic scenery and dominant organizational and pedagogical style (*Erziehungsstil*)—testify to the co-occurrence of elements specific to young leaders' summits with cultural forms widely associated with the Soviet summer camp tradition. Forms of self-improvement and group competition that were central to Soviet pedagogy are repurposed at these establishments, testifying to the state's neotraditional investment in human capital. In keeping with the advice proffered by students of political ritual—to include audience responses in order to grasp a ritual's fuller meaning—I have woven campers' narratives of their experiences into this chapter, juxtaposing their views on and emotional responses to aspects of camp life with my own observations.

To conclude this chapter, I will explore how the camps influence civic life in Russia more generally, arguing that these establishments are a mainstay of Russian youth and local development politics because they teach young campers "entrepreneurial literacy." Like the concept of "financial literacy," which denotes citizens' ability to participate in financialized social security arrangements, entrepreneurial literacy refers to citizens' capacity to develop their own business projects and to participate in public grant competitions for project funding.[1]

Who attends these youth-leadership summer camps in provincial Russia, and how are campers selected? At the camps that I visited, all attendees were there voluntarily. Most were between eighteen and thirty years old, enrolled in higher education institutions—more than eighty percent of Russian high school graduates start a tertiary education[2]—and most were residents of the areas where the camps took place. To attend the camps, applicants were required to complete an application form and sketch out an idea for a project to support local development. Actual examples of such proposals included a redesign of a small park, and the creation of a business selling energy-efficient home design. Access to participation in these youth-leadership camps appears easy for local young adults: several campers told me that they did not know of anyone whose application had been rejected. Moreover, the cost of a one-week stay was only 500 rubles per camper, the price of a pint of beer at Krasnoyarsk's Irish Pub at the time. This included transport to the site, meals, accommodation, and trips to nearby nature sights, as well as training sessions. Thus, becoming a camper did not require highly specialized skills, membership of the ruling party, or wealthy parents. This makes the camps a real exception to the general lack of easily accessible high-profile educational sites for young people from different socioeconomic backgrounds in contemporary Russia. Indeed, many campers spoke of their participation in camp in terms of an opportunity: to get some valuable training, and maybe even a chance for upward social mobility by presenting their project ideas to the VIPs that regularly visited the camp sites, all while enjoying an affordable summer holiday.

These establishments offer a number of compelling attractions for the young adults who attend them: a contemporary ambience, opportunities to meet interesting peers, and an educational program that addresses actual challenges on the job market as well as in the start-up sector. For many of the campers that I interviewed, the attendance of business experts and personal development coaches with a nationwide or even international reputation—such as Dr. Sam Potolicchio, a Georgetown and Harvard graduate who runs an NGO, the Preparing Global Leaders Forum[3]—indicated a high-level program.

This chapter's discussion of youth-leadership summer camps draws on my own participation in the Krasnoyarsk-based camp "Territory of Youth Taking Initiative *Biriusa*," and in another, *SakhaSeliger*, which took place in the Republic of Sakha (Yakutia) in Russia's so-called Far Eastern district. At the time of writing (early 2023) *Biriusa* still exists; *SakhaSeliger* was renamed *Sinergiia Severa* (Synergy of the North) in 2016, and took place in 2019 for the final time before the introduction of antipandemic restrictions the following year. I participated in both camps, much as ordinary campers did, in 2013. (Appendix I features a discussion of certain ethical and organizational considerations related to my participation, as well as a detailed account of the number and quality of participant observations and interviews conducted.)

In 2014, I returned to *SakhaSeliger* to conduct interviews with campers. The difficulty of meeting campers from the previous year for interviews on their home turf, given the inaccessibility of many parts of the vast republic via public transport, was the main reason for my return visit. In hindsight, this return trip proved a crucial window onto ways in which the regional youth-leadership summer camps *could* be used as forums for the government's direct political propaganda.

As outlined in Chapter 3, the founding of the federal youth-leadership camp *Seliger* had been a direct reaction on the part of the Russian government to the Ukrainian Orange Revolution in 2005, when young Ukrainians successfully protested against electoral fraud, leading to the inauguration of a president who sought to further integrate the country with the European Union. That a similar scenario could take place in Russia, however, seemed unlikely after Vladimir Putin's position was secured in 2008 and Ukrainians elected a pro-Russian president in 2010. Even mass Russian protests against electoral fraud (2011–2013) did not shake the Putinist government's foundations. After 2008, *Seliger* was opened to all young Russians, and came to emphasize innovation and an entrepreneurial spirit, much as the Krasnoyarsk-based *Biriusa* camp did from its inception in 2007 (see also Chapter 3).

However, in 2014 *Seliger*'s focus returned to political support for the regime.[4] In the winter of 2013 the Ukrainian government's sudden intensification of economic and political ties with Russia, in stark opposition to the parliament's earlier decision to sign a European Union–Ukraine Association Agreement, sparked massive protests in Kyiv, leading to the ousting of Ukraine's pro-Putin president in February 2014. In the aftermath of this revolution, which was framed by the governing Russian authorities as a fascist coup d'état, Russia annexed the Ukrainian peninsula of Crimea and started a frozen conflict in Eastern Ukraine as well as a massive media campaign designed to prove that the new government in Ukraine was fascist—and that Western governments were supporting it anyway. It was in this context of a low point in relations between Russia and Euro-American states that the youth-leadership summer camps were—once again—used to spread Putinist propaganda, denouncing the government's enemies as fascists.

Novel lecture formats and a renaming of the 2013 working group "Politics" (*Politika*) as "We are Multinational Russians" (*My Rossiiane*) immediately communicated this change when I returned to *SakhaSeliger* in 2014. The term *Rossiiane* denotes all members of Russia's constitutive multinational people and is not reserved for ethnic Russians. The renaming mirrored the intensification of a Putinist nationalism that mixes imperial and classic nationalist elements. The Russian political scientists Alexander Verkhovsky and Emil Pain have aptly characterized it as a civilizational nationalism,[5] for it chimes with Vladimir Putin's crafting of Russia as a unique state civilization with a specific set of values.[6] However, overt political appeals to support the government's anti-Ukrainian, anti-Western stance still did not dominate the camp's educational program in quantitative terms. The bulk of the working groups, lectures, and workshops were devoted to making young Russians fit for the economic challenges of the twenty-first century, with a focus on project management and grant writing.

Analyzing Youth-Leadership Summer Camps as Political Spectacles

Political spectacles such as rallies, parades, outdoor concerts, and commemorative events are inherently bound up with political legitimation. They are key to the staging of political support, to making tangible experiences out of abstract politics.

If organized by a government, such events—also called political rituals in the relevant literature—symbolize support for the political leadership. In her study of the political culture of interwar Italy, sociologist Mabel Berezin argues that the fascists' spectacles needed mainly to "give the appearance of enthusiastic mass support" for the government.[7] That simple attendance might matter more to those in power than *actual* local support for government policies is argued by anthropologist Sally Moore through the example of political meetings in socialist Tanzania. Participants' attendance was key for substantiating the notion that ordinary citizens approved of the new political leadership.[8]

Such staging of support is especially important in a socio-political context such as Russia's, where for decades emigration to more affluent world regions has been a regular part of promising young peoples' career plans.[9] Long before the full-scale invasion of Ukraine, Putin started to portray the ensuing brain drain as resulting from a secret plan led by Western foundations to "'hook' children on 'grants' to get them to leave home and work for the benefit of foreigners, who presumably cannot do without Russia as a source of intellectual as well as natural resources."[10] Investing in programs that get potential strategic elites to stay in the country is economically and symbolically central for the regime's survival. Crucially, such programs, and youth-leadership camps in particular, not only aim to address young people's material interests, but also seek to instill in them an identification with the state's flexible authoritarian project. In order to make abstract ideals, such as that of the Russian citizen as an entrepreneurial patriot or that of the patriotic entrepreneur, feel real to young people and part of their own conception of the good life,[11] they need to be invested with emotional significance. Political spectacles are thus also central to regime legitimation, because they can endue abstract political ideals with affection. Rallies, public concerts, and national holiday celebrations can produce excitement and emotion among those attending, engendering temporary "communities of emotional attachment" that eventually result in long-lasting bonds of solidarity.[12]

The summer camp as a form of political spectacle is uniquely suited for creating such communities of feeling. Not only does it bring campers outside of their usual environment,[13] it also creates a temporary microcosm with its own time schedule, its own symbolic scenery, and its own objectives. Immersion in this cosmos is likely to forge new social bonds.[14] Several social movements and youth groups with extremely divergent political aims—such as the *Lebensreform* movement, the Nazis' *Hitlerjugend*, the Soviet Young Pioneers, Zionist organizations in today's Israel, or the Arab Palestinian scout movement[15]—have relied on the form of the summer camp to make their ideals experienceable, and to enhance close ties of a kind that form through temporary communities of attachment, among their followers.

As students of political spectacle caution, the outcome of all ritual is elusive and uncertain.[16] Both observers and social researchers may conflate the display of political support with participants' *actual* support. It would be naïve to infer from the observation of a political spectacle the unanimous support of its participants: as political scientist James C. Scott points out, "Just as subordinates are not much deceived by their own performance there is, of course, no more reason for social scientists and historians to take that performance as, necessarily, one given in good faith."[17] Thus, differentiating between the meaning that a spectacle may have for its creators and its meaning for participants is a critical analytical task.[18]

What is more, independent of how well choreographed and staged political spectacles are, there are limits to their capacity to forge new social bonds and endue political ideals with affection. These limits, as social psychologist Margaret Wetherell convincingly argues, "are to do with the perspectives, identities and affective 'know how' people carry forward from past practice."[19]

Indeed, many of the young campers I interviewed were critical of the current Russian leadership, though not fully opposed to it. Though their participation indicated loyalty to the flexible authoritarian regime that was in place, their narratives caution against interpreting it as an expression of straightforward, devoted support for Putin and his entourage.

Studying political spectacles requires a focus on their formal aspects. Mabel Berezin describes political spectacle as the "play-form" of politics, "which communicates the boundaries of political legitimacy."[20] Anthropologists assume that the medium of a ritual—that is, its form—is part of its message.[21] In the post-Soviet context, state-promoted political spectacles often perpetuated Soviet forms of entertainment and staging while their political content might have little in common with Soviet ideology.[22]

SakhaSeliger's History

Unlike the youth-leadership summer camp *Biriusa*, which was founded as early as 2007 in response to the local governor's concern for local economic development (see Chapter 3), *SakhaSeliger* was directly inspired by the federal *Seliger* camp initiated in 2005. According to Artem Nikolaev Baranov, a local organizer of *SakhaSeliger*, in 2011 the Republic's governor, Yegor Afanasyevich Borisov, visited the federal *Seliger* and, impressed by the format, gave orders for a replica of *Seliger* to be established in the Sakha Republic.[23] Young adults from the region who had attended *Seliger* that same year became subsequently involved in organizing a local version of the federal camp in the Sakha Republic.[24]

The first *SakhaSeliger* camp, which took place in 2012, was organized mainly by the Federal Youth Agency *Rosmolodezh* in close cooperation with the pro-government "Foundation for National Perspectives" (*Natsional'nye Perspektivy*), which financed several of the youth organization *Nashi*'s projects (*Nashi*, or "Those on Our Side," is the pro-government youth group that was founded in 2005 and met regularly at the federal-level *Seliger* camp).[25] Unsurprisingly, the working groups offered at *SakhaSeliger* in 2012 primarily followed the existing range of *Rosmolodezh* projects, such as "Young Entrepreneurship," "Innovation and Technical Creativity," "Volunteering," "Politics," and "Our Army." This close relationship with *Rosmolodezh* continued in subsequent years. Though the funding through *Rosmolodezh* was starkly reduced, federal influence remained evident in 2013 when I visited.

Despite this greater political influence from the federal center, *SakhaSeliger* was not connected in the minds of local campers to the pro-government youth group *Nashi*. Two *SakhaSeliger* campers, Aleksandr and Evgeniia, who were in their mid-twenties at the time, shared their vague ideas about *Nashi* in our interview:

> Evgeniia: "I think people who live in Yakutia, youths, do not have a clue about what this is–*Nashi*."
> Aleksandr: "Yes [he nods]."
> Evgeniia: "To be frank, I do not exactly know myself what *Nashi* is. I know *Molodaia Gvardiia*—it is the young United Russia [the ruling party's youth wing]. But I have no idea what *Nashi* is."
> Aleksandr: "I even know their hymn, well: '*Nashi*—this is a movement forward.' I even know their hymn!"
> Evgeniia: "Maybe this is something European, which did not make it to us?"
> Aleksandr: "*Nashi*, *Stal'*, *Khrushi protiv*, *StopKham* [the other designations refer to other government-sponsored youth projects]."[26]

SakhaSeliger did not even feature a working group reserved for members of the governing party's local youth-wing branch. While several members of the Young Guard of United Russia participated in the camp in 2013 and 2014, their presence did not stand out. As at *Biriusa*, the non-partisan character of the event was important for its organizers. Artem Baranov, the local organizer of *SakhaSeliger*, stressed in our interview that the camp's main aim was to provide education, not to create political cadres for the governing United Russia party:

> The main task of this forum is to offer young folks an education program. As you can see, we do not shout [the names of the political parties] "United Russia," "Communists," "Just Russia." There is no hidden political motive whatsoever. Young people of all kinds participate: some love the president, some do not.[27]

Federal influence was, however, especially noticeable in 2014, when teaching staff sent from Moscow replicated the patriotic lectures that marked the federal *Seliger* that year. Unlike at *Biriusa*, in both years the head of the educational program and most teaching staff met in Moscow to fly into the remote national republic. Due to *SakhaSeliger*'s greater dependence on the Federal Youth Agency *Rosmolodezh* and its more modest funding through the local budget, a change in federal-level politics seems to have had a more immediate effect there.

This difference in funding might also have influenced decisions about *SakhaSeliger*'s physical location. While the site where *Biriusa* has taken place since 2007 is especially designed to accommodate the camp, *SakhaSeliger* moves between different sites each year. The folkloric style of some of these sites—in 2014 the camp took place at *OrtoDoidu*, the ritual site of the traditional Sakha celebration of the beginning of summer—combined in an interesting way with the camp's focus on innovation, communicating that local tradition was compatible with twenty-first-century innovations. Another reason why *SakhaSeliger* (or *Sinergiia Severa*) is not conducted in the same place every year is surely the enormous size of the Sakha Republic and the difficulties faced by young people traveling to camp on a limited budget and reliant on public transportation.

The Symbolic Scenery at the Youth-Leadership Camp *Biriusa*

Because *SakhaSeliger* takes place at different historical sites each year, it does not feature its own specific symbolic scenery. (By this I mean the general style of its setup, location, and the naming of streets and tents, as well as auditory features such as the jingles that are played several times a day to remind campers of the schedule.) Therefore, my analysis of camp scenery covers only *Biriusa*, the site of which had never been the base of a pioneer or children's summer camp, but was designed especially to host the summer youth-leadership event.

Biriusa's location is on the shore of a large and beautiful barrier lake of the Yenisei River amid seemingly endless woods. With its state-of-the art tents for training sessions, lectures, and evening concerts, and its spacious setup, with ample room for activity and relaxation, it challenges stereotypical notions—be they Euro-American or Muscovite—about provincial Russia. Like the *Sporteks* Center for Extreme Sports, the site's stylish modernity stands in contrast to the relatively run-down and somewhat antiquated state of public facilities in many other places in Russia.[28] This up-to-dateness is certainly intended to showcase the ruling local government, yet it also appears to have been designed to communicate to young people that the government is interested in them, the young and talented, and that it does not spare expenses because it believes in their abilities. As Stepan Petrovich Smirnov, a teacher who regularly lectures at youth-leadership summer camps such as *Biriusa*, put it:

> Young people understand now that the government does not exist somewhere out there, but [have the feeling that] "we can participate in these summer camps, and they will hear us." This of course influences young people's inner image of Russia. They have suddenly come to understand— thanks to the summer camps—that there is a huge variety of opportunities and prospects for them in this world.[29]

Indeed, much of the site is designed to create a modern image of Russia and its internationally significant achievements, as well as to invite young people to stay in Russia and bring their ideas to fruition within the country of their upbringing.

The entire camp site is organized into several broad areas with different functions: sleeping and living take place in *Biriusa-siti*—"*Biriusa*-city"; education and trainings in the University area; sports in an activity area; and cultural events and gatherings at *prem'er-stsena*—the main stage, which is surrounded by an amphitheater that can seat about 1,000 people.

In 2013, the streets that make up *Biriusa* city were named after uncontroversial and internationally famous Soviet and Russian figures. In line with the Putinist notion of a "millennial history of Russia," streets were named for people such as the eighteenth-century polymath Mikhail Lomonosov, the composer Pyotr Ilyich Tchaikovsky, and the Nobel-prizewinning physicist and Soviet dissident Andrei Sakharov, as well as Yuri Gagarin, the Soviet cosmonaut who was the first human to journey into outer space. Correspondingly, the camp site's *dialog-kholly* (Dialog Halls), which are part of the University area, were named after Central Siberian figures of national and international renown. They commemorated Vasily Surikov, a fin-de-siècle Krasnoyarsk-born realist painter; the Soviet writer Viktor Astafyev, known for his uncompromising depictions of the everyday atrocities of war (and a famous critic of the Chechen war)[30]; the Soviet physicist of Sakha nationality Leonid Kirensky, who co-founded the Krasnoyarsk Institute for Physics[31]; and Mikhail Reshetnev, an aerospace engineer after whom the minor planet 7046 Reshetnev was named.

Why this nomenclature? In the context of other motivating and activating features that make up *Biriusa*'s symbolic scenery, one answer is that young people lack internationally acclaimed local and Russian role models. Given that most trainers at the youth-leadership summer camps referred in their presentations mostly to US-American entrepreneurs such as Michael Dell and Steve Jobs as paragons for the young campers, this nomenclature emphasized the significance of both Russia and the region for achievements of world importance that connect to the present. In combination with Russianized loanwords from English such as *siti* (city) or *khol* (hall), such nomenclature is intended to inscribe Russian history within a global story of modernity. Invoking figures of national and international fame conveyed the notion that young Russians, including those from the region, could also excel in spheres as varied as science, aerospace engineering, fine arts, music, and literature like those celebrated individuals before them. Simultaneously, in commemorating outstanding Siberian and Russian personalities and their achievements, the nomenclature reminded campers that there was reason to feel pride in Russia, for it had contributed to development and modernization on a global scale.

The trendy, luxurious features of the camp site's University area highlighted the continuation of this distinguished local history into the here and now. This area featured *dialog-kholly* (Dialog Halls), small studio tents, and huge *kongress-kholly* (Congress Halls)—pavilions with wooden floors and white canopies, whose design resembled the aesthetics of co-working spaces. The year that I visited *Biriusa*, one of the Congress Halls featured a snack bar; another was furnished in a manner often advertised in Russia as the "European style," with stylish bookshelves, vintage lamps, beanbag chairs, and blankets for chilling out. A café called "Intelligence Place" served barista coffee, which could be consumed on comfortable sofas. There was also a tent, called *SUVENIRitet*, selling souvenirs with the *Biriusa* logo.

Like several other regional youth-leadership camps, *Biriusa* featured its own corporate identity on t-shirts and other *Biriusa* souvenirs. The perception of *Biriusa* as a brand was developed still further by an alumni gallery, closer to the lake, that displayed photo portrayals of successful former *Biriusa* campers, so-called *Biriusintsy*. Besides these souvenirs and alumni stories, signature songs and jingles, which I will discuss below, added to the creation of a unique *Biriusa* brand.

In addition to *Biriusa*'s branding, the technical setup—adjusted to the digital and social-media age—contributed to the staging of contemporaneity at camp. The covered main stage was equipped with a huge screen and a powerful PA system to amplify speech and music across the outdoor site. Wi-Fi and mobile-network access were available across the camp. The University area featured an IT-center (*IT-tsentr*) with about thirty computers, as well as a media center where a fifteen-person youth media team reviewed and sorted video clips, photographs, and campers' selfies. These were published in abundance on the camp's social media pages and featured in *Biriusa*'s own news coverage, called *Biriusa Today*.

Taking photographs and selfies was encouraged by the very design of the site. Upon arrival, campers could borrow a sign reading "Evolutionize!" (*Evolutsionirui!*)—the main theme that summer at *Biriusa*—to embellish their photographs. They could also be photographed next to a mime artist dressed up as the goddess of Justice. Another popular motif was provided by billboards communicating motivational messages of a neoliberal register, such as: "Dreams don't work if you don't work" (*Mechty ne rabotaiut poka ne rabotaesh' ty*)," "Don't be afraid to start afresh! To get the best result, you won't succeed straight away!" (*Ne boisia nachinat' zanovo. K nailuchshemu rezul'tatu udaetsia priiti ne srazu!*), and "No one said that it's gonna be easy!" (*Nikto ne govoril chto budet legko!*).[32]

These permanent billboards appealed to campers' work ethic, much like the various jingles reminding camp attendees that a new phase of the day's schedule would soon begin. Like the billboard slogans, these auditory reminders were often linked to motivational messages. The jingles directly addressed campers, some employing first-person narratives—speaking from the viewpoint either of an individual camper or of the collective of *Biriusintsy*. The curfew jingle (*otboi*), for instance, was based on a first-person narrator, an active and creative subject:

The whole day I've been a hero	[*Tsely den' ia byl geroem*]
But now I close my eyes	[*A teper' glaza zakroiu*] [...]
I fell asleep—this became clear	[*Ia prosnulsia eto iasno*]
Sleep came by like a beautiful film	[*Son prishel kak fil'm prekrasnyi*]
I'm the main actor in this film	[***Ia** v etom fil'me glavnyi akter*]
I'm the script writer, **I'm** the director	[***Ia** stsenarist v nem, **Ia** rezhiser*].

The text communicates that the narrator—having been "a hero" for the whole day—is creative even as the writer, director, and main actor of his own dreams (the text is written in the generic masculine). The pronoun "I" (*Ia*) is especially prominent in the final verse, when the meter forces its accentuation three times in a row—suggesting that "no one else but me" is the boss now. The jingle thereby portrays the typical *Biriusa* camper as an active doer and creator but, at the same time, as someone who observes the rules.

In a post-Soviet inflection on positive thinking, the morning call jingle urges campers to forget their grief and idleness (*nam segodnia pozabyt'/ pora svoiu pechal' i len'*). Instead of giving in to such feelings, the jingle seeks to motivate campers to open their eyes, because "great deeds" await them (*otkryvat' glaza pora/ zhdut velikie dela*), as well as a summer day during which they will become smarter (*prishel odin is letnikh dnei/ kogda vy stanete umnee*). The jingle ends with the imperatives "wake up!"; "get up!" Again, an image of campers as heroes engaging in great deeds goes hand-in-hand with a reminder to follow the prescribed schedule for sleeping and waking. As we will see in Chapter 5, many young campers considered the biggest obstacle to development to be other people's apparent depressive mentality and idleness, the persistence of which they often ascribed to low levels of willpower. Jingles such as the morning call conveyed that one could easily fight such feelings through a positive attitude to the day and by observing a daily routine.

A motivational address to campers was most pronounced in the university jingle, which asserted that if there was only one thing that the listener could do better than other people—even a minor skill such as building "houses out of matchsticks"—this was already a resource. This empowerment overtone is accompanied by a utilitarian thrust in the verse that emphasizes the usefulness of such a talent in life, and that learning things will pay off ("you don't take pains for nothing").

> If you can do anything better than others [*Esli ty chego-to luchshe vsekh umeesh*]
> If you glue houses out of matchsticks [*Domiki prikol'nykh iz spichek kleesh'*]
> [...]
> This will undoubtedly be useful in life [*Eto budet besuslovno v zhizni prigoditsia*] [...]
> If you learn something for some reason [*Esli ty pochemu-to uchish'sia*]

It means that you don't take pains for nothing [*Znachit ne naprasno muchish'sia*] [. . .]
Study! Come on, study! [*Uchis', davai uchis'!*]

The applicability of individual talent and the possibility of transforming a special skill into a marketable project were emphasized as a special feature of the new youth politics in my interview with youth political organizer Daria Glazkova. "Every person is unique, and every person has a set of skills; he just might not accentuate them," she told me. She and her colleagues were therefore tasked primarily with simply helping a young person "to understand what he wants in life and give him the possibility to experiment in different spheres."[33] Glazkova offered the example of a housewife who needs to be taught that her ability to run a household is already a powerful resource that can help her find a job. Such resource-oriented workforce development is not without a certain humanistic quality: the addressee of such assistance is a priori regarded as capable, unique, and by no means a problematic case. At the same time, workforce development is a means to an end, designed to "upskill workers for long-term success."[34] In the context of youth-leadership camps, the goal was to enable a young person to become competitive on the job market and to build something that the region or state needs. Nevertheless, this resource-oriented approach—discernible in the university jingle and highlighted by Glazkova—also emphasizes young people's power to shape the world and leave their unique mark on it.

Jingles and songs that were regularly played at *Biriusa* were also intended to heighten young campers' can-do spirit by identifying them as part of a community of active, positively-minded people. The song that always accompanied the camp's opening ceremony, for instance, encouraged campers to see themselves as part of a larger "we"—be it a collective of *Biriusintsy*, Siberians, or Russians.

Today, here [. . .] we [with you] will do everything in our power/ for Siberia, for Russia [*Zdes', segodnia my s toboiu . . . sdelat' vse chto v nashikh silakh/ dlia Sibirii, dlia Rossiia*] [. . .]
Here, we are many proactive people/ we, together with our friends, are for the positive [*my mnogo zdes' initiativ/ my s druz'iami za pozitiv*].

The grammatical form of the instrumental case in Russian is used twice in the above text. The form *My s toboi* in particular, which literally means "we with you," is unique in communicating commonality. Unlike "we *and* you" (or "we *and* our friends"), it conveys that the two entities belong to a single collective. In this vein, the verse states that "we together with you, who is *already* a part of us, will do everything for Siberia and Russia." Moreover, the jingle defines those present not only as proactive people, but as friends who together favor "the positive."

The message that "you are now part of a team of talented and self-developing *Biriusintsy*" was most overt in a song called the *Biriusa* hymn, which portrayed *Biriusa* as primarily the sum of its smart campers. As the refrain goes:

"*Biriusa*—this is us young brains" (*Biriusa eto my, molodye umy*), or "*Biriusa*—this is us in the very center of the country" (*Biriusa eto my v samom tsentre strany*). The hymn's verse portrays the *Biriusintsy* as young geniuses:

> How many ideas and new discoveries [*skol'ko idei i novykh otkrytii*]
> We create developments in the ocean [*my sozdaem v okeane sobytiia*]
> We believe in ourselves and surpass ourselves [*verim v sebia i rastim nad soboi*]
> We with you breathe one *Biriusa* [*dyzhem s toboi my odnoi Biriusoi*]

Again, the instrumental case in the last line powerfully invokes a collective entity, one which "breathes one *Biriusa*."

Like the jingles, these songs read almost like a psychological empowerment program with a regional or national communitarian undertone. They appear to have been composed against the backdrop of an assumption that young Siberians and Russians suffer from depression regarding their future, and therefore lack the kind of self-belief and ego necessary to succeed in conditions of flexible capitalism. Young people are represented as needing the state's or a local authority's "activation"—a term that denotes attempts by businesses and government agencies to engender individual initiative.[35]

The jingles urged campers to discover their full potential and act, motivating them not just through readable slogans, which might simply be ignored, but via memorable pop tunes loudly broadcast over the PA. These musical exhortations invited young campers to sing along, especially during collective spectacles such as the opening and closing ceremonies. Indeed, catchy, well-known pop tunes accompanied the songs' textual messages, facilitating recognition and encouraging campers to join in through sing-alongs. The jingle "Breakfast," for instance, was sung to the tune of the international hit *Pretty Fly* (by the Offspring); the jingle for the evening program was based on Blur's *Song 2*. The interplay between these hits' distinctive hooks—"uh-huh, uh-huh" in the case of *Pretty Fly*, and "woo-hoo" in the case of *Song 2*—and the motivating appeals in Russian lent the jingles an air of youthfulness, style, and of being cool.

> Woo-hoo—we will rock now Biriusay [*raskachaem Biriusy*]
> Woo-hoo—I wait to party every day [*Kazhdyi den' tusovku zhdu*]
> Woo-hoo —I go there already-ey [*Ia uzhe tuda idu*].[36]

Jingles that were not based on English-language hits likewise incorporated elements that are widely associated with Anglo-American popular culture, so as to popify the banal disciplinary messages of the texts.[37] The final seconds of the general assembly jingle featured a rapped "*yeah*—everyone to the general assembly" (yeah—*vse na obshchii sbor*). The jingle signaling the start of the teaching program was also rapped. Mimicking hip-hop culture, it started with a male voice announcing: "The best MC introduces . . . " (*Luchshii EmSi predstavliaet . . .*) and closed with the words "Welcome to *Biriusa*" in the English original. Like many other English loanwords in Russian, these accentuated the camp's hip and contemporary character.

Unlike the jingles, other features of the camp site's symbolic scenery were more reminiscent of the Soviet summer camp tradition—which does not mean that they pertained to the tradition's authoritarian *Erziehungsstil*. These included a fire pit where campers could meet in the evening to sing songs and have conversations around the bonfire, a beach at the shore that featured only a small, designated swimming area (akin to the *liagushatnik* in Elem Klimov's movie *Welcome, or No Trespassing*, discussed in Chapter 3), as well as a huge activity area where campers could play soccer, volleyball, basketball, and table tennis, or use a trampoline and gymnastics equipment.

These features tied in with the propagation of a healthy lifestyle among young people (generally called *zdorovyi obraz zhizni*) which is frequently referred to by its abbreviated form "*ZOZh*" and which gained momentum in the mid 2000s in Putinist state youth politics. These health-related public exhortations, among them a program called "Run with Me" (*Begi za mnoi*), advertised a healthy lifestyle as an "extra advantage" to a young person's career, because "obviously, a healthy and beautiful person has more chances of being successful."[38] *ZOZh* speaks to those practices of bodily self-improvement that, as Angela McRobbie argues in her analysis of "makeover" TV programs, are central to career-advancement in neoliberalism.[39]

Similarly reminiscent of the summer camp tradition, the site featured numerous services providing for the safety and health of campers and guests: security guards; an emergency service (named after the Russian Ministry for Emergency Situations "*MChS*"); a lifeguard to oversee swimmers and designate swimming times; and a medical team, which had two extra tents that functioned as isolation rooms for preventing the spread of infectious diseases. Another safety feature were danger signs, installed on the border of a forest area that was forbidden to campers, emblazoned with the words "Do Not Enter" and images of ticks. As I had learned when registering at *Sporteks*, ticks had been eradicated before our arrival from the meadows, the shore, and the beach, but not the forest. Upon registering, we needed to purchase, or provide proof of, special medical insurance against tick-borne encephalitis, as well as a few other health-related certificates. Other required documentation included vaccination records, a "fluorography" of the chest—an x-ray method that is used in mass radiographies—and a confirmation issued by a physician that attested to one's "sanitary living environment."

Overall, *Biriusa*'s symbolic scenery was designed to instill a can-do spirit in campers, emphasizing that they could shape the world around them as a community of *Biriusintsy*, of Siberians, and of Russians. And yet, even as the symbolic scenery aimed to inspire campers, it also attempted to control and discipline them. The slogans and jingles called upon campers to exert themselves and to obey the set daily regime. The site's physical borders limited free movement and restricted the autonomy of—from a legal perspective—perfectly responsible young adults.

Spectacle and Communities of Feeling: Entertainment and Show at Camp

Political spectacles often attempt to create, albeit temporarily, communities of feeling that are ideally capable of generating more durable bonds of solidarity.[40] The offers of entertainment at both camps were aimed at generating a community spirit through the collective experience of positive emotions.

While in many respects *Biriusa* resembled a multi-day pop festival, with top acts and show masters on the main stage during its evening program, *SakhaSeliger*'s entertainment lineup featured more traditional summer camp activities. Campers themselves staged evening events, usually in the form of a competition between working groups. This comparatively low-key entertainment at *SakhaSeliger* appeared to further the aim of getting young campers to take the initiative for an exciting evening program, and was key to creating a feeling of commonality through collective organization. To that end, finding out who could contribute and how was crucial. Campers' collective process of self-sorting into complementary roles became a solidarity-building activity in itself. Some working-group members, for example, especially enjoyed making trinkets, decorations, and costumes out of flowers, plants, or paper; others preferred to engage in choreography and directing; still others were very good singers or dancers, whose outstanding performance could make the difference in front of the jury.[41] After our working group *Politika* won the dance contest, we experienced a palpable sense of collective pride and mutual connection. Unlike at *Biriusa*, where campers took on the role of spectators at the evening program, those at *SakhaSeliger* were, as co-creators, much more invested in the evening activities. Several campers mentioned during interviews how organizing their working group's contribution to the evening program helped unite its members, and how much they enjoyed this. Alla, Nikita, and Nadezhda, for instance, offered the following thoughts:

> Alla: "When you prepare for the evening events, a collective is created [*Kogda gotovish'sia k vechernym meropriiatiiam, to eto uzhe idet kollektivizatsiia*]. This is great. Sixty people aiming at the same, are on the same wavelength [*napravleny na odnoi volne*]; all are rehearsing, preparing; all want to perform well. And the performances are super!"
> Nikita: "There is one aim . . ."
> Nadezhda: ". . . yes, one aim. I really like this."
> Alla: ". . . many different people and one aim."[42]

At both camp sites, social bonding among campers was most encouraged by the "final evening" parties. After campers had defended their project proposals and some had received awards during the official closing ceremony, the atmosphere loosened up and most enjoyed moving to the tunes of electronic dance music (at *SakhaSeliger*) or party hits (at *Biriusa*). While the closing ceremonies were reminiscent of the traditional Parents' Day at summer camps for children, these after-parties more closely resembled clubbing or organized tourist activities for young adults.

During *SakhaSeliger*'s final evening, campers of all working groups danced to techno music on the platform in front of the main meeting place. When the music reached a peak, the collective exaltation was palpable, the sort of moment that the French sociologist Émile Durkheim characterized as collective effervescence: "Once the individuals are gathered together, a sort of electricity is generated from their closeness and quickly launches them to an extraordinary height of exaltation."[43] In this atmosphere, "showing oneself and looking at the others"—as Maksim, the young farmer from the Sakha Republic, put it—was a central element of party.[44] During this event, there was no strict control—yet in accordance with the camp rules, alcohol was not consumed in public (though it was probably imbibed in private, which was also forbidden), and most campers smoked only at the bonfire, the officially designated smoking area, though smoking was generally discouraged.

Unlike at *SakhaSeliger*, where the party was more akin to a self-organized rave, entertainment on stage was central to *Biriusa*'s last evening party. The rap song "We Are *Biriusa*" (*My Biriusa*) was a peak moment. The song's lyrics, written especially for *Biriusa*, referred to the collective of *Biriusintsy* with the pronouns "we" and "us." Like several of the official camp jingles, the chorus featured an affirmation "*Daa!*" (Yes!)—which invited campers to shout in concert with the rap, lending their voices to its message. The chorus went as follows:

> Entertainers on stage: "We are the camp at the river [*My eto lager u reki*]"
> Dancing campers: "Yes!" [*Daaa!*]
> Entertainers on stage: "We are Siberian youth [*My molodezh Sibiriaki*]"
> Dancing campers: "Yes!" [*Daaa!*]
> Entertainers on stage: "We are ready to self-develop/ We will try harder than all [*My vse gotovy razvivat'sia/ My budem bolshe vsekh starat'sia*]"
> Dancing campers: "We are *Biriusa* 2013!" [*My Biriusa Dvadtsat' trinadtsat'!*][45]

The text emphasizes the campers' membership in a community of young Siberians alongside the conviction that they, as *Biriusintsy*, strive toward self-development. The question-answer format of the refrain recalls one of the ways in which musicians and entertainers seek to motivate audiences at rock, pop, and hip-hop concerts, or at tourist resorts, to support the onstage performance by singing along.[46]

That the last evening at *Biriusa* traditionally featured a foam party (*pennaia vecherinka*) was one of the features that more experienced campers would tell peers about early on. Like pool parties, foam parties have a highly sexualized reputation.[47] The choice of a sexualized party format might not have been accidental. Summer camps for young adults are known to be potential places for flirtation and maybe even finding a partner. As the Russian scholar of education Boris Kupriyanov recently pointed out with regard to the Soviet period: "the pioneer camp offered a place of relative freedom where adolescents could express their first romantic feelings."[48] *Seliger* in particular has been discussed as a place where intimate heterosexual relationships are promoted and homosexuality is opposed.[49] Although none of the interviewees mentioned flirtation as a motivation for participating in the summer camp, several said that they had met a partner in previous years at camp. Moreover, clips of *Biriusa Today*, the camp's own news coverage created by the young media team, point to this feature of the camp experience. In one clip, the reporter, a young female, investigates how campers spent their last night, insinuating that they might not have spent it alone. At the collective sinks, the reporter approaches a female camper who has just got up—an impression given by a two-second still zooming in on the camper's bleary eyes, accompanied by a fanfare sound:

Reporter: "Good morning, please introduce yourself!"
Camper: "Nastia."
Reporter: "Nastia, tell us how you spent the last night?"
Camper: "Well [laughs]."
Reporter: "What did you do [*Chto vy delali*]?"
Camper: "I slept. [*Spala.*]"
Reporter: "With whom? [*S kem?*]"
Camper: "[Laughs]. Alone! [*Odna!*]"
Reporter: "All alone?" [*Voobshche odna?*]"[50]

The camper asks, laughing, "What do you mean?" and a cut closes the scene. Through such teasing the media team deliberately cultivated suspense concerning the possibility that sexual encounters might have occurred, and alleged that they were a normal part of life at camp.

Camp staff never directly addressed intimate relationships. Unlike entertainers at holiday resorts who encourage young tourists to drink lots of alcohol, thereby lowering their inhibitions toward casual sex,[51] staff acting as entertainers on *Biriusa*'s main stage did not encourage any kind of sexualized romance during parties. The final evening party at *Biriusa* was, in contrast with such organized tourist activities, controlled, and ended with the curfew. Female campers adhered to the dress code restricting the wearing of bikinis to the beach, while the party was an occasion for male campers (for whom no such restriction existed) to dance only in shorts. Another feature of foam parties—the invitation to dance and loosen up, and to experience feelings of liberation through childish behavior or looking funny—appears to have been more relevant to the *Biriusintsy* that I interviewed.[52]

For several *Biriusintsy*, the foam party was among their most memorable summer camp experiences. They usually portrayed its impact as the feeling that one was part of a crowd "in the open air." In the words of Oleg:

> There was the foam party and to me, a person who never had been to such a party before . . . There at *Biriusa* in the open air, where there's so many people [*kucha narody*], proactive, young, developing, that is people who came to relax, to develop. And so, they are all in that crowd, and you are in that crowd. I liked that a massive amount. This was just super.[53]

This and other depictions of campers' experiences suggest that these parties were much more powerful in engendering temporary communities of feeling and collective effervescence than the compulsory calisthenics (*zariadka*) that the *Seliger* youth-leadership camp in particular became known for.

In many respects, the calisthenics sessions at both camps resembled those often found at children's summer camps, with an onstage trainer demonstrating movements for campers to imitate. Here, however, it was young adults replicating movements to music played at high volume, with fitness trainers seeking to entertain campers with jokes—and that made a difference, rendering an old summer camp tradition youthful and hip. Nevertheless, despite the lighthearted informality, this morning ritual established a certain uniformity. Campers wore nearly identical t-shirts displaying the camp's logo, which differed only in color according to the wearer's working group.[54] All campers received these shirts upon arrival and were asked to wear them throughout their stay. While this uniformity of dress reinforced that of the exercise motions, it also marked a popular-cultural break from pioneer uniforms or neckerchiefs.

While interviewees found the evening competitions and parties especially memorable and often mentioned how these events created a feeling of togetherness, none of them described similar feelings for *zariadka*. One interviewee from the Krasnoyarsk Region, Vlas, even shared his disdain for the attempt to stage a regimented uniformity, describing his "aversion to those moments, when people show themselves as being part of a crowd [*kogda liudi proiavliaiut sebia kak chast' tolpy*]."[55] When interviewees mentioned *zariadka*, they did so to accentuate that *Biriusa* or *SakhaSeliger* were in many instances a "typical camp." As Mikhail put it:

> Camp, this is always camp, because it is a bounded space, assembled people, and the regime of the camp, meaning morning call, *zariadka*, breakfast—all the same as in a children's summer camp. Naturally, there is a different program. *Biriusa* and children's summer camps are basically the same thing, it's just [that *Biriusa* is] a variant for older youths.[56]

That only one interviewee mentioned having been irritated by the compulsory calisthenics indicates that most campers likely accepted them as a common feature of camp life, pointing to the tacit effect of what I call the summer camp tradition.

One might assume that most campers decided to participate in the camps primarily in order to have a good time and party. Nearly all interviewees asserted, however, that they were most interested in *obshchenie*—which can be translated as conversation[57]—with active people who could influence them positively. For example, Lidiia and Vera, two friends who had decided to attend *SakhaSeliger* together, described themselves as rather passive; what they liked about camp was the opportunity to get to know a large number of very active people who knew "what they wanted in life."[58] Others, such as Alla, apparently considered themselves active, and wanted not only to get to know new people at camp, but also to meet *svoi*, that is, those "of their own kind,"[59] and to make themselves known: "I came to get to know folks, to show myself and get some experience, because at *SakhaSeliger* there are many very interesting folks."[60] Alla further accentuated the excitement of meeting so many new and interesting people so easily. Aleksandr, who evinced a conviction during our interview that he would make a successful career for himself, described fellow campers as "active, strong, smart folks; those who are leaders by nature" (*lideri po svoei prirode*).[61] Igor, a young man from the Krasnoyarsk Region, told me, "First of all I liked that there are many proactive people [*mnogo initsiativnykh liudei*]. All the people there are very open; there are no withdrawn people. If there are, they open up there like a flower. There are many interesting ideas, ideas that you would not hear of otherwise."[62]

Margarita shared Igor's assessment, pointing out her "joy that young people are ready to go forward, to strive for something." She recounted how easy it was to get in touch with other campers:

> You listen to their ideas, and you understand that it's interesting and even, maybe... you hadn't thought of this before and you think—'wow, well done!' and this causes joy that young people are ready to go forward, to strive for something. You arrive at *Biriusa* and you see this activity, when everyone's running around, everyone's happy, and everyone's pursuing something interesting. You just approach any person, get to know them, talk, tell them about your ideas, and they tell you about their own, and all that takes place absolutely easily, easy-going [*absoliutno spokoino prokhodit*].[63]

Most interviewees regarded their fellow campers as more interesting than "average peers"—an assessment I had previously encountered at multi-day seminars in Western Europe for students deemed especially talented. Both of these establishments address young adults as the future elite, pointing to their attendance as proof of their specialness. At camp, the feeling of belonging to a special crowd, to tomorrow's elite, was especially supported through the visits of VIPs.

Indeed, the presence of VIPs and the television broadcasting of Q&A sessions with these individuals communicated to campers and the outside world that this was a high-level event. The special modes of transportation used to bring such visitors to the remote camp sites underscored the guests' exclusivity and, indirectly, attested to campers' above-average status. At *SakhaSeliger*, VIPs often arrived by helicopter—a popular background among those campers who were keen to be photographed with the guest. At *Biriusa*, VIPs arrived by motorboat. When the governor of the Krasnoyarsk Region arrived, campers were organized to greet him at the shore. Most VIPs visiting the camps were successful businessmen or politicians; their presence was important to most of the campers I interviewed. "Here [at *SakhaSeliger*], there are several ministers, people who have founded their own business,"[64] Serafima said admiringly, while Lidiia noted that "the president [as the post of governor is called in the Sakha Republic] came by, the vice-president and so many politicians."[65]

Official visits are highly symbolic acts, serving to unite the peripheries with the center, and have a ceremonial meaning: that those governing the region communicate directly with the (young) people.[66] Some VIPs gave lectures, while others talked to campers in a more intimate format around the bonfire. When the Sakha Republic's president, Yegor Borisov, visited *SakhaSeliger*, his Q&A session with campers mirrored the style of the Q&A TV show *Direct Line with Vladimir Putin*.[67] Campers raised pressing questions about such topics as the long-awaited start date for construction of a bridge across the river and the introduction of liquor stores, meant to regulate the sale of alcohol as a prevention against alcoholism among minors. The president's replies made him appear—to use communication scholar Natalia Kovalyova's characterization of Putin's self-representation during *Direct Line with Vladimir Putin*—as a "capable task manager of multiple projects and an ultimate problem-solver" who was "equally attentive to all concerns."[68] After promising several quick solutions to structural problems, Yegor Borisov appealed to campers to support his actions. He insinuated that change would occur when campers' "initiative from below" came to match his pressing for improvements "from the top down."

Education and the Dominant *Erziehungsstil* at Camp

Entertainment was also an important tool for enlivening educational content. At *Biriusa*, for instance, several "special effects" were used to introduce that year's guiding theme of evolution. During a gathering at the main stage, we were shown a short movie clip featuring a timeline of human evolution. It depicted this process as primarily one of technical and scientific development—accentuating innovations such as the steam engine and the emergence of preeminent scientists such as Albert Einstein. It ended in an Asian city with interactive street maps and visions of fully digitalized medical care. As soon as the clip ended, a remix of the song *It's Bigger than Hip-Hop* by Dead Prez resounded, theatrical fog began to cover the main stage, and professional dancers appeared, mimicking robots. Their breakdancing made for a spectacular show.

Although educational presentations were seldom pepped up with such professional entertainment as this one, most of the campers that I interviewed found the training sessions refreshingly different from the lectures they had experienced in public educational institutions. They expressed an emphatic appreciation for the dialogical teaching atmosphere and the applicability of the content, as well as the use of techniques such as storytelling and simulation games.

Project Management and Self-Improvement Training

Indeed, the camps' educational program had more in common with corporate human-resources training than with typical university lectures. This assessment was shared by Aleksei Ivanovich Orlov, a senior staff member of *Rosmolodezh*, who characterized education at youth-leadership camps thus: "The forums [that is, youth-leadership summer camps] are most similar to human-resource training sessions in huge companies aiming at the motivation and determination of staff and the teaching of leadership skills."[69] Correspondingly, trainers at camp were often entrepreneurs who had successfully started their own businesses, heads of philanthropic organizations, or politicians. Camp presenters included, for example, Bari Alibasov, the co-founder of the pop group *Na-Na*; Vasilii Afanas'ev, the founder of several bread factories in the Sakha Republic; Galina Bodrenkova, the president of the National Volunteer Center and a member of Russia's civic chamber; and Boris Khasan, a renowned psychologist at the Siberian Federal University in Krasnoyarsk.

The training sessions' refreshing difference from university lectures was emphasized by nearly all interviewees.[70] Many were especially amazed by how easy it was to approach trainers and how effortlessly they could follow them. As Galina put it:

> There haven't been such lively teachers at my institute. Here they are lively, and you can reach them, be in touch with them [*do nikh mozhno dotianut'sia, sotronut'sia*]. Whereas in my institute [. . .], they were higher [more formally removed from students], and you were afraid to ask about fundamental elements of the lecture—even if you didn't understand something. Also, here they are lively, they are real—and you don't sleep, you listen, you consider carefully, you understand [*ty slushaesh', ty vnikaesh', ty ponimaesh'*]. [...] There, we have chairs, desks, a warm and big auditorium—but you sleep. Here, it is hot, it is cold—but you *don't* sleep. They [teachers at camp] are approachable, they are lively. I really like our teachers.[71]

94   FLEXIBLE AUTHORITARIANISM

Moreover, most campers that I spoke with were impressed by the trainers' careers and status. Some were highly paid specialists whose training sessions would normally not be affordable for the average camper. That such renowned specialists addressed campers as equals impressed many. As Igor said approvingly:

> There, all are equal [*po urovne ravny*]. There are people of the administration, prominent entrepreneurs, and there are very young folks, and all communicate in the same language, meaning in an informal way [*oni obshchaiutsia na odnom iazyke, to est' v neformal'noi obstanovke*].[72]

That such informality impressed campers has to do with the style of organization in Russian higher education institutions. Strict hierarchies structure the relationships in many such institutions, not only between professors and students, but also between administrative staff and students.[73] In the interview with Aleksei Orlov, the senior *Rosmolodezh* staff member, I learned that the departure from standard higher education modes of communication was intentional at the youth-leadership camps. Because the state had still not managed to reform the curricula of public educational institutions—whose contents Orlov regarded as mostly worthless for business needs—camp education was designed to plug the gap:

> So, the state, not touching the fundamental system of higher and secondary education, constructs a parallel where great freedom and variation is possible, where experiments are permissible. And this is indeed the reason for why this [the format of the youth-leadership camps] spread to this extent. [. . .] And it becomes clear that the universities don't teach what a young person needs to make a successful career. [. . .] At the same time, as common practice shows, education must be maximally adjusted to the demands of the job market, so that businesses can hire the specialists who are in demand.[74]

That the training sessions were practically applicable was especially appreciated by those campers who wanted to start their own businesses. Serafima, for instance, planned to do so after finishing medical school. She told me how much she preferred to attend lectures taught by practitioners: "Excuse me [for saying this], but lecturers who teach philosophy—they are not philosophers *themselves* . . . But Bari Alibasov owns so many companies and he conveys his direct experience to us!"[75]

While techniques such as dialogical teaching, storytelling, and simulation games break with an authoritarian *Erziehungsstil*, they can nevertheless also be employed to convey authoritarian and neotraditional values. Several trainers based their teachings on highly problematic assumptions about human nature and the social world, invoking racist stereotypes and often drawing illogical inferences. The trainings that struck me most in this respect were those conducted by Kirill Davydenko, the founder of a coaching business called "Strong People" (*Sil'nye liudi*). He was then a man in his early thirties, whom campers called by his first name, without the patronym. At one of Kirill's first lectures, which I attended as a participant in my working group, he claimed that success in one's job very much depended on body language. Since, as he reasoned, people basically function like apes, communicating one's strong will through (an apparently universal) body language is key. For instance, as he explained, if a person looks at you and you look away first, you have lost psychologically. One of the first exercises we were to practice was looking into the eyes of other campers as long as possible without averting our gaze. As Kirill told us, this technique would not only be lucrative in business meetings, but also effective against what he called the "pestering of gypsies (*tsigany*)." According to him, the latter could not hold somebody's gaze, insinuating that ethnicity determined psychological strength.

Such power plays impressed several campers. Mikhail, an aspiring teacher from the Krasnoyarsk Region, was particularly taken with the eye-contact exercise:

Kirill told us how to become a strong personality, a master [*sverkhchelovek*]. As he said [at camp]: "You will leave here as a totally different person; you will perceive yourself differently and react differently to others."[76]

The technique assured Mikhail that he would have the status of the master in relationships (literally "to be above other people"—*byt' sverkh liud'mi*) and be able to resist manipulations. As he added later in the interview, he had attended a similar training—organized by his university—called "Discernment of Lies and Operative Psycho-Diagnostics." Mikhail believed that it was possible to recognize a person's psychological character simply by reading his facial expressions or body language, and that this knowledge would further his career. Such dubious assumptions do not only risk engendering false, and potentially dangerous, judgements of human interaction, but also promote a worldview according to which all people manipulate each other and success is understood as achievable primarily through asserting one's power over others.

Over the following days, we engaged in more of Kirill's training exercises, all designed to change our personalities by boosting our strength and leadership. Self-awareness games included the task of holding up one's arms at a forty-five-degree angle for several minutes as a way of heightening our willpower. In a confidence-boosting exercise, we were taught to receive and accept compliments from others. Kirill recommended that we tell ourselves these compliments daily, reminding ourselves that we were great, that we were winners, and that we believe in ourselves. We also learned to imitate the behavior of upper-class people—though only of our own gender—in order to maximize our chances of upward social mobility.

Kirill's trainings present an ideal example of how neoliberal modernization and neotraditional ideals may be integrated into educational content. As I argue in Chapter 6, the diffusion of these ideals may subtly stabilize flexible authoritarianism on an ideological level. During an interview with *Biriusa Today*, Kirill introduced the very model of leadership he taught in camp, entailing the pursuit of a healthy lifestyle, the rejection of all kinds of drugs, and the readiness to take responsibility through initiative.[77] The homepage of Kirill's "Strong People" coaching business presents the company goal as "forging clean, bright people who do not drink, do not smoke and continuously self-develop under the strict supervision of the experienced trainer for personal growth, Kirill."[78] The business's other arena of activity is that of classic career coaching: trainings for personal development, SPIN selling ("Situation—Problem—Implication—Need-Payoff"—a technique developed by the British-American consultant Neil Rackham), and financial success strategies.[79] While some campers were, like Mikhail, taken by the trainings' authoritarian promises—such as to be "the master" in relationships—it was Kirill's teaching style that led most to name him, in a poll conducted at camp, as their favorite trainer.[80] Oleg and Mitislav were both part of Kirill's unofficial fan club at camp:

> Oleg: "There [at camp], I heard a lecture by a person I had never heard of before—Kirill Davydenko..."
> Mitislav: "... our favorite trainer, the favorite trainer of all!"

Oleg: "From Novosibirsk..."
Mitislav: "We all remember him affectionately and lovingly... [*s dushoi, s liuboviu*]"
Oleg: "Yes, he was just a super trainer. I was crazy about the exercises."[81]

Trainings such as Kirill's, merging neotraditional ideals with neoliberal ones, were not the rule. At *SakhaSeliger* in particular, I witnessed more classic project-management and personal-development forms of training. Stepan Smirnov's trainings at *SakhaSeliger* were a good example. Smirnov, who also works as a coach, told me that he promoted neoliberal ideals among young people in order to help the (Russian) economy function more effectively:

> And when you start to teach these things to young people [thinking in projects (*proektnoe myshlenie*)], the majority want to become entrepreneurs. This means that [through the teachings/spread of project-thinking] we receive hundreds of thousands of projects which have their own lifespan [*srok godosti*]. And accordingly, when one project ends, a new one starts. As it turns out, the entrepreneur or employee is not a person who will fulfill one function for forty-five years, but a person who for forty-five years will, roughly speaking, fulfill ninety functions, he will complete ninety projects. And in that way occurs the maximum surplus of the economic sphere's development [*I takim obrazom idet maksimal'noe pokrytie ekonomicheskoi zony razvitiia*].[82]

Stepan Smirnov's training sessions introduced many of the time- and self-management tools that are increasingly taught at soft-skills workshops around the globe, some of which I was familiar with through my graduate school. These included tips for setting realistic aims and increasing one's self-discipline—for instance, through the S.M.A.R.T. (Specific/Measurable/Assignable/Realistic/Time-related) tool,[83] which in its Russian translation *KIPRO* (*konkretnost', izmerinost', podkontrol'nost', realistichnost', opredelennost'*) featured prominently in the *SakhaSeliger* exercise book handed out to all campers free of charge. This book had been created especially for *SakhaSeliger* campers and contained mostly time- and self-management tips—so that readers could work on their self-improvement—but also project-management tools.[84]

Lidiia and Vera especially liked a lecture given by Smirnov that taught campers how to set goals for themselves. They wanted to make use of this for their diploma theses. "I apply this [goal-setting] now," Vera told me eagerly. "You keep thinking of something you want in an *exact* way, you set yourself the aim and imagine the result; I mean then you will certainly achieve it." And Lidiia added: "We will soon write our diploma thesis. This is a project in any case, and some of the knowledge is effective for that—how to set aims, how to develop all this."[85] Moreover, Smirnov taught us campers to formulate aims positively and to envision that our career would be successful.

Trainings such as Smirnov's amounted to the "theologizing approaches to personal change" that anthropologist Sonja Luehrmann has described as combining popular self-help tips with appeals to lead a happy, purpose-driven life.[86] The promotion of personal change for a happy life was intertwined with that of strategies for economic success.[87]

Aleksandr Abramovich, a high-ranking Krasnoyarsk youth politician, affirmed during our interview that the creation of happy young citizens was a major aim of his—in part because their happiness was key to economic innovation. As he told me, youth politicians like himself "want young adults to be positive, happy, open. A sad and boring person will not create anything new. Therefore, we support all kinds of undertakings so that folks smile more, are more positive and more kind to each other."[88] Positive thinking was deliberately fostered at camp in order to enhance young adults' motivation to realize and marketize innovative project ideas.[89]

Language that emphasized the possibilities for self-improvement, the payoffs of a protestant work ethic, and the need to make deposits in another person's "Emotional Bank Account"[90] to build trust was ubiquitous in the training sessions. Trainers and camp organizers regularly addressed us campers using such language. For instance, during the very first general assembly at *Biriusa*, organizers exhorted us to make "the best possible use" of the state's investment in us, the country's talented youth. Thus, we needed to learn to discipline ourselves and win a victory over ourselves (*pobeda nad samim soboi*). Self-discipline implied keeping one's promises to oneself, especially in terms of the organizers' recommendations to make the most of our time at camp. We should promise ourselves to "always be on time!" "Always have pen and paper!" and "keep a diary of our progress!" Such a diary should ideally include a section for one's friends to sign off on one's self-promises, so as to heighten one's commitment to one's own self-improvement goals. This strategy implied that sharing our self-promises with others increased our capacity to stick to them. Punctuality was—according to the organizers—particularly essential, to allow us to "make the most of" our stay.

Such instructions were also given against the backdrop of assumptions about purportedly Russian characteristics, such as the notion that a Soviet or Russian way of doing things carelessly—a stereotype we will encounter again in Chapter 5—was impeding economic development. Trainers regularly spurred campers on by sayings like "promised, done" (*obeshchal, sdelal*) or "promise less, do more," and similar take-home messages. They used as a foil the assumption that Russia had always been and would always be a "country of connections" (*strana sviazei*), emphasizing the need for campers to stay in touch with "important" people and cultivate such relationships by continuously paying into an "Emotional Bank Account."[91] The presence of VIPs at camp presented an ideal opportunity to initiate such practices right away.

This mixture of stimulating didactics, the likeability of the trainers, and the applicability of content enabled several of my interviewees to recall some of the training sessions' content without difficulty during our conversations—which in some cases took place about a year after camp. Only a few campers disliked the educational program, and even they could mention at least one lecture that they remembered well and had found inspiring. Campers stated that they cherished the dialogical teaching styles, rife with examples relating to their life-worlds. They enjoyed how the trainers treated them as equals and encouraged them to pursue their own visions—a style of teaching commonly associated with empowerment and democratic group atmospheres.[92]

This atmosphere stood in sharp contrast to the authoritarian values promoted in some trainings, but also to the authoritarian *Erziehungsstil* that characterized the camp experience outside of the lecture tents and *dialog-kholly*. It also contrasted with several lectures that sought to instill in campers neotraditional values and a veneration of the motherland. While such presentations could be counted on the fingers of one hand in 2013, they gained a prominent position at the 2014 *SakhaSeliger*, which took place after Russia had annexed the Ukrainian peninsula of Crimea. Indeed, that year, lectures conveying Russia's leading role as a political and economic power—one that was allegedly misunderstood and repressed by the West—were mostly inspired by an exercise book called "Russia and the Contemporary World" (*Rossiia i sovremennyi mir*).[93]

Campers had varying opinions about these indoctrinating lectures, and several, either publicly or privately in conversation with me, conveyed that they disapproved of such attempts to instill in them a particular political view. In contrast, few found fault with the authoritarian *Erziehungsstil* of the camp's overall organization. Most seemed to accept this *Erziehungsstil* as being typical for camp.

An Authoritarian *Erziehungsstil*

At both camps, young campers were expected to obey rigid rules of conduct, follow a strict daily routine, wear their camp ID badges visibly at all times, and remain on site; otherwise, they were expelled from camp. Active attendance at workshops, general assemblies, and calisthenics was compulsory. Swearing and the consumption of alcohol and illegal substances were strictly forbidden. A special camp site security service or patrols made up of campers monitored compliance. Every transgression resulted in cutting off one edge of a camper's ID badge, if made of paper, or puncturing it, if made of plastic. A camper who accumulated three such marked transgressions was required to leave the site for good. I heard of three campers at *Biriusa* who were made to leave the site for this reason during our themed session.

At *SakhaSeliger* all rules were stated in a booklet, while the rules for *Biriusa* could be downloaded from the homepage in advance.[94] The *SakhaSeliger* booklet outlined in detail how every subgroup should organize itself: it recommended the designation of "managers" who would be in charge of certain pieces of equipment, the election of campers who would carry out guard duty, and the assignment of *dezhurnye* (meaning "those on duty") to prepare tables for meals.

Rigid hierarchies, strict rules of conduct, and attempts to control campers' movements reflect the law-and-order character of authoritarian Putinist rule; they might also have been inspired by the Soviet summer camp tradition discussed in Chapter 3. The strict daily routine, for instance, paralleled the daily schedules common in pioneer camps and children's summer camps, which featured rituals such as the morning call (*pod'em*), calisthenics (*zariadka*), a general assembly followed by an evening program, gatherings around the bonfire, and a curfew (*otboi*).

How did the campers perceive of this authoritarian *Erziehungsstil*? Zinaida, a regular camper at youth-leadership summer camps for years, was a downright fan of the daily routine. According to her, it showed that camp was "not about sunbathing, barbecuing, and beer."[95] In 2013, she even found herself missing the digital monitoring and rating of campers' attendance that had been present at the 2012 *Biriusa*. For her, such strictness added to the experience of full immersion in daily life at camp:

> This routine is interesting; it carries you into a completely different life. [...] And when you return to the city, it's just bizarre—you don't have to go to the *zariadka*, no one plays jingles for breakfast or lunch, you don't wear your ID badge, you don't swipe in [*ne propikivaesh'sia*]. [...] In 2012 it was so cool; we had this rating. On one side of the ID badge was a barcode and when we went to lectures, everyone was swiped in, and all information was automatically registered in the computer. [...] It was just cool, you attended, swiped, attended, swiped.[96]

A similar rating system was re-introduced to *Biriusa* in 2014 as youth political organizer Daria Glazkova told me. The so-called team contest (*olimipiada druzhin*) rated a team's activities "quantitatively and qualitatively," and measured its performance in sports, cultural events, competitions, its observance of rules, its participation in general assemblies and trainings, and its activity in online social networks (though only positive comments on social media were rewarded). Team members' transgressions resulted in deductions for the whole team.[97] This practice may have been inspired by Soviet scholar of education Makarenko's observation that discipline is best achieved when fellow youth reprimand each other.[98]

Other campers were much less impressed than Zinaida by the daily routine, yet they accepted it as a standard feature of camp life. Fedor observed that as a grown-up, one simply accepted this state of affairs, having consented to the rules as part of being a camper: "There [at the children's camp] you don't like this daily routine. At the forum [youth-leadership summer camp], you consented to all this yourself, and so this doesn't bother you at all. The daily routine is just perceived as something that should be that way."[99]

In addition to the daily routine, the rules of conduct also recalled the summer camp tradition. Campers were not entitled to leave the site of their own accord. At *Biriusa*, campers who left without permission forfeited their right to participate in the camp, just as non-participants were not allowed to enter without prior authorization. Staff or control-group commands had to be obeyed, and refusal could result in the termination of one's stay.

The ID badges, or *beidchiki*, served a purpose like that of the pioneer uniforms: to immediately distinguish campers from unauthorized visitors.

Zinaida described the *beidchik* as a central feature of camp, calling it "*Biriusa*'s passport":

> At *Biriusa* your passport is your *beidchik*. Besides a photograph, it states who you are, your team [*druzhina*]. When you return to Krasnoyarsk [after camp] you understand that you practically slept wearing the *beidchik*, you wore it while washing yourself, so many things you did with this *beidchik* for seven days, and then, it hangs just there, and it feels just so strange [*neprivychno*] to take it off and hang it on the wall.[100]

Most campers endorsed the camp's rules of behavior. Like Fedor, they described the rules as an aspect of camp experience that they had known about beforehand. Zinaida's enthusiasm stood out—as did, at the other end of the spectrum, the critique offered by Arkadii, a camper who had been active with the Communist Party's youth wing. When I asked him one of my standard questions—how he would change the camp if he were its main organizer—he immediately replied that campers should "not be chased to trainings and lectures," but "go of their own free will."[101]

Yet while Arkadii found it important to let campers freely decide whether to attend lectures, the same principle did not apply for him regarding the consumption of alcohol. Like several others, he strongly supported its prohibition at camp.

> Of course, it's good [that people do not drink at camp]. And it's good that people are not allowed to bring any drugs. A "territory of proactive youth" must be attended with a clear mind [*Territoriia initsiativnoi molodezhi dolzhna byt' na svezhuiu golovu*]. If you drank at night, how would you attend lectures afterwards?[102]

Ethnologist Ina Schröder's study of a Russian summer camp for Khanty and Mansi youth, a program that sought to empower them as representatives of non-Russian nationalities in an environment that still devalues their specific cultural heritage, is informative in this regard. She argues that many campers who experienced the damaging effects of alcoholism in their communities appreciated the prohibition of alcohol at camp, interpreting the ban as freeing them from the social pressure to engage in drinking with their peers.[103]

Mikhail, a camper at *Biriusa*, was of the opinion that a full ban on alcohol could not be upheld; in any case, he found no fault with the prohibition either: "It's clear that you cannot stop everyone from drinking, because there is a mass of young people, singing songs and playing guitar. All those who were okay with it [the ban] didn't drink."[104]

Mikhail found that the prohibition of alcohol at camp had not been rigorously enforced (*Tam byl sukhoi zakon, no ne byl zhestochaishim*). As he made clear, the fact that the security guards sometimes turned a blind eye constituted an easing of the rules:

> And even the security guards, who came to check what was going on, said: "Folks, we are also human. It's your birthday, we understand that [you want to celebrate], we have nothing against your party, but you should not spoil everyone else's stay on the island. You can drink and have fun, but do it quietly." That was it, deal, we found a compromise.[105]

Mikhail also saw the punctures given to ID cards for transgressions as a fair warning mechanism: "They didn't just catch you and kick you out," he told me. "If you don't accept the rules, that means this is not your place. If you collect three punctures—goodbye."[106] The only prohibition he disliked was the ban on swimming on the day the governor visited the camp: "They forbade us from going swimming—what kind of nonsense is that? It's 35 degrees, heat, everyone's flagging, everyone's feeling the stuffiness; yet swimming is forbidden; because the head of the region is coming."[107]

With the exception of Arkadii and Mikhail, none of the campers I met objected to the authoritarian *Erziehungsstil* that characterized the general organization of the camps. Rather, several campers at the 2013 *SakhaSeliger* favored an extension of the transgression system to monitor punctuality and attendance. One suggestion went as far as returning to a rule that had been common in pioneer camps during the 1950s, requiring that team members always be with their leaders when crossing the camp site. Such suggestions were rooted in campers' discontent over poor organization. Lower-ranking team instructors sought to ward off the criticism directed at them, contending that the root cause of the disorganization was campers' non-compliance with their requests, such as showing up on time or answering their phones—a last-minute strategy to discipline one's group. To me it was noticeable how quickly the young adults turned to extending the camp's transgression system. This seemed to chime with most campers' acceptance of the strict rules of behavior—sometimes in stark contrast to their open criticism of the events' overall political purpose. One interpretation of their inclination to see threats of punishment as a solution might simply be their previous experiences of seeing educational and political institutions turn to law-and-order practices in attempts to eradicate organizational or motivational problems.

Governing through Soft Techniques and Overt Political Appeals

An authoritarian *Erziehungsstil*, informed by a preoccupation with culturedness—that campers should behave in a polite manner, engage regularly in calisthenics, care about cleanliness, and refrain from swearing as well as from alcohol and nicotine consumption[108]—dominates the organization of young-leadership camps. In addition, "soft" governance techniques, as opposed to overt political appeals or commands, were used to persuade campers to behave in a way that was sanctioned by camp organizers and state authorities alike.[109]

Such soft techniques included governing through project grants. At camp, sessions called "project conveyors" (*proektnyi konveier*) gave those in attendance the opportunity to discuss their proposals with teaching staff. Feedback was mostly given in a way that maximized campers' chances of receiving grant money. For instance, a young woman attempting to realize an information project for young families, motivated by her own experience of a lack of well-structured information about childcare, was encouraged by our trainer Kirill to frame the project as a countermeasure to "homosexual propaganda"—echoing a term frequently used by Russian government officials to disparage mobilizations for the rights of LGBTQI people. That would, Kirill explained, underscore the project's topicality.

Several campers were aware of attempts at camp to shape their political views. Vlas, the interviewee who was most critical of the government (he was inclined to see white supremacism as a solution for current shortcomings), concluded that the biggest problem was that "the majority of these forums—no matter if we take *Seliger* or *Biriusa*—are conducted by the state." And, he added, "the state just does it in such a way that this youth will think in the way that's needed."[110] In a similar vein, Arkadii observed that many trainings tended to legitimate the government's policies, telling campers that "Power [*vlast'*/the government] acts correctly, like 'You have to behave as Power does and never judge our Power.'"[111] Timur and Valentina, campers who like

Arkadii were members of the Communist Party's youth wing, noticed that the future candidate for the governor's post had visited *Biriusa* to solicit political support from campers.

Aside from these examples, most campers that I interviewed did not comment on the camps' attempts to manipulate them. Either they did not notice such attempts or they regarded them as simply to be expected. Others might have feared raising this topic during the interview, or perhaps simply did not feel like touching on the issue.

Overt political appeals and attempts to influence campers were much more pronounced in 2014 at *SakhaSeliger* than at both camps during the previous year. This was evident primarily in speeches by *SakhaSeliger*'s main educational instructor, Viktor Stepanenko, a history lecturer at the North Caucasus Stavropol branch of the Moscow State Pedagogic University M.A. Sholokhov—the institution that edited the 2014 patriotic exercise book "Russia and the Contemporary World" (*Rossiia i sovremennyi mir*) for the *Seliger* camp. In 2013, Stepanenko had added some neoliberal toppings to his neotraditional speeches—such as the notion that because today's economy was driven by creators (*sozdateli*), young people should focus on action (*predprimimat' deistvie*) and thereby become entrepreneurs (*predprinimateli*). Apart from that, he promoted an all-Russian patriotism that defined Russia and its different nationalities as a unique state civilization. For instance, using Oswald Spengler's notion of a Siberian-Russian civilization, he alleged that Russia's various ethnic groups (*natsional'nosti*) had learned to live together in peace, to nourish each other, and to share their riches over centuries. The Russian state civilization was, according to him, threatened by large-scale immigration from neighboring, high-birthrate China, whereas in Russia the population was continuously decreasing—a trope that has been widely discussed in Russia since the early 2000s.[112] At the 2014 *SakhaSeliger*, he replaced China as the main external threat with the United States and the European Union. Using clips from Marcel Theroux's 2006 *Death of a Nation* documentary, he attempted to show that Western powers had anticipated Russia's death and would, unfairly, try to keep Russia down.[113] During *SakhaSeliger*'s 2014 opening ceremony, Stepanenko recited Alexander Pushkin's poem *To the Slanderers of Russia*, which tells the story of how all of Russia's *natsional'nosti* united against Western enemies, promising them a humiliating defeat.[114]

Two interviewees related positively to Stepanenko's opening speech, which confirmed their belief that the West would act against Russia. Yet there were also some campers who actively objected to the views Stepanenko expressed. During a seminar based on a chapter entitled "Geopolitical and Geo-Economic Image of the World" in the patriotic exercise book, Stepanenko claimed that implementing democracy was impossible in Russia due to the country's size. One camper openly and eloquently countered during the seminar itself that the size of the United States had not impeded the introduction of checks and balances there. Other campers distanced themselves from such speeches less openly. During the same seminar, one camper handed me a piece of paper on which he had written in German—probably so that others would not understand, or as a gesture of sympathy to me as a representative of the West, which was presented as Russia's enemy by the lecturer—"How do you like the lecture?" When I replied "horrible," he added his opinion: "too much politics." Some campers indirectly conveyed that they understood what was going on. When I asked a fellow camper in 2013 what a particular part of a lecture by Stepanenko was about (Stepanenko was *SakhaSeliger*'s main educational instructor at that time), he used the formulation "*nam pytaiutsia vnushit'*", meaning "they try to inculcate or instill into us," revealing that he distanced himself from the content and was critical of how it was conveyed.

The changes at the 2014 *SakhaSeliger* notwithstanding, most training sessions were still devoted to project management and grant writing. That overt political appeals were rather the exception than the rule should not be taken to mean, however, that teaching "entrepreneurial literacy" to campers was not intended to spread the government's neotraditional ideals—for instance, via governing through project grants.

Summer Camp as Spectacle and Hub for Spreading Entrepreneurial Literacy

Flexible authoritarianism operates at concrete sites such as youth-leadership summer camps, which offer promising youth a unique experience. My cultural analysis of the nature of this experience through images, symbols, music, and routines points beyond an understanding of flexible authoritarianism as mere ideology. Flexible authoritarianism, as it can be experienced at these sites, also constitutes a lived political reality, albeit one that is bound to the time and space of camp. Similar to the rally, the public concert, and the national holiday celebration, the summer camp is a form of political spectacle especially suited to the creation of temporary "communities of emotional attachment" that eventually result in long-lasting bonds of solidarity.[115] Relatively isolated from the usual affirmations of their identity, campers may be more inclined to enter a state of liminality—that is, a transitional stage between one's separation from a present state of being and entry into a new one.[116] Because campers sleep, play, and work at the same site, carrying out all activities with the same co-participants and according to a planned schedule, their conceptions of themselves might be more prone to change at camp.[117] This may then be accompanied by a change of what Mabel Berezin has called the felt hierarchy of identities:

> There are some identities that we value more than others, that we experience as 'hypergoods,' and some we experience as essentially 'contingent.' The felt force of some identities is so potent that we might be willing to die for them. It is those identities that generate powerful emotions carrying political importance.[118]

Youth-leadership camps seek to instill in campers an identification with the state's flexible authoritarian project so that campers make the state's aim of becoming an entrepreneurially-minded and patriotic person part of their own conception of the good life. This goes hand in hand with the teaching of entrepreneurial literacy.

As mentioned at the beginning of this chapter, what I call entrepreneurial literacy denotes citizens' capacity to develop their own business projects and to participate in public grant competitions for project funding. This kind of literacy is intended to prepare young campers to become entrepreneurs of their life plans, transform their ideas into marketable business models, or participate in public grant competitions. Being entrepreneurially literate after camp attendance enables young people to become co-creators of a government-sponsored civic life that seeks to elicit, but also tightly control, civic action.[119] By applying for government sponsorship to realize their projects, young people become active co-creators of a civic life that allows for various forms of engagement. As long as they comply with government-approved neoliberal modernization and neotraditional ideals in their project proposals, applicants have a good chance of obtaining funding for their visions. Entrepreneurial literacy is indeed a precondition for becoming a co-creator of government-sponsored civic life, as the example of the government-sponsored vigilante project *StopKham*, discussed in Chapter 6, demonstrates. The teaching of entrepreneurial literacy by and in authoritarian states to potential strategic elites exemplifies how forms of what has been called "new public participation"[120] are incorporated in non-democracies. It illuminates how "soft" techniques of governance such as grant competitions and activation can be used to spread the government's neotraditional ideals.

The spectacular character of the youth-leadership summer camps is also meant to stage youthful support for the regime to the larger public. Photographs and movie clips shown on TV displaying large crowds of young people in enthusiastic conversation with high-level politicians, businessmen, or NGO leaders show that Russia's future generation is on board with the current leadership.[121] While local camps are covered by regional media, Russian national TV reports from federal-level summer camps such as *Seliger* and its successors—the "Territory of Thoughts" (*Territoriia Smyslov*) and *Tavrida* (the historical designation for parts of Crimea, originating from the time of the Russian Empire). The latter two were both founded, not accidentally, in 2014, when Russia annexed the Crimean peninsula and proclaimed a new Cold War against Western powers in the aftermath of Ukraine's Maidan Revolution.

Neoliberal modernization and neotraditional ideals co-exist, combine, and merge at regional youth-leadership summer camps. The symbolic scenery and entertainment on offer aim to activate campers by appealing to their dreams. The ubiquity of empowerment slogans ("you are the best," "the state invests so much in you—get the most out of this," "you can do it," "realize your potential") testify to the state's ambition to motivate potential strategic elites. Dialogical teaching atmospheres and participatory teaching formats—reminiscent of the workforce development programs of human resource departments—are as characteristic of these idiosyncratic establishments as an authoritarian *Erziehungsstil*.

As I have shown, a Soviet summer camp tradition is repurposed for flexible authoritarian ends at these youth-leadership summer camps. Soviet-type values of culturedness (polite behavior, no swearing, no alcohol), ideas about effective group self-management, and standard precautionary measures against accidents and epidemics shape the general rules at these establishments. The notion of the summer camp tradition, developed in Chapter 3, illuminates how an authoritarian *Erziehungsstil* can influence, often unquestioned, the authoritarian organization of present-day youth-leadership camps. While some camp features were certainly used intentionally to control campers, others do not appear to have been deliberately chosen, but rather applied by regional youth political organizers according to their tacit assumptions about what such a camp should be like and how it should be organized.

What is more, the summer camp tradition shapes young people's assumption about what to expect at these contemporary camps, partially explaining why campers acquiesced to strict regulations and accepted a militaristic-seeming daily regime and a hierarchical camp organization—even though several registered their objections, at least among each other or with me, to authoritarian lectures and attempts at manipulation. Campers' acceptance of this authoritarian *Erziehungsstil* contrasted with their enthusiasm for the project management and self-development trainings. They were taken in particular with dialogical teaching atmospheres and participatory teaching formats that broke with the hierarchical chalk-and-talk approaches they knew from their university lectures.

Numerous campers described their overall summer camp experience in terms of an inspiring, feverish activity: "Just adrenalin," said Elena of her stay at *SakhaSeliger*. "When there is hardly time to go to the restrooms; you shoot a video clip, you stage a dance, memorize a song, although you cannot even sing. And all this takes place in these extremely short time frames, but it works out."[122] Even campers who, like Arkadii, criticized the attempt to manipulate young people so that they would support the governing party, were impressed by such activity. "I will participate again [in *Biriusa*]," Arkadii told me. "It's cool there, interesting. And it struck me very much that all people there try to defend their projects with such zeal."[123]

While these statements testify to the fact that the experience offered at camp certainly resonated with campers, they do not amount to any evidence that the camp experience had a long-lasting effect. What is nevertheless worth noting is that it was not the authoritarian *Erziehungsstil* that inspired campers, but the impression that they were surrounded by people who, like them, wanted to become active and develop their neighborhood, region, or country.

5

Loyal Youths' Individualist Quests for Change

Self-Development for the Good of All

The complicity of promising young people with flexible authoritarian regimes tends to involve ambiguities, and that is certainly the case in today's Russia. Ambitious young people seek to align themselves both with the demands of the market, which targets them as individuals, and with those put forward by the authoritarian state, which addresses them collectively as potential members of tomorrow's strategic elites.

The individualist quests for change I discovered in the campers' narratives arise from a complex coexistence of criticism of and loyalty to the Russian state. While campers repeatedly and fiercely criticized corrupt politicians, businesspeople, and public institutions, their quests for change often failed to respond to the social ills they condemned. Most of them found little fault with government-promoted narratives that justify authoritarianism and the government's neotraditional ideals. For instance, numerous interviewees regarded authoritarian practices as necessary responses to foreign threats, or to what they, like government officials, saw as deficiencies in the mentality of ordinary Russians. While campers condemned wrongs of a systemic nature—the intermingling of politics and business, double standards in law enforcement, and the intimidation of business rivals or political opponents—they also echoed the moral analyses favored by ruling politicians, laying the blame on those who passively lived off the state or those who used the country's riches solely for their individual wealth. What united these two categories of people, according to both interviewees' stories and government proclamations, was their indifference to the common good.

Government-sponsored youth-leadership camps are designed to legitimate the regime, in part by bringing the glamour of Silicon Valley start-ups to Siberia. They combine both carrot and stick by conveying to young people that they can break new ground in diverse sectors, such as business, social work, and politics, as long as they do not question the political status quo. Nevertheless, campers were able to see behind some of the regime's shiny promises and unlikely depictions of reality. Some, for example, noted that launching a business was often impossible in sectors where newcomers were subject to intimidation by already-established rivals—a situation not touched upon in business start-up training sessions at camp.[1]

However, this did not mean that campers held liberal views or criticized the government's neotraditional ideals. On the contrary, in some policy areas their stance could be even more conservative or nationalist than the government's. For instance, several interviewees from the Krasnoyarsk Region were highly critical of immigration from Central Asia and viewed the lack of stricter immigration policies as a governmental failure. Wishes for greater democracy only featured in very few instances.

To be sure, not all campers held the same views, especially when it came to issues such as immigration and racism. Galina, a young teacher from the Sakha Republic, was outraged by the way she had often been treated in Central and Western Russia: "I always want to show them my passport: I am a citizen of the Russian Federation! They all say: '*Ponaekhali*.'"[2] This verb, when used in the past tense, literally translates as "they came here," and pejoratively denotes labor migrants. It is usually employed with reference to people like Galina, from a Sakha family, who do not look like ethnic Russians, and it carries a derogatory connotation. Galina continued: "Excuse me, but I live in *my* country (*v svoei strane*), and I can travel wherever I want to. [...] This is what annoys me [in Russia]: '*Ponaekhali*.'"[3] For Galina, though, these experiences and her anger about them did not lead to alienation from the Russian state: she had deliberately chosen the working group "We Are Multinational Russians" (*My—Rossiiane*) at the 2014 *SakhaSeliger* because she regarded herself as a real patriot, having grown up in a communist, patriotic family and having always, as she emphasized, been an activist. She was active in several organizations, including student clubs and the governing body of her university, but she did not engage in government-critical antiracist projects or similar endeavors. Like many others, she was hesitant to touch upon such large-scale problems, which appear, as some of her Sakha peers put it with regard to racism, eternal and inevitable.

Though campers could be deeply divided on issues such as migration or same-sex partnerships, they all related similarly to the regime, to Russia's underlying order of economic and political life.[4] Despite their severe criticism of "how things work" in Russia under the current rule,[5] these young people are largely loyal to the country's regime.

A conceptual differentiation which helps to illustrate my argument about the complex coexistence of criticism and loyalty in young campers' narratives is that between specific and diffuse political support, which was made in the 1970s by political scientist David Easton. He developed this distinction in response to his finding that the simultaneity of discontent and approval was a regular phenomenon in political systems:

> Typically, members of a political system may find themselves opposed to the political authorities, disquieted by their policies, dissatisfied with their conditions of life and, where they have the opportunity, prepared to throw the incumbents out of office. At times such conditions may lead to fundamental political or social change. Yet at other times, in spite of widespread discontent, there appears to be little loss of confidence in the regime—the underlying order of political life—or of identification with the political community.[6]

The latter constellation described by Easton accords exactly with my argument: while the campers I interviewed are dissatisfied with ruling politicians and conditions in their own lives, they still evince confidence in the regime. Easton speaks of two different kinds of "political support." While he defines political support in general as a situation in which people orient themselves favorably toward a party in power or act on its behalf, he distinguishes between specific support—peoples' satisfaction with a particular government's performance—and diffuse support—people's general approval of a regime—that is, a political system's "underlying order of political life."[7] While few campers supported local or federal politicians, indeed several found politics to be little more than a business carried out by old men in suits, almost all accepted Russia's political and economic setup. The vast majority found no fault with a political system lacking checks and balances, the government's "normalization of the Soviet past" (discussed in Chapter 3), or the annexation of Crimea in violation of international law. Even those who in principle favored democracy over Putin's strongman rule were reluctant to side with opposition parties and movements that criticize Russia's authoritarian regime.

The uncritical political stance of the campers toward authoritarian practices and neotraditional ideals was accompanied by a belief that everyone has equal opportunities to advance professionally and socioeconomically, echoing the promise put forth at the youth-leadership summer camps, for instance, through the career stories of visiting VIPs: that those who make every effort to succeed and do not shy away from hard work will be rewarded. The summer camps, and state youth political programs more generally, cultivate young people's loyalty by appealing to their personal career ambitions and hopes for raising their own living standard as well as that of their families. These establishments stoke young people's belief in the possibility of a professional future in Russia and prevent them—at least in part—from developing a more critical perspective toward the regime.

Young people in Russia's provinces have often had little choice but to leave home for more prosperous regions in order to make a living. During the 1990s, young and ambitious people in particular left remote regions for the centers of Western Russia or, more often, Europe or North America. Promising youth from regional Russia still face the dilemma of having to choose between either staying home or leaving for better wages and professional self-realization. The training sessions at the youth-leadership summer camps that I discussed in Chapter 4 thus respond to a pressing situation for ambitious young people, making the case that it is possible to engage in fulfilling work "despite" staying in their region or Russia. The camp-based training promises an alternative to both the monotonous, underpaid jobs available at home and the difficulties involved in moving to more prosperous places.

Today's potential strategic elites desire to create the conditions that will allow them to lead a Western-style life "at home," meaning—depending on the interviewee—in their city or region or in Russia at large. In peripheral places, where emigration to burgeoning centers is the silent imperative for the young, well-educated, and ambitious, the possibility of development in the here and now is dazzling. My interviews revealed that young people from the Sakha Republic in particular preferred staying in their region, which is mainly inhabited by Russian citizens of non-Russian ethnicity. Many of these young people associated living in other parts of Russia, but also in Western countries, with poor treatment arising from widespread racial profiling affecting those with stereotypically Asian features.

Many campers were keen to self-develop, not only to further their career, but also to improve the overall quality of life in their regions. Their individually conceived quests for change arose from their dual wish to enjoy the same conveniences available to the middle classes in economically prosperous liberal democracies and at the same time see the flourishing of their own region. That regular individuals can initiate larger changes simply by changing themselves is a powerful notion in places that are associated by many of their inhabitants with backwardness and stagnation.

In this regard, young campers' individualist quests for change are informed by a deep-seated trust that their individual initiative can serve the common good. Similarly, their quests speak of the unquestioned beliefs that all must share in the task of developing the country, and that any socioeconomic development can benefit all citizens. Campers affirmed development as a value in and of itself and had a markedly apolitical understanding of social change. Most supported government-enforced public narratives portraying patriotism—to love one's home even if it is underdeveloped—as a precondition for development. In keeping with these stories, their self-presentation was as people keen to groom themselves to become successful professionals, in the process furthering the development of the region and, in some cases, the country. They understood "being active" as an indispensable personal quality for all those who, like them, want to change themselves, the region, and Russian society for the better. They thus shared in the belief, promoted by the government, that the country needs people actively taking initiative so as to spur development.

This apolitical stance toward social change was mirrored in the kind of activist engagement campers mentioned when I asked them about their previous or current personal efforts for "a better life." Few of them told me about having actively campaigned for greater accountability of deputies, fairer bidding procedures for public contracts, more equal conditions regarding medical services, equality before the law, or a reform of labor market policies. An exception in this respect were those campers who were engaged in the Russian Communist Party's youth wing—which, claiming the role of heir to the Soviet Youth League *Komsomol*, calls itself the Russian Federation's Leninist Communist Youth League (*Leninskii kommunisticheskii soiuz molodezhi Rossisskoi Federatsii, LKSM RF*).[8] This group's members, calling themselves *Komsomoltsy*, asserted that they repeatedly protested against inequality before the law and for greater accountability of deputies.

I seldom met campers who had become involved in organizations or parties that are known to overstep the boundaries of the government's narrow political course—such as the Left Front, the *Yabloko* party, or the NGO *Memorial*. The *Komsomoltsy* mentioned several actions in which they were pitted against injustice or socioeconomic inequality, but were also, generally speaking, more inclined than their peers to find credible the government's story of a fascist *coup d'état* in Ukraine, a narrative that builds on Soviet-era propaganda portraying Ukrainian nationalism as necessarily fascist and supported by the United States.[9] During the late-Soviet period, the clash between fascism and antifascism was used by Soviet politicians to mark a boundary between a malign Western capitalism, allying with fascists, and a benign Soviet socialism, firmly opposed to fascism.[10] As I observed during my participation in a gathering of several Central Siberian *Komsomol* groups in 2014 (see Appendix I), several participating *Komsomoltsy* criticized the Putin government for its "overly lax position" regarding what they found to be Western "historical falsifications" about the Soviet period. Some of the *Komsomoltsy* present at that gathering sought to convince me that the Stalinist purges had been necessary to clear the Red Army of potential Nazi collaborators and ensure the Soviet victory over fascism; or that the Holodomor, a famine produced by Stalinist politics in today's Ukraine, had been a natural disaster.[11] Aside from the *Komsomoltsy*, along with a camper who identified as a member of the *Yabloko* party, and another who held white-supremacist views, the interviewees were usually involved in organizations that presented themselves as apolitical, hewing to the government's course.

Most campers I interviewed were active in the self-management bodies of their university or other higher education institutions. Those bodies—student councils or student unions—are known to offer very limited opportunities to influence even university-related matters.[12] A similar situation exists in local, government-sponsored groups such as the student brigades in the Krasnoyarsk Region that I discussed in Chapter 3, regional youth parliaments, and state-funded volunteer initiatives, as well as in state-funded non-commercial groups that are part of federal or regional state registers for youth organizations. Since the mid-1990s the so-called register mechanism profits only those non-commercial organizations whose activities match the political course of the government.[13] The principle of adding only "loyal organizations" to this central register—membership in which is the precondition for receiving state support—has persisted with Putin's rise to power, while the political course has not only changed considerably since then, but is also defined in much narrower terms. This is also reflected in the falling numbers of organizations included in the register: whereas in 2001, thirty-two youth organizations received state support, this had dropped to only ten by 2010.[14]

The register mechanism means that organizations refuting the narrow governmental course are very unlikely to receive funding because power over budgetary decisions resides with local or federal government organs. What political scientist Natal'ia Beliaeva demonstrates in the case of regional youth parliaments' draft bills may well hold true for most other government-sponsored initiatives: "organs of power [*vlast'*] support projects that correspond to the general strategy of the region's or the state's political course," and there are "numerous examples of youth parliaments not admitting representatives of oppositional youth organizations."[15] Unsurprisingly, the range of activities that such state-funded organizations support is usually limited to charity work, commemoration activities, or small-scale urban activism such as planting trees or painting public buildings.[16] Overall, most campers were active in organizations that foster what political scientist Alexander Libman calls compliant forms of activism that "support existing social norms" and "complement state activities."[17]

This chapter is based on narrative interviews conducted with thirty-seven campers of youth-leadership summer camps in the Krasnoyarsk Region and the Sakha Republic. I met all of these campers either during my on-site participation in the camps or via so-called snowball sampling, in which I asked those that I interviewed to refer me to any acquaintances who had participated in youth-leadership camps and would be willing to talk to me. I have summarized the details of how I organized the interviews in Appendix I.

I have organized this chapter along the lines of three main themes that emerged from a close analysis of the interview narratives: campers' negative stereotypes about Russia, their trust in the benevolence of socioeconomic development and an active ethos, and their portrayal of an unconditional love for their home region or country. I have arranged subthemes according to a variety of sayings that young campers invoked in interviews to illustrate their concerns or hopes. I thereby discuss several common cultural understandings that lie behind potential strategic elites' loyalty to the regime and how they interpret these in relation to their life and career plans.

We Are Corrupt, Indifferent, and Behind in Development

Positive portrayals of life in Russia were rare in the interviews. Above all else, most campers associated Russian society with corruption and backwardness, as well as with the indifference and lack of initiative that they believed characterized the majority of Russian citizens.[18] Despite several campers' indignation over what they found to be Western provocations in Ukraine in 2014, all associated desirable aspects of development—be they technical, infrastructural, social, or aesthetic—with conditions in the Euro-American world. To be sure, when campers began to feel that they might have been talking too much about shortcomings in Russian society, they were quick to emphasize that not everything was so bad: for example, that Russia was special due to being a multinational country, or that they loved their region due to its unique nature.

When the interview conversations touched upon conflicts with Western powers, almost all campers indicated that they were loyal to the Russian state's interests, previous criticisms notwithstanding. Nevertheless, they kept a firm interest in the West as an ideal. Even though I conducted all interviews with campers in mid-2014, when a possible war between NATO states and Russia was being discussed in Russian media as a consequence of the country's annexation of Crimea (several campers told me that they indeed feared the prospect of war), most campers regretted this low point in relations with the West. They largely interpreted the tensions as arising from an unfortunate misunderstanding of Russia's good intentions in world politics. The West, for everyone that I interviewed, remained a role model of socioeconomic development and a destination they desired to visit and explore.

Nevertheless, many campers rejected what they viewed as pro-immigration stances and support for same-sex relationships from European governments. Several campers from the Krasnoyarsk Region told me that they had traveled to Europe and had returned with mixed opinions. Some found fault with litter in the streets and what they perceived as a lack of social order. Others shared their disillusionment over not having encountered a racially white society in Western Europe. Visits to Paris seemed to have been especially disappointing: interviewees shared the same disdain for non-white Parisians as Moscow's mayor Sergey Sobyanin, who stated in a 2011 radio interview that because "there are people whose skin is not Paris-colored and the number of migrants [...] has, I think, reached nearly half the population of Paris," he had allegedly experienced trouble realizing he was in Paris.[19] These campers were particularly surprised and annoyed by the prevalence of "migrants"—here, as elsewhere in Europe, code for people of color—and the visibility of same-sex couples holding hands. Though white-supremacist views were relatively rare among campers from the Sakha Republic, Galina did tell me that many Sakha youth were appalled by the growing number of labor migrants from Central Asia seeking work in the region. Likewise, several respondents from the Sakha Republic spoke with derision about same-sex relationships.

One might assume that negative characterizations of Russia and the notion that the country was backward would provide fertile ground for criticizing government politics. Yet many campers found the current governmental trajectory to be much more promising than the policies that had determined the two preceding "historical periods"—the 1990s and, before that, the Soviet era. Their views of the 1990s were largely negative and informed by government narratives, widely circulating public stories, and family stories of economic downturn and impoverishment. In contrast, campers' evaluations of the Soviet period were highly ambivalent. Many were well aware of the purges and atrocities that had taken place during Stalinism—especially when family members had suffered or died. Numerous campers associated the Soviet period with a life characterized by aesthetic and cultural monotony, daily drudgery, rigid doctrines, and a lack of freedom to choose one's profession or travel. Nevertheless, several interviewees, referring to stories they had been told by their grandparents and parents, emphasized that the Soviet period had been one of socioeconomic development and collective social cohesion. For them, the Soviet period was significant because it had been a time when "Russia" had developed before the country's 1990s turn to democracy, which—widely associated with economic stagnation—would have caused Russia once again to fall behind in comparison with the Western benchmark.

The idea that Russia was backward was mirrored in campers' evaluations of their own regions. Among Sakha respondents in particular, the idea circulated that the Republic lagged far behind the development of Western Russia. This critical attitude toward local standards notwithstanding, when campers criticized the haphazard completion of tasks, the power of informal ties, and the corruption they saw in business and politics, as well as ordinary people's indifference to the common good, they construed these not as localized problems but as traits characteristic of all of Russia or its residents.

Doing Things Carelessly: *Spustia Rukava*

Quite often, my role as an interviewer from Germany prompted campers to compare Russian standards of living to what they assumed to be German ones. Expressions such as "you have" or "where you live" (*u vas*) usually introduced such comparisons, followed by the contrasting pair "we have" or "where we live" (*u nas*). Assumptions about life in Germany created an ideal or actual background against which interviewees measured realities in Russia. Thus, the (imaginary) West figured as a benchmark.

Evgenia and Aleksandr, for instance, asked me whether government-sponsored vigilante groups such as Stop Rudeness (*StopKham*) or Piglets Versus (*Khrushi Protiv*) were active in Germany as well. When I said they were not, they came up with the explanation that because problems such as illegal parking or the selling of expired food would not occur in Germany, there was no need for such vigilante groups to emerge:

> Aleksandr: "You have this as well, right? *StopKham* and these kinds of movements?"
> Interviewer: "You mean in Germany?"
> Aleksandr: "Yes."
> Interviewer: "No, we don't."
> Evgeniia: "Sure, because there are no problems with parking."
> Aleksandr: "Where *you* are from everything is normal, *you* don't have problems. That's why you neither have *Khrushi protiv*, nor *StopKham*."[20]

This understanding of Western Europe as a model for smoothly operating, relatively uncorrupted societies was especially noticeable when conversations touched upon the quality of products or public infrastructure. Igor, an interviewee from the Krasnoyarsk Region, remarked, for instance, that during Soviet times leading politicians had driven locally manufactured cars, such as the *ZiL* or the *Chaika*, and then added, "But *now* our president drives *your* car, a Mercedes." When I asked him why the incumbent president did not drive a Russian car, he explained that Russian people could not manufacture autos "the right way," and referred to a TV broadcast to substantiate his point. "Yesterday I watched this movie about the new *ZiL* for the president. It [the car] started only after the third attempt, and when the film team was sitting on the back seat, the whole car was jolting, it was really loud. And, I mean, this car is for the *head of state!*"[21]

His view refers back to the idea that anything conceived or produced in Russia was not accomplished thoroughly, lacked systematic planning, and ultimately displayed the haphazard and slipshod manner with which people had approached the task. The topos of the poor quality of Russia's roads, most frequently expressed in the saying that Russia's flaws are roads and fools (*dorogi i duraki*), is a case in point. The taxi driver who collected me early in the morning from the home of my couch-surfing host to drive me to the meeting place for departure to the *Biriusa* youth-leadership summer camp, for instance, used that saying to curse the quality of the roads in the suburb where I had stayed. Then he added that the biggest problem, however, was that the fools *made* the roads—alluding to the careless construction of public infrastructure. Thus, the association between the West and high-quality products is by no means specific to the potential strategic elites I interviewed. Not only the streets, but Russian products in general, are often considered synonymous with poor quality. For example, the Russian roommates with whom I shared an apartment in 2015 and 2016, when I lived in Moscow to conduct archival research on the summer camps, would never buy the cheaper Belarusian washing powder that was sold for half the price of the standard one and was available next-door, but rather chose the branded one from the more distant supermarket, arguing that only the latter would be of decent quality.

Daria, a student of pedagogy from the Sakha Republic, expressed this view explicitly: "Where you live, in Germany, everything is solid [*stabil'no*]. With us, here, everything is *spustia rukava*—made without zeal, carelessly and haphazardly."[22] The expression *spustia rukava* goes back to the fifteenth- and sixteenth-century fashion of very long sleeves (*rukava*) that would interfere with the wearer's activities if they slipped down (*spustit'sia*). Unlike the English expression "left-handed," *spustia rukava* connotes psychological aspects underlying the improper execution of a task: a lack of zeal and motivation to do a job in the proper way.

The image of the West held by Sakha campers Daria and Liubov was not only one of a place where products were solid and infrastructure was stable; it was also associated with respectful treatment of ordinary citizens like themselves in public institutions. Daria elaborated on what *spustia rukava* meant to her by drawing on her experiences in Russian public hospitals:

> Let's take an example. We pay in the same way as you for our health insurance. But your services and ours are different because people think that we receive them for free, as a donation [*na khaliavu*]. So, when you have paid for health insurance in Germany, people will relate to you as a person who paid for this service. In *your* country, you go to the hospital and it's like you are the boss [*khoziain*]: you paid, you are the person they serve. But when

we go to the hospital here, it is as if we were the ones serving *them* [*kak budto my obsluzhivaiushchie*]. There's this attitude toward us "you're ill; sit here in the waiting line and just don't start disturbing anyone [*nechego tebe rypat'sia*]." But in your country, you sit in the waiting line like "Please, come in"; it's respectful like that. Here nothing like that exists. People do not respect each other.[23]

Notably, Daria ascribes the negative treatment people receive in Russian public institutions to a social-psychological condition she assumes to be generally characteristic of most Russians: that they do not treat others with respect. The brusqueness of customer service interactions in Russia is often interpreted as a remnant of the Soviet period.[24] Daria, however, locates these disrespectful interrelationships in a new individualism, which she connects to Russia's extreme socioeconomic inequality. She relates disrespectful treatment to a social setting in which "people would not work for the sake of other people, but primarily for their own sake," and in which those who possess money have this "particular attitude," which she cannot pin down (*esli u menia den'gi, tipa ia . . . Kak-to ia ne mogu vyrazit'*).[25]

Research on how such inequality plays out culturally in Russia suggests that, as in many places, the rich do receive much more respectful treatment. Sociologist Liudmila Khakhulina shows, for example, that paid medical services for the relatively wealthy are not only of a higher quality but also stand out in terms of the "conditions under which they are received,"[26] meaning that the way patients are treated by doctors and nursing personnel is, on average, much more respectful. Neither Daria nor Liubov brought up alternative explanations for the problem of disrespectful treatment in such places, such as poor working conditions or an overburdened health system. They seemed not to be familiar with the opinion that "sometimes bad service is class struggle."[27]

Informal Connections: *Nuzhnye Liudi*

Another theme that interviewees related to Russia's being "behind in development" was what they called corruption: how it permeated Russia's political system, business, and society. Fedor, a law student from the Sakha Republic, shared his own detailed analysis of the various informal practices in politics that were used to keep alternative candidates off the ballot or prevent their election. These authoritarian practices included the fielding of pseudo-adversaries as well as negative PR campaigns and legal pressure against unwanted candidates. "In the end, they [powerful incumbents] make something up [*vytvoriaiut*], which they can show on the news," he told me.[28]

As many interviewees illustrated, starting anything new in business, politics, or the cultural sphere required having influential acquaintances or a protector, a so-called *mokhnataia lapa*—literally, a shaggy, hairy or fleecy paw. Aleksei, a technician from the Sakha Republic, explained that if someone's *mokhnataia lapa* had a government post, he could climb the career ladder. He portrayed such a career as "artificial," as unrelated to one's merits or skills, as would characterize a truly competition-based system. To substantiate his point, he described how businessmen with close ties to Putin—not those with the best offers—won the open bidding for general contractors to construct buildings for the Sochi Olympics:

> Who participated as general contractors? Oligarchs and close friends of Putin: Gennady Timchenko; then there is, I do not recall all of them, but Oleg Deripaska, Potanin... the close entourage of Putin. They suddenly won the open bidding, became general contractors, and appropriated huge amounts of money, not forgetting about their personal enrichment. We can observe that a competition-based system does not work in Russia.[29]

While campers' criticism of corruption was fierce, they accepted that there was no other way of making things happen under the current conditions. As a former law student at *SakhaSeliger* told me, there was often simply no viable formal path by which to enter certain professions. Vlas, an interviewee from the Krasnoyarsk Region, was also outspoken in his view that nepotism was one of the biggest problems for Russia's development. Like Aleksei, he referred to Putin's entourage—what he called the leader's circle of confidants (*krug priblizhennykh*)—to illustrate this:

> You can observe this very well in the organization of our political system and the interrelationship between Power [*vlast'*] and business. Let me take an example: Putin has a circle of confidants. If you are somehow connected to this circle, everything will turn out well for you. If you are not connected to it, everything will turn out not particularly well for you; and if you relate to them negatively, everything will turn out not at all well for you.[30]

And yet Vlas had told me earlier in the interview that he himself participated in a local volunteer initiative that renovated orphanages expressly in order to get to know what he called *nuzhnye liudi*.[31] This expression, which literally means "needed people," denotes contacts who are useful for obtaining services, goods, or job positions.[32] Vlas explained the function of such "needed people" through another special Russian term: "We have this word in Russian *kumovstvo*. It means that some of your acquaintances, they may be relatives or old friends, support your career development."[33] So, while Vlas may have been critical of the seemingly inexorable cronyism in Russia's informal system of career advancement, he freely acknowledged his own participation in this system.[34]

Several campers were also aware that newcomers to a business field were often scared off by intimidation tactics on the part of those who were already established in the field and did not want competition. The conversation with Aleksei on what *mokhnataia lapa* meant blended into his explanation about why it was so hard to start one's own business in established branches: "It's just like some people come to you and say: 'don't do this kind of business, because we do it already.'"[35] When I asked what happened if you continued anyway, he explained, "Then already open intimidation starts, pressure—not only from these people you do not know, but also from those who they know in the state apparatus [*gosudarstvennoi mashiny*]."[36] In his view, "the absence of an independent juridical system"[37] was to blame for the popularity of such intimidation practices.

Flaws in the juridical system were especially criticized by those campers who were active in the Communist Party's youth wing. They shared stories of glaring injustices in the legal system, such as the example of defense minister Anatoly Serdyukov. If a defendant came from an influential family or had an influential patron or protector, that alone would result in low penalties. The criminal investigation of Serdyukov, who was suspected to have been involved in the selling of state-owned real estate at cheap prices to "well-connected" insiders, costing the state about 60 million US dollars (about 3 billion rubles at the time), had simply ended with the president pardoning him.[38] Arkadii referred to a dismissive adage about the Putinist concept of a "Sovereign Democracy" to characterize the ubiquity of those double standards in Russia under Putin: "There is even this sarcastic saying: Sovereign Democracy means that the freedom of a person ends where the freedom of a bureaucrat begins."[39] As Denis, one of Arkadii's friends, accentuated, these double standards in criminal prosecution would continue to exist, because unlike Europe, Russia did not have an "active society." He saw such a society as characterized by uncompromising citizens who are not cowed by people in power, but, rather, willing to stand up for their rights and interests: "All people in power know that they [themselves] are murderers, criminals, and so on [he refers here to his disparaging view on developments during the 1990s]. Here, where we live, there is not such an active society as in Europe. Here, people fear losing the last thing they have."[40] When I asked what exactly this meant, he added that many people were threatened by local bureaucrats: " 'If you do not vote for us, we will cut off your electricity [*svet*].' People fear losing the little bit they possess; they have nowhere to go or to turn to. Many do not know the laws."[41]

While many campers criticized double standards and practices of intimidation, few mentioned, as Arkadii's friend Denis did, difficult socioeconomic circumstances or an absence of knowledge about or trust in one's rights as the reason for citizens' passivity. On the contrary, most campers I interviewed found passivity and indifference to be merely psychological traits. They were convinced that most people were simply unwilling to act for the common good or take care of themselves.

The training sessions at the youth-leadership camps took the same line. They conveyed a sense that young people's life trajectories were largely dependent on their own efforts and engagement. It is not possible to know what came first—the summer-camp education or campers' prior familiarity with slogans such as "life is what you make it." In campers' final analysis, people's passivity was the root of social ills. Thus, it was not so much the government, informal networks, or socioeconomic conditions that needed to be changed, but people's attitudes.

Indifference and Passivity: *Nichego ne Znaiu, Moia Khata s Kraiu*

Maksim reserved his most elaborate criticisms of passivity and indifference for his fellow citizens. For him, democratizing Russia meant abolishing such character traits among them. When I asked him what needed to be done in order to democratize Russia, he was initially unsure, but then answered after a pause for reflection that, first and foremost, Russians needed to get rid of laziness, which he defined as a Great Russian Problem (*velikaia russkaia problema*).

Maksim: "Laziness is our scourge [*eto nash bich*], which permanently stops us."

Interviewer: "Do you mean that this is a trait of Russianness [*cherta russkosti*]?"

Maksim: "Yes, but this is not just a trait of Russianness, this is a Great Russian Problem."[42]

He went on to say that the root of the problem was that most people tended to live according to the saying *nichego ne znaiu, moia khata s kraiu*, literally meaning "I don't know anything, my hut is located at the village's edge." He explained the saying to be an individualist principle:

> It's like they don't care what happens beyond their house. He knows that he is in his house and receives his salary; knows that the salary suffices to feed [*nakormit'*] him and his family and that's it. And all that is connected to, let's say, the good of the population is not interesting to him because of ordinary laziness![43]

Most interviewees shared this notion that Russian citizens were lazy. To make that point, Oleg, a schoolteacher-to-be from the Krasnoyarsk Region, paraphrased a joke by the famous clown and comedian Yuri Nikulin, remarking that Russians would only start acting if someone "kicked them in the backside."[44] The original joke features three prisoners of war—an American, a French, and a Russian soldier—who are held captive by German fascists. The fascists allow them each a last wish before their execution. While the first two wish to receive a glass of whiskey and champagne, respectively, the Russian asks for a kick up the backside—which he receives. Propelled forward by the kick, he manages to wrench a machine gun from one of the German soldiers and escapes together with the other two captives. As they flee, they ask him why he had not acted earlier: "That's [our] character," he shouts, gasping; "unless you kick us in the butt, we cannot do anything [*kharakter takoi, kharakter. Nam poka po zhope ne dash', nichego delat' ne mozhem*]."[45]

Several other campers also saw indifference, as expressed in "*nichego ne znaiu, moia khata s kraiu*," as part of a Russian (and Sakha) national character. Aleksandr referred to such a character in a discussion of his fellow citizens' possible reaction to war and their unwillingness to fight for the motherland:

126 FLEXIBLE AUTHORITARIANISM

> At least Russians and Yakutians have it here [he points to his chest] . . . It's in the soul: "I don't give a damn about there being war . . . Who cares; at home everything's all right, I got food in my belly, a place to sleep. And everything else."[46]

I was surprised that campers used stories of indifference to warfare to illustrate the kind of egoism among their fellow citizens that they so fiercely criticized. This might have been related to the timing of the interviews, which took place shortly after the shooting down of a Malaysian passenger plane in Ukrainian airspace in 2014, when commentators were speculating about the possibilities of a war between NATO and Russia.[47] It might also point to the centrality of commemorations of war in Russian memory politics.[48] Like Aleksandr, Liubov underlined how little ordinary Russians cared for the common good through the example of war in a conversation with Daria. Both contrasted today's lack of decency, sincerity, and community feeling with the Soviet period, alleging that Soviet people would have cared for their surroundings, for poorer people, and for the community at large, as evidenced by the deeds of the Soviet Youth league *Komsomol*:

> Daria: "Then, people were more kind-hearted (*otzyvchivye*). For example, today young people can just pass by some poor people, or people who are in need. But back then something like that caused a general panic, all were informed that somewhere something had happened to a person: right up to the *Komsomol* and to all-all-all."
> Liubov: "In the past people were generally more humane."
> Daria: "Yes, they were more compassionate."
> Liubov: "During which years was World War II? Then all went to fight. But if today there was a war, no one would go."
> Daria: "Yes, without being paid, no one would go."
> Liubov: "No one would go there voluntarily. They probably would say things like 'Why do I need this? Why should I die for this country?'"
> Daria: "For this reason one has to change the customs, just changing the culture, that's it."
> Liubov: "Today no one is a patriot. They all have become egoists."[49]

Their assessment that "today no one in Russia would defend the country at war without being paid" chimed with a feeling held by other interviewees that in this day and age most people in Russia were egoistic and lacked "patriotism." Many campers defined a patriot in positive terms as a person who cared, like themselves, for other people and the common good. Lidiia, a law student from the Sakha Republic, characterized the Soviet period as one during which people were more benign and there was more patriotism: "there was this outspoken patriotism, there was this open attitude that everything was shared."[50] Like her, Liubov and Daria used the term patriotism to denote a sense of altruism, care for other people and one's surroundings,[51] and an "active disposition toward life" (*aktivnaia zhiznennaia pozitsiia*), an expression dating back to the Soviet period.[52]

Oksana, a *Biriusa* camper who was active in the Communist Party's youth wing, disparaged what she saw as a lack of this "active disposition toward life" among her fellow citizens. She alleged, with a nationalist overtone for which the Communist Party in Russia is known, that people who have no consideration for the common good would "not like Russia, but at the same time do not do anything to either leave or change something. They just live and hate [. . .] Who is stopping you doing something so that it [life] would be good in Russia? It all depends on the person."[53]

Oksana's quote exemplifies how neotraditional ideals—specifically, a tendency not to badmouth the motherland—were intertwined with the kind of positive, individualist thinking that is commonly associated with neoliberal self-government, namely, that "everything depends on the person." Such a view was also shared by Fedor, who was convinced that many people simply lacked the motivation to develop themselves. While he had stated earlier in the interview that many people did not speak up because it could cost them their jobs due to arbitrary law enforcement and the absence of worker protection, he later stated that "other people's passivity" resulted from their laziness and lack of willpower:

> Fedor: "What annoys me in society is that people don't want to develop, they don't engage in personal development."
> Interviewer: "Why do they not develop, what do they lack?"
> Fedor: "They lack strength, will, desire. They do not want [to develop], because they are lazy."[54]

While Fedor considered passivity to result from an individual's insufficient willpower, he did not connect it to an immorality that set in after the demise of the Soviet Union. Others, however, clearly made this connection. They attributed the loss of qualities such as compassion and a communitarian orientation—often subsumed under patriotism—to the injustices and social dislocations of the 1990s. *Komsomoltsy* in particular were indignant about all the inequities that had occurred during that period. Igor, for instance, shared what had happened during the privatization of the Norilsk combine, which would become the mining company Norilsk Nickel (whose general manager Aleksandr Khloponin went on to become governor). Igor's father had worked there as a crane operator in the 1990s, but did not profit from the piece of paper he received that was considered to be his share of the combine[55]:

> Only those people who were interested in these matters, that were those who principally knew what happened, they took possession of many shares; and now they have lots of money. But those people who worked more than others were left with nothing.[56]

The privatization of state-owned companies and the formation of a stratum of rich politicians who were *also* businessmen constituted, for him and many other campers, the unjust basis of today's politico-economic order. As he continued, "When the privatization was over, when everything was already divided (up), no one started to make a fuss about that anymore. Now it is already useless to say: 'They did not give me my shares in 1996. Give them back to me.'"[57]

Although this critique was most clearly expressed by *Komsomoltsy*, it was also common among most other campers. For many, the demise of the Soviet state was inherently connected to the demise of communitarian principles. Most suggested that individualism had spread alongside the acceptance of inequality during the 1990s, when, they believed, people had started to think only about themselves—as Liubov had put it, "all have become egoists." Fedor saw this expressed in the popularity of McDonald's, or the possession of foreign cars by many of his fellow citizens.

For Timur, who like many *Komsomoltsy* found that "Russia" (not the Soviet Union!) had achieved the apex of its development after the October Revolution—"the apogee of state construction"[58]—the most pressing problem was also this shift in orientation away from a common future and toward individual well-being. He located this shift as having occurred with the advent of democracy in the 1990s:

> In the past everything was built on the idea that we must unite, that people must unite and together approach a bright future. But later, when this all

disintegrated, when democracy emerged, it kind of started that everyone was just for himself [*vrode kak kazhdyi sam za sebia*].[59]

Almost all interviewees found that a concern for other people had been fundamentally missing since the advent of the 1990s, or that it was only slowly reappearing. Interviewees from both the Krasnoyarsk Region and the Sakha Republic regarded the 1990s as the birth of egoism, inequality, and disunity. While scattered instances of positive associations with the 1990s are discernible in the interview data—the 1990s as the start of trade and business, as a period when new styles and subcultures emerged as well as the possibility of free travel—these appear to matter little given campers' overall condemnation of the period. Their perceptions align with public stories that have been dominant in Russian discourse and media since the late 1990s,[60] upon which the Putin government seized in order to construct its narratives of a new stability guaranteed through law-and-order and a strong leader in both domestic and international affairs.

Notably, such negative evaluations of the 1990s are at odds with the Sakha Republic's actual economic performance during the decade. In fact, the national republic was thriving during the 1990s. This was because its president (the equivalent of a regional governor; the head of each national republic is called "president" in Russia), Mikhail Efimovich Nikolaev, did not privatize state-owned companies but transformed them into businesses owned by the Sakha Republic. As Aleksei explained:

> Our president, instead of distributing all this [state property/combines] to private people, made it into the property of the Republic so that some people wouldn't become oligarchs later on. [. . .] This meant that very large companies worked for the sake of Yakutia and huge funds were spent on the development of the Republic, on the construction of medical and educational facilities and different social programs.[61]

Aleksei ardently criticized how Putin's construction of an authoritarian "power vertical" in the early 2000s completely destroyed federalism and replaced it with "a unitary state, in which everything is subjugated to the Kremlin."[62] This also meant that many of the educational and infrastructural programs benefiting the Sakha Republic came to a halt. Nevertheless, he concluded, that "in general" the 1990s had constituted a time of downturn.

130 FLEXIBLE AUTHORITARIANISM

An interview conversation among Nikita, Alla, and Nadezhda, all campers from the Sakha republic, is revealing in this regard.

> Nikita: "My own impressions of the 1990s are good. *But in actual fact* it turned out later when I was already studying history [in school], that in the country horrible things were happening. Not only in the country, everywhere, in private relationships, between people. [. . .] It turned out [as Nikita probably learned in school] that after 7 pm it was impossible to go out of the house. If you went out, you would be beaten up by those drug addicts and alcoholics [*tam tebia prib'iut eti narkomany, alkogoliki*]."
> Alla: "... yes, everywhere people were waiting for you ... "
> Nikita: " ... it is said that no one went out after 7 pm, all sat at home in all cities."
> Nadezhda: "In the 1990s there was especially theft, robbery..."
> Alla: "... hooliganism..."
> Nadezhda: "... in broad daylight!"[63]

They associated the 1990s, as did many people throughout Russia, with general lawlessness.

Most campers' evaluations of the Soviet period were much more ambivalent. Several rejected the Soviet period because they associated it with a life characterized by aesthetic and cultural monotony, daily drudgery, and restrictions on free movement, as well as, for some, the atrocities of the Soviet state against ordinary people. Two interviewees used the terms "repressions" and "terror." When campers brought up forced dispossession and persecution, they often used family stories to convey their point. A recurring theme was that of how sharing food during the war famines was punished by the Soviet authorities:

> Egor: "I also have a grandfather like hers, who slaughtered his cattle, one cow, to feed the neighbors and did not return from prison."
> Galina: "Because it was not allowed to give it away like that. Because the cow gave milk to the state, and not to him."
> Elena: "And that way you've already become an enemy of the people."[64]

Even though most interviewees were more ambivalent than completely negative about the Soviet period, no one desired a full return of Soviet rule. While the *Komsomoltsy* expressed the criticism that the Soviet leadership had forgotten Russians in their quests for international revolution and support of the international proletariat,[65] other campers criticized the lack of freedom. Serafima, a young medical student who wanted to open her own business one day, believed that "if there had been a *SakhaSeliger* in the USSR, I don't think that we would have come here—like, that we would have been selected."[66] She observed that "today everything is free, we can go wherever we want to go."[67] Liubov and Daria likewise interpreted Russia's becoming a free country after communism to mean that one was free to move wherever one wanted to.

While most valued the current freedom to travel and choose one's profession very highly, their final assessment was—consistent with the Putin governments' dominant narrative—that the 1990s were a period of overall downturn.

This dominant narrative depicts a "Russia" that had risen (during the Soviet era), fallen (during the 1990s), and rises again (under Putin).[68] Russia scholar Elliott Borenstein finds that this dominant story "always reaffirms Russia's role as the hero of history while emphasizing its status as the world's victim or offended party."[69] Alla was one of several campers who clung to this common characterization of Russia's rise and fall. She interpreted the year 1990 as the moment when Russia was orphaned (echoing the indoctrinating welcome lecture at the 2014 *SakhaSeliger* during which Viktor Stepanenko, that year's main educational instructor, had used the same formulation). For her, the demise of the Soviet Union also proved Russia's strength, because it reflected Russia's uniqueness for having risen again after this historic moment of purported weakness.[70]

Much as Alla reinterpreted this historic moment of weakness, turning it into one of strength, Oleg reevaluated the Stalinist repressions. He found that the Red Army's successful fight against fascism—taking place during and after the repressions—demonstrated an exceptional Russian spirit.[71] In a peculiar way, both reinterpretations chime with the advice given to us campers during the career training sessions, that we should always frame our concessions of weaknesses as statements ultimately conveying our personal strengths.

We Stay! Development as Societal Vision and the Meanings of "Being Active"

Campers held the view that indifference, passivity, and egoism not only corrupted Russian society but also impeded local development. Not unlike government officials, they attributed systemic shortcomings to deficiencies in the average Russian's mentality and believed that the country needed more people with an "active disposition toward life" to improve societal cohesion and spur development. But how did they characterize development; what did the term mean to different campers? And how should development be brought about?

Most campers defined "being active" and "being patriotic" as personal qualities. As their narratives made clear, most regarded career development and patriotism as going hand in hand, and a few even interpreted patriotism as an orientation that included an entrepreneurial spirit on behalf of the country and its economy. The traits of an active and entrepreneurially-minded person blurred with those of a good patriot in my interviews.

Developing Oneself and the Country to Move with the Times: *Idti v nogu so vremenem*

Interviewees' notions of what was meant by development depended on their characterizations of Russia and the degree to which they saw their region lagging behind in terms of development. Hence, development—*razvitie*—meant creating conditions so that everyone could lead a better life in terms of material well-being (*zhit' luchshe*).[72]

For Lidiia and Vera, it was important that "everything develops, moves with the times [*chtoby shli v nogu so vremenem*]."[73] They raised the example that every time they returned from Moscow, where they studied, to Yakutsk, they always noticed how much the two cities diverged in terms of development and wished that Yakutsk would also develop. At the same time, they did not want to badmouth their home soil. Their way of appreciating it was to promise themselves that they would invest in its development upon their return.

For these two young women as for most interviewees, living in a developed place meant enjoying good infrastructure—including paved roads without potholes, a reliable public transportation network, and contemporary safety standards—and up-to-date equipment in the workplace. Inhabiting a developed place meant living in an environment that accorded with standards perceived as contemporary, modern, and comfortable, both materially and technically.

In fact, "development" was often used as a shorthand for *technological* development. This narrow understanding of the concept was most explicit in my interview with Volodia, the former head of a state-run youth center in Krasnoyarsk who had recently visited *Biriusa*. He envisioned the transformation of Krasnoyarsk from, as he put it,

> an industrial region into an innovative one, which is characterized by IT and tourism. I don't want to live in a city of factories. I want to live in a city of computer programmers, computer scientists who are good and orderly, who earn plenty of money.[74]

Instead of smoking chimneys, he imagined an innovative place populated by new media and IT businesses that paid their employees high salaries.

While several campers shared Volodia's vision, others understood development in social terms. In their view, development promised the opportunity to be treated with respect and have access to more secure jobs. Indeed, campers' views of development sometimes amounted to a cure for all kinds of societal ills. As Maksim believed, development would lead to a quasi-automatic drop in poverty and societal problems such as alcoholism: "Development is important for every country, because then the country will be internationally competitive. When it develops, problems such as hunger or alcoholism will disappear, or rather they will decrease."[75]

Aleksei was one of the very few interviewees who considered development to be inherently connected to democracy. In his opinion, real development would be possible only if Western-style democratic institutions were fully implemented in Russia. Referring to the tsar Peter the Great, widely known for his attempts to Westernize imperial Russia, he urged that copying the "most developed political institutions and practices" from the West and implementing them in both his region and the country at large was the key to development. Unlike him, however, the majority of interviewees did not see a democratic political system as a precondition for development. Rather than seeing development as resulting from systemic changes, they considered it to emanate from individual initiative and self-improvement. Echoing Maksim's idea that things would get better if *everyone* just stopped being lazy, most interviewees maintained that changing behavior on the level of the individual would suffice to bring about those large-scale social changes they wished for. This implied that the pursuit of one's own interests—whether it be a business prospect, a career as an artist, or a clean-up campaign in one's neighborhood—would as a matter of course lead to the improvement of life for everyone.

Margarita, a member of the local youth parliament, was one of the campers who believed that the pursuit of self interest would naturally lead to general betterment. As she put it, while "maybe, in the beginning, everyone has his own interest," this would "in any case" lead to a "unified result which follows from the fact that you seek after something and start going... in any case you make something better."[76] In her opinion, markedly different individualist quests for change and projects would connect if only they were conceived in the spirit of developing a local place:

> So, let's say, one person needs help with business to make a specific commodity competitive on the world market, another person is just interested in improving life here to ensure higher salaries. So, because salaries rise there are also more social support measures. This is all connected. As soon as you set yourself the aim of improving the place where you live, this will start bringing people together.[77]

In my interviews, such notions of unity often connected self-development with the development of the country or the imagined community to which an interviewee felt most attached. For Oleg, this was the most salient take-home message from *Biriusa*: "There [at *Biriusa*] is this atmosphere of unity, that we are unified, we develop, our country develops thanks to our own development."[78] For several interviewees, engaging in forms of self-development that they considered to be tied to national development reflected a spiritual-economic ascent of the country which, for them, had begun in the early 2000s. As Zinaida put it: "Russia has struggled more than fifteen years to lift itself up [*podniat'sia*]."[79] Oleg also believed in such a rise, which he thought depended largely on young and active people like himself: "Naturally, we ourselves will revive, create, and build up [*Estestvenno, sami vozrozhdat', sozidat', stroit'*]. Just us by ourselves. Who else can do it for us? [*Tol'ko my sami. Kto eshche mozhet eto sdelat' za nas?*]."[80]

Although far from all of the interviewees defined being active as participating in Russia's spiritual-economic rise, several nevertheless found that having an "active disposition toward life" meant giving concrete form to their feeling of duty to their immediate surroundings or region. Their understanding of "being active" was intrinsically connected to their understanding of patriotism.

The Changing Meanings of "Being Active"

Following a usage that was common during the Soviet period, campers used the term "activist" synonymously with "active person" to refer to people who are lively, energetic, productive, athletic, or on the move. In Soviet parlance, an "activist" (*aktivist*) commonly denotes a person who demonstrates zeal. According to Soviet scholar Anton Makarenko, it would be such "activists" who activated and disciplined passive members of a group—taking responsibility for the group and for society at large.[81] Those "active people" or "activists" were further portrayed as taking an "active disposition toward life" (*aktivnaia zhiznennaia pozitsiia*). They were also very much thought of as "cultured people," driven by enthusiasm associated with a commitment to personal growth in physical, social, and intellectual terms and a fundamental rejection of unhealthy habits, passivity, and cynicism.[82] It was assumed that the late-socialist person—being allegedly freed from economic restraints and preoccupations with social security—would direct her zeal to all-round (self-)development (*vsestoronnee razvitie*).[83]

In a similar vein, campers perceived being active as an inherently good character trait, independent of the kind of actions a person pursued. Put differently, campers did not reflect upon the possibility that contradictory political objectives could cause activists' actions to cancel each other out. For instance, activist A might mobilize for the construction of a nuclear power station, believing in its importance for local development, while activist B fights against its construction, fearing that it could destroy local livelihoods and existing developmental achievements. Such possible contradictions did not trouble campers in their conversations among each other and with me. They seemed to believe simply that a tendency toward action was inherently good, and likely to bring about desirable development, while young people who lacked that tendency were simply indulging in indifference and passivity.

Elena, a young farmer who had recently started her own business, complained that there were too few active young people in the villages. She saw local young people as having no initiative: they "immediately want a high salary," but were deeply unmotivated to work. Thus, she preferred to employ elderly men, who she said were ready to work because they wanted to earn something on the side. As she continued:

It annoys me that so many youths in the village have no initiative. Many live off the pensions of their parents and spend their money on alcohol. They think that it is beneath their dignity to do hard work. [...] The majority has no zeal, no aims in life [*bez stremleniia k zhizni*]. I would say they lack a positive attitude. Young people, they should strive for something bright, bring something to perfection, develop themselves. But the majority is not like that.[84]

Most interviewees cherished the prospects of making a career and engaging in continuous self-development, including the pursuit of a healthy lifestyle. They highly valued being an activist[85] and, as mentioned in Chapter 4, found the youth-leadership camps attractive as a place to meet people of their own kind. But campers who considered themselves less active also found it a source of pride to be among so many activists at camp. Iana, a schoolteacher from a small Sakha village, was amazed by the preponderance of such individuals among her fellow campers. Upon being asked what was special about *SakhaSeliger*, she highlighted their presence:

"All who came here have, how is it called, an active disposition toward [life] ..., I mean they are all activists [*Aktivnaia zhiznennaia ..., kak skazat' ...; aktivisty vse priekhali po-moemu*]."
Interviewer: "What is this, an activist?" [*Chto takoe aktivist?*]
Iana: "Well, leaders [*lidery*]. For instance, our Liubov [a woman in the same working group], she totally seems to be a leader. Like, she right away proposed that we all play this one game to get to know each other."[86]

Like Iana, many interviewees frequently used key terms of Soviet pedagogy to describe themselves or fellow campers.

Echoing the camps' leadership training sessions, interviewees valued enthusiastic commitment to personal growth and cultured behavior. Within today's context, these commitments are meant to boost one's employability and worth in the national capitalist economy. For the promising youth attending these camps, personal growth and holistic self-development appeared not to be the result of a life freed from concerns over income, as was imagined during socialism, but a necessary precondition for earning money and ensuring a happy life in the current socioeconomic conditions.

A striking example of this inversion of late-Soviet reasoning came from Anton, a camper of the working group "Run After Me" (*Begi za mnoi*). He worked as a trainer for the youth political program with the same name.

Anton explained that cultured behavior, including an active way of life, and especially a healthy lifestyle, mattered because it increased "a person's general capacity for work, his efficiency."[87]

> Imagine, you go to an employer—stooped, wheezing, with a pale face, and you look altogether strange. How long will the employer talk to you for? This is one question. The other question is: if all is in order, there is a smile on your face, your shoulders are in place, and your spine is straight, how much time will the employer spend talking to you, how will this first impression be? So, this is the employer's first impression [guiding decisions about possible employment]: if the person doesn't look healthy, he probably smokes and will often take breaks; if he [the person] is ill then he will take more sick leave [*brat' bol'nichnye*] and this will disrupt deadlines.[88]

For Anton, being healthy was an instrument for becoming or remaining employable. His instrumentalist view of health, though unique among interviewees, indicates how Soviet concepts of activism can be reinterpreted to suit neoliberal capitalism. Campers' narratives reflected the ways in which trainers at camp employed Soviet notions of activism and adapted them to the neoliberal parlance of self-improvement books and podcasts.[89]

Margarita, the youth parliament member we met earlier, saw an active disposition toward life as the binding fabric among those she called patriots. Her narrative reveals the blurring of notions of activism and patriotism. According to her, all patriots strive for the same goals: a well-developed and comfortable place where "life was good," where everyone sees an economic future for themselves and their children. Activists, she argued, were those people who noticed the "things disturbing these [universal] wishes" and were ready "to correct them." She regarded as patriots those who were "striving toward the point that life will be better, that there will be even more comfort."[90]

Alla presented herself as a dedicated activist—a trait she said was instilled in her by her communist grandmother, a former deputy in the Supreme Council of the Yakutian Autonomous Soviet Socialist Republic (ASSR). Alla understood being active in terms of "participating in all kinds of actions" [*vezde uchastvovat'*] and striving to excel [*otlichnik/otlichnitsa*]. Responding to a question about what motivates her to be active, she directly linked her participation in numerous pro-government initiatives to her grandmother's imperative to excel, which was part of her education of her granddaughter in a patriotic spirit:

Already during childhood, I was educated in this way. My grandmother was in her day [*v svoe vremia*] a deputy in the Supreme Council of the Yakutian ASSR; today this is called *Il Tumen*. And she educated me—starting in early childhood—in the spirit of patriotism, to actively participate everywhere."

Nikita: "And [when you do that] already everything works out by itself, automatically [*I uzhe samo po sebe idet.*]"

Alla: "And already you take the course all by yourself [*I uzhe samo po sebe beresh' kurs*] and you cannot stop it anymore. And certainly, you see the shortcomings of society. And I myself do have shortcomings, very many shortcomings. And in order to work on oneself and to be of whatever use to society at the same time, I started to join different movements and I'm already organizing my own events."[91]

Echoing her grandmother's Soviet-era interpretation of activism as "participation in all kinds of organizations," striving toward excellence and personal growth, Alla regarded her own activism as a mixture of patriotic duty and self-development. Notably, she did not differentiate between Soviet-era and Putin-era patriotism.

Alla continued to explain how she became an activist in a way that suggested that activists are also high-achievers, striving to excel in physical, social, and intellectual activities and earning only the best grades in school. As she noted, this was also what her parents had wanted her to be: "In school, I only received a four [the second-best grade in Russia] once and they [her parents] scolded me because of that. So, this is why there are these high standards and why you advance, advance, advance [*dvizhesh'sia, dvizhesh'sia, dvizhesh'sia*]."[92]

In Alla's definition of activism, shared by several campers, career advancement and upward mobility are aims pursued by patriots. To be engaged in ambitious pursuits was a way to prove one's excellence, to distinguish oneself (*proiavit' sebia*) and make one's mark on the world as an activist and patriot.

The Systemic Limits of Individualist Quests for Change

Aleksandr was another camper for whom upward mobility and the quest for excellence were the natural traits of a patriot. He used a popular Russian proverb, the meaning of which is close to "always aim for the stars!," to justify his parents' desire for him to always be the first—the manager of managers (*nachal'nik nachal'nikov*) or director of directors, as he put it. When I asked about his plans for himself, he, his friend Evgeniia, and I engaged in the following conversation:

> Aleksandr: "I have the same [as his parents' plans for his future].
> Because: only a bad soldier does not want to become a general... [*Plokh tot soldat, kto ne khochet byt' generalom*]. The one who does not want to be the best [who does not aim for the stars] is a bad soldier."
> Interviewer: "Okay, so you always need to try to be the best."
> Aleksandr: "Yes, you need always to *be* the best. Grow."
> Evgeniia: "[You need] always to become the boss [*vsegda stat' nachal'nikom.*]"
> Aleksandr: "The boss of the boss of the bosses [*nachal'nikom nachal'nikov nachal'nikov*]—like that. [...] We, guys like me [*rebiata*], we run forward, we mount the horses and ride toward the battering ram."[93]

Aleksandr portrayed himself as a typical careerist; his main aim was "moving forward," climbing the career ladder so that he would be the one to dominate others. He struggled to express what "moving forward" meant more concretely in the current political and social conditions. What path would he take as the "boss of bosses"? He tried to explain how difficult it was to discern the right or righteous path of action by contrasting complex reality with the plot of the *Lord of the Rings*. In the movie, he told us, "Aragorn, Legolas, Gimli, Gandalf—they are all the good ones. The orcs are all the bad ones. It is clear which side is right and which is wrong."[94] Yet he struggled to find that clear line in reality:

> Aleksandr: "I myself could be one of the orcs and rush to Gondor, but I don't suspect that I could be that orc. [...] Or I am Aragorn who wants to become king."
> Evgeniia: "So, in actual fact, you don't know..."
> Aleksandr: "I don't know if I am good or bad, just in the movie this is all much simpler. It is so much more visible in the movie, who is not right and who is right, but in life it's not visible [discernible]."[95]

His confusion about right or wrong was accompanied by a seeming lack of alternative ways to make sense of the social world beyond a Manichaean view. The *Lord of the Rings*, rooted in the premise of an eternal struggle between good and evil that does not allow for moral ambiguity, corresponds to the Manichaean logic that political scientist Michael Urban and other scholars found to characterize Russian domestic politics since the early 1990s.[96] Aleksandr's lack of a clear basis for distinguishing the right path from the wrong was influenced by his radical doubt in the possibility of establishing any truths, partly because history would be, as he said, written by the victors. Moreover, he believed that world politics, not only those in Russia, were decided by two or three people alone, whom he would call "the center."[97]

Like many of his fellow campers and most people susceptible to conspiracism, he applied this radical doubt only selectively.[98] The widespread notion that one "could not know anything for sure" was often used by campers to avoid any more profound reckoning with their own participation in the reproduction of power. Likewise, as I alluded to earlier in the chapter, they did not reflect on the political meaning of their activism and its broader implications.

For interviewees, "activists" could be people who are skilled at creating and leading successful projects. A telling example in this regard is Alla and Nikita's portrayal of a VIP guest at the 2014 *SakhaSeliger*: Vasilii Afanas'ev, a local politician and successful businessman. After having been a rather lazy student, Afanas'ev told the campers, he became an activist after a change of school—even rising to the position of school president, the highest post within a school's student self-management body. Alla was impressed that he had eventually "realized so many projects," including the Niurbinsk bread factory.

> Alla: "Vasilii Afanas'ev spoke yesterday in his role as the head of the Khangalasskii district [*glavy Khangalasskogo ulusa*]. [...] He realized so many projects, even *Niurbinskii khleb* [Niurbinsk Bread], the bread factory."
> Nikita: "They deliver bread across the whole republic!"
> Alla: "Already after a very short time [after opening the factory] they started to deliver bread to all parts of the republic. The example of his biography was striking because he said that he did not do *anything* until the eighth grade. It seems that he was even expelled from school. Then he was sent to his aunt [...] He said that the gymnasium gave him such a boost that he even became the president of the school in the end."[99]

Their depiction of Afanas'ev's biography shows that any kind of initiative, whether civic, business-related, or political, can be seen to distinguish a person as a real activist. Nikita and Alla's account traced Afanas'ev's career as a typical success story, even echoing the rags-to-riches myth with respect to his bad performance in school. Afanas'ev's biography could be a textbook example for how to build one's career—to show one's initiative by excelling in extracurricular as well as academic activities. The first step of his career was to prove his leadership skills in a societal organization, the school's student body.

Certainly not all interviewees were as zealous as Alla and Aleksandr, yet all campers saw "being active and taking initiative" as useful for their personal development. The *Komsomoltsy* discussed self-development in a way that was more critical of capitalism. None of them mentioned starting their own business as a way to self-develop. However, they used the same term, self-development (*samorazvitie*), as their peers and were eager to engage in the kind of self-development that was offered at camp. Arkadii, for instance, articulated his readiness to participate in a potential new working group on "family life": "Why not? It's interesting. When you try many different things, you develop yourself. You don't just sit over your books and think; you communicate with people, you find out something new, and because of that you develop yourself, you develop other people."[100]

Interviewees seldom connected activism with a quest for more democratic, just, or inclusive decision-making. Likewise, their solidarity with underresourced groups—such as the residents of orphanages who were the most frequent target group of campers' volunteer projects—hardly took the form of a rallying cry for structural change that would extend beyond the borders of charity or the language of gift-giving.[101] Instead, they told how they staged events for orphans and those in children's homes (*detskie doma*), collected New Years' presents for them, or refurbished parts of the building or courtyard for them; not how they engaged with the reasons for why orphans in Russia live in such establishments in the first place. None of the interviewees elaborated on the limits of this charity activism or mentioned the structural problems that lie beneath the very existence of children's homes. Likewise, notions of how to empower the inhabitants and do something *with* them, not only *for* them, were absent in campers' discussions about giving support and assistance to the less privileged.[102] While campers were enthusiastic about cultivating a can-do spirit and, as I argued in the previous chapter, pleased to be treated as equals, their own good works seldom testify to the application of democratizing elements or attempts to give a voice to the historically marginalized.[103]

Campers appeared to adopt rather unsophisticated, sometimes banal-seeming empowerment parlance. Beliefs such as "everything depends on a person's will" were widespread and often informed their conviction that the achievement of one's aims depends only on individual willpower and persistence. As Vera put it, in order to achieve something, you just needed to really want it:

> If a person really knows that he can change something, when he really has this wish and really wants it, he can achieve anything. [. . .] Let's take the example of people with limited abilities [the fate of people with disabilities was a theme she had raised in response to a question about what she could change in Russian society]. If this is something which really worries you, you can participate in *Seliger*, for instance, you can go there for this specific purpose with your project. All depends on the person, his thinking. If he really wants something, he will change everything. Nothing is impossible.[104]

While this conviction that personal ambition makes everything possible may be a good psychological tool for self-empowerment, it obscures the vast differences in opportunities in today's world, especially within markedly unequal societies such as Russia's. Such notions thus shift responsibility for people's well-being from the polity to the person.[105] They pave the way for a greater acceptance of the delineation between people categorized as "working and deserving" and people categorized as "workless and undeserving" that characterizes much social policy under flexible authoritarianism.[106]

While the belief that every problem can be solved by willpower was widespread among the campers, it was, again, only very selectively applied. Interviewees provided few examples of their actual experiences challenging societal shortcomings, even if they themselves had sharply criticized such shortcomings and identified them as obstacles to development and a better life. Anton, the activist for a healthy lifestyle, was, for instance, convinced that "every problem could be solved" and deeply preoccupied with increasing the population's health, yet he rejected any possibility of decreasing the level of pollution in Norilsk, the industrial city north of Krasnoyarsk where he had grown up. As described by a journalist in 2016, the Norilsk metallurgical plant next to the city "belches so much acid rain-producing sulfur dioxide—two million tons a year, more than is produced in all of France—that it is surrounded by a dead zone of tree trunks and mud about twice the size of

LOYAL YOUTHS' INDIVIDUALIST QUESTS FOR CHANGE   143

Rhode Island."[107] When I asked Anton how he felt about the implications of the pollution for public health, we engaged in the following conversation:

> Anton: "I lived there; I know that this is this negative thing [*ia znaiu eto takoe negativnoe*]. Every inhabitant of Norilsk would respond negatively if the neighboring factory installed a chimney which continuously smokes. Certainly, this is inconvenient, at the very least. But I do not have the possibility in this case, right now, at this moment of my life, to make these chimneys [*truby*, literally tubes] disappear, because these are factories which provide many resources for Russia. This is a different level of communication, totally different people deal with this."
> Interviewer: "And who deals with it?"
> Anton: "Those who own these factories, the state to some degree, higher ranks—let's say it like this."
> Interviewer: "And it's not possible to influence them?"
> Anton: "Generally you can influence everyone, but how to bring it about that a factory produces less exhaust gas . . . Either they don't want to, or they don't want to decide."
> Interviewer: "You don't feel that there is a possibility to actively affect such a development?"
> Anton: "I don't deal with factories. But in order that something goes on benefitting the people there, it's possible to work together. There are also people who deal with healthy lifestyle issues [*zanimaiutsia ZoZh*]. For instance, extreme sports [*ekstremal'nyi sport*] develop very well there."[108]

Anton's reluctance to engage with this large-scale problem in the interest of local people's health was the most striking example of the contradictions inherent in government-sponsored compliant activism, complementing state activities.[109] Promoting a healthy lifestyle program in a place so polluted that even trees can hardly grow seems, depending on the point of view, cynical or simply ineffectual.[110] Certainly, Anton's rejection of any activism that would challenge those whose activities generate pollution ("I don't deal with factories") testified to his reluctance or even fear to become a government-critical activist protesting against environmental damage. Fighting factory owners and state officials who made up those "higher ranks" would mean risking inconvenience, unemployment, and even arrest.

Some interviewees were more explicit about the implications of such government-critical activism and their reluctance to engage in it. Aleksei, for instance, shared the story of a worker at the mining company *ALROSA* (the abbreviated form of *Almazy Rossii-Sakha*, i.e. Diamonds Russia-Sakha) who organized an independent workers' union that pushed through a strike for higher wages and better working conditions. This union organizing was countered, as Aleksei put it, by a "campaign of lies" and other actions against him: "The police search his home, supposedly because he was taking drugs, they find a small package. And that's it, they imprison him for five years because of drug possession. Yet afterwards he was awarded an international prize for the assertion of civic rights [by the Norwegian trade union *Industri Energi*]."[111]

Evgeniia, another interviewee who did not refrain from criticizing the Putin government, conceded that she did not have enough strength to press for systemic changes and that, moreover, she was not even sure about the point of doing so. She admitted that while she wished there were truly critical analyses of current events, she would herself not voice them.

> Maybe, smart people who analyze [what's going on], they just don't want to speak up. [...] They simply keep their opinion to themselves. Like I do. Usually I never comment, I never start conversations on the internet, because it leads to a kind of trolling.[112]

Evgeniia preferred to "improve or impair" her own life alone. Like many others, she was disappointed by what she described as the corruption of almost every sphere of social or public life by narrow economic or political interests. She was frightened by the conspiracist idea that "the whole world was governed by a few people. All presidents are puppets."[113]

Besides such conspiracism—or the somewhat less sinister notion that there was simply nothing one could do about purportedly eternal and inevitable problems—the scale of social problems led campers to shy away from engaging with possible solutions or concrete actions. One example of this is the racist exoticization experienced by Russian citizens who are not ethnic Russians, or are not considered as such. Several interviewees from the Sakha Republic shared their deep irritation and indignation about such experiences, yet profoundly doubted the possibilities for change.

> Egor: "Probably this [racism] will stay and always exist."
> Elena: "Yes, even when I ask, for instance, about racism in Soviet times... because many of my friends' parents studied in Moscow then. So,

I ask them: 'was there racism?' 'Yes, there was,' they say. So even in these peaceful times, even in the Soviet Union there had been racism. In Russia there is and there will be racism. To change that... I don't know."[114]

However, some interviewees did believe that small-scale actions would probably affect large-scale problems in the long run. They suggested, for example, that information and education—about the multinational history of the country and region, for instance—could counter discriminatory exoticization. Others suggested that it was important to counter the stereotypes associated with one's own non-white appearance by behaving non-stereotypically.

Such belief in the potential of small-scale actions was also raised by interviewees regarding other social ills that they identified. Regarding what campers called corruption, several observed that watchdog oversight could help to replace informal interactions in business and politics with formal ones. Egor, a camper from the Sakha Republic who was preoccupied with health-damaging toxins used in mining for cleaning noble metals, expressed his confidence that further research initiated through projects could help to replace these toxic chemicals with safe alternatives. Change through innovative projects was often mentioned as a possible way to tackle problems more creatively or to implement alternatives. Following this belief, several interviewees stated that they had submitted project proposals to found businesses specializing in solar heating and solar power. In line with the campers' overall admiration for scientific and technological development, these project proposals testified to their belief that technological innovations could improve life, especially at the level of one's neighborhood, village, or region.

An Unconditional Love for (Local) Place

While many interviewees were dissatisfied with what they called the backwardness of their regions and of Russia as a country, very few considered emigrating to more developed places. Rather, they took pride in their decision to stay and contribute to the development of their region, cultivating an "equally good life at home." Young campers' wish to develop "this place" in order to live as good a life "here" as one would "there" (in more developed places) was not only their most common justification for staying; it was also the most common definition of what many framed as "being a patriot of the country."

Naturally, the subject of emigration to more developed countries often engendered controversies in group interviews: did emigration constitute an egoistic act in itself? Under what conditions was emigration compatible with patriotism?[115]

Most campers I interviewed thought of remaining in their region, or in Russia, as a patriotic avowal of their unconditional love for the motherland and a commitment to developing it—not a fate imposed by the lack of opportunities. As Aleksei put it: "I want my people [the Sakha] to live as well as people in the United States, Japan, or South Korea. After all, they have achieved this in Korea; they live much better now, can travel the whole world, and they did so by developing their region."[116]

Akin to the idea of unconditional love for a person, interviewees described their commitment to their region in terms of love "regardless of the shortcomings" of their local area. Often, they would use terms like "despite," "regardless of," or "although" in their description of attachment: they would stay *despite* the poor infrastructure, the underresourced municipalities, the scarcity of career opportunities, the harsh climate, and the exoticization of their region in Western Russia.[117] Similar constructions were used when "Russia" was the object of interviewees' patriotic feelings: Even though it might be better for their career to leave Russia, and even though they could earn more elsewhere and have greater chances of advancement, they would stay in order to contribute to the common good. Such expressions communicated a kind of sacrifice those ambitious young adults were making for their place and the people who inhabit it. As one *SakhaSeliger* camper observed: "When you're from a poor country, you need patriotism, otherwise hardly anybody would stay. Rich countries can afford to go without patriotism."[118] In her view, the only thing that would prevent further brain drain—that is, the emigration of young people who could help the region to progress—was patriotism in the sense of unconditional love for one's home.

Timur, an interviewee from the Krasnoyarsk Region, even compared the love of one's country to unconditional love for one's mother: to him, patriotism was "when you love your country, no matter what [*kogda liubish' svoiu stranu, kakaia ona ne byla*]."[119] In this vein, patriotic self-descriptions also served as noble justifications for non-emigration, given that emigration to Western Russia or developed countries has not ceased to function as a template for career-oriented decisions among ambitious youth. As elsewhere, a job in a business located in Western Europe, Canada, or the United States is regarded as more significant, in terms of both symbolic and material value, than one at a company with headquarters in an emerging national economy. A declaration that one was choosing to stay because of patriotism preempted the potential criticism that the decision was motivated by a lack of skills, motivation, or talent. Non-emigration was portrayed not only as an altruistic and sensible choice, but also a contemporary one: designating oneself a patriot stressed one's readiness to invest labor power and creativity in the development of the region or country. It communicated one's willingness to be "of use" to society through one's innovative ideas.

The Place Where You Were Born Is Where You'll Be of Use: *Gde rodilsia, tam i prigodilsia*

Often when conversations touched upon the theme of emigration, campers, as well as camp staff, employed a popular Russian proverb: *Gde rodilsia, tam i prigodilsia*. Literally meaning "the place where you were born is where you'll be of use," the saying affirms that a person is most needed, or is of greatest benefit to society, in the place where they grew up.[120]

Given the significance of the West as a benchmark for a developed life in campers' narratives, the adage emphasizes that it is not a disgrace to stay in one's region, but a decent thing to do—especially when most people are leaving. Among others, Aleksei expressed his affection for his home in these terms: "We have something to strive for here," he told me. "I wish not to just move somewhere where life is good [*gde khorosho zhit'*] . . . Like, 'okay, I'm off.'"[121] If too many young people were to depart in this manner, he suggested, the republic itself would be in danger. Instead, he proposed to make the republic into an "economic, financial, political, cultural center," even an international one; he believed this endeavor would be more fulfilling to locals than developing a place far away:

> If all youth leaves for other places, then who will develop this land [*etu zemliu*], what will become of her [this land] later, what will we keep for future generations? What about it? If I will endeavor that *here*, where we live [*u nas*], everything will become like *there*: this will be of greater use overall; and it will mean more to you, to make the place where *you* live a better place.[122]

Thus, for Aleksei, as for many others, staying was closely connected to a fundamental commitment to development. Certainly, most interviewees also preferred to stay because they liked where they lived, wanted to stay close to their friends and relatives, and felt comfortable there.[123] Yet statements about non-emigration also appeared inextricably linked to notions of modernization and the overcoming of a place's supposed backwardness. This link might have been reinforced by the presence of an interviewer from Western Europe.

At the same time, emigration had a difficult and ambiguous reputation among campers. Igor, a camper from the Krasnoyarsk Region, contrasted young people wishing to emigrate with those who had not given up hope for Russia (to him the regional aspect was of less importance): "We have these people here who shout: 'I don't like Russia, I'm leaving to live in another country' [*zhit' za granitsu*]. But there are also people who hope for a bright future for Russia, who love their country, love the people who surround them."[124]

Because Igor seemed to suggest that people who emigrate do not love their country, I asked him whether a patriot would never move to another country (*ne uekhal by za granitsu*). The question engendered the following argument between him and a friend of his who was sitting next to us in the café and only occasionally joined the interview:

> Igor: "No, a patriot would never move to another country [*nikogda ne uekhal by za granitsu*]."
> His friend: "There are refugees from Ukraine—you suggest that they are not patriots? [*Oni chto, poluchaetsia, ne patrioty, chto li?*]"
> Igor: "No [they are patriots], they still love their motherland [*Oni zhe vse ravno liubiat svoiu rodinu*]."
> His friend: "But they rescue themselves by fleeing."
> Igor: "Yes, they are forced [to leave]. When I go to Turkey for a holiday, this doesn't mean that I'm not a patriot. [. . .] I return in any case. This means that those people from Ukraine who live here in Russia now [after the Maidan Revolution/the annexation of Crimea], will likely return home when everything calms down. *This* is patriotism [*Vot chto takoe patriotizm*]."[125]

So, the boundaries between non-patriotic and patriotic emigration were contested. Most often, interviewees defined patriots as those emigrants who would "still return, despite everything (*vse ravno vernutsia*)."[126]

In such debates, many campers raised the example of people whose emigration appeared to be justified by their contribution to the good of the country (or region) from afar, or by other special circumstances such as a violent conflict. Timur, for instance, found that Kostya Tszyu, the boxing world champion, was a patriot although he had lived for many years in Australia. That Tszyu, who was born in the provincial Siberian town of Serov, had returned to Russia after the most successful part of his career was a fact Timur used to substantiate his argument: "He trained there [in Australia], appeared on the international stage, defended the country, defended the Russian flag. [. . .] But afterwards he naturally returned. Anyways, there are various circumstances when people emigrate."[127]

Many interviewees considered career and self-development to be an important enough reason for leaving—to obtain new experiences and skills in more developed places—but only if they ultimately put those acquisitions to use for Russia. Aleksandr, for instance, had already decided to move to Moscow or St. Petersburg after his studies, which he saw as a necessary step in his career, which he was convinced would end in the Russian State Duma. He did not indicate whether he would study abroad during our interview, but, judging from his zeal to make a career and his wish to be of use to his country, he probably would consider doing so, if it benefited those aims.

For a few interviewees, moving temporarily to another country was not primarily connected to their career, but driven by curiosity and a deep wish to see the world. Liubov stated that she did not want to simply "be satisfied" with living in her own country (*dovol'stvovat'sia svoei stranoi*)—though she was sure that she would yearn for the motherland while in China, her destination of choice. Egor's dream was to leave the Sakha Republic temporarily to volunteer in an African country, because, as he reasoned, he was Black [*chernyi*] himself and loved heat. While there is research on the tendency among Armenian and Adyghe youth in Russia to self-identify as Black, I could not find evidence for similar self-perceptions in the Sakha Republic.[128] Egor's identification as Black might have stemmed from a political reading of the concept that, as in the South African Black Consciousness movement, subsumes all non-white people suffering from racist discrimination and oppression under that rubric.[129] In other parts of the interview, Egor shared experiences of racism elsewhere in Russia, also noting that he had been taken into custody several times, including by local police, because he was mistaken for a Chinese citizen and had no documents in his pockets to prove that he was not. He responded to these incidents not with irritation at the government's politics privileging ethnic Russians; rather, he identified the police officers' lack of knowledge of the peoples and cultures of "our multinational Yakutia," as he put it, as the main cause.

Aleksei, who was among those most critical of the incumbent government but strongly committed to self-development and the future blossoming of his region, had found a way to reconcile his dream of living in a more developed country with his commitment to helping improve life in the Sakha Republic. In his view, the key was to return to one's home place with novel skills and visions:

> In the past I had this wish, to finish studying, move to another country like the United States and stay there. I still do have this dream, but it changed. I want to live there not for all my life, but for some years, to adopt this spirit, all their achievements, their technologies, their way of thinking—how they achieved all of that and bring it here. So, this place will also be transformed into a center.[130]

Nevertheless, for the majority of interviewees, emigration and patriotism were not easy to reconcile. Oleg, for instance, stated that while he could understand the Soviet scientists who escaped their likely assassination during the Stalinist terror, he struggled with the fact that they had worked for the benefit of other states. He had far fewer problems criticizing most contemporary emigration. People who left Russia today just for the sake of convenience, he said, simply lacked a patriotic ethos: "When a person just leaves, like for the reason—'they pay more over there'; or 'there, it is good, clean, delicious'—I don't understand that; I think this person is just not a patriot, he just has no moral values."[131]

The Grass Is Always Greener on the Other Side: *Vezde khorosho gde nas net*

At the youth-leadership summer camps, lecturers often portrayed young Russians' wish to emigrate as resulting from very naïve notions of life in the West. As Viktor Stepanenko, *SakhaSeliger*'s main educational instructor, put it during a general lecture in 2013:

Do you think that Hans, Ulrich, John, and Paul [typical non-Russian names] are just sitting and waiting to hand over their well-paid jobs to you? [. . .] Even such celebrities as the great engineer Nikola Tesla, who worked in America in his day . . . half of his innovations have been appropriated by others, by Americans.[132]

Correspondingly, many interviewees explained the longing for emigration in terms of another popular proverb, *vezde khorosho gde nas net*, literally meaning "life is good where we are not," mostly used in the sense of "the grass is always greener on the other side." In this view, emigration was seen as childish and naïve, while plans to stay were considered mature: life elsewhere would not be a picnic.

Daria inverted the saying "life is good where we are not" to justify her desire to stay in the Sakha Republic:

I did not reflect upon living beyond the borders of our Republic. For whatever reason, nothing draws me there. I don't think that it is better there, where I am not. I think it is good where I am [*Mne ne kazhetsia, chto luchshe tam, gde ia net. Mne kazhetsia, chto khorosho tam, gde ia est'*].[133]

At other times, emigration was depicted as the consequence of peoples' denial of their inner problems. Stories in this register suggested that the dissatisfaction leading to emigration was rooted not in poverty, political persecution, or simple curiosity, but in an inability to be happy. In such stories, emigrants were cast as the never-satisfied, always on the run to avoid facing their "real" problems. This depiction corresponds to another interpretation of the proverb, which chimes with the nineteenth-century topos of the superfluous man (*lishnii chelovek*), who is often characterized as socially passive, idle, and bored. There is evidence suggesting that the proverb goes back to a literary figure from the nineteenth-century play *Woe from Wit* (*Gore Ot Uma*), by Alexander Gryboedov. The play's main protagonist answers the demand of his former lover, Sophia—"tell me where things are better [*Gde zh luchshe?*]"—with the words, "Where we are not! [*Gde nas net*]."[134]

Oleg Vasil'evich Kozlov, another teacher at *SakhaSeliger* who worked at the time for *Rosmolodezh*, stuck to this interpretation of the emigrant as the idle, never-satisfied layabout:

I know these people who move from country to country. In fact, they are not happy; they try to run away from themselves. Wherever you run, wherever you move, you will always take yourself with you. You can never run away from yourself.[135]

He made the case for a "culture of creativity" in Russia that would allow young people to "found something, do something, create something in *every* place [including Russia]."[136]

In a similar fashion, several interviewees connected emigration to a subsequent deep yearning for the motherland. Mikhail, a camper from the Krasnoyarsk Region, believed that he could not live in a country other than Russia, because he would miss the vast open space, though he would not be missing the state:

> I am ready to travel like a tourist, to observe and be interested, but not to live there, because I would miss Russia very much [*potomu chto mne budet ochen' ne khvatat' Rossii*]. This might sound patriotic [. . .] I mean, those white oligarchs from Russia who made *so much* money and left the country for a better life in America. [. . .] Now they are bored, feel lonely, sit at the beach and look at the emptiness [*smotriat v pustotu*], look into nowhere with empty eyes, read newspapers from Russia which they order. [. . .] There is not this freedom and openness [as there is here].[137]

While for many interviewees Russia was the home they would long for, others defined the place they would miss in geographically narrower terms. Serafima, for instance, said that she had started to miss the Sakha Republic, studying medicine in Western Russia: "Lately, patriotism draws me back more to the Republic [*menia patriotizm bol'she tianet k respublike*]."[138] In some instances, such attachment to the Sakha Republic was connected to experiences of exoticization, or racism, in other parts of Russia. This attachment to what some called their small motherland (*malaia rodina*) was also common among some interviewees from the Krasnoyarsk Region. Oleg explained that because "many Russian people have this developed sense of home, sense of motherland [*razvitoe chuvstvo rodiny*]," they "return to the place where they were born despite unlimited opportunities."[139]

The notion of a small motherland dates back to the late-Soviet period, when it was intended to promote the idea of a homeland as a tangible entity rather than an abstract category. The development of patriotic feelings was conceptualized as evolving organically from the love of one's birthplace to the love of one's country.[140] The distinction between a small and a big motherland goes back to an influential figure of thought that Lenin used to guide early Soviet nationality policies, advocating for unity when it comes to socialist ideas, but diversity regarding the setup of the Soviet state:

> By "fostering national cultures" (*nasazhdat' natsional'nuiu kul'turu*) and creating national autonomies, national schools, national languages and national cadres, the Bolsheviks would overcome national distrust and reach national audiences. "We are going to help you develop your Buriat, Votiak, etc. language and culture, because in this way you will join the universal culture [*obshchechelovecheskaia kul'tura*], revolution and communism sooner."[141]

Historian Francine Hirsch has aptly referred to this approach, which also informs the distinction between a small and a big motherland, as the Soviet policy of double assimilation, by which she means "the assimilation of diverse peoples into nationality categories and, simultaneously, the assimilation of nationally categorized groups into the Soviet state and society."[142] This principle of unity through diversity has been revived under Putin, as has the distinction between a small and a big motherland with its goal of strengthening identification with the federal state through the strengthening of local identifications.[143] Several interviewees from the Sakha Republic, such as Liubov, embraced this distinction to highlight the idea that being of Sakha nationality was not opposed to being Russian (note that she uses the term *russkii*—which some speakers deliberately use to mark ethnic Russianness—when contrasting Russians and Yakuts, but also when collapsing the difference between the two entities, referring to herself as being Russian):

> We have very good relationships with Russians [*K russkim my ochen' khorosho otnosimsia*]. I mean we live with them for so many years, since 1800 or so [sic], when Dezhnev the earliest Russian explorer arrived. He showed and disclosed to us so many things. We have very good relations with Russians [*s russkimi*], because our second language is Russian. It is already our native language, Russian [*svoi rodnoi uzhe russkii iazyk*]. We speak it fluently, have normal conversations. It is accepted unquestioningly [*i tut voobshche bez razgovorov*]. We were born in Russia, so this also means we have to. We are both Russians and Yakuts [*My i russkie i iakuty*].[144]

As this narrative and that of other Sakha interviewees suggest, the distinction between a small and a big motherland does aid in the Putinist effort to integrate local patriotism with allegiance to what he framed as the Russian state-civilization.[145]

Only a small number of campers countered notions of patriotism that tied one to place or the country. Maksim, the Sakha farmer, used the quote "the motherland is there, where we stay warm" (*rodina tam, gde my v teple*), which he had picked up from a movie, to account for his indifference to patriotism. He saw himself as carrying his sense of home with him wherever he might go:

> Wherever my future children or my dear relatives (*rodnye*) have it better, wherever all those close to me have it better, wherever they can self-develop, increase their material well-being, there will be my motherland. [. . .] As I said, I am a citizen of the world [*chelovek mira*].[146]

Andrei, a camper from the Krasnoyarsk Region, was struggling with his status as a soon-to-be emigrant whose departure from home could be read as non-patriotic. He felt that one problem was an outdated, rote understanding of patriotism: "this commonplace opinion about 'the patriot' as a person who serves in the army for eighteen years and maybe remains there all his life or remains working in the factory all his life, and goes to the public holiday in celebration of paratroopers wearing a sailor's shirt and jumps into the fountain."[147] His statement is especially significant with regard to how he reconciles the imperative to be a patriot with the flexible demands of the international economy:

> But maybe this [commonplace] understanding is changing right now. Everybody decides for himself what makes a patriot a patriot—whether a patriot could also be the person who works for an international corporation but pays taxes here. Maybe he does this in order to achieve something in the future and help his country in another way, in another sense. Everyone determines this for himself in his own way.[148]

Like many other campers, Andrei tried to show that being patriotic was not outdated, but aligned with the entrepreneurial spirit commonly associated with start-up business culture. In this understanding, patriotism entailed regional and national development. It reconciled the individual pursuit of one's career interest with the wish to do good for the region or country at large. Patriotism in this sense is not a counterpoint to career advancement, to a Western lifestyle, or to the belief in scientific and technological progress. On the contrary, it is, in this reading, capable of motivating creativity and marketable innovations that can benefit the motherland. A patriot, then, is a developer, a person interested in the forward movement of both the local community and the larger one.

Striving for Development and Patriotism

Young campers' individual quests for change are animated by the wish to live in a modern, developed region and country. Their notions of what this might entail ranged from a functioning infrastructure to respectful treatment in public institutions to the opportunity for young people to realize their work-related ambitions while engaging in personal growth.

Campers imagined development toward such a flourishing region as a modernization process in a particular area or in Russia as a whole. Their reverence for the scientific, economic, and social stage of development that economically advanced liberal democracies are known for was accompanied by their desire to improve the socioeconomic situation around them. Many believed, or wished, that through self-initiative and disciplined work they could one day enjoy the same conveniences as the middle classes in economically advanced liberal democracies.

Such wishes contrasted with campers' negative evaluations of "Russians" and "Russia" in response to questions about what irritated them about society or politics. As I have tried to show, these stereotypes of an imagined Russian national character that deviates from a supposed Western standard are not unique to campers. Critiques abound among most Russian citizens regarding the relatively poor quality of Russian manufacturing and the enormous influence of informal networks on Russian business and politics.[149]

Most campers shared in this negative view of Russians and Russia. Numerous interviewees located Russian citizens' initial turn to egoism and indifference in the 1990s. In part, they blamed the major politicians and "selfish oligarchs" of that period for having created the conditions that led to such a general decline in care for others.

Many longed for a more egalitarian and, especially, a more moral society, one they claimed had existed in the past. Aside from the *Komsomoltsy*, who regarded the Soviet period as having been the golden age of Russia as an empire and wished for it to return (albeit without the Soviets' internationalism, which they saw as having especially harmed Russian workers and peasants), most campers viewed that time with ambivalence. While they wished that their romanticized image of kind-hearted Soviet customs and altruistic patriotism could be transposed to the present, they rejected that period's limited possibilities for self-realization and the lack of personal freedoms, such as unconstrained travel and choice of profession.

Campers' criticism of present conditions was softened by a government-approved philosophy that frames the history of the Russian state in terms of recurrent ups and downs. Within this philosophy of history, every historical low point accentuates the unlikeliness of the following upswing, mythologizing an ideal Russian collective spirit that enables victory "against all odds." This kind of historical pride might be the most substantial mode of alleviating the various negative definitions of Russian national character. Notably, it also figures in the popular joke by Nikulin, in which the Russian soldier escapes the German fascists: this is not only a story about Russians' alleged passivity, but also conveys that when Russians do act, the outcome is heroic.

Campers' criticism of systemic flaws was offset not least by their love for Russia as a place—a landscape, a special color of the sky, a climate, or the courtyard of one's childhood. In the words of Daria: "It is the people that are bad, not the air, not the soil, not the sky above us. Russia is a good country."[150] Many campers' love for "their" place and the wish to see it flourish in the future motivated them to stay and work for local, not necessarily national, development. Contrary to accounts emphasizing ordinary Russians' psychological craving for the Soviet Union's lost Great Power status,[151] I found that many campers were primarily concerned with developing their region, city, or district.

In this vein, campers framed patriotism as an unconditional love for their home region and a necessary precondition for its development.[152] Almost all of my interviewees self-identified as patriots in these terms. They understood *real* patriotism as entailing altruistic deeds and a communitarian attitude to a common "we"—be it the village, the Republic, or the Russian Federation at large. Being a patriot meant being disposed toward action and development *here*, versus a longing to be *there*, where life is allegedly better. Calling oneself a patriot was also a way to indicate that one was morally good and decent—respectful and supportive of one's neighborhood, home region, or Russia at large *despite* them being perceived as backward. Calling oneself a patriot emphasized that one belonged to a category of active, caring people, distinguishing the speaker from fellow citizens who were inclined toward indifference and laziness.

While campers had no difficulty framing their career advancement and individualistically conceived plans for self-development as patriotic acts, they struggled to evaluate emigration that resulted from such career-advancement decisions. Many campers assumed that honest investments in their career paths could benefit the collective. I see this understanding of patriotism as rooted in the acceptance of an entrepreneurial approach to shaping one's life. A patriotism that is to conform with the principles of economic competition needs to accommodate capitalist values such as the individual pursuit of happiness. Economic development under capitalist conditions requires the participation of patriots who accept both the pursuit of individual success and its apparently glamorous benefits. It also demands that patriots blame themselves and others for their own insufficient economic performance if they lack these material blessings and societal privileges.[153]

In accordance with this reformed, capitalist-friendly patriotism, most campers had no objection to the simple pursuit of individual success but expressed their annoyance at those who pursued their personal aims *without* any communitarian orientation or respect for other people's lives. Campers strongly criticized anti-communitarian values and behaviors: egoism, greed, obsession with money, the maximization of individual success, and above all, indifference toward other people.[154] Their most intense indignation was aroused not by socioeconomic injustices, but, as several interviewees put it, by "all those people" who would just "sit on the bench" all day—drinking, smoking, complaining. Campers characterized oligarchs, politicians, and successful people who received patronage from informal networks as self-serving, corrupt, and greedy. Yet, when asked about what was to be done about those systemic wrongs, most did not address the problem of self-serving laziness and indifference in the higher echelons of power. They stated only that it was necessary to re-educate their indifferent, passive, lazy fellow citizens so that the latter would care for other people and their immediate surroundings, and engage, like them, in working for the common good.

While campers were uncertain about the nature of the common good that they sought, they were clear about its opposite. Many interviewees' classist distaste for those imagined others whom they called "passive" and "lazy" amounted to an equation of personal worth with the ability and "willingness" to engage in hard work. They appeared to be adapting Soviet social ethics—with their emphasis on work and a prohibition against becoming a burden to society—to national capitalist imperatives for economic competition and nationwide solidarity.

In line with this, most campers did not regard government policies or international economic conditions as the root cause of what they sometimes called the backwardness of their region. On the contrary, they identified the "bad qualities of other people" as causes for corruption and idleness in Russian society, which in turn were seen to be the greatest obstacles to the country's economic and technological development. Thus, campers' moral diagnosis of social ills often led them to engage in what they themselves rejected—a lamentation.

Their analysis largely coincided with that of official state youth politics, which seeks to train more patriotically spirited "activists" who would stay in the region or country to serve as tomorrow's strategic elites. As such, campers showed strong allegiance to those government-promoted narratives that justify authoritarian practices and neotraditional values to counter what they saw—just as government officials do—as deficiencies in the mentality of the average Russian. In keeping with David Easton's differentiation between specific and diffuse political support, young campers hardly engaged in gestures of specific support for politicians in office, yet they usually did affirm those narratives legitimating Russia's flexible authoritarian regime.

Adding to campers' acceptance of the flexible authoritarian regime was their belief that there was "nothing to be done" about power imbalances and inequality that exceeded community-level concerns. Such thoughts were usually justified with regard to various conspiratorial notions regarding the secret or hidden nature of power that would render it impossible to rally for changes on a state-wide or worldwide scale.

Yet this disaffection toward change pertained only to large-scale issues: All interviewees were clearly convinced that one could accomplish much individually or at the community level. They regarded immediate actions such as litter clean-up campaigns, renovations of public neighborhood spaces, making public buildings accessible to the disabled, and organizing concerts or New Year's visits to orphanages as meaningful and unequivocally positive. The organizations and projects that most interviewees supported focused on single issues, addressed in isolation, without regard for the larger social context and its power imbalances—organizations that eschew seeking structural changes or a re-evaluation of dominant norms.[155]

6

Professionalizing Patriots

The Branding and Staging of Heroic Masculinity

In this chapter[1] I show how the law-and-order youth initiatives Stop Rudeness (*StopKham*) and Lion Versus (*Lev Protiv*) marketize and popify[2] neotraditional and neoliberal modernization ideals promoted by the Russian government through video productions uploaded to YouTube and similar online platforms. In the previous chapter I explored how potential strategic elites negotiate both the flexible demands of the market and the authoritarian demands of the state in their quests for a better life. Here, I demonstrate how the figure of the "vigilante-entrepreneur," who performs the ideal of the financially successful heroic patriot engaged in "doing good" for society at large, fuses flexible and neotraditional elements.

This figure of the patriotic vigilante-entrepreneur corresponds to the Putinist vision of an economically and politically strong Russia, with ideal future generations imagined as being devoted to the regime.[3] The flexible authoritarian vision evokes a country that is modern, prosperous, and internationally competitive, but also a bastion of traditional order and heterosexual gender relationships. Its flexible aspect encourages economic growth and development, while its neotraditional aspect romanticizes images of the past, including Soviet forms of patriotic vigilantism, to legitimate the pursuit of a conservative future.[4] The packaging of conservative morals into video clips by Stop Rudeness and Lion Versus supports these political aims, thereby helping to stabilize the regime ideologically.

The law-and-order initiatives whose video productions I analyze here combat what they regard as rude behavior in Russia's streets and public places. In order to do this, they film people violating traffic rules, or those flouting the prohibition of public alcohol or tobacco consumption, and challenge those responsible to change their ways. Those who refuse are punished with a huge sticker on their windscreen saying "To hell with everyone, I drive where I want,"[5] or by having their cigarettes extinguished with spray bottles. This often results in heated arguments and violence between the young vigilantes and those they target. Hyping these violent encounters and promoting a youth-focused brand has helped the two projects amass more than 2.5 million followers each on their YouTube channels. They are widely considered Russia's best-known contemporary youth initiatives.[6]

The vigilantes' video productions help to legitimate flexible authoritarianism, incentivizing young citizens to take the initiative in service of a more moral and entrepreneurial society (according to the Putinist flexible authoritarian vision), while expanding authoritarian aggression—"the tendency to be on the lookout for, and to condemn, reject, and punish people who violate conventional values"[7]—against alleged norm offenders. Not only do they reflect the regime's neotraditional and flexible ideals back at itself, they also popularize a new ideal of heroic masculinity that fuses patriotism with entrepreneurialism.

I build on bodies of scholarship about masculinity that ask how the staging of male heroism might help to legitimate both authoritarian governments and neoliberalism. Performances of heroic masculinity by ruling politicians or successful entrepreneurs are often used to cast nation-states as strong and independent—traits commonly associated with traditional masculinity. As Marion Fourcade-Gourinchas has shown, personified images of nation-states and unquestioned stereotypes of their alleged national character have real effects in business and politics.[8] It is therefore not surprising that political leaders increasingly associate their countries with specific personified images through "the tools, techniques, and expertise of commercial branding," in order to attract foreign investors and arouse citizens' "loyalty to the territory" and "national priorities."[9]

Stop Rudeness and Lion Versus are similarly engaged in a type of branding that has the capacity to strengthen loyalty to the flexible authoritarian state, specifically among young people. Expanding on Sarah Banet-Weiser's research, I understand a brand as a story told to consumers that promises a specific experience across a range of articles, art works, or video clips.[10] Increasing a brand's resonance can create loyalty to the regime on an ideological level among young people who are otherwise disaffected when it comes to politics. I argue that the vigilantes help to transform public discontent with systemic social ills into moral indignation against supposedly asocial and indifferent people through "popifying" video content.[11] In that regard, the vigilantes' videos build on a widely held belief among ambitious youth loyal to the Russian regime, who, as I showed in Chapter 5, find other people's passivity and indifference to be the main problem in contemporary Russian society. To reinforce the repackaging of neotraditional ideals as hip and youthful, the videos incorporate humorous dialogue, footage from popular movies, effects such as fast or slow motion, and especially rebellious-seeming music ranging from rock to metal to hip-hop.

Thus the vigilantes' video clips perform critical ideological work: they help to stabilize the regime by making neotraditional ideals tangible and "cool" among an age cohort that is commonly more concerned with breaking traditions than with conforming to them. Responding to this notion of youthful defiance, the video clips employ a rebellious style that contrasts starkly with their aim of enforcing conservative morals.[12] The packaging of law-and-order ideals into a novel format of social-media entertainment supports flexible authoritarianism on a day-to-day basis. As Rashid Gabdulhakov has shown, Russia's big TV channels largely support the vigilantes' depiction of violent encounters with norm offenders, using as evidence footage from the vigilantes' clips—not recordings made by the vigilantes' targets.[13] The vigilantes' depiction of reality is therefore affirmed on TV and spills over into more established media formats. Unlike most media formats on TV, the social media entertainment format established by these law-and-order initiatives (in many aspects akin to an online influencer business model) is consumed primarily by young people and offers a skillfully staged authenticity.[14]

State Funding of Social Media Entertainment Businesses and Its Limits

The enterprising character of these law-and-order initiatives is crucial to understanding how vigilante practices that ideologically support the state coincide with entrepreneurial motives under flexible authoritarianism. Presidential grants were important sources of funding for Stop Rudeness, and indirectly, as we will see later, for Lion Versus.[15] That the young vigilantes are carrying out ideological work in support of the flexible authoritarian regime is crucial to making sense of why they still receive symbolic support from government officials, including Vladimir Putin, despite large-scale scandals—involving, for instance, a brawl between Stop Rudeness and the bodyguards accompanying the wife of Chechnya's deputy presidential plenipotentiary to a shopping center in Moscow, or the former Olympic champion

Alexei Nemov's verbal abuse of Stop Rudeness vigilantes. Such scandals led to the exclusion of Stop Rudeness from Russia's Unified State Register of Legal Entities (see also my discussion of the so-called register mechanism in Chapter 5).[16] For this reason, Stop Rudeness has been unable to apply for presidential grants since 2016. However, the group continues to receive symbolic if not financial support from government officials, including Vladimir Putin, who praise their engagement for a more orderly society.

Since then, both initiatives have successfully sought alternative funding sources. Indeed, their recent estimated monthly revenue could support several people, if Russia's monthly minimum wage of 490 USD is used as a point of comparison.[17] Stop Rudeness's monthly YouTube revenue, according to estimates by Social Blade in 2021, is somewhere between 2,300 and 36,600 USD,[18] and similar Social Blade estimates exist for Lion Versus. During a televised debate in 2020 with Vitali Milonov, a deputy of Russia's ruling party, Lion Versus's founder, Mikhail Lazutin, stated that he earns between 2,300 and 2,450 USD per month.[19] Revenues from Russian online platforms, donations, and sales of branded merchandise may add another few hundred dollars per month to these estimates.

Stop Rudeness in particular reached out to transnational audiences, gaining international visibility under the name "Stop a Douchebag"—not so much as a Kremlin-backed law-and-order youth initiative but as a creator of "Citizen Activism videos," as the initiative's webpage on the crowdfunding platform Patreon puts it.[20] While lawsuits filed by famous targets against the initiatives' transgressions have had legal repercussions for Stop Rudeness, in 2017 Vladimir Putin once again publicly endorsed their vigilante actions and condoned police protection for the initiatives by asking the Ministry of Internal Affairs to collaborate with "citizen activists."[21] This loyalty is of a two-way nature: Dmitry Chugunov, the founder of Stop Rudeness, occupied an influential position in the Public Chamber, a public consultation body financed by the presidential administration with members largely appointed by Putin, as well as on the advisory board (*obshchestvennyi sovet*) of the Ministry of Industry and Trade. He openly stated his support, and that of Stop Rudeness, for the president, since, as he put it, "Putin can't do everything alone."[22]

As other researchers studying the two groups' vigilantism have highlighted, their relationship to the state is complicated.[23] Stop Rudeness started as a state youth political project at the Kremlin-backed youth-leadership summer camp *Seliger* in 2010. Chugunov—then a high-ranking member of the pro-government youth movement *Nashi* ("Those on Our Side"), and called a "commissar" in allusion to the Soviet period—presented the project during his participation in the *Seliger* youth-leadership camp. That his idea gained widespread support among state officials appears to stem from several overlapping circumstances. For one, it came at a time when the attention of Russian youth politics shifted to making potential strategic elites entrepreneurially literate and enabling them to become co-creators of government-sponsored civic life (see my discussion of these terms in Chapter 4). Moreover, the project's ideological proximity to flexible authoritarian ideals appealed, as we will see later on, to government leaders. Finally, popular mobilizations against traffic lawlessness during the first half of 2010 explain why the law-and-order initiative might have received government sponsorship at that time.

Support for Chugunov's project from *Rosmolodezh* (the Federal Agency for Youth Affairs) and other government sources certainly owes to his previous activities in *Nashi*. Despite *Seliger's* opening to all Russian youth in 2009 and its novel focus on project management,[24] evidence shows that the youth-leadership summer camp continued to be dominated by a network of former and current *Nashi* activists.[25] For one thing, many *Nashi* commissars had become employees of the newly founded "State Committee of Youth Affairs," which was transformed into *Rosmolodezh* only months later.[26] Replacing *Nashi*, *Rosmolodezh* became the main organizing body of *Seliger* and similar youth-leadership summer camps in 2008. This turn to officialdom—*Nashi* had no legal status as an organ allowed to use government funds—was accompanied by the strengthening of informal ties between the ministerial agency and the youth movement, with considerable personal continuities and administrative overlaps. In 2010, *Nashi* and *Rosmolodezh* still shared a common press service; work contracts, so-called *goskontrakty*, worth more than 3 million USD, were issued by *Rosmolodezh* for current and former *Nashi* commissars.[27]

Likewise, many of the projects that were developed at *Seliger* from 2008 to 2011 and that gained considerable government support were designed by current and former *Nashi* commissars. A telling example for this selection bias is Elena Bocherova's project "Youth School for Entrepreneurship" (*Molodezhnaia shkola predprinimatel'stva*). At the time when she presented her proposal, she was both a *Nashi* commissar and regional deputy.[28] Renamed "You Are an Entrepreneur" (*Ty predprinimatel'*), the project not only received considerable state funding and formed the basis of an entire themed session at *Seliger* in 2009, but was subsequently transformed into an official *Rosmolodezh* project.[29] A similar privileging of projects conceived by *Nashi* commissars is likely to have played a role in the selection of Chugunov's proposal to found Stop Rudeness. This is substantiated by the degree to which the organization was able to rely on government funding between 2010 and 2015. Stop Rudeness's first cameras, along with what would become its signature feature—the car-wheel-sized stickers that are used to punish intransigent drivers—were sponsored by *Nashi*.[30] In the years to follow, so-called presidential grants were important sources of funding for Stop Rudeness, which apparently transferred part of almost 300,000 USD it received from the state budget between 2013 and 2015 to its sibling initiative Lion Versus.[31] As investigative journalists have alleged, the network of former *Nashi* commissars appears to have been crucial for this channeling of money to Lion Versus.[32]

Chugunov's proposal to establish a traffic-related, government-loyal vigilante youth group, using online platforms such as YouTube, probably gained support because of growing public discontent over the use of so-called *migalki*—"those flashing blue lights on the tops of so many public officials' cars, which evidently empower them to barrel down public thoroughfares, endangering and enraging others."[33] A movement that became known as the "Blue Buckets Society" emerged in response to a deadly car accident in February 2010, during which two female doctors died in a collision with the car of the vice-president of the Lukoil company, one of the world's largest enterprises and closely connected to the Kremlin. It remains disputed which party was at fault.[34] Many people engaged in flash mobs to protest against what they perceived to be the lawlessness and arrogance of officials on Russia's streets.[35] In spring 2010, more and more Russian citizens followed the instructions of a viral YouTube video and started to mount blue children's buckets on the roofs of their cars in imitation of the flashing lights so often misused by government officials and influential businesspeople.[36]

Chugunov's idea to found Stop Rudeness most likely responded to the "Blue Buckets Society," another of who's aims was "stopping rudeness," though in a much more government-critical fashion. Stop Rudeness expressed the same outrage against lawlessness, but, unlike the blue bucket protests, it did not explicitly target government officials and influential businesspeople, and set out to punish relatively minor transgressions of a kind that seldom cause injuries, disability, or death: that is, parking violations. As with the kind of activist engagement prevalent among participants of the youth-leadership camps discussed in Chapter 5, Stop Rudeness and Lion Versus constitute instances of a "compliant form" of activism.[37]

Stop Rudeness and Lion Versus are run by young people acting as both vigilantes reinforcing neotraditional morals alongside the state and entrepreneurs seeking to gain from social media monetization; hence my term "vigilante-entrepreneurs." That the roles of vigilante and entrepreneur coincide here bespeaks the logics that drive ambition under flexible authoritarianism. Under such regimes, politically conformist, neotraditional activities promise both symbolic and material rewards. At the same time, entrepreneurial success promises to be rewarding not only materially but also symbolically, because it can be read as a new way of showing one's patriotic spirit by contributing to Russia's economic strength.[38] Thus, the vigilante-entrepreneurs' material rewards, gained through online monetization, blur with the symbolic rewards of recognition for doing good for the country as both economically independent, active young entrepreneurs and "activist heroes," helping to uphold neotraditional morals.

Legitimating Flexible Authoritarianism: Moralization and the Performance of Heroic Masculinity

The video clips produced by Stop Rudeness and Lion Versus have the capacity to channel young people's discontent with Russia's social ills toward social groups deemed "undeserving." Like the lectures and training sessions at the youth-leadership camps—which convey that being active and entrepreneurial should be the goal of decent people—the stories told in the videos help to legitimate flexible authoritarianism among new publics. This is especially true of clips produced by Lion Versus. The vigilantes tend mainly to cast as villains those that they label *bydlo*, meaning "trash," while those they deem to be suffering from bad luck through no fault of their own (purportedly unlike the former) are cast as victims. I will provide examples for both types of character work in the analysis of Lion Versus's videos below.

This presumption of moral innocence explains why such "victims" appear in the clips as deserving the vigilantes' mercy. The categorization of people into "deserving" and "undeserving" groups is also characteristic of other flexible authoritarian regimes, such as Hungary's, where, as Dorottya Szikra argues, "social rights are not based on 'needs' any more but rather on 'deservingness' measured according to one's performance" in the sense of hard and honest work."[39] Not only are those whom the government considers a "burden on society" portrayed as undeserving of mercy, but alleged egoists and non-patriots are shown to unjustly benefit from the privileges of a lawless society as it emerged during the 1990s. A good example to illustrate this point is the origin story of Stop Rudeness. As founder Dmitry Chugunov tells it, he became motivated to put a stop to rude behavior on Russian streets when his own car was blocked in for more than two hours by a double-parked Porsche Cayenne. When the Porsche's driver—"a beautiful girl"—returned, failing to offer an apology or excuse for the inconvenience and even shrugging off her transgression, Chugunov found himself thinking, as he stated in an interview, "B*tch, this is unfair! Lawlessness and privilege is everywhere, and people think that they can park wherever they want just because they have the bigger car."[40]

As I showed in Chapter 5, even young adults who are loyal to Russia's political regime are largely discontent with the functioning of many things in the country, including lawlessness. Their evaluations correspond with domestic and transnational narratives of an "allegedly traditional Russian culture of lawlessness and informal relations," as Vadim Volkov puts it.[41] Informal relations do indeed shape public life in Russia today, as Alena Ledeneva's meticulous analyses show.[42] At the same time, Russia's reputation for lawlessness is also a popular cultural theme in literature and movies. Alexei Balabanov's neo-noir *Brother* crime blockbusters (from 1997 and 2000), for instance, famously portray post-Soviet Russia as a state that "has proven itself incapable of establishing a minimal level of security and social justice."[43] As media scholar Anthony Anemone argues, the post-Soviet vigilante hero emerges in these movies as a person who is "selfless, and sometimes self-sacrificial," struggling against "the unscrupulous and powerful elements that dominate a lawless society."[44]

The heroic and "cool" self-styling of Stop Rudeness and Lion Versus corresponds to this popular cultural notion of self-acclaimed vigilantes who protect those that *they* define as most vulnerable in a lawless society. The latter, who appear in the clips as victims, are portrayed as being endangered by apparent "villains." Much like the campers we met in Chapter 5, the vigilante-entrepreneurs of Stop Rudeness and Lion Versus pursue a moralizing agenda to create a better society. They position themselves as complementing the state's law enforcement while also stepping in when the police fail to carry out their role—as a force for moral oversight on behalf of society as a whole. In this regard they perform a heroic social role that corresponds to the pop culture ideal of the incorruptible rebellious vigilante, acting according to the credo that "strength lies in righteousness, not in money."[45] Echoing this ideal, the vigilante-entrepreneurs of these two groups insist that they are motivated primarily by "doing good" for Russian society, not by the prospect of career opportunities in state institutions or of financial gain from video monetization.

It is critical in this context to understand the role of gender norms for legitimating flexible authoritarian regimes and their ideological foundations—in Russia, but also transnationally. Russia's mainstream media present the country's economic strength as being reinforced by Putin's masculine authoritarian leadership and alleged protection of Russia's unique "civilization" (a term intended as a substitute for the contested concept of "nation" in a polity where multinationalism is constitutionally enshrined).[46] Thus, "civilizational uniqueness" and national economic strength are presented not only as being in a reciprocal relationship, but also as requiring the state's protection—authoritarian if necessary—from destructive liberal and foreign influences. As several scholars argue, such protection is increasingly framed in terms of masculine strength, particularly since the 2014 annexation of Crimea. Oleg Riabov and Tatiana Riabova show, for example, that besides the establishment of Vladimir Putin as a symbol of masculine strength, the country itself is increasingly presented as strong due to its preservation of moral principles (which also relate to the country's adherence to a strict gender binary): "Russia appears as a bastion of 'moral principles,' and the current Russian authorities as guarantors of the preservation of the nation's normalcy."[47] In contrast, as the authors argue, the derogatory neologism "Gayropa," used by government officials, serves as a tool to "demasculinize" the figure of Europe by alleging that granting the right to same-sex partnerships would weaken the nation.[48] This government line was echoed at the 2014 *SakhaSeliger* camp, when staff leader Viktor Stepanenko showcased drag queen Conchita Wurst's first prize at that year's Eurovision song contest in one of the (few) indoctrinating lectures. Using the same language of normalcy and moral principles described by Riabov and Riabova, Stepanenko described the conferring of this prize on a drag queen as evidence of what he, alongside government officials, labeled Europe's decay—a form of alleged decline that would also surface in European governments' support for Ukraine's Maidan Revolution and their criticism of Crimea's annexation.[49]

The aforementioned *Brother* movies prove a popular cultural role model in this respect as well. Media scholars interpret these films as conflating heroic masculinity—incarnated in the figure of a young male vigilante hero fighting against malevolent, rich businesspeople—with national authority.[50] In a similar fashion, historian Elizabeth Wood identifies Putin's performances of hypermasculinity, as she calls them, as having the capacity to legitimate his strongman rule.[51] The appeal to traditional gender norms in PR campaigns "emphasizing Putin's outward physical signs of masculinity" can "symbolize not only his own, but also the country's masculine strength," writes Valerie Sperling.[52] Traditional gender norms are invoked to legitimate not only authoritarian rule, but also—as political scientist Birgit Sauer shows for liberal democracies—neoliberal restructuring. As she points out, arguments for neoliberal restructuring are often couched in terms of restoring states' independence, self-sufficiency, and competitiveness, characteristics commonly associated with masculinity.[53]

Besides adding to the legitimation of a regime—that is, the underlying order of political life in a society—performances of heroic masculinity are also marketing and branding strategies. Bearing this in mind, when I analyze vigilante-entrepreneurs' performance of heroic masculinity, I do not make a claim about who they are, but rather about the *personae* they strategically construct in order to attract wider audiences. I use Philip Auslander's conceptualization of persona, which he developed against the backdrop of changes in popular music industries, but which is equally illuminating for social media entertainment formats in which online self-presentation is key to gaining more views. His concept of persona denotes a "person's representation of self within a discursive domain,"[54] emphasizing that it results from the strategic choices of producers, agents, or publicists, and that it is guided by a cultural industry's specific rules of how to gain visibility and become successful.[55] Stop Rudeness and Lion Versus's brand management draws considerably, and strategically, on the transnational salience of performances of heroic masculinity. Their vigilante brands promise both Russian and transnational audiences the opportunity to identify with young, entrepreneurially successful heroes.[56] The video clips appeal to audiences because they have the capacity to elicit schadenfreude in response to an outgroup's misfortunes, especially when perceived transgressors get their "just deserts."[57] The brands' success therefore needs to be understood in the context of growing transnational social-media audiences who take pleasure in watching heated arguments, aggression against alleged norm offenders, and, in several cases, violence—for instance, when drivers try to remove vigilantes from their radiator hoods with physical force or people hold onto their beer bottles when vigilantes attempt to confiscate them. As Anatoly Papp of the Moscow-based organization Public Verdict puts it, the problem with vigilante initiatives such as Stop Rudeness and Lion Versus is not only their harassment of targets, "but that there are millions of people who will watch these videos with pleasure, where one person messes with the other."[58]

Such performances of heroic masculinity also attract wide audiences due to the increasing dominance of what gender scholars call "neoliberal masculinity" or "transnational business masculinity." According to Birgit Sauer, entrepreneurs—especially those who work in creative industries— are increasingly "forced to at least simulate neoliberal masculinity and to practice competition, risk-taking and the marginalization of others to succeed in daily struggles of survival."[59] She posits a reciprocal relationship between the tendency to understand social relations primarily through the lens of competition and gestures of discrimination against others.[60] Thus, discourses of deservingness and undeservingness, which I discussed as being characteristic of flexible authoritarian regimes, are fueled by transnationally shared ideologies of competition.[61] Within the context of a globalizing neoliberal culture of success, economic success depends increasingly on the "transnational business masculinity" that sociologist R. W. Connell identified as being hegemonic among internationally influential business executives.[62] As we will see, the specifically post-Soviet discourse of a "crisis of masculinity" relates to this understanding of men as being in need of economic independence to feel and act like real men.

While the entrepreneurial activities of the two law-and-order groups correspond to the youth political emphasis on fostering young talents, which set in around the year 2009, their vigilante actions coincide with the revival of Soviet forms of youth activism that accompanied Putin's rise to power in the early 2000s. As discussed in Chapter 3, a change in memory politics under Putin allowed for a re-evaluation and partial rehabilitation of the Soviet past—including the revival of then-popular forms of youth activism and their repurposing for flexible authoritarian ends. The spread of law-and-order initiatives in Russia since the early 2000s—among which Stop Rudeness and Lion Versus are a special variant—directly relates to neoliberal ideas of sharing responsibility for security and well-being with private citizen initiatives.[63] Similar to programs that facilitate cooperation between local citizens and police in Britain or the United States, the field of privately organized law-and-order initiatives in Russia appears as "a site where neoliberal thinking about crime prevention combined with more traditional forms of conservatism, permeating, albeit unevenly, into everyday life."[64] As historian Gleb Tsipursky argues, support for law-and-order initiatives in Russia spread after the 2008 world financial crisis, when local volunteers compensated for a shortage of police officers.[65] As Tsipursky stresses—substantiating my argument in Chapter 3—the proponents of such initiatives emphasized the revival of a Russian-Soviet tradition in a neoliberal spirit.[66]

Indeed, the enterprises discussed here resemble the voluntary law-and-order initiatives that were endorsed by the Communist Party's leadership during the late Soviet period, after Stalin's death in 1953.[67] Various "volunteer patrols" then emerged under the aegis of the Soviet Youth League *Komsomol*. Besides fighting petty crimes, their members were on the lookout for non-conformists, persecuting not only legal transgressions but also activities that ran counter to established, cultured, norms of behavior.[68] As historian Juliane Fürst puts it, the patrols "concerned themselves with every little small misdemeanor ranging from drunken and lewd behavior to garish trousers or rubbish on the pavement."[69]

The history of these volunteer patrols during the Soviet era is still well known in Russia. So is their fight against so-called hooliganism, a concept then denoting apparently motiveless and therefore superfluous pleasure in acts of disobedience and non-conformism, "such as the singing of songs with dubious text, willful destruction of public and private property, cruelty to pet animals, display of disrespectful behavior towards women, and so on."[70] With the social dislocations of the 1990s, which led among other things to a sharp increase in drug use and crime, preoccupations with the loss of moral standards in society rose—a process fueled by conservative civil-society groups.[71] Such moral panics fitted a more general framework, shared by many Russian citizens at the time, of considering social and political relations to have fallen into a state of deep crisis.[72] This led, as early as the late 1990s under Boris Yeltsin, to federal legislative acts facilitating the legal operation of local law-and-order initiatives.[73] Times of moral panic provide opportunities for the strengthening of the authoritarian state. Indeed, the need to quell hooliganism has been cited by Russian authorities to delegitimate artistic expression, non-heterosexual intimate relationships, and also—as in the case of Pussy Riot—government-critical protest.[74]

Concern for lawful and "cultured" behavior in accordance with conservative norms was also practiced in the early 2000s by pro-government youth groups, such as *Rossiia Molodaia* (Young Russia) or *Mestnye* (The Locals), and by patrols forming within the youth wing of Russia's ruling party, *Molodaia Gvardiia Edinoi Rossii* (the Young Guard of United Russia). They campaigned against the consumption of alcohol and nicotine and engaged in raids on migrants allegedly lacking work permits.[75] *Mestnye* in particular aligned themselves with far-right organizations who sought a Russia for ethnic Russians only, such as the Movement Against Illegal Immigration (*Dvizhenie protiv nelegal'noi immigratsii* or *DPNI*).[76] As the head of *Mestnye* stated in 2006, while the far-right *DPNI* only talked about the problems produced by "migrants," his organization would take concrete action.[77]

Lion Versus's digital vigilante practices in particular appear to have been inspired not by Kremlin-backed youth politics or a nostalgia for the Soviet past, but by the far right.[78] The group *Restrukt*, for example, of which Lion Versus founder Mikhail Lazutin had been at least a sympathizer and potentially a member, and which was led by the neo-Nazi Maxim Martsinkevich (alias Tesak), aroused attention beyond Russia. Under the slogan *Okkupai-pedofiliai* (Occupy Pedophilia), its members harassed and brutally humiliated homosexual people (perjoratively called "pedophiles") in front of a live camera.[79] *Restrukt*'s other vigilante projects, *Narkofiliai*, *Alkofiliai*, and *Vyseliai*, used similar means to target people suffering from an addiction to drugs or alcohol and immigrants lacking documentation.[80] *Kamen' Protiv* (Rock Versus) was the name that Mikhail Lazutin, the founder of Lion Versus, and the openly neo-Nazi Andrei Makarov, a *Restrukt* member, gave to their first digital vigilante project. Like Occupy Pedophilia, Rock Versus targeted and humiliated homosexual people in front of a live camera.[81] Lazutin started his own digital vigilantism projects, *Lev Protiv Pedofilov* (Lion Versus Pedophiles)[82] and Lion Versus, after Lazutin was detained by the police for theft alongside Makarov in January 2014. Although Lazutin was quickly released, the two apparently parted company.[83] That same year, Makarov was prosecuted in connection with the murder of an Azerbaijani citizen.[84] Lazutin now claims that he never held neo-Nazi views, and has produced clips testifying to his antifascist stance and his support for state-sponsored imperial ("antifascist") Russian nationalism.[85] One example is his highly popular video clip "Lion Versus Skinhead Nazis [Scuffle] against racism" (*Lev Protiv Skinkhedov Natsistov [Potasovka] protiv rasizma*), which has garnered fifteen million views.[86]

Lazutin's personal connections to the neo-Nazi scene correspond to the ideological overlap between state-sponsored civilizational nationalism and anti-state far-right nationalisms, as Marlène Laruelle has studied.[87] Increasing overlaps between the Putinist moral vision of what constitutes a good society and that of the far right are especially noticeable in the state's shifting position on gender and sexual freedoms. The depiction of LGBTQI activists and feminists as a threat to the nation, once a distinguishing feature of Russian far-right ideology, has become central to state-sanctioned civilizational nationalism since the 2010s.[88] With regard to the legitimation of authoritarian aggression against those who allegedly harm society with "immoral behavior," it is notable that Putinism integrates the far right's sexual, gender, and reproductive norms into its neotraditional ideals of a good society.[89]

Analyzing Vigilante-Entrepreneurs' YouTube Videos and Their Political Meanings

While previous chapters have focused on the voices of young people and youth political staff, here I am more concerned with representations of society in vigilante video clips and their political meaning. What is the overarching moral story communicated by these vigilante brands, I ask—and what experience do they promise? What is the political meaning of such mediatized vigilante actions? In what ways do they bolster the legitimacy of flexible authoritarianism?

I contend that one can extrapolate the unquestioned beliefs underpinning vigilante-entrepreneurs' video productions from their choices of actions, targets, and immediate goals. This undertaking builds on the thesis that activists' political visions, even those that remain unspoken, shape their action repertoire. Such repertoires are thus not neutral tools, but expressions of the activists' "political identities and moral visions."[90] My analysis is guided by the question of how these choices make sense within a prevailing political logic[91] shared by the activists and—in this case—by politicians in power who offer them symbolic sponsorship. Because the videos tell stories, they are based on plots—that is, the structures that order the sequence of events in a story and thereby lend it plausibility.[92] In analyzing stories told through videos, identifying characters—heroes, villains, and victims—is crucial. They, as James Jasper, Michael Young, and Elke Zuern argue, "tell" audiences through examples that they can emulate "who and what to admire or pity, fear or reject," and give guidance on how to lead "our moral, emotional, and cognitive lives."[93]

More concretely, I consulted the thirty most-viewed videos on each of the groups' YouTube channels (I assumed that past successes in view counts guided the vigilante-entrepreneurs' aesthetic and action repertoire choices for future productions), and scrutinized them according to the following questions: who are the main characters and what are the general plotlines and techniques used to create suspense across individual videos? What do these elements tell us about vigilantes' unquestioned beliefs concerning who is to blame for social ills and how to tackle them? What kind of experience or feeling do the brands established by these law-and-order youth initiatives promise to audiences?

The Styling of a New Heroic Character against the Backdrop of a Lawless Society

Russia's political incumbents welcome youth activism as long as it supports the broad aims of flexible authoritarianism. Stop Rudeness and Lion Versus fashion themselves (literally) as moral entrepreneurs, encapsulating flexible authoritarian ideas in social media brands. Their brands present a youthful, hip way to police conservative morals. Their clips call on their peers to fight—side by side with top-level politicians who publicly endorse their activities—immoral and apathetic behavior. At the same time, the initiatives' main protagonists are start-up entrepreneurs who, while educating the badly behaved, run a self-sustaining business based on their innovation of a novel social media entertainment format. In this way, they carry out important ideological work. Not only do they popularize both law-and-order values and a positive image of entrepreneurship; they also help to fuse the two by fashioning a new kind of heroic character.

Like the traditional hero, this new character performs his brave deeds, meant to rescue others and protect the community from harm, by engaging in combat.[94] However, this novel persona is crafted according to pop culture cues, such as cool behavior and a youthful, seemingly subcultural appearance.[95] In the post-Soviet context, the combination of these traits with the figure of the independent entrepreneur contrasts sharply with the so-called "crisis of masculinity" discourse, which depicts both men and the heterosexual family as being in a state of crisis. The economic downturn of the 1990s and the loss of private ownership during the Soviet period are thought to have "left men unable to fulfill the role of breadwinner and therefore robbed them of an authoritative role in the family."[96] Worries about low birth rates link this discourse to patriotic concerns about the future of the nation. The new hero persona builds on the figure of the "muzhik," which has signified "real" manhood in Russian popular culture and advertising since the mid-1990s.[97] Indeed, in several respects, the "muzhik" is antithetical to the notion of the post-Soviet man in crisis, but also to the image of the liberal Western man. As Tatiana Riabova and Oleg Riabov explain,

> This type [of masculinity] is founded on self-sufficiency, economic independence, [and] respect for private property (in that sense, a "muzhik" is anti-communist). It is also far from 100-percent support for liberalism—values that are interpreted as a cult of individualism and egoism—while comradeship (tovarishchestvo) and male brotherhood are crucial components of the image of a "muzhik". [...] A "muzhik" is hardy, strong, and powerful; he doesn't say much, but always stands by his word. Finally, he is a patriot—he prefers the values of his own national culture, and expresses his readiness to defend the Motherland.[98]

The various acts of self-fashioning by the vigilantes of Stop Rudeness and Lion Versus are telling performances of this heroic masculine character. Their dedication to the motherland, rebellious appearance, esteem for male comradeship, and entrepreneurial zeal make them the antithesis of those weak and apathetic male characters who inform the "crisis of masculinity" discourse.

Self-fashioning as rebels is particularly crucial for the vigilante-entrepreneurs' construction of heroism. While a rebellious attitude is often read as a sign of opposition to the regime, presenting oneself as a rebel may also integrate well with a form of compliant activism that focuses on combatting minor social shortcomings. As such, it may stabilize the regime by channeling everyday grievances. According to Libman and Kozlov, such critical-but-compliant activism "limits the toolbox of potential opposition: if the public cannot clearly distinguish between the (apparently similar) forms of compliant activism pursued by groups loyal to the regime and actions of the opposition, it becomes more difficult for the latter to mobilize mass support."[99] For instance, in a 2016 interview, Stop Rudeness's founder Chugunov attributed the court decision to exclude his initiative from the state register, thereby preventing it from applying for presidential grants, to his group's profound incorruptibility. According to him, he and his fellow vigilantes would not close their eyes when members of informal power networks broke the law:

> We are the only organization in this country that does not make exceptions for anyone.... Who haven't we caught? ... Bandits, staff of the police, the public prosecutor's office. All of them have some kind of influential circle of friends who can play dirty tricks.[100]

Chugunov's criticism of power networks and even of the governing party in this interview should not, however, be taken as a sign of opposition to the regime.[101] Not only was the interview conducted by PASMI.RU, an anticorruption organization sponsored by the Russian government, but immediately following the above statement, Chugunov expresses his support for the president, signaling his loyalty to the regime. I read Chugunov's emphasis on incorruptibility as an element of his self-fashioning as a heroic rebel—a character that is well received in post-Soviet pop culture. The vigilante violence of rebels appears ethical and heroic against the backdrop of a lawless state. As Elizabeth Wood argues, Putin bolstered his rule through self-fashioning as an incorruptible rebel early in his presidency. For instance, he announced his intention, using expletives, to "rub out" [*mochit'*] bandits and oligarchs, "excluding the possibility of anyone sucking up to power [*prisosalsia*]" in order to fight the actual and perceived lawlessness widely associated with Boris Yeltsin's rule.[102] In a similar fashion, Stop Rudeness and Lion Versus vigilantes construct their rebel image in opposition to a context of lawlessness, as I will show through an interpretation of Stop Rudeness's video "Without Court and Consequences" (*Bez suda i sledstviia*).[103]

The video vividly portrays Russia's state of injustice. Departing from Stop Rudeness's usual formats, which tell the story of individual transgressors, it shows the degree of helplessness many Russians experience vis-à-vis the unlawful decisions of authorities. The demolition of garages depicted in the clip can be seen to precede the 2016 Night of the Long Shovels, when the Moscow city government ordered the destruction of several hundred makeshift shops in the city center that the authorities considered an eyesore. As mayor Sobyanin put it, the city needed "more modern," uniform designs for kiosks and trading pavilions.[104] Often, the shop owners did not even have time to rescue their goods. Demolitions of such shops were preceded by those of garages in several Moscow districts in 2014. As suggested in an account of the garage demolitions by a supporter of *Yabloko* (a liberal democratic opposition party), the private demolition squad, acting in the video as if it were the executive branch of an official city organ, has close ties to a club of military officers, some of whom are connected to federal incumbents.[105]

To contextualize "Without Court and Consequences," Artyom Leonov—dubbed Stop Rudeness's "wrestler" because he is famous among fellows and fans for his throws and takedown combat-sports techniques—explains the background story of the demolition in an introductory section. Pensioners, veterans, and disabled people had called Stop Rudeness for help because their garages were being demolished without warning. These people make for perfect victims in a post-Soviet setting, since respect for veterans is high, and pensioners and disabled people are known for often being among the poorest people in the country. The vigilantes thus play the role of heroes fighting for the vulnerable. The main video (3.9 million views on the Russian-language channel; 1.2 million on the English one where the video is called "Garage Wars"[106]) starts with shots of the demolition. We then see a young Stop Rudeness vigilante nervously asking the burly man heading the demolition squad to show him the official papers ordering the demolition. "Who are you, the owner?" asks the latter. "No, I am not the owner, I am a Russian *citizen*, I have the *right* to ask this," replies the young vigilante. To no avail: "Continue the demolition!" orders the foreman. In the next scene, big men in black jackets, black hats, sunglasses, and stocking masks approach. Working for a private demolition squad, these men make for ideal villains in a country where corporate raids are common. A cut, and Leonov points to the bulldozer behind him demolishing the garages. Talking directly to the camera, he again explains the situation: "There is the bulldozer tearing down the garages of *pensioners*. And the *policemen* just went away, maybe solving some other problems." In less than fifty seconds, these few scenes show us a lawless society in which the meager possessions of citizens, presented as helpless victims, are literally being destroyed before our eyes. The state, represented by the police, is turning a blind eye to the injustices. The only ones left to support the pensioners are the Stop Rudeness vigilantes.

In the remainder of the video, we witness violent fights between the vigilantes and the demolition squad. The vigilantes try to keep the bulldozer from starting the demolition, while the squad members force back the vigilantes using pepper spray and sticks. Several scenes underline the vigilantes' manly heroism. We see Mikhail Lazutin, at that time a member of Stop Rudeness, with a bleeding wound to his face, arguing with police officers that they should detain the person who beat him. He, like others, is advised to file a complaint, and told that it is not possible to arrest the person on site. The inaction of the police contrasts with the heroism of the vigilantes. Dmitry Chugunov, having been beaten and pepper-sprayed, tells the paramedics: "No, I can't go with you [to the ambulance]. If I leave, they'll tear it all down." The version of the clip on the Russian-language YouTube channel ends with an on-screen caption directing a rebellious question to the authorities: "Dear heads of the prefecture and the administration—if something is forbidden by law, but someone just wants it so much, does that mean that it's allowed?"[107] The subtitled version on their English-language channel, published about two years after the incident, adds a final scene showing a police van. A narrator tells us: "The real police had come. The thugs who had been crushing the garages . . . were taken to the police department. . . . This was a great scandal with criminal prosecution on both sides of the conflict."[108] As there is no information regarding the outcome of the prosecution or the results of investigations conducted by the vigilantes themselves, it remains unclear whether the vigilante-entrepreneurs' rebellious gestures amounted to a genuinely successful political opposition.

This portrayal of the police as a force aligning with "thugs" is not a standard theme of the two groups' clips. In general, the police as *the* symbol of the state play a more ambiguous role.[109] In most clips, they appear to collaborate closely with the vigilantes, punishing transgressors and bringing rough fights to a halt. These clips match the vision of collaboration expressed by the Minister of the Interior at the 2010 *Seliger* camp, when Stop Rudeness was first presented to the public: "This [project] will raise awareness of boors [*khamov*] in traffic and increase discipline. *GAI* [the official Russian traffic patrol] supports your project. An employee should be part of all [vigilante] groups to patrol the streets together with you."[110] In these clips, the police embody the rule of law, the importance of which Putin, often styling himself as commander-in-chief, has highlighted throughout his presidency.[111]

Besides "Without Court and Consequences," however, several other clips also present a less favorable picture of official law enforcement. Take, for example, the Lion Versus video "Smoking and Assault by Police" (*Kurenie i rukopikladstvo politsii*), which has more than five million views.[112] It starts with Mikhail Lazutin reprimanding two very young policemen who are smoking not far from the entrance of a metro station—which is forbidden. A typical Lion Versus story unfolds in which the transgressors are chased to the sound of heavy metal. The shots of the police station where Lazutin ends up clearly seek to discredit the local police. Besides zooming in on a pack of cigarettes on the desk and cigarette butts in a bucket of water, the camera shows us a police force lacking the modern equipment that usually symbolizes competent law enforcement.[113] Instead, we see a small room and a narrow corridor lit by fluorescent tubes; the walls are coated in the same washable paint that can be found in underresourced homes for orphans and public hospitals across post-Soviet countries. The young policemen who were seen smoking passively watch the argument unfolding between Lazutin and the officer in charge. The clip ends with Lazutin explaining that he won the argument and has ensured that the two transgressors will be reprimanded. He further highlights how such "trash behavior" gives the police a bad reputation. While the clip shows on the one hand the "authentic reality" of local police stations, Lazutin's epilogue nevertheless frames the whole endeavor as supportive of the police as a respected institution. He presents himself as a dashing hero, morally incorruptible due to his outsider status and acting for the good of Russian society.

Unlike "Smoking and Assault of Police," the "Without Court and Consequences" video does not show actual winners. Can the vigilantes be identified as the clips' heroes even though they could not rescue the garages? The outro song, *StopKham*, of the "Garage Wars" clip, written by the amateur rapper *Frast*, at least conveys the vigilantes' heroic aspirations:

> We are all heroes here. What we possess we created ourselves [*chto imeem poradili sami*]. . . . We are not ashamed to defend justice/truth [*pravda*], but it's shameful to be a boor [*kham*]. . . . A grown-up muzhik does not act like a lad. To act [simply] to deny it afterwards [is like] dishonoring mother and father.[114]

In contrast to the villains they fight, the song identifies heroes as self-made men who have acquired everything they have through their own work and who stand by their word: they are real *muzhiki*. The song contrasts heroes not only with those who became rich by birth or crime, but also with those who possess things that have been given to them by the state, their spouse, or well-meaning others. They by definition cannot be heroes—they are either thugs (villains) or victims.

The videos themselves reveal little about the ways in which the vigilantes self-fashion their entrepreneurial persona in the online public sphere—a significant element of their activity. Several Stop Rudeness raid leaders have achieved fairly widespread recognition and started their own YouTube channels. An interview with Lazutin, conducted by Stop Rudeness's Artyom Leonov and produced for Leonov's YouTube channel "Life in Russia" provides an excellent example of how the figure of the entrepreneur is fused with common patriotic heroism. The channel's pilot presents Leonov as a strongman who served in the army. Leonov wears a shirt from the patriotic brand motherrussia featuring a portrait of Ivan the Terrible and the word *oprichnik*, which refers to a member of the first tsar's special police corps.[115]

For the interview, Artyom Leonov has switched his oprichnik shirt for a white one. The backdrop is Moscow's hip Gorky Park. Blond and cleanshaven, wearing a silver necklace and a backwards LA Lakers baseball cap, Artyom introduces us to the meeting with Lev (meaning "lion" in Russian) Lazutin. He greets Lev (whose real name is Mikhail) with a handshake that turns into a hug. Lazutin wears a grey Nike hoodie. His shaved head contrasts with his long beard. The two vigilantes call each other "brother." Their greetings, speech, and gestures are reminiscent of rappers: relaxed, cool, showing mutual respect. Contrary to the stereotypical image of the rapper, however, the video emphasizes their straight-laced position and law-abiding behavior—their virtue. When Lazutin is approached by a teenager (stylish haircut, branded T-shirt, iPhone) asking him how he can join Lion Versus, Lazutin immediately checks whether he is underage. The teenager, who is a minor, asks in reply "You should not drink and not smoke, that's the criteria?" Lazutin, seemingly surprised by this question, answers "What's the point of it all if folks [vigilantes] smoke and drink themselves?" On leaving, the teenager adds that he will join Lion Versus as soon as he turns eighteen. Lazutin turns to Leonov: "Look, it's like in the army, once they're eighteen they're coming."

Comparisons to the army are frequent in the clip. In another scene, Lazutin paraphrases the comment of a fellow vigilante who had compared the initiatives' raids to his army service:

> With you it's in principle like in the army . . . you kill your legs, walking six hours every day, approach people, who all the time try to hit you, you go to the [police] department trying to sort things out. . . . And all of that solely for the good of the country![116]

The army comparisons underline the manliness of the raids and the vigilante-entrepreneurs' bravery. And they emphasize that what is at stake here is more than individual gain: "doing good" for the community at large inspires Lazutin's raids, as he emphasizes several times. Whereas his main motivation lies, as he explains in a key scene, in the feeling that he is a "worthy person," his second aim is to change the hearts and minds of young viewers through visible examples.

> I upload a video clip, a social clip, which young people are watching. And that is what I count on. That there might be one, just one young guy out of 500 000 viewers, who sees this. And what he sees creates an aversion to alcohol in his heart, in his soul, an aversion to swear words, to aggression.[117]

Fashioning oneself not only as strong, but also as making sacrifices for the common good, is a defining trait of hero characters.[118] The display of a virtuous self is another principal ingredient of classic heroism: one of Lion Versus's most successful videos (6.5 million views) features Lazutin rescuing a sick cat by taking it to a vet (*Spasenie kotenka ot smerti*), underlining his good intentions and fundamental compassion for victims.[119]

In the interview, Lazutin also makes it clear that anyone could follow his example. Reproducing a promise popular in start-up culture—that anyone can become an entrepreneur, a producer, or an individual activist[120]—he argues:

> If a person really does cool things, then it's not important who he is or where he started [*ne vazhno kto on*], he becomes popular.... When a person starts to do something, ... he starts to develop. But the most important thing is your spirit, your belief in your undertaking.[121]

Lazutin again appeals here to his young viewers to choose the path of (male) virtue, this time by calling upon their innate ability to live up to their full potential. His words sound as if they have been taken from an advertisement clip produced for the state youth political program "You Are an Entrepreneur" (*Ty predprinimatel'*):

> Everyone said, you don't have money for travel—but *you* went on foot; [...]
> Everyone said, this is a small town, there's no future—but *you* became the first in your business; [...]

Everyone said, it's time to stop—but *you* started.
You are an entrepreneur!¹²²

The interview makes clear that Lazutin is famous and respected. He is twice approached by teenage boys who tell him that they adore his initiative. Both Lazutin and Leonov are presented as young men who are not only strong and fearless (evidenced by footage from the raids), but also virtuous, economically successful, and possessing a good fashion sense. The fact that they look like bourgeois hipsters may normalize the authoritarian, misogynistic, and, at times, racist overtones of the law-and-order initiatives. Altogether, their self-fashioning illustrates how the flexible and authoritarian dimensions of Russia's current political order are fused in a new heroic persona.

Creating Suspense through Plot, Popification, and Character Work

The plots of Stop Rudeness's videos closely follow the deeds of the male heroic figures. Except for clips that were produced prior to 2016, all follow a standard five-act storytelling structure: Action—Background—Development—Climax—Ending. The well-structured videos begin with a teaser, featuring the most dangerous or funny situations. The main "villain" appears, at the latest, during the third quarter of the video—the climax. Plots and casts remain almost the same across videos. The heroic vigilantes fight against immoral villains who often turn violent; regardless of whether they drive taxis, mini trucks, or luxury cars. The clips never feature instances in which the vigilantes initiate violence, yet recordings from targets suggest that this does occur. Bystanders usually support the heroes, but sometimes cast their lot in with the villains. When passersby are pensioners, mothers with children, or trolleybus drivers, they are often presented as the victims of those who violate traffic rules. Footage from popular movies, effects such as black-and-white sequences, fast or slow motion, the replaying of scenes from another camera angle, and above all rebellious music (from rock to metal to hip-hop) create entertaining variations on the repetitive plots.

Suspense across videos is also created by varying the targets. Clips that prominently feature women as targets are among the most popular on the Stop Rudeness channels, and some of these have more views than those showing heavy fighting scenes. For instance, Stop Rudeness's second most popular video on the Russian channel is "*Krasnogorskaia Niasha*," with more than 15.8 million views[123] (translated as "Cutie Worldstar" on their English-language channel with 7.3 million views).[124] It features a woman who beats the vigilantes with her shoes to prevent them from attaching their sticker to her car's windscreen and drives off with several young men still clinging to the hood of her car. The initiative's Moscow branch created a highly successful compilation video called "Female Top 10" (*Zhenskii Top 10*) on their channel which has had almost 7.3 million views.[125] Unlike male targets, women are never depicted as serious opponents even if they fight back. This is underlined by the vigilantes' designations of women: "*devushka*" (girl), "cutie," "miss," "sloppy mommy," or "representative of the weaker sex." Suspense is created by revealing their behavior as unfeminine, unmotherly, or hysterical. For instance, in "A Muscovite Born and Bred"[126] (called *Moskvichka v tret'em kolene* on the Russian-language channel, almost 9 million views),[127] which also features in the top ten compilation, raid leader Kirill Bunin appeals to a female driver with the words "girl, darling" and asks her to re-park her car to be "a real girl [*bud'te devushka do kontsa*]." When the argument intensifies (the woman is using offensive language herself), he shouts to all present: "Who wants to marry that one? Who needs her? You can bet on it, a hamburger is preferable . . . simply trash." When the female target's husband shows up, raid leader Bunin asks him to reprimand his wife, and seems disappointed by the lack of male comradeship when he refuses.[128]

In many clips, women as villains underline the vigilante-entrepreneurs' manliness by means of contrast. Among Stop Rudeness's most popular videos are those that feature attractive women, often focusing on their childlike and innocent appearance (large eyes, small chin, carefully dressed and styled), which is taken to contrast with their use of obscene language and rude behavior in response to the vigilantes' harassment. In particular, Bunin's raids present such female villains as weak and hysterical, as for instance in the two videos of the "Family Escalation" series (*Semeinoe Obostrenie*), 4.9 and 2.8 million views, respectively.[129] At the end of the second of the two videos, Bunin addresses the audience: "As you also see, the psychological sanity of this woman is to be doubted. . . . We hope that both her sanity and her driver's license will be inspected."[130] Female villains are depicted as people who cannot be taken seriously and need the guidance of men.

Depicting women as inferior to men is one way to emphasize the vigilante-entrepreneurs' supposed virility. Another is demonstrating superiority in combat against male villains. Yet only when the vigilante-entrepreneurs regard those villains as sufficiently manly do they engage in a fight; if male targets behave in a way that can be interpreted as feminine, they need not be defeated in combat to emphasize the vigilantes' virility. Rather, these men's inferiority is signaled by the use of misogynistic language (see Stop Rudeness's "Mama's Boy").[131] Yet even the physically strongest male opponents show signs of weakness. Their seemingly unjustified aggression, their screaming and swearing, is typical in displays of weak characters. When villains turn remorseful *after* a physical fight or the arrival of the police, this can come across as a double victory for the heroes. Not only do the transgressors defer to the vigilante-entrepreneurs' interpretation of the situation; they also change their minds, unlike "real *muzhiki*."

Interestingly, Lion Versus's videos focus much less than those of Stop Rudeness on women as a special type of "villain." This is already indicated by the videos' titles, which do not advertise female villains and their physical attractiveness. Instead, they link public places popular among either young or homeless people with behavior described as "trash" (*bydlo*), "horror," "hell," or "disorder." Stop Rudeness's focus on drivers often means that targets are perceived as economically successful (luxury and middle-class cars mark economic success; poorer urbanites seldom own cars). In contrast, Lion Versus's raids target primarily those who cannot afford to drink in bars and may lack a private space to which to invite friends. Young and poorer people who drink, especially males, thus make up the majority of villains in Lion Versus clips. While female targets are treated more politely than men by the Lion Versus vigilantes, they are nevertheless portrayed as suffering from the same weak character as their male counterparts. An exception to this is the video "I Am Queen" (*Ia koroleva*)[132] which shows a young woman with a deep voice who breaks established gender norms, sometimes deliberately to provoke the Lion Versus vigilantes, who harass her with the camera: she uses obscene language and behaves in a highly sexualized way. The camera focuses almost solely on her, although she is part of a larger group of young people. Close-ups emphasize her non-compliance with the traditional gender binary. The raid leader questions several times whether she is a woman and, in the outro, calls her behavior "devilish"—suggesting that people who do not fit the gender binary or act according to established gender norms are "bad people" and undeserving of respect.

Contrary to the basic schema that strong heroes fight strong villains, the targets of Lion Versus appear less as misbehaving individuals than as social types.[133] As such, they function as visible reminders of what one should not become.[134] The video "Crowd of Trash and VDV" (*Tolpa bydla i VDV*)[135], with over 10 million views, simply thrives on the depiction of middle-aged drunk people during a public holiday in celebration of paratroopers (VDV is short for *Vozdushno-desantnye voiska Rossii*). "There's nothing you can do about such people," Lazutin explains in the middle of the clip; "they've fully lost a human character [*chelovecheskii oblik*]. They don't care at all how they behave and what they do."[136] The villains that Lion Versus vigilantes fight are presented as weak, their conduct as subhuman. A clip uploaded on March 25, 2022, called "Trash yells about Ukraine and Donbass in Moscow's Center!" (*Bydlo oret pro Ukrainu i Donbass v tsentre Moskvy!*)[137], employs the same language to delegitimate criticism of Putin's attack on Ukraine—uttered in the clip by a homeless person who uses several expletives and drinks alcohol—as something only indecent people would do.

It is telling that for Lazutin drinking in public places (which is against the law), swearing (which is mainly, if anything, a moral transgression) and being aggressive (which is only illegal if it involves physical violence or insulting behavior) are all part of the same syndrome—asocial and rude behavior. In another part of the interview with Leonov, he makes it clear that he has no illusions about his targets: "My main goal is not to change the people who we are approaching. A man who is thirty-five years old, swears and drinks . . . I know he might swear at us and maybe even start a fight. He probably drinks alcohol again the next day."[138] Lazutin never reflects on his and his fellow vigilantes' aggressive behavior. He believes that the syndrome of what he identifies as asocial behavior can be effectively fought among youth by *showing* how his own virtue contrasts with the—ultimately unmanly—inconsiderateness and lack of self-discipline of his targets.[139] His contempt for the latter is mixed with despair; their fate seems already to be sealed. People suffering from an addiction to alcohol and homeless people function in Lion Versus clips as visible reminders of what one should not become. Portrayed as *social types*, they symbolize the danger that Russian society may degenerate. In another register as female villains, these categories of people and their stereotypical depiction enables the vigilante-entrepreneurs to seem heroic, manly, and virtuous.

Acting in an exemplary manner and publicly shaming those who are guilty of minor misdemeanors is these groups' strategy to "do good" for Russia. Their self-fashioning as masculine heroes, allegedly serving the community as a whole, justifies their vigilante behavior, including harassment and the instigation of violent encounters. In the self-styled vigilante heroes' moral universe, belligerence can be virtuous, as long as it is instigated by people who, like themselves, know which behaviors are morally correct. The vigilante-entrepreneurs' character work reinforces the gender binary, especially among young people who consume their videos. It stabilizes a patriarchal hierarchy in which men are punished for behavior that can be read as feminine, are responsible for the actions of their wives, mothers, and daughters, and need to prove their masculinity through economic independence. Russian mainstream TV reinforces this character work by reproducing the characterization of women targets as inadequate representatives of their sex and ridiculing them as "missy" or "blonde,"[140] and presents as natural the patriarchal hierarchy inherent in misogynistic language and visuals. This hierarchy helps to legitimate strongman rule and authoritarian aggression as necessary forces to weed out feminine and dependent behavior that might weaken the state—and the economy.

Vigilante Videographers' Enforcement of Flexible Authoritarian Rule

What picture of the world is conveyed by Stop Rudeness's and Lion Versus's video clips; what story do the vigilante brands tell their viewers? They suggest that society's main problems lie in the immorality and indifference of people who are too rich and egoistic, or too poor and apathetic, or who do not behave according to purportedly gender-appropriate norms. The videos thereby obscure larger social ills—a reform deadlock in transport policy, for example, or increasing poverty and its corollaries. By zooming in on the minor transgressions of individuals, they attribute structural problems in Russia and the world to personal choices and apparently innate character types. The vigilante brands' character work has an important ideological function: it shifts responsibility for social ills onto individual citizens. If *everyone* strove to become more moral, caring, and active—this is the brands' moral story—many problems would simply not exist. In this regard, they communicate a similar analysis of the root causes of Russia's social ills as that held by the young campers that we met in Chapter 5, and which informs Russian state youth political programs. The brands also tell the tale of young male heroes whose bravery, incorruptibility, good behavior, and entrepreneurial spirit stand in sharp contrast to the villains' apparent weakness. The vigilante-entrepreneurs' heroic masculinity is constructed in opposition to weak characters—passive, dependent, and frequently changing their minds: traits that are historically associated with femininity and regularly used to characterize welfare states.[141] Again, this juxtaposition of active, resourceful, heroic people with passive and weak others characterizes the vigilantes' self-fashioning as much as that of the young campers I interviewed at the youth-leadership camps.

But how does this relate to Russia's flexible authoritarianism? It chimes with the government's strategy to respond to people's everyday grievances by blaming civil servants' corruption and ordinary people's immoral behavior or reluctance to take responsibility. By portraying heroic masculinity as the antithesis of the alleged problems of dependence and apathy, the vigilante brands perpetuate the myth that masculine strength benefits society at large, and that heroic individuals should be at the helm. Most importantly, they fuse the masculinity and down-to-earth character of the post-Soviet *muzhik* with the—internationally salient—figure of the successful entrepreneur who makes his way to the top against all odds. Rather than appearing as an independent or unpatriotic liberal, however, this entrepreneur is invested in doing good for Russia.

The vigilante brands have succeeded internationally in part because they promote new types of masculinity that fuse the figure of the heroic, combative rebel with that of the successful entrepreneur—a trope with widespread appeal. Many gangster-rappers successfully fashion their personae in a similar way—as outlaws who have achieved fame and economic success in a hostile world. Yet the vigilante brands discussed here are different, in that they promise the possibility of retaining what they define as a virtuous, heroic self by shaming and punishing those who transgress norms while being gentle with "innocent" victims. What is more, through digital diffusion, the brands can incentivize young people to emulate "good" and eschew "bad" social types. They promise their viewers the positive feeling of identifying with today's heroes. They offer international audiences suspenseful, often funny, social media entertainment and allow them to enjoy the moment when alleged transgressors get their "just deserts"—thereby popularizing flexible authoritarian explanations for social ills and remedies to cure them.

Such experiences of schadenfreude are based on psychological processes that dehumanize perceived transgressors.[142] Dehumanization is easier when targets represent categories of people that are often devalued in the context of patriarchy and flexible capitalism.[143] Indeed, as Richard Sennett notes, today's neoliberal regime "treats those who are dependent on the state with the suspicion that they are social parasites, rather than simply helpless."[144]

This contempt for dependent individuals, whether they are regarded as parasites or "trash," is often coupled with a corresponding suspicion of those rich people who are not the originators of their own wealth. Their dehumanization is facilitated by flexible capitalism's celebration of the ideal entrepreneur, who starts from scratch, is independent, takes risks, and succeeds in the face of great challenges. Stop Rudeness and Lion Versus's packaging of authoritarian aggression into brands that offer entertaining do-it-yourself justice are capable of attracting many viewers not only within Russia but, increasingly, beyond Russia's borders, because it chimes with the authoritarian elements of flexible capitalism.

7
Conclusion

Russia's full-scale invasion of Ukraine in February 2022 and the ongoing Russo-Ukrainian war put this book in a new light, requiring that its findings be measured against the shaking of beliefs that have governed Euro-American security politics vis-à-vis Russia since the demise of the Soviet Union. One of the beliefs called into question by Putin's aggressive invasion was that the Russian government would mainly direct its overt authoritarian aggression toward members of the opposition (those not represented in the parliament) and, avoiding escalations that would put the domestic economy at risk, practice only covert aggression against those neighboring states seeking a closer integration with the European Union or NATO. Close economic ties and joint infrastructural projects between Russia and European states, especially with Germany, were continued on the premise that economic interdependency would keep peace and that—despite an increase in Russia's authoritarian practices, systematic suppression of dissent, and increasing conflicts with neighboring sovereign states—the Putin government would not jeopardize economic ties with economically prosperous liberal democracies.

This premise rests on a perspective that construes Russia's policies of economic development, understood by many governments to be rooted in internationally accepted templates and scientific knowledge about emerging economies, as separate from authoritarian restructuring and neotraditional ideals. Neotraditional policies—such as the subjugation of individual rights under what the government claimed were the collective rights of the Russian imperial nation, and the suppression of feminist and LGBTQI organizing to enforce a heterosexual norm—were treated as issues pertaining to a world of cultural values unrelated to that of business.

In contrast, this book's notion of flexible authoritarianism introduces a framework that treats authoritarian-neotraditional restructuring and neoliberal economic modernization as connected. Present-day authoritarianism—not only in Russia, but also in Hungary and China—is often of a flexible nature, combining the expansion of authoritarian practices that systematically sabotage accountability and suppress dissent with attempts to implement an innovation-based development agenda for ensuring long-term economic growth. Notably, the flexible element of this governmental style demands a more active citizenry and a social climate of openness that rewards autonomous thinking and incentivizes an entrepreneurial, can-do spirit—conditions that *seem* at odds with authoritarian expansion. Attempts to implement an innovation-based development agenda rely on certain unquestioned beliefs, such as that of a society populated by entrepreneurial individuals, that are shared by international financial institutions and governments across the globe.[1]

As I argued in the introduction, several theories underpinning the current excitement about innovation-based economies accord with authoritarian thinking. Joseph Schumpeter, in particular, was highly critical of democracy. The democratic ideal of equality clashes with the division of labor and rights that Schumpeter envisaged, which pits innovative geniuses—deserving personal freedom in order to remain creative—against semi-skilled laborers who must be tightly disciplined in order to carry out dull, routine work. Several tenets informing the models of innovation-based development reproduce authoritarian thinking, often tacitly, and such tenets enter contemporary politics. For instance, the latest Hungarian education reform reduces the minimum period of compulsory school attendance, singles out a few talented students to be further educated, and introduces vocational training for the rest. This vocational training is designed to provide multinational companies such as car manufacturers that produce parts in Hungary (an industry dominated by German corporations) with cheap and specifically trained laborers.[2]

In today's re-nationalizing world, it is critical to recognize those transnationally circulating beliefs and cultural forms that legitimate authoritarian values. Directing attention to the role of transnationally held beliefs in the legitimation of authoritarian practices is particularly relevant in studies of Russia and Eastern Europe, where culturally sensitive research has historically been plagued by stereotypes about alleged national cultures that would propel people to support authoritarian leaders.

In Chapters 4 and 6 in particular, I analyzed how authoritarian rule in Russia is legitimized by exploiting the aesthetics, promises, and techniques of cool start-up capitalism. Both the youth-leadership summer camps and the vigilante-entrepreneurs active in the groups Stop Rudeness and Lion Versus employ visual designs and language intended to give these enterprises an air of contemporaneity. Since 2009, if not before, the youth-leadership summer camps, catering to Russia's potential strategic elites, have been designed to keep young, educated, forward-looking people in the country. Their mission is to instill in the country's best brains an optimism for Russia's future and to inculcate in them what I have called entrepreneurial literacy. As I argued in Chapter 4, not only does such literacy foster a business start-up culture, it also lays the foundations for soft governing through incentives. At these camps, young people are motivated to become the co-creators of a government-sponsored civic life and to engage in bottom-up participation—participation that is welcomed by the authorities as long as it does not question the regime's consensus.

The vigilante enterprises Stop Rudeness and Lion Versus exemplify how such government-sponsored civic activity supports the government's neoliberal modernization and neotraditional aims in the form of social media entertainment. Even though the vigilante-entrepreneurs' relationship to the authorities has been more antagonistic since 2016, when they began outing the boorish behavior of influential people such as former Olympic champion Alexei Nemov, their videos, which revolve around the heroic persona of the vigilante-entrepreneur, further a view of the social world that stabilizes the current regime. They suggest that heroic individuals, who are simultaneously patriotic and entrepreneurially spirited, should be at the helm of society. What is more, they shift attention away from systemic flaws and suggest that certain groups of people—those who are not the originators of their own income or wealth—are to blame for Russia's societal dysfunction. The male heroes of the videos, "doing good" for society at large, are styled as successful start-up entrepreneurs. The persona of the heroic vigilante-entrepreneur crafted by these initiatives fuses neotraditional and flexible elements, and combines the down-to-earth masculinity of the post-Soviet "*muzhik*" with the internationally salient figure of the entrepreneur, autonomously making his way up the ladder of wealth and influence against all odds.

What Stop Rudeness and Lion Versus have in common with less controversial examples of government-sponsored civic life—such as student brigades or volunteer initiatives—is their revival of Soviet forms of extracurricular youth activity in a neoliberal spirit. The vigilantes' actions, for example, are reminiscent of the *Komsomol* troops fighting minor misdemeanors and so-called hooliganism during the Soviet period. Their endorsement by top-level politicians owes as much to their ideological stabilization of the regime's neotraditional ideals as it does to the neoliberal ideal that private citizen initiatives should support the state's policing activities. In a similar vein, the revival of the Krasnoyarsk Student Brigades through the business manager-turned-governor Alexander Khloponin in the early 2000s exemplifies how Soviet traditions of extracurricular youth engagement have been reinvigorated for market purposes. As I showed in Chapter 3, local politicians created the student brigades, equipped with Soviet-style uniforms and badges, so that the young labor fighters, as the brigades' participants are called, could develop entrepreneurial skills and work as interns for the region's major companies.

The story of Alexander Khloponin's introduction of neoliberal youth policies to the Krasnoyarsk region testifies to the local enforcement of globally circulating neoliberal templates.[3] It reveals the reductionism of claims that neoliberalism primarily amounts to a force from outside that would destroy local livelihoods, highlighting how such notions neglect the role of local players in supporting neoliberal restructuring. This insight is also true of federal-level politics in Russia that further an agenda of flexibilization with neotraditional means. For this reason, this book cautions against interpreting authoritarian developments in Russia as a backlash against neoliberal capitalism. Instead, as I have shown, flexible authoritarian regimes exploit neoliberal techniques both for market purposes and to diversify their governing techniques.

Another point I make in this book is that a better understanding of authoritarianism requires a study of its social foothold. While much reporting has sought, especially since Russia's invasion of Ukraine in early 2022, to explain Russian politics (and society) through the lens of a ruling dictator, it is crucial to signal the limits of such an approach. As Samuel Greene and Graeme B. Robertson have convincingly argued, the current regime depends on a "social consensus around the inevitability and righteousness of Putin's rule."[4] Hence, especially if we are interested in assessing which tropes and constructs legitimate this regime, our analysis must focus on what is happening beyond the circles of the ruling class—for instance, among the country's potential strategic elites.

My interviews with up-and-coming young people participating in youth-leadership summer camps revealed that they are invested in the idea of developing their region. Campers believed that the standard of living in their localities could be raised by making their region a dazzling economic center and Russia a competitive player on the world market. Even though several interviewees were averse to identifying as patriots of the Russian state, and some were even opposed to Putin, they were generally all motivated to participate in this collective endeavor by pursuing their career plans and realizing small-scale projects or starting their own businesses financed by public grants.

The youths that I interviewed found the government's neotraditional and neoliberal modernization ideals appealing. In their view, becoming a "normal country" would entail elevating Russian citizens' respect for their places of origin and their compatriots, abolishing informal social interactions, and reducing "uncultured" behavior such as drinking, smoking, and (welfare) scrounging. They saw becoming competitive on the world market in terms of scientific-technological development. Though they seldom spelled this out in detail, they associated development primarily with the vision of achieving a contemporary infrastructure and an entrepreneurial start-up culture that would offer them well-paid positions with attractive labor conditions, aesthetic appeal, and relief from monotony.

The majority of interviewees saw a commitment to self-development as quasi-automatically benefiting their local area and the country at large. For them, being active often meant being patriotic, and being a patriot almost necessarily entailed adopting an active stance. The campers that I talked to tied their wishes for development in a patriotic spirit (or patriotism in a developmental spirit) to hopes that the regions they cared about would ultimately allow them to realize their career ambitions and dreams of material well-being. They valued staying at home—not in order to retain Russia's Great Power status, but to be able to lead a life similar to that of the Euro-American middle classes without having to emigrate to more prosperous places. For most of these young people, the essence of patriotism lay in unconditional love for less-developed places, in contrast to what they viewed as superficial "hooray-patriotism"—the waving of flags or pledging of allegiance, unsupported by development-oriented deeds.

As I have underlined, the positions of these potential strategic elites did not preclude severe criticism of the flaws besetting their country, including corruption and favoritism. Nevertheless, neither their project ideas nor their visions of change fundamentally called into question those narratives that legitimate the underlying order of political life in Russia—such as the notion that permanent emigration is unpatriotic, that many of the country's problems result from the passive mentality of average citizens, or that Russia has the unique capacity to rise again and succeed against the odds. Thus, young campers' individualist quests for change remained largely within the boundaries of permitted speech, as policed by the incumbent government, and their hopes for a better life seldom included wishes for greater personal freedom or the inclusion of marginalized people in political processes. In keeping with David Easton's differentiation between specific and diffuse political support, interviewees seldom showed specific support for politicians in office, but their stories did affirm those narratives that legitimate Russia's flexible authoritarian regime as a neotraditional and modernizing one.

This complex combination of criticism and loyalty is exemplified in a detailed Facebook post by a Russian émigré, Katia, regarding difficult conversations with her mother following Russia's full-scale invasion of Ukraine.[5] Katia's mother, who remains in Russia, is subject to the Russian government's official narrative that it would free Ukrainians from fascist occupants supported by Western governments, with the United States as both a new and old enemy leading the way. As Katia stresses, her mother is a Jewish-Russian survivor of the Second World War who "knows about Nazism and how important it is to defeat it." She describes how her mother, anxious about the fate of Ukrainians and believing that her government is rushing to help them through what it frames as a special military operation, has difficulty explaining why there are tanks around Kyiv. "I don't know, Katia," she says. "That's what they say on TV. Why should they be lying?" Her daughter replies, "So why do they [government officials] lie about other things? Are you really content with how they treat you [in Russia]?" Her mother, prompted by Katia's question, goes on to decry the government's stupidity, greed, and dishonesty. Nevertheless, the idea that the Russian army could be waging an aggressive war against a former "brother people"—a term from the Soviet period—appears impossible to Katia's mother, and to others who share a faith in the grand narratives that underpin Russia's regime. The sacralization of the Red Army's victory over German fascism and its inscription into a history of a millennial Russian statehood is a centerpiece of the Putin government's neotraditional symbolic politics.[6] Many in Russia take for granted the notion that the Russian government is a successor to the Soviet one, on the right side of history when it comes to fascism.

On a very different scale, what I have described as a Soviet summer camp tradition also amounts to a taken-for-granted, unquestioned set of beliefs—in this case, one that shapes expectations about the nature of summer camp experience. As I showed in Chapter 4, most campers found the authoritarian organization of the youth-leadership summer camps to be a normal and expected trait of camp life. Their familiarity with typical camp rules shaped their expectations and explains, at least partially, why they did not complain about the strict rules. Similarly, they did not appear irritated by the mismatch inherent in an overall camp organization that required them to be submissive to authority while attending training sessions designed to motivate them to think independently and solve problems creatively, develop a can-do spirit, and take initiative. Sessions that were conducted in a dialogical format and gave campers the impression that their views and opinions counted featured among their most vivid memories—alongside recollections of their fellow campers' zealous enthusiasm about polishing their project proposals and organizing their contributions for an evening competition, or the way a sense of community permeated the party on the last evening of camp. While not a single interviewee mentioned the compulsory calisthenics during morning sports as memorable, many were eager to share with me how the leadership trainings, conversations with like-minded peers, and entertainment had inspired them.

Campers' fascination with the neoliberal-modernization elements of the youth-leadership camps can be attributed to the humanistic heritage underlying motivational theories of self-determination, which are often invoked in forms of training designed to engender initiative. It remains to be seen whether such humanistic seeds, carrying the democratic ideal that humans are capable of self-governing, may be a latent resource for change in today's Russia. They may appear insignificant given the ubiquity of the law-and-order approaches employed by Russian authorities, the severe crackdowns on any form of opposition to the government, and the widespread notion that the hidden nature of power renders social change beyond the community level impossible. Nevertheless, it bears keeping in mind that humanistic beliefs were appealing to those young people who were loyal to the Russian regime (though not necessarily to the government) in the past.

It is unclear whether these seeds might yet bear fruit in a society that the Russian government has attempted, since around 2021–2022, to mobilize in a narrowly nationalist, patriotic, and military fashion. This mobilization accords with the ideals of previously marginal far-right ideologues, marking a radicalization of earlier decades' neotraditional ideals and a clear shift away from a neoliberal modernization agenda that presupposes peace.[7] There is evidence that some of those young people who made a name for themselves as government-loyal activists before Russia's full-scale invasion of Ukraine have been among the first to voluntarily relocate to Russian-occupied territories in that country in order to promote state youth political formats, such as youth-leadership summer camps or student brigades, among young Ukrainians.[8] It also remains to be seen to what extent a war economy—capitalizing on neo-colonial territorial gains in neighboring states and aligning with the government's nationalist and civilizational-imperial ideals—will replace the previous innovation-based development agenda.[9]

APPENDIX I

Methodological Approach and Description of Empirical Research

Following a logic of discovery, the main topic of this study changed during the research process, as I constructed the research object while in the process of learning about the case of government-sponsored youth-leadership summer camps in today's Russia. Appendix I traces this evolution.

My initial research interest concerned the ideological motivation of young adults in government-sponsored youth groups in today's Russia. In what ways did they find Putinist ideology meaningful? How did they connect that ideology with their everyday beliefs? How was it legitimated in their eyes through public stories shared by friends, family, or colleagues?

I began by consulting several academic accounts on the pro-government group *Nashi* ("Those on Our Side") that relied on participant observations at the annual meeting of *Nashi* activists at the federal *Seliger* summer camp.[1] Following the example of these studies, *Seliger* appeared to be an ideal event at which to get in touch with members of government-sponsored youth groups. Besides reading more of the thematically relevant scholarly literature on the topic, I collected information that was available online—on *Nashi* itself and *Seliger*, but especially on various subgroups of *Nashi* that had developed since about 2008. Newspaper articles and YouTube videos posted by activists in these groups were my primary sources of information on the subject. A first insight from preliminary web and literature searches in 2012 and 2013 revealed the existence of several government-sponsored organizations that relied on volunteering or vigilante techniques, portraying themselves as independent from Russian state youth politics and the Putin government yet apparently sharing their ideals.[2]

These web searches were laborious: it was hard to make any sense of the entanglement of those new subprojects within *Nashi* and the themed sessions at the *Seliger* summer camp. Moreover, the web searches also revealed that a number of summer camps similar to *Seliger*, apparently copying its model, were organized on the regional level (for an overview of youth-leadership summer camps across Russia see Appendix II). This partial similarity was discernible via the naming of the events (unmissable, for instance, in the designation *SakhaSeliger*) and the themed sessions or working groups on offer, which often mirrored the naming of *Nashi* subgroups. Existing regional versions of *Seliger* were not part of the academic literature I knew at the time.[3] Regional youth-leadership summer camps appeared to be even more interesting than *Seliger*: Although support for the Putinist government was known to be especially high in the country's provincial regions, existing research on *Seliger* focused on Western Russia and the Tver' Region. Most astonishing to me at the time was the discovery that some provincial youth-leadership summer camps (such as *SakhaSeliger* or *Mashuk*) were designed to garner support for the Putin government among the country's young people of non-Russian nationalities— those Russian citizens who are not ethnic Russians, but whose ancestors had often been subjects of the Russian Empire, the Soviet Union, and the Russian Federation. I came to ask myself how these citizens would perceive the increasingly national tone in government discourse and the rising prejudice against so-called *migranty* (migrants) and blue-collar workers from Central Asia. While *Nashi* had organized alternatives to the nationalist Russian March on the one hand, its activists had also participated in raids against undocumented workers (see also Chapter 6). This discrepancy prompted me to get more familiar with the different currents of nationalism that have structured official politics in Russia since the early 1990s.

The official dissolution of *Nashi* in 2013 had already made it unlikely that I would meet actual members of that organization at the summer camps. However, in the wake of the organization's dissolution, after pondering whether to change the research topic altogether, I decided nevertheless to visit provincial youth-leadership summer camps as a start. At the time it was completely unclear whom I would meet at these camps—party militants, Putinists, careerists, local youth in search of entertainment?[4] I expected to encounter at least some former *Nashi* members or participants in *Nashi* subprojects. I also expected that I would meet young party militants with thick commitments[5] to the ruling party and the incumbent president. I expected that lectures would primarily feature Russia's messianic role in world politics, traditional family values, and praises of Vladimir Putin.

Initial Sampling and Gaining Entrée

Studies following a logic of discovery usually face the challenge of where to begin. Though theoretical sampling is often mentioned as a feature of such studies, consciously sampling on the dependent variable (what is to be explained in the study) is only possible after that variable is known. To put it another way, a detective aiming to uncover what she initially perceived as theft might suddenly find herself investigating a family feud. Only after she identifies that theft is an epiphenomenon of family feud will she be able to adapt her collection of evidence accordingly.

The same is true for theoretical sampling, which can never start at the beginning of a study. Theoretical sampling presupposes knowing what a case "is a case of."[6] Nevertheless, one needs to start gathering evidence somewhere. Thus, initial sampling means developing a plan that will necessarily be overturned. As outlined above, I received the ideas and sensitizing concepts for my initial sample from existing literature, web searches, and news coverage. In accordance with the information I could obtain, my initial sampling was based on the assumptions that:

- my units of analysis are clearly bounded government-sponsored youth groups with a relatively stable constituency
- (former) members of government-sponsored youth groups constitute the bulk of campers at youth-leadership summer camps in the regions
- regional subgroups of *Nashi* (or at least former *Nashi* groups which had been 'rebranded' after the organization's official dissolution) are present at youth-leadership summer camps, along with young people affiliated with *Molodaia Gvardiia Edinoi Rossii* (the youth wing of the ruling party United Russia), or young adults who are active in similar types of organizations existing on the regional level
- straightforward political lectures dominate the educational input at government-sponsored youth-leadership summer camps

These assumptions also informed my decisions regarding gaining entrée to the field of government-sponsored youth groups. Emulating the approach of other researchers, I planned to acquire a first empirical overview by participating in regional youth-leadership summer camps. Instead of visiting *Seliger*, I chose to compare two provincial summer camps.[7]

I selected regional youth-leadership summer camps to visit on the basis of several theoretical and practical criteria:

- Choosing sites in different major territorial units in the Russian Federation—that is, the Urals, Eastern Siberia, and the Russian Far East (I excluded Moscow, St. Petersburg and Western Russia, which are extremely well studied)[8]
- Avoiding regions in the chosen territorial units that are comparatively well researched (e.g. Novosibirsk)
- Applying only to camps *without* a special session for international participants, because I wanted to get in touch with local young adults
- Ensuring that session schedules allowed for travel from one camp to the other
- Favoring summer camps and themed sessions that took place after the end of the German semester—that is, in July—to allow me to accomplish my course work
- Favoring summer camps that confirmed my participation early on (participation required a successful application), enabling me to book flights as soon as possible

I expected that participating as a foreign PhD student with an interest in youth activism in Russia would be rather difficult. Yet all I had to do was to fill in online application forms and suggest an idea for a project I would like to realize, one that fit the themed session or the working group. I stated in my application's cover letter that I was pursuing a PhD and that my aim was to get an idea about the summer camps and youth activism beyond the headlines of Western news coverage. I also emphasized my previous research on youth activism in the US and Germany.

In the summer of 2013, I applied to three regionally-based youth-leadership summer camps:

- *TIM Biriusa* (meaning "Territory of Youth Taking Initiative *Biriusa*") in the Siberian Federal District, *Krasnoiarskii Krai*
  Themed session (*smena*): Civic Society and Volunteering
  Working group (*napravlenie*): Civic Society
  Dates: July 12–17, 2013
- *UtroUral* 2013 in the Ural Federal District, *Sverdlovskii Oblast'*
  Working group: Patriotic and political Ural
  Dates: July 13–17, 2013
- *SakhaSeliger* in the Far East Federal District, Republic of Sakha, Yakutia
  Working group: Politics
  Dates: July 19–27, 2013

In case applications to these regional youth-leadership summer camps were rejected, I also applied to the federal camp

- *Seliger* in the Central Federal District, *Tverskaia Oblast'* (Federal Level Status)
  Themed Session: Civic Forum
  Dates: July 28–August 5, 2013

I applied mainly for sessions and study groups devoted to civic society and politics, because I expected (former) members of *Nashi* mainly to visit those sessions or working groups.

I received the first acceptance letter from the organizers of *TIM Biriusa* and decided to partake in that session, which practically precluded my participation in *UtroUral*. In the end, I received acceptance letters in response to all four applications. Finally, I decided to participate in *TIM Biriusa* and *SakhaSeliger* in summer 2013.

Ethical Considerations Regarding My Participation in Youth-Leadership Summer Camps

Sociologist Kristin Luker notes that interview researchers and participant observers are, in the first place, a cost to organizations, and not a benefit:

> I take for granted that no organization, like no human being, lives up to its ideals all of the time. Organizations, like people, cut corners. But would you want someone checking out your closets and kitchen drawers to see how clean they are? That, in essence, is what you are proposing to do when you ask an institution to let you come in and hang around.[9]

Yet I suppose that in the case of the summer camps, this unwritten rule does not apply. Contrary to expectations, the organizers appeared very happy to welcome foreign participants. As I understood later, and especially when conducting interviews with organizers, the participation of (Western) foreigners was widely regarded as an asset. Their presence gives the events an international image, which arguably makes them more interesting for local young adults, especially in places where one would not regularly meet a young person from a Western country.

Moreover, given that the youth-leadership summer camps—also contrary to my expectations—had much in common with business trainings and summits for young leaders, hosting international participants heightened the events' modern image. For sure, being a university researcher from a Western European country probably made a huge difference with regard to the welcome I received from organizers; a factory worker from Turkmenistan might have met with quite a different reception. So, given my status as a Western foreigner with a university degree, my participation seemed to be beneficial for representational purposes. At *SakhaSeliger* that summer, my participation had been advertised on the camp's social media pages.

In 2013, when I embarked on my first field trip to *TIM Biriusa* and *SakhaSeliger*, my research question was not yet finalized, nor did I plan to write an ethnographic account about the behavior of campers at youth-leadership summer camps. In my application letter to the organizers, I had openly stated the reason for my participation—that I was a PhD researcher who was interested in youth activism in the Russian regions and had heard of the regional versions of the *Seliger* camp. I had emphasized my experience as an observer of youth activism in Germany and the United States. At the time, my intention was to get in touch with (former) members of *Nashi* or similar government-sponsored groups on the local level. I was already planning to build the study primarily on in-depth interviews with activists, focusing on how they interpreted their activism and their participation in government-sponsored youth groups.

My main concern about my participation in the camps in July and August 2013 was that I lacked a proper affiliation with a Russian university at that time. My official affiliation with a Russian university, the Russian State University for the Humanities (*RGGU*), began only in the fall of that year, in combination with an Erasmus scholarship for PhD students. Receiving a research visa only for the summer months was difficult, given that my contacts had written me an invitation letter for the fall, when the Erasmus Mundus Mobility Program, which was connected to a cooperation with the Russian State University for the Humanities, started. Thus, I could only obtain a tourist visa. More precisely, I feared that my lack of a research visa could lead to an official complaint about my not possessing the correct visa for conducting research at the youth-leadership summer camps. Such a complaint could have jeopardized my reception of the research visa for fall (when I planned to be conducting interviews), or even the prospect of receiving future research visas at all. In hindsight, I think it's unlikely that negative consequences would have arisen from a mismatch between my juridical status and a cover letter to the organizers describing my participation as a "participant observation." The overall attitude of organizers was indeed very welcoming. This was affirmed in 2014, when I conducted interviews with some of them and distributed the description of my research project as part of the informed-consent letter.

At the time, though, I found it safer simply to describe my research interest, rather than a not-yet-existing, full-fledged research project, in my cover letter. (*Nashi* had been dissolved as an organization a few months before my visit in 2013, so my initial project idea had been negated by *Nashi*'s dissolution and was now up in the air.) Thus, I decided to introduce myself only as a PhD student with a research interest in youth activism in Russia.

Kristin Luker continues her discussion about gaining entrée with a strong ethical caveat never to do research on individuals without their active consent:

> Both Human Subjects Committees and good manners insist that you must never do research on individual people without getting their permission ahead of time. (To go back to the closet and drawers metaphor, think how you would feel if you walked into your own bedroom during a party and found one of the guests rifling through your sock and underwear drawers. That sense of betrayal should give you a taste of how betrayed organizations and individuals feel when you study them under false pretenses).[10]

Keeping this in mind, whenever meeting new people, I introduced myself as a PhD researcher with an interest in youth activism and youth-leadership summer camps; I did not enter the field to observe the campers without their knowledge. For this reason, when I depict the summer-camp experience from the viewpoint of campers, I do not draw on my observations of campers' behavior at the sites, but on the interviews I conducted with them in 2014. For those conversations, all interviewees had been thoroughly informed beforehand about the study and had given their human-subject consent to being interviewed.

However, I did not refrain from making use of observations concerning the words and behavior of lecturers and VIP guests, as well as observations regarding the general organization of the youth-leadership summer camps. Unlike rank-and-file campers, the staff, lecturers, and VIP guests attended the forum as professionals or public personae, who intended their words to be heard, not only locally but also on TV broadcasts. Moreover, staff, teachers, and guests were accommodated in special tents or rooms, had private sanitary installations for their use, and did not share meals with me, so I had few opportunities in any case to observe them in private moments.

Yet, for sure, my informal talks with campers in 2013 and the impressions gained via my visits to the youth-leadership summer camps as a rank-and-file participant heavily influenced the further course of my research. In particular, my impression that it was not young people with thick political commitments who attended the summer camps, but rather average young adults with ambitions who were loyal to the regime, shaped my framing of this study. From an investigation of activists in pro-government youth groups, it turned into an inquiry into the ambiguity and complexity of loyalty to the political status quo in Russia.[11]

Another ethical aspect that must be discussed is the sponsoring of a flight from Moscow to Yakutsk and back in 2013. During the application process for the *SakhaSeliger* camp, I accidentally *posted* my application on the web page. I had intended only to submit the document for a second time, but had clicked the wrong button. There was no possibility of deleting the post. It included my cover letter, my full name and my institutional affiliation. A few days later I received a message via the social network *Vkontakte* asking whether I wanted to participate in *SakhaSeliger*. The sender was a former trainer at the Yakutian School for Public Administration (*Institut upravleniya pri prezidente Respubliki Sakha, Iakutiia*). After I confirmed that I was, indeed, interested in attending *SakhaSeliger*, he replied that I could participate and even join the official delegation of teachers from Moscow. They would be flown in with a charter flight from Moscow and I could join them for no cost. After discussing the issue in my supervisor's research colloquium, I agreed to take the flight—but I think it important to consider why it might have been offered to me. One possibility is that my participation was regarded as an asset. Besides the official announcement of my visit on *SakhaSeliger*'s social media page, a variety of local journalists, but also the camp site's media team, were eager to conduct interviews with me. As stated above, foreign participants made for a good advertisement. Another possible explanation is that I received the initial *Vkontakte* message because the trainer had just opened a youth hostel in Moscow and was looking for potential guests to stay there. He sent me an invitation to join the *Vkontakte* group of the hostel, and, several times, sent an advertisement for the place (I did not stay at this hostel in Moscow though). My personal guess is that the two reasons complemented each other: The sponsoring of a flight ticket did not bother the organizers and my presence was a good form of advertisement; and the hostel owner—probably having good connections to the organizers—wanted to advertise his hostel with a potential guest who might recommend his new place to people in Western Europe.

A final clarification I need to make concerns an article about my participation in *SakhaSeliger* in 2013, published in the Sakha-language newspaper *Eder Saas*.[12] As I mentioned above, there was a huge interest in my person when I arrived at the camp site which I had not expected. Besides not being able to remain in the background as I had planned, I was also concerned about my visa status, and was therefore not interested in attracting too much attention from the authorities. Due to these insecurities, I tried to keep interviews with external journalists to a minimum. The supposed interview with me that was published in *Eder Saas* a few days after my arrival actually never took place. The author of the interview claims that I did not speak Russian and that my translator had answered the questions. Although the possibility might be very slim that someone will ever read this newspaper article, I nevertheless would like to clarify that I did speak (and more importantly understood) Russian at the time, and that I visited *SakhaSeliger* without a translator. Two campers, the same two who showed me the article, orally translated it for me from Sakha to Russian. I was shocked that someone had simply fabricated a story about me, but one of these campers reassured me that things like that were just normal in Russia and that I should not worry.

Surprises and Consequences: My Participation in *TIM Biriusa* and *SakhaSeliger* in 2013

The classical literature on participant observation stems from anthropology and ethnology. The ethnographic method traditionally involves studying an entire society or ethno-linguistic group by observing and participating in daily life, routines, and rituals.[13] Ethnographers usually study whatever is happening in the field.[14] Sociologists who employ participant observation are instead interested in observing micro processes, exploring macro-theoretical questions on the ground, or studying a specific milieu.[15] Though more and more anthropologists are now departing from classic approaches to ethnographic research, the main difference between the two disciplines may lie in the significance of giving a holistic depiction of a setting. Sociologists prioritize the analysis of specific phenomena and processes and care less for holistic description.[16] The same is true for the present study.

From the onset of my participation, it became clear that several of my initial assumptions had been wrong: Most of the campers were not organized in pro-government organizations akin to *Nashi*, but were in fact university students who did not appear to be deeply committed members of pro-government youth groups. I had expected to meet party militants, but the observations I made in the summer camps indicated a more complicated texture of loyalty to the government and the regime.

Apart from some members of the ruling party's youth wing, most campers at *Biriusa* were members of their universities' student unions or councils, so-called student brigades, or the local youth parliament, or else they had been involved with the municipal youth centers in their city district's or town's youth center. Apparently, some had only registered with a youth center in order to receive a permit for participation in the summer camp (*putevka*). The impression that there were very few members of pro-government groups or former *Nashi* members among campers was substantiated at *SakhaSeliger*. My working group "Politics" (*Politika*) was by far the most political of the working groups present. Other working groups included "Youth of the Countryside" (*Molodezh sela*), "Innovation and Invention" (*Innovatsii i izobretatel'stvo*), "Run With Me" (*Begi za mnoi*), "Art Square" (*Art kvadrat*) and "Youth Entrepreneurship" (*Molodezhnoe predprinimatel'stvo*). Yet besides a few who were active in the ruling party's youth wing, even the campers who had chosen this working group appeared not to be participants of any stable pro-government organizations. Very few, in fact, seemed to be fully committed supporters of the incumbent government. Again, most campers at *SakhaSeliger* were active in student groups and youth clubs, often with a focus on practicing *Sakha* traditions if they were studying outside the borders of the Sakha Republic. At both events, I heard no boisterous statements regarding love for Putin, the ruling party, or the like. There was, for once conforming to my expectations, also no resounding or open critique of the political elite.

The most surprising discovery at the two youth-leadership summer camps was that most educational inputs were reminiscent of self-development trainings and introduced the basics of project management. Presentations about positive thinking and self-improvement were far more dominant than lectures or speeches concerned with Russian patriotism, Putin's rule, or Russia's role in the world. Self-development trainers made up a large part of the teaching staff. And several of the trainings and recommendations for self-improvement—including time management—reminded me of the soft-skills workshops I could attend at the graduate school of my home university. Equally, the symbolic scenery at *Biriusa* was akin to that of innovation hubs and business start-ups. The ways in which teaching staff conducted workshops and lectures had little to do with the chalk-and-talk approach that is common at many facilities of higher education in Russia. Rather, the lectures and workshops employed various means to let everyone participate and create an atmosphere of empowerment. They thus mirrored forms of activation that have been analyzed by scholars of neoliberal governmentality.[17] I was most astonished that the big silver letters affixed in the hallway of the Krasnoyarsk state-funded autonomous institution (*gosudarstvennoe avtonomnoe ucherezhdenie*) called Center of Youth Initiatives "Forum" (*Tsentr molodezhnykh initiativ "Forum"*), which organized *TIM Biriusa*, displayed a quotation not from Vladimir Putin, but from Apple founder Steve Jobs.[18]

Regarding the general conduct of the summer camps, however, it struck me that the strict rules and the daily routine stood in sharp opposition to the innovation-hub feeling of the overall events. Some rules seemed simply arbitrary to me, others fully incomprehensible. Why would we need to wear badges visibly all the time, even when just going to take a shower? Why were only women, and not all campers independent of gender, advised to wear "proper" swimming clothes at the beach? Why could we not go swimming during the whole day, just because the governor was visiting in the afternoon? Why weren't we supposed to leave the campsite even to go for a walk? Why were we expected to stick to our (sub)groups? Though informal talks with other campers revealed quite a bit of variance of opinion on political and societal topics, the acceptance of strict rules, arbitrary changes of regulations, and predefined gender roles at the camp sites appeared to be universal and unequivocal. Campers seemed also to be fully at ease with the hierarchical setup of our group (descending from the leader of the group to instructors on different levels) and the routine of the day. They seemed completely comfortable with the camps' over-regulated organizational and pedagogical style.

In light of these observations, the direction of my study changed considerably. An early decision was to shift the focus from activists in pro-government groups to campers at youth-leadership summer camps. Most campers were, contrary to my expectations, not members of politically organized pro-government groups akin to *Molodaia Gvardiia Edinoi Rossii* or *Nashi*, but rather part of organizations and clubs that are indirectly or directly sponsored through state institutions such as city governments, universities, or state youth political programs. A central aim of my new focus was to better understand the nature of campers' loyalty to Russia's government, political status quo, and regime— that is, to the underlying order of political life. Moreover, I became more interested in the youth-leadership summer camps as cultural forms. On the one hand, these seemed to be establishments where young people applied what they had come to see as "normal" rules of behavior at official events. Why did everyone know, and at least superficially accept, these unwritten rules? On the other hand, these establishments were interesting to me as sites where neoliberal modernization and neotraditional ideals promoted by the Putin government became tangible. Their educational content, show and entertainment elements, and strict rules of behavior (which stood in sharp contrast to the horizontal teaching methods) testified to an entanglement of classic authoritarianism and neoliberal logics.

Theoretical Sampling, Comparisons of Summer-Camp Styles, and Cultural Insider's Support

At this point, I started to sample *theoretically*. Kathy Charmaz recommends starting with theoretical sampling when preliminary categories have emerged and can be further developed.[19] Studies following a logic of discovery do not share the concern of mirroring as exactly as possible the distribution of categories in a general population. Theoretical sampling means, on the contrary, consciously sampling on the dependent variable. This is quite logical, because the goal of this kind of research is to explain distinct outcomes. Therefore, the researcher deliberately selects cases in which these outcomes do occur.[20] The aim of theoretical sampling is to determine where and how data can be obtained that might be conducive to understanding one's (shifting) conundrum. According to Charmaz, "engaging in theoretical sampling prompts you to predict where and how you can find needed data to fill gaps and to saturate categories."[21]

My decision to change the focus of the analysis was also a decision to investigate further why my perception of rules and hierarchies did not at all match the perceptions of fellow campers. This discrepancy would be expectable in a setting where thick political commitments prevailed among campers; but because campers' political commitments turned out to be of a thin quality, I found it in need of explanation.[22] I gained some insight into this matter when, during my stays in Moscow, where I was affiliated with the Russian State University for the Humanities, an acquaintance called my attention to the *similarities* of the rules and procedures common at youth-leadership camps to those she knew from her work as an educator at children's leisure camps.

In order to find out which of the observed rules and regulations were specific for the youth-leadership summer camps, I decided to visit a children's summer camp organized by the Russian Union for Railway Workers and also participated in a multi-day gathering of Siberia-based groups of the *Leninskii Komsomol*, the youth wing of the Russian Federation's Communist Party (*KPRF*). By means of the comparison, I wanted to find out which features of the youth-leadership camps were specific to these establishments and which were commonly assumed to be part of a summer camp.

My acquaintance organized a visit to the children's leisure camp for one day in June 2014. Organizing my participation in a gathering of the *Leninskii Komsomol* was more complicated. There was information available about previous years' gatherings, but no announcements of future meetings. As I learned later, dates and meeting places are deliberately published *after* the events. Apparently, this practice results from concerns that meetings could be prohibited or disturbed by regional government or rival political formations. Again, access was made possible by existing contacts: a Russian American friend happened to have relatives close to the Communist Party of the Russian Federation (*KPRF*). I contacted the regional Russian Federation's Leninist Communist Youth League (*Leninskii kommunisticheskii soiuz molodezhi Rossisskoi Federatsii, LKSM RF*) in Krasnoyarsk, as the party's youth wing is called, with a support letter from a former member of the *KPRF*, and asked for permission to join their gathering, which would be taking place near Omsk in July 2014.

Throughout the field research and data analysis, I was preoccupied with questions about the degree to which my observations were case-specific or occurred more generally in Russian society—questions that bear on the findings' social relevance: how did my observations relate to Russian citizens' average opinions? While surveys existed on average opinions about issues such as immigration from Central Asia to Russia, there were hardly any data regarding obedience to authority or the acceptance of hierarchies and strict, often arbitrary, rules (and even less about the beliefs on which such acceptance is based).

Such preoccupation with the distribution of a phenomenon connects to a feeling that is common among field researchers: the fear of not being able to do justice to the material one collects as a cultural outsider. Anthropologist Barbara Myerhoff shared her concerns over not being knowledgeable enough, not being the right person to do the kind of research she wanted to conduct:

> In the beginning phases of my work with the elderly I too suffered severe pangs of guilt. At first it focused on questions concerning my competence in the task I was embarking upon. Did I know enough Judaica? Did I know enough Yiddish? Was I too young? Was I too emotionally involved? Should I be working for the old people's welfare instead of studying them? and the like.[23]

Similar self-doubt accompanied my field research, starting from the question of whether my Russian-language skills were good enough and the recognition that I was not knowledgeable about Sakha culture. I also asked myself whether it would not have been better to do research only on members of the youth wings of the ruling party and that of the *KPRF*—an approach that would have allowed me to deal with clearly bounded categories of actors and compare them. However, with time I became convinced that studying loyalty in its complexity among people who are not party militants was key to making sense of the reproduction of political power in today's Russia. Conversations with acquaintances and colleagues, as well as attempts to read more about, for instance Sakha cultural traditions, were key to resolving such concerns.

Talks with acquaintances such as the educator (whose comments led me to visit the children's summer camp in *Kratovo*) significantly affected how I interpreted my field experiences in relation to average beliefs in Russian society. Similar encounters and exchanges were enormously helpful to put my observations and hunches in perspective. For example, my short stay with my Krasnoyarsk couch-surfing host in 2013, before I participated in *Biriusa*, illuminated the fact that the small talk in local bars differed little from that among the campers at the youth-leadership summer camp. In both cases, the hot topics to discuss with a visitor from Western Europe were the whistle-blower Edward Snowden, who was staying at a Moscow airport at the time; the legalization of same-sex marriage in Europe (at a time when Russia had introduced a law criminalizing the visibility of same-sex relationships), and the activist-punk group Pussy Riot's staging of a prayer that protested the Russian Orthodox Church's support for the Putin government in Moscow's Cathedral of Christ the Savior. Thus, insiders such as the Moscow-based former educator at children's' summer camps and my couch surfing host played, at least temporarily, a role similar to that of the informant Shmuel in Myerhoff's study. She characterized Shmuel as having been her "teacher, critic and guide,"[24] a characterization that aptly describes my relationship to these people. In the course of the research, a whole range of individuals took on that role, with varying influence and for quite dissimilar time spans. What they all had in common was that they were, on the one hand, insiders, in that they had lived in Russia for most of their lives, and yet they were interested in explaining and differentiating between social conventions and political changes. Contrasting their opinions with mine amounted to a theoretical engagement with my observations. My conversations with these cultural insiders were marked by switching back and forth between observational and explanatory units, a method called comparative by Charles Ragin.[25]

I also learned a great deal from Russian acquaintances' childhood summer-camp memories as well as from their accounts of other experiences—for example, of living through the 1990s in a poor Russian province, dwelling in student homes in the early 2000s, or experiencing the social hierarchies in Russian society. In particular, conversations with fellow PhD students who had emigrated to the US and Western Europe but had grown up in Russia, and were, like me, visiting the country to conduct field research, helped me to translate my more promising theses into social-scientific categories and ponder their relevance to ongoing debates. Not least, staying as a guest researcher at the student home of the Russian State University for the Humanities provided me with valuable experiences relating to the authoritative style of conduct in institutions of higher education and their adjunct student homes—such as the authoritarian-command style of communication practiced by our floor's female resident assistant, a position that is called, aptly, commandant (*komendantsha*) in Russia.

So, although the actual participant observation for this study was restricted to youth-leadership summer camps, my outsider status prompted me to compare my data implicitly with daily experiences during my two long-term research stays in Moscow at the Russian State University for the Humanities and during the shorter stays in Central and Eastern Siberia.[26] Conversations with individuals who acted as teachers and critics led me to discard or modify my developing theses. These people provided me with the background information necessary to abandon old convictions and seek new ones in a context they knew much better than I did. This is why my analyses of the summer camps and campers' narratives draw on some of these observations from outside the narrower field of youth-leadership camps.

Semistructured In-Depth Interviews

A key thesis I derived from my first participant observation in the two youth-leadership summer camps in 2013 was that these establishments intended to promote both neoliberal modernization and neotraditional ideals among campers. Such ideals entailed expectations for young Russian citizens' behavior and ideological orientation. Campers appeared well acquainted with such expectations *prior* to their departure to camp, a fact reflected in the research question that I developed on the basis of the 2013 observations: How do campers at youth-leadership summer camps relate to the government's neoliberal modernization and neotraditional ideals?

This research question formed the basis of my interview guide. Through in-depth interviewing I wanted to learn how young campers understood and framed their participation in the youth-leadership summer camps, but also in university clubs, youth parliaments, student brigades, and other extra-curricular activities. How did such experiences relate to their understandings of self and society? And what did recurring concepts such as "activism," "improvement," and "development" mean to them?

While I treat interviews as highly subjective accounts of reality, as "stories about what the person being interviewed *thinks* happened, or thinks *should* have happened, or even *wanted* to have happened,"[27] I hold that this methodological tool can reveal meaningful patterns. In other words, interview data elucidate more than the subjective view of an individual person; they show what kind of thinking is common among many people and therefore is of a social quality. In the words of Kristin Luker:

> The point of interviews, however, is not what is going on inside one person's head, but what is going on inside lots of people's heads. When you hear the same thing from people all over the country who don't know one another, you can be reasonably sure that you are tapping into something that is reliably social and not just individual.[28]

Thus, my aim was to compare many interview narratives and to understand which beliefs were widely shared among campers even though they had never met or, in some cases, never met until they encountered each other at camp.[29]

The Interview Guide and Recruitment of Interviewees

When I speak of semistructured interviews, I do not have in mind what Robert Weiss calls "fixed question, open response" interviews, which are closer to surveying.[30] I mean interviews that leave room for debate, meaning-making, and interviewees' priorities,[31] but are subtly directed by an interview guide that has been carefully crafted by the interviewer beforehand. By interview guide I mean, following Weiss, "a listing of areas to be covered in the interview along with, for each area, a listing of topics or questions that together will suggest lines of inquiry."[32] In contrast to question-response interviewing, this approach allowed me to re-order subject areas and questions in a way that was conducive to building rapport with interviewees. Likewise, it allowed me to change the wording of questions—for instance, to pick up on a particular term or saying used by the interviewee. While in theory I aimed to cover all of the subject areas laid out in the interview guide, I prioritized building rapport with interviewees and leaving them room to develop their thoughts.

I constructed the interview guide on the basis of the observations I had made at the youth-leadership summer camps in 2013. I also relied heavily on existing social-scientific analyses of Russian public and governmental discourse, most significantly on political scientist Olga Malinova's analyses of symbolic politics and public discourse in Russia, which she published in a Russian-language volume in 2013.[33] Reading discourse researchers' analyses, I came to realize how closely the setup and content of the youth-leadership summer camps replicated key themes of government discourse and their seeming contradictions, such as the combination of tradition and modernization. Given my ethical concerns about the participant observations in 2013, the interview guide also included questions about campers' evaluations of their camp experience. This way, it was possible to include their voices in my analysis of the summer camp without drawing on my 2013 field notes.

After introducing myself and presenting the research project, I informed interviewees about the confidential and anonymous handling of the data and asked them to sign the human-subject consent form. Given that almost all interviewees were (former) campers, my first question was usually how they had first heard about the camp. The remainder of the interview guide covered the following subject areas:

1. **Campers' experiences with and definition of activism and their evaluation of today's society**

Their participation in voluntary organizations, local or student self-government, youth political programs such as youth parliaments or student brigades, their project ideas, and their definition of "activism" (when they used the term). Questions interrogating what irritates campers about today's society and what should be done to change society for the better

2. **Campers' camp experience**
Summer camp participation as extra-curricular education/as springboard for one's career, summer camp as a cultural form, campers' relationship among each other and to teaching staff; their views on leisure, education, and the camp's *Erziehungsstil* (organizational and pedagogical style)

3. **Campers' understanding of politics and sources of information (media)**
How they understand "politics"; preferred ways to obtain information, habits of media consumption. How they draw the line between political and nonpolitical issues

4. **Campers' identification with place, nationality and/or Russia**
Views on emigration/the preferred place to live, explanations of the term patriotism, campers' relationship to their nationality and to people of other nationalities

5. **Campers' assessments of the past**
Their assessments of important historical events and periods (especially the Great Patriotic War and the 1990s, due to these periods' significance for the legitimation of Putinist rule)

6. **Campers' notions of a happy and morally correct life and their plans for the future**
Dreams of self-realization and future (career) plans, visions of the ideal family, questions on sex education (who should teach it to young people)

The final or cooling-down part of the interview concerned campers' prior experiences at other youth-leadership summer camps or children's summer camps. My very last question was always whether they wanted to add or correct anything.

After the interview I handed out a survey that inquired into interviewees' sociostructural situation (age, gender, and ethno-linguistic identification; education, occupation, and income)—information that would allow me to detect any pronounced patterns with regard to these markers during the analysis. I constructed this survey drawing on examples from the Centre for Youth Studies at the St. Petersburg branch of the Higher School of Economics, and with the kind support of sociologist Ivan Klimov at the Moscow branch of the Higher School of Economics.[34]

I used a similar interview guide and survey—adjusted to the person's occupational position, the extent of their involvement with youth-leadership summer camps, and the nature of our prior contact—for interviewing teaching staff, summer camp organizers, and youth political officials. For those interviewees, the warming-up and cooling-down questions differed: I asked either about the person's typical workday or about her or his professional biography. I usually started the cooling-down part of those interviews by asking for a general evaluation of youth-leadership summer camps. I had obtained contacts with teaching staff, organizers, and youth political officials either from personal meetings at the camp site or by contacting them via email.

The selection of interviewees largely took place through my participation in the summer camps, but also through snowball sampling—that is, asking people I interviewed to refer me to any acquaintances who had been campers or organizers at youth-leadership camps and would be willing to talk to me.

Regarding the regional comparison, my selection of interviewees was influenced by local specificities. In early 2014, I realized that it would be beyond my capabilities to travel to the homes of interviewees who lived in the Sakha Republic's remote villages, given the region's vast extent and infrastructural limitations. In order to arrive at a less biased city-village sample, having asked and received the organizers' permission, I decided to participate in *SakhaSeliger* for a second time in 2014 in order to conduct interviews at the camp site. At the 2014 *SakhaSeliger* I did my best to recruit participants from most of the various working groups in order to discern any significant differences among them, given that I had mostly gotten to know people from the working group "Politics" in the previous year. In 2014, I decided for the same reason to apply for the "Volunteering" working group, rather than the most political working group, "We Are (Multinational) Russians," which replaced the 2013 "Politics" group.

My participation in the gathering of Siberian *Leninskii Komsomol* groups, the youth wings of local chapters of the *KPRF*, in Omsk in 2014 was very revealing: Many Krasnoyarsk-based members of the *KPRF*'s youth wing had also participated in *Biriusa*. Thus, several interviewees from the Krasnoyarsk Region were not only campers at *Biriusa*, but in some way related to the local *Leninskii Komsomol* group. The secretary for ideology of the Central Committee of the *KPRF* youth wing, who visited the Omsk gathering for two days, explained to me that the party's general policy was to use the youth-leadership summer camps as forums to popularize the *KPRF*'s ideology among young people.

The Interviews in Numbers and Sociostructural Data on Interviewees

All interviews with both *SakhaSeliger* campers and *Biriusa* campers were conducted in the summer of 2014. The interviews, including several breaks, lasted between 50 minutes and three hours. The longer durations were an exception, and usually involved group interviews. While I usually invited interviewees to a coffee place (one I knew to be relatively quiet), such places were hard to find for evening meetings. An advantage of interviewees recommending places they liked—such as a local bar or pub—was, however, that they very much enjoyed being there, shifting more quickly into a talkative mode. This facilitated their forgetting about the recording, informed consent, and other formal aspects of the interview setting. Those interviews I conducted during the 2014 *SakhaSeliger* were much easier to organize, though sometimes, because we were often sitting outside, the wind or other noises lowered the quality of the recording.

This sense of greater convenience for the interviewees was one of the reasons why I tried to conduct group interviews whenever possible. Unlike in focus-group interviews, the compositions of these groups were not deliberately created by me; rather, they emerged when people suggested bringing along friends who remembered me as a fellow 2013 camper. Sometimes, a friend who had not attended camp was simply interested in joining. Another benefit of conducting group interviews was to check whether the conversation in this setting would differ significantly from the one-on-one interviews with me, the foreign interviewer. (I did not observe any striking differences.) Finally, group interviews allowed debates to play out among interviewees, revealing a heterogeneity of opinions and convictions.

In total, the interview data collected through interviewing campers amounts to a corpus of twenty-three texts, of which ten are based on group interviews and thirteen on one-on-one interviews. Twenty of the thirty-six interviewees were from the Sakha Republic (though some of those interviewees were studying in other Russian cities), sixteen from the Krasnoyarsk Region. Given that some interviews were conducted during the summer camps themselves, in two cases the boundaries between one-on-one interview and group interview became blurred when a friend of the interviewee joined in. I always informed those who joined about the interview and the tape recording. Unfortunately, I accidentally deleted two interview recordings on the digital recorder during the 2014 *SakhaSeliger* summer camp. Although I discovered the loss right after the deletion (after the second interview that day) and was able to write down all major points in memory minutes, any possibility of a verbatim analysis of the interviewees' stories and the expressions they used was lost.

Of the thirty-five interviewees who completed the participant survey, twenty-five were between eighteen and twenty-four years old during the interview, and ten between twenty-four and thirty-one years old. Sixteen interviewees stated that they were female, nineteen male. The majority of interviewees were not married; few had children. Most interviewees from the Sakha Republic identified as Sakha, most of those from the Krasnoyarsk Region as ethnic Russians. Only five interviewees stated that they were religious non-believers (though two others wrote that they believed in science and free thought). Most of the Sakha interviewees stated that they practiced the Sakha religion (sometimes mixed with Christian-Orthodox beliefs) and twelve of the Krasnoyarsk interviewees stated that they were religious (nine Christian-Orthodox, two Muslim and one "multi-religious.") Most interviewees stated that their own or their family's income sufficed for food, clothes, and household appliances, but not for buying a car, an apartment, or a house.

One should be cautious with regard to interpreting the data on income. It is unclear to what extent interviewees counted themselves as belonging to the household of their parents. Moreover, it could well be the case that their answers were influenced by the social desirability of appearing affluent.

Of the interviews with youth political officials as well as with teaching staff, all but one took place in the form of one-on-one interviews. Two interviews with teaching staff were conducted via Skype, because the teachers lived in other parts of Russia (far from Moscow, the Sakha Republic, and the Krasnoyarsk Region). Of the nine youth political officials and staff, three were working for the Moscow-based Federal Youth Agency *Rosmolodezh*, two for Sakha youth political institutions, two for youth political institutions in Krasnoyarsk, and two at so-called youth centers in Krasnoyarsk. All but two had taught at least once at youth-leadership summer camps.

I had met two youth-leadership summer-camp teachers accidentally at a sociological discussion group in Moscow, which I visited thanks to the forwarding of the invitation by a sociology professor. The event took place in an apartment in central Moscow and was attended by only about twelve people. When I stated that I was researching youth-leadership summer camps similar to *Seliger*, the host (a man in his fifties) and a young visitor told me that they were both involved with state youth politics and had indeed been working as teaching staff at *Seliger*. The host of the discussion group even showed a number of ID badges he had obtained at the different youth-leadership camps (for an overview of youth-leadership summer camps across Russia see Appendix II). I excluded the interview I conducted with the host from the sample for several reasons. He would not answer any of my questions. Instead, he told several conspiracy stories (several of them openly anti-Semitic), asserted that he had magic powers, and claimed that he had been haunted by the Russian secret service, but then decided to collaborate with the ruling authorities. The only findings from this interview relevant to this study are that the selection of teaching staff for youth-leadership summer camps is apparently guided by informal relationships between teachers and youth political organizers (a thesis which was affirmed by interviews with other staff).

The Interview Situation and Building Rapport

Given that successful interviewing requires empathy and rapport, interviewing people who hold political views and opinions with which one deeply disagrees places an interviewer in a difficult professional, emotional, and political position. Researchers making use of participant observation and in-depth interviewing deal with these issues in a variety of ways. For example, sociologist Kathleen Blee, who studied women on the far right in the United States, made her political convictions clear to interviewees before the conversation started.

> From the beginning, when I asked women if I could interview them, I made it clear that I did not share the racial convictions of these groups. I explicitly said that my views were quite opposed to theirs, that they should not hope to convert me to their views, but that I would try to depict women racist activists accurately. I revealed my critical stance but made it clear that I had no intent to portray them as crazy and did not plan to turn them over to law enforcement or mental health agencies.[35]

Unlike Blee, I decided not to state my political convictions at the outset, because I wanted interviewees to express their opinions independent of my political convictions, but I did tell interviewees the truth about my own political convictions whenever they directly asked me. I usually tried to put such requests off until the interview had finished. Given that interviews took place during the height of the 2014 Ukraine crisis, I used this tactic quite often, because my very presence prompted people to ask about my opinions on the sanctions and the status of Crimea. For this reason, I had omitted any questions regarding Russia's relationship to the West from the interview guide.

Despite this deliberate omission, the Ukraine conflict arose as a topic in most interviews, especially given the fear of a pending war between Russia and the West. This fear was especially pronounced after the shooting down of a Malaysian passenger plane over Ukrainian airspace in summer 2014. Despite the political tensions, I met absolutely no hostility toward me as a representative of the West. On some occasions my being from Germany prompted topics and themes that would not have arisen with an interviewer from Russia. Most notably, these were comparisons between, to put it bluntly, the good life in the West and the hard life in Russia.

It is hard for me to judge the influence gender may have had on the interview situation; I could not find any pattern in the interview data or in my reflection memos that would indicate any specific influence. There was one interview with a male interviewee (not a camper) who was about my age that felt tense, probably because my disagreement with his comments surfaced. He found writing books, as he told me, superfluous, because what mattered were short summaries about best-practice examples.

I often probed more deeply into apparent contradictions or sentiments that irritated me by asking pointed questions, including leading questions. In one case this led the interviewee—a young man from a Sakha village—to fall silent, so in that case I changed tactics, suspecting that I might have embarrassed him into thinking that I was trying to reveal his lack of education. In other cases, co-interviewees took over the role of probing or criticizing their peer's opinions. Overall, I found that combining open-ended, pointed, and leading questions was fruitful. Almost all interviewees felt free to object to my suppositions.[36]

Yet sometimes, when my anger was rising and probing did not help, I switched to provocative questions. Oddly enough, in most cases my provocation was not understood. In one interview, for example, a young member of *Rosmolodezh* had just shared his opinion on the alleged proper place of a woman: in the kitchen. In reply, I asked him whether it would not be of utmost importance that Russian official memory should commemorate the many internationally famous Russian feminists. He paused for ten seconds, then answered with full conviction that he did not know of any of those individuals, but that if they were famous this would be not because they were emancipated women, but because they were Russian: Being Russian meant being successful.

Precisely because I often disagreed with interviewees' opinions and convictions, it was very important to me to make the interview process as transparent as possible. This included, besides completing the human-subject consents, sending interviewees the transcripts of their interviews to allow them to detect any mistakes that might have occurred during transcription.

Transcription and Analysis of Interviews

A professional transcription agency based in Moscow transcribed the bulk of the interviews, which are all in Russian. Professional transcription by native speakers ensured a correct understanding and allowed for a more thorough analysis of the interviews.[37] Each interviewee received a copy of their interview transcript, though a few of them had (accidentally or deliberately) not provided their contact details.

Beyond its ethical desirability, this practice aided the study in two ways. First, if interviewees reported minor errors in the transcripts, a comparison with the audio recording could reveal possible mistakes (which were not unlikely due to the background noise in cafés, bars, and at the camp site). Second, I planned to regard complaints about the transcripts as additional data, though such complaints have not arisen to date. Certainly, if an interviewee had withdrawn consent altogether (none did), I would not have used that person's transcript for analysis.

I should note at this point that I decided to use the interviews with youth political officials and staff to get a better understanding of the relationship between federal and regional state youth politics, and the staff's interpretations of government-promoted ideals. The relatively low number of these interviews and the interviewees' very different functions (youth political officials, administrative staff dealing largely with organizational issues, independent trainers for self-development and project management, history teachers, and people affiliated with the Federal Youth Agency *Rosmolodezh*) made it difficult to draw more rigorous conclusions from the obtained data. However, conducting these interviews and analyzing them provided considerable help in testing my assumptions about a Soviet summer-camp tradition and obtaining insider knowledge about the history of regional youth-leadership summer camps. It revealed the desire, shared by staff and youth political officials, to emphasize the non-partisan, non-political nature of the events.

The interview data were processed according to an issue-focused (as opposed to case-focused) analysis, which "would concern itself with what could be learned about specific issues—or events or processes—from any and all respondents."[38] Given the broad range of topics involved, I started to code the interview transcripts deductively, corresponding to the subject areas of the interview outline, creating so-called code families. Every code family was assigned a specific color. I coded with the software Atlas.ti.

I subsequently coded inductively within each code family—yet I did not follow the word-by-word and line-by-line coding scheme commonly used by grounded theorists (who often follow a purely inductive line of inquiry).[39] Regarding the inductive type of coding, I followed this advice:

> I don't try to make sense of every 'meaning unit'—every utterance that provides a complete thought—nor of every sentence of paragraph. But as I go through the material I do ask myself what I am seeing instances of, what I am learning about, and what questions the material raises.[40]

This meant that I coded all those instances that I found revealing in relation to an emerging category. As a next step, I inquired whether the singular instances I had coded were actually variations of one theme.[41] This theme then became the meso-level code. These meso-level codes consisted of several low-level codes. I used in vivo codes (in which the name of the code replicates the wording of an interviewee) for innovative ways to capture a thought, for insider terms, and for recurrent proverbs.[42] I found the frequent use of proverbs especially intriguing. When different interviewees used the same proverbs, I created in vivo codes. Several of those became meso-level codes in subsequent steps of analysis.

This means that during inductive coding I connected lower-level codes to higher-level ones by using the link "is a." This involved specifying the boundaries of meso-level codes—meaning what they entail and, more importantly, what they do not entail.[43] My codebook is structured along the lines of these broad code families. For example, one such code family, "What is to be done," comprises all suggestions raised by campers in response to my question of what they would like to change. The meso-level codes within this code family specify the target of such actions (activism against indifference, against racism, against corruption, for a better society), while the lower-level codes within the family specify how or by what means interviewees suggested bringing such changes about (care for surroundings, refute racial stereotypes, public control and education, youth must stay in home region).

While the delineation between different code families was helpful for coding inductively within a code family (other code-family examples include "Activism," "Patriotism," and, "We Are Sakha"), it was not conducive to arriving at a better understanding of relationships across code families. This is why, in a second step, I created analytically structured groups of codes, at which I arrived by what grounded theorists call axial coding. Charmaz defines it as follows: "Axial coding relates categories to subcategories, specifies the properties and dimension of a category, and reassembles the data you have fractured during initial coding to give coherence to the emerging analysis."[44] I used axial coding to create the categories that made up the building blocks of my argument about the main vectors of loyalty among campers. The code group "Development" entails all codes that connected to the theme of development.

An important tool for the analysis in Atlas.ti was the so-called code co-occurrence table. It resembles the table that indicates the distances between major cities in a territory—a feature often included as a page in day planners before online maps rendered it superfluous. The co-occurrence table works to a similar logic as the distance table, but instead of distances, it indicates the frequency of co-occurring codes. Using this table, I could, for example, check how often participants' identifications with Russia co-occurred with mentions of the Great Patriotic War and contrast this result with the frequency of co-occurrences between identifications with one's small motherland and the Great Patriotic War.

Although no other researchers coded my interview transcripts to check for intercoder reliability, I discussed emerging codes and categories with fellow researchers during the process of analysis. Given that the interviews were in Russian (and I had not had them translated into English), the circle of people with whom I could discuss the analysis was relatively small back in Germany, and it was not an option to join interpretation groups. I had looked out for such an interpretation group while living in Russia, but had not found one.

Participant Observations and Collection of Additional Data

This book draws on a variety of data. Besides the types of data already described in detail above, I collected strategy papers, legislation and statutes of state youth politics, newspaper articles, web pages, and YouTube clips. Given that much information on youth-leadership summer camps, but also on organizations initiated or sponsored by state youth politics, is distributed across social networks, several of the web pages I have referenced belong to the Russian social network *Vkontakte*.

As described above, observational data for this study were mainly gathered in the summer of 2013 at two youth-leadership summer camps: At *TIM Biriusa* (Territory of Youth Taking Initiative *Biriusa*), which has taken place in the Krasnoyarsk Region since 2007, and at *SakhaSeliger*, which was organized for the first time in the Republic of Sakha, Yakutia, in 2012. Since 2016 this camp has been called *Sinergiia Severa* (Synergy of the North), and the last installment of the camp took place before the pandemic in 2019. While *Biriusa* was continued after the restrictions were loosened, *Sinergiia Severa* has not been revived since then.

Additional participant observations included my visits to the 2014 gathering of Siberian Komsomol groups and to the children's summer camp *Kratovo*, close to Moscow. Shorter visits included one at the Representation of the Sakha Republic in Moscow (*Postoiannoe predstavitel'stvo Respubliki Sakha (Iakutiia) pri Prezidente Rossiiskoi Federatsii*) in June 2014. A guided tour of the Representation's museum was revealing. The person who accompanied me—a woman from the Sakha Republic living in Russia whom I had met through a common colleague—along with her acquaintance at the Representation who had facilitated our visit, and the head of the museum, engaged in discussions of the Republic's future, its historical specificities (such as Stalin's early repressions of Sakha communists due to their alleged overly-nationalist orientation), and the possible importance of neotraditional policies such as the maternity capital program for small peoples and nationalities in Russia.[45] In 2015, I visited the Moscow-based Public Chamber of the Russian Federation during the fourteenth AICESIS international conference on September 17th. AICESIS stands for Association internationale des conseils économiques et sociaux et institutions similaires (The International Association of Economic and Social Councils and Similar Institutions). This visit was pivotal for my understanding of the ways in which the Russian government aimed at creating a civil society that was good for the market and loyal to the state. A friend of my former roommate worked there at the time and had organized the trip. In 2016, I visited the Moscow-based Komsomol archive (*Rossiiskii gosudarstvennyi arkhiv sotsial'no-politicheskoi istorii—RGASPI*) to obtain more information on summer camps for leisure during the Soviet period. During my visits there I became acquainted with a group of former troop leaders, *vozhatie*, of the famous pioneer camp *Artek* who met there to work on edited volumes about *Artek*'s history. Together with the archivist on duty, they kindly organized for me a visit to the Moscow Humanitarian University (*Moskovskii Gumanitarnii Universitet—MosGU*), the successor organization of the Higher Komsomol School (*Vysshaia komsomol'skaia shkola*), in spring 2016. Both visits were fruitful for gaining a better understanding of Soviet extra-curricular activities and their revival in the 1990s and early 2000s.

APPENDIX II

Overview of Youth-Leadership Summer Camps in Russia

There are no official figures on the total number of youth-leadership summer camps in Russia. The Russian Youth League (*Rossiisskii Soiuz Molodezhi*) states that in 2022 more than 20,000 young adults between 18 and 35 years participated in youth-leadership summer camps.[1]

Forum Name	Previous name/ eponymous programs	Type	Federal Level Status as of 2022	Federal District (Federal'nyi Okrug)	Region	Date of Initiation	Taking place annually	Did not take place in	Existed (from-to)
1 Baikal'skii molodezhnyi forum "BuZaN" (Budushchee za nami)		Modeled after Seliger		Sibirskii Federal'nyi Okrug	Respublika Buriatiia	2003	x		
2 Seliger		Original Seliger		Tsentral'nyi Federal'nyi Okrug	Tverskaia Oblast'	2005			2005–2014
3 Mezhdunarodnyi molodezhnyi lager' "Baikal 2020"	"Molodezh' Pribaikal'ia" in 2006 "Molodezhnyi kadrovyi rezerv" in 2007	Modeled after Seliger		Sibirskii Federal'nyi Okrug	Irkutskaia Oblast'	2006	x		
4 Territoriia initsiativnoi molodezhi Biriusa, TIM Biriusa		Modeled after Seliger		Sibirskii Federal'nyi Okrug	Krasnoiarskii Krai	2007	x		
5 Vserossiiskii lager'- seminar LIGA		Initiative of conservative civil society organization, cooperation with youth political institutions		Privolzhskii Federal'nyi Okrug	Nizhegorodskaia Oblast'	2007	x		
6 Ostrova	"SeliSakh" until 2013	Modeled after Seliger		Dal'nevostochnyi Federal'nyi Okrug	Sakhalin	2008	x		
7 SeliAs		Modeled after Seliger		Iuzhnyi Federal'nyi Okrug	Astrakhanskaia Oblast'	2008	x		

8 Forum-festival' molodezhi My za mir vo vsem mire		Modeled after Seliger	Ural'skii Federal'nyi Okrug	Iamalo-Nenetskii avtonomnyi Okrug	2009	x
9 Interra		Focus on Innovation/ Year of Youth 2009	Sibirskii Federal'nyi Okrug	Novosibirsk	2009	x
10 Kazan OIC Youth Entrepreneurship Forum		Focus on Innovation/ Year of Youth 2009	Privolzhskii Federal'nyi Okrug	Respublika Tatarstan/ Kazan	2009	
11 Mezhdunarodnyi molodezhnyi upravlencheskii forum ATR "Altai Territoriia Razvitiia"	Altai Tochki Rosta until 2019	Modeled after Seliger	Sibirskii Federal'nyi Okrug	Altaiskii Krai	2009	x
12 Mezhregional'nyi molodezhnyi forum "Komanda Tuvy 2030"	"Durgen" (2009-2014) "Tuva—Territoriia Razvitiia Durgen" (2014-2016)	Modeled after Seliger	Sibirskii Federal'nyi Okrug	Respublika Tyva	2009	x
13 Molodezhny Obrazovatel'ny Forum Ladoga		Modeled after Seliger	Severo-Zapadnyi Federal'nyi Okrug	Leningradskaia Oblast'	2009	x

2009–2013

(*continued*)

Forum Name	Previous name/ eponymous programs	Type	Federal Level Status as of 2022	Federal District (Federal'nyi Okrug)	Region	Date of Initiation	Taking place annually	Did not take place in	Existed (from-to)
14 Molodezhnyi innovatsionnyi forum		Focus on Innovation/ Year of Youth 2009		Privolzhskii Federal'nyi Okrug	Ul'ianovsk	2009			2009–2011; 2015–2016
15 Molodezhnyi kar'ernyi forum "Professionalizm—2020: upravlenie razvitiem"		Focus on Innovation/ Year of Youth 2009		Sibirskii Federal'nyi Okrug	Tomsk	2009			2009–2009
16 Okruzhnoi obrazovatel'nyi forum "Volga"		Modeled after Seliger		Iuzhnyi Federal'nyi Okrug	Volgogradskaia Oblast'	2009			2009–2013
17 Patriot		Modeled after Seliger		Tsentral'nyi Federal'nyi Okrug	Kostromskaia Oblast'	2009	x		
18 Smola		Modeled after Seliger		Tsentral'nyi Federal'nyi Okrug	Smolenskaia Oblast'	2009	x		
19 Utro	"UtroUral" until 2020	Modeled after Seliger		Ural'skii Federal'nyi Okrug	Altering regions: Cheliabinskaia Oblast', Sverdlovskaia Oblast', Tiumenskaia Oblast', Iugra…	2009	x		
20 Baltiiskii Artek		Modeled after Seliger		Severo-Zapadnyi Federal'nyi Okrug	Kaliningradskaia Oblast'	2010	x		
21 Inerka	Since 2021 the competition "Inerka" takes place in the region, designed to create a cadre	Modeled after Seliger		Privolzhskii Federal'nyi Okrug	Respublika Mordoviia	2010	x		

22 Mashuk	Modeled after Seliger	x	Severo-Kavkazskii Federal'nyi Okrug	Stavropol'skii Krai	2010	x
23 Molodezhnyi forum "RITM"	Modeled after Seliger		Sibirskii Federal'nyi Okrug	Omskaia Oblast'	2010	x
24 Oblastnoi molodezhnyi forum "Start"	Modeled after Seliger. Since 2017 there is an eponymous program to economically develop the region		Sibirskii Federal'nyi Okrug	Kemerovo	2010	2010–2017
25 Mezhdunarodnyi molodezhnyi forum Kaspii"	Modeled after Seliger		Dagestan	Makhachkala	2011	x
26 Molodezhnyi etno-turistskii forum "Etnova"	Modeled after Seliger		Sibirskii Federal'nyi Okrug	Respublika Khakasiia	2011	x
27 Molodezhnyi forum "Tomskii kollaider"	Modeled after Seliger		Sibirskii Federal'nyi Okrug	Tomskaia Oblast'	2011	x 2011–2017
28 Rabotaiushchaia molodezh'	Modeled after Seliger	x	Privolzhskii Federal'nyi Okrug	Nizhegorodskaia Oblast'	2011	x
29 Rostov	Modeled after Seliger		Iuzhnyi Federal'nyi Okrug	Rostovskaia Oblast'	2011	x
30 Mezhdunarodnyi molodezhnyi forum "Targim"	Modeled after Seliger		Severo-Kavkazskii Federal'nyi Okrug	Respublika Ingushetiia	2012	x 2013
31 Sinergiia Severa	Modeled after Seliger		Dal'nevostochnyi Federal'nyi Okrug	Sakha Republic	2012	x
32 iVolga	Modeled after Seliger		Privolzhskii Federal'nyi Okrug	Samarskaia Oblast'	2013	x
33 Oblastnoi Forum Molodaia Volna	Modeled after Seliger		Iuzhnyi Federal'nyi Okrug	Rostovskaia Oblast'	2013	x

(*continued*)

Forum Name	Previous name/ eponymous programs	Type	Federal Level Status as of 2022	Federal District (Federal'nyi Okrug)	Region	Date of Initiation	Taking place annually	Did not take place in	Existed (from-to)
34 Mezhdunarodnyi mezhreligioznyi molodezhnyi forum		Forum of the Russian Orthodox Church		Severo-Kavkazskii Federal'nyi Okrug	Respublika Dagestan	2014	x		
35 Rossiia Studencheskaia Vesna		Focus on Student Self-government		Different places		2014	x		
36 Tavrida		Modeled after Seliger	x	Ukraine: Crimea Federal'nyi Okrug	Ukraine: Crimea	2014	x		
37 Vyshe kryshi	"Vsmysle" until 2019	Modeled after Seliger		Severo-Zapadnyi Federal'nyi Okrug	St. Petersburg	2014	x		
38 Arktika. Sdelano v Rossii		Modeled after Seliger		Severo-Zapadnyi Federal'nyi Okrug	Arkhangelsk	2015	x	2016	
39 Nashi Ostrova	"Iturup" until 2019	Modeled after Seliger	x	Dal'nevostochnyi Federal'nyi Okrug	Kuril'skie Ostrova	2015	x		
40 Territoriia Smyslov		Successor of Seliger	x	Tsentral'nyi Federal'nyi Okrug	Until 2018 in Vladimir; Since 2019 in Solnechnogorsk, Moskovskaia Oblast' (on the coast of Senezh Lake and next to the new state-run educational center "Senezh")	2015	x		

41 Dal'nevostochnyi molodezhnyi obrazovatel'nyi forum "Amur"	Modeled after Seliger	Dal'nevostochnyi Federal'nyi Okrug	Khabarovskii Krai	2016	
42 Evraziia Global	Modeled after Seliger	Privolzhskii Federal'nyi krug	Orenburgskaia Oblast'	2016	x
43 Regional'nyi forum "Iugra—Territoriia vozmozhnostei"	Modeled after Seliger	Ural'skii Federal'nyi Okrug	Khanty-Mansiiskii Avtonomnyi Okrug—Iugra	2017	x
44 Ekosistema	Modeled after Seliger	Severo-Zapadnyi Federal'nyi Okrug	Vologodskaia Oblast'	2021	x
45 Samolva	Modeled after Seliger	Severo-Zapadnyi Federal'nyi Okrug	Pskovskaia Oblast'	2021	x
46 Biznes-lidery Budushchego	Focus on Start-up Businesses	Moscow	Moskovskaia Oblast'	2022	
47 Forum sotsial'nogo prizvaniia	Modeled after Seliger	Severo-Zapadnyi Federal'nyi Okrug	Leningradskaia Oblast'	2022	x
48 Iug Molodoi	Modeled after Seliger	Ukraine: Zaporizhzhia Oblast'	Ukraine: Zaporizhzhia Oblast'	2022	x
49 Predprinimatel'skii molodezhnyi forum BizONN	Modeled after Seliger	Privolzhskii Federal'nyi Okrug	Nizhegorodskaia Oblast'	2022	x
50 Shum	Modeled after Seliger	Severo-Zapadnyi Federal'nyi Okrug	Kaliningradskaia Oblast'	2022	x
51 Sreda	Modeled after Seliger	Tsentral'nyi Federal'nyi Okrug	Belgorodskaia Oblast'	2022	

2019

Notes

Chapter 1

1. Maksim, Personal interview with participant of "SakhaSeliger," interview by Anna Schwenck, July 23, 2014.
2. Maksim, Personal interview.
3. Maksim, Personal interview.
4. Wendy Brown, *Undoing the Demos: Neoliberalism's Stealth Revolution* (New York: Zone Books, 2015), 222.
5. Brown, *Undoing the Demos*, 95.
6. Edgar Cabanas and Eva Illouz, *Manufacturing Happy Citizens: How the Science and Industry of Happiness Control Our Lives* (Cambridge: Polity Press, 2019), 5.
7. Tom R. Tyler, "Psychological Perspectives on Legitimacy and Legitimation," *Annual Review of Psychology* 57, no. 1 (2006): 375–400.
8. Cf. Samuel A. Greene and Graeme B. Robertson, *Putin v. the People: The Perilous Politics of a Divided Russia* (New Haven, CT: Yale University Press, 2019).
9. Gert Pickel, "Die kulturelle Verankerung von Autokratien—Bestandserhalt durch ideologische Legitimationsstrategien und ökonomische Legitimität oder Demokratisierung?," in *Autokratien im Vergleich*, ed. Steffen Kailitz and Patrick Köllner (Baden-Baden: Nomos, 2013), 183.
10. Ivan Nechepurenko and Anton Troianovski, "Mass Beatings and Detentions in Belarus as President Clings to Power," *The New York Times*, August 13, 2020, https://www.nytimes.com/2020/08/13/world/europe/beatings-detentions-belarus-lukashenko.html.
11. Milan W. Svolik, *The Politics of Authoritarian Rule*, Cambridge Studies in Comparative Politics (Cambridge: Cambridge University Press, 2012), 10.
12. Jeffrey C. Alexander, *Performance and Power* (Cambridge: Polity Press, 2011), 1.
13. For a theoretical reflection on that question see Peter Graf Kielmansegg, "Legitimität als analytische Kategorie," *Politische Vierteljahresschrift* 12, no. 3 (1971): 400. For an earlier version of the idea see Anna Schwenck, "Russian Politics of Radicalisation and Surveillance," in *Governing Youth Politics in the Age of Surveillance*, ed. Maria Grasso and Judith Bessant, The Criminalization of Political Dissent (London: Routledge, 2018), 170.
14. Erica Frantz and Andrea Kendall-Taylor, "A Dictator's Toolkit: Understanding How Co-Optation Affects Repression in Autocracies," *Journal of Peace Research* 51, no. 3 (2014): 2, https://doi.org/10/f54qr6.
15. David Easton, "A Re-Assessment of the Concept of Political Support," *British Journal of Political Science* 5, no. 4 (1975): 435–57, https://doi.org/10/b5phsd.

16. Jan Fagerberg, Martin Srholec, and Bart Verspagen, "Innovation and Economic Development," in *Handbook of the Economics of Innovation. Vol. 2*, ed. Bronwyn H. Hall and Nathan Rosenberg, Handbooks in Economics (Amsterdam: Elsevier, 2010), 865.
17. Fagerberg, Srholec, and Verspagen, "Innovation and Economic Development," 842.
18. Mariia Pliusnina, "Kak ANO 'Rossiia—strana vozmozhnostei,' sozdannaia ukazom Putina, potratit R3 mlrd subsidii," *Znak*, September 17, 2019, https://web.archive.org/web/20210413043148/https://www.znak.com/2019-09-17/kak_ano_rossiya_strana_vozmozhnostey_sozdannaya_ukazom_putina_potratit_3_mlrd_subsidiy. The legal form in Russia is that of an "Autonomous Non-Commercial Organization" (*Avtonomnaia nekommercheskaia organizatsiia, ANO*).
19. "Rossiia — strana vozmozhnostei. Kak prezidentskaia platforma zapuskaet novye sotsial'nye lifty," *Lenta.ru*, December 29, 2022, https://lenta.ru/articles/2022/12/29/platform/.
20. Suzanne Keller, *Beyond the Ruling Class: Strategic Elites in Modern Society* (New York: Random House, 1963), 4. I am grateful to sociologist Christian Schneickert for introducing me to Keller's concept of strategic elites.
21. Novel evidence suggests that most high-level government and military officials were not in the picture of Putin's war plans: Erin Banco et al., "'Something Was Badly Wrong': When Washington Realized Russia Was Actually Invading Ukraine. A First-Ever Oral History of How Top U.S. and Western Officials Saw the Warning Signs of a European Land War, Their Frantic Attempts to Stop It — and the Moment Putin Actually Crossed the Border," *POLITICO*, February 24, 2023, https://www.politico.com/news/magazine/2023/02/24/russia-ukraine-war-oral-history-00083757.
22. Francesca Ebel and Mary Ilyushina, "Russians Abandon Wartime Russia in Historic Exodus," *Washington Post*, February 13, 2023, sec. Europe, https://www.washingtonpost.com/world/2023/02/13/russia-diaspora-war-ukraine/.
23. Reuters, "Kremlin: Many People in Russia Are Showing Themselves to Be Traitors," *Euronews*, March 18, 2022, https://www.euronews.com/2022/03/18/us-ukraine-crisis-kremlin-traitors.
24. Novel evidence suggests that most high-level government and military officials were not in the picture of Putin's war plans: Banco et al., "'Something Was Badly Wrong.'"
25. Aleksandr Bikbov, "Travma Neomerkantilizma i zadachi novoi kul'tury," in *Pered licom katastrofy: sbornik statej*, ed. Nikolaj Plotnikov, Philosophie: Forschung und Wissenschaft 57 (Münster: Lit Verlag, 2023), 65.
26. Aleksandr Bikbov and Asia Leofreddi, "Inequalities and Resistance in Putin's Russia," *OBC Transeuropa*, November 15, 2022, https://www.balcanicaucaso.org/eng/Areas/Russia/Inequalities-and-resistance-in-Putin-s-Russia-221607.
27. Bikbov, "Travma Neomerkantilizma i zadachi novoi kul'tury."
28. Bernard Gert, "Loyalty and Morality," in *Loyalty*, ed. Sanford Levinson, Paul Woodruff, and Joel Parker (New York: New York University Press, 2013), 3–21; Johannes Gerschewski, "Legitimacy in Autocracies: Oxymoron or Essential Feature?," *Perspectives on Politics* 16, no. 3 (2018): 652–65, https://doi.org/10/ggjpf4.

29. Lisa M. Hoffman, *Patriotic Professionalism in Urban China: Fostering Talent, Urban Life, Landscape, and Policy* (Philadelphia: Temple University Press, 2010); Li Zhang and Aihwa Ong, eds., *Privatizing China: Socialism from Afar* (Ithaca: Cornell University Press, 2008); Ágnes Gagyi and Tamás Geröcs, "The Political Economy of Hungary's New 'Slave Law,'" *Lefteast*, January 1, 2019, https://lefteast.org/the-political-economy-of-hungarys-new-slave-law/; Ágnes Gagyi and Tamás Geröcs, "Reconfiguring Regimes of Capitalist Integration: Hungary since the 1970s," in *The Political Economy of Eastern Europe 30 Years into the 'Transition'*, ed. Ágnes Gagyi and Ondřej Slačálek, International Political Economy Series (London: Palgrave Macmillan, 2022), 115–31, https://doi.org/10.1007/978-3-030-78915-2_7.; Gábor Scheiring, *The Retreat of Liberal Democracy: Authoritarian Capitalism and the Accumulative State in Hungary*, 2020; Adam Fabry, *The Political Economy of Hungary From State Capitalism to Authoritarian Neoliberalism* (London: Palgrave Macmillan, 2019), https://doi.org/10.1007/978-3-030-10594-5.
30. Marion Fourcade-Gourinchas, "State Metrology: The Rating of Sovereigns and the Judgment of Nations," in *The Many Hands of the State: Theorizing Political Authority and Social Control*, ed. Kimberly J. Morgan and Ann Shola Orloff (New York: Cambridge University Press, 2017), 103–27.
31. Jim McGuigan, *Neoliberal Culture* (London: Palgrave Macmillan, 2016).
32. Suzanne Keller, *Beyond the Ruling Class. Strategic Elites in Modern Society* (New York: Random House, 1963), 97.
33. Joseph Rothschild, "Observations on Political Legitimacy in Contemporary Europe," *Political Science Quarterly* 92, no. 3 (1977): 499, https://doi.org/10/fgdx5r.
34. See for instance Hilary Appel and Mitchell A. Orenstein, *From Triumph to Crisis: Neoliberal Economic Reform in Postcommunist Countries* (Cambridge: Cambridge University Press, 2018).
35. Gábor Scheiring, *The Retreat of Liberal Democracy: Authoritarian Capitalism and the Accumulative State in Hungary* (London: Palgrave Macmillan, 2020), 52.
36. Aron Buzogány and Mihai Varga, "Against 'Post-Communism': The Conservative Dawn in Hungary," in *New Conservatives in Russia and East Central Europe*, ed. Katharina Bluhm and Mihai Varga (New York: Routledge, 2019), 70–91.
37. Gagyi and Geröcs, "The Political Economy of Hungary's New 'Slave Law'"; Adam Fabry, *The Political Economy of Hungary from State Capitalism to Authoritarian Neoliberalism* (London: Palgrave Macmillan, 2019).
38. Emília Barna, "Managing the Eastern European Position in the Digital Era: Music Industry Showcase Events and Popular Music Export in Hungary," in *Eastern European Music Industries and Policies after the Fall of Communism*, ed. Patryk Galuszka (London: Routledge, 2021), 149.
39. Aleksandr Bikbov, "Neo-Traditionalist Fits with Neo-Liberal Shifts in Russian Cultural Policy," in *Russia: Art Resistance and the Conservative-Authoritarian Zeitgeist*, ed. Lena Jonson and Andrei Erofeev (New York: Routledge, 2017), 65–83; Ilya Matveev, "Russia, Inc.," *OpenDemocracy*, March 16, 2016, https://www.opendemocracy.net/en/odr/russia-inc/.

40. Alexandra Dmitrieva and Zhanna Kravchenko, "Unhealthy, Deviant and Criminal: Drug Control Policies in Russia," *Baltic Worlds* IX, no. 4 (2016): 12–22; Gilles Favarel-Garrigues and Ioulia Shukan, "Perspectives on Post-Soviet Vigilantism. Introduction," *Laboratorium: Russian Review of Social Research*, no. 3 (2019): 4–15, https://doi.org/10/gm7mtm; Julie Hemment, "Soviet-Style Neoliberalism? Nashi, Youth Voluntarism, and the Restructuring of Social Welfare in Russia," *Problems of Post-Communism* 56, no. 6 (2009): 36–50, https://doi.org/10/d5gbxs.
41. Richard Sakwa, *The Putin Paradox* (London: I.B. Tauris, Bloomsbury Publishing, 2020), 221.
42. Harley Balzer, "Managed Pluralism: Vladimir Putin's Emerging Regime," *Post-Soviet Affairs* 19, no. 3 (January 1, 2003): 189–227, https://doi.org/10/ftk423. On the importance of analyzing official speeches and declarations, especially since February 2022, because they provide clues of possible political trajectories see Gwendolyn Sasse, *Der Krieg gegen die Ukraine: Hintergründe, Ereignisse, Folgen* (Munich: Beck, 2022), 67.
43. Aleksei Levinson, "O molodezhi staroi i novoi," *Vedomosti*, May 22, 2017, https://www.vedomosti.ru/opinion/columns/2017/05/23/690975-molodezhi.
44. Ilya Kalinin, "The Struggle for History: The Past as a Limited Resource," in *Memory and Theory in Eastern Europe*, ed. Uilleam Blacker, Alexander Etkind, and Julie Fedor, Palgrave Studies in Cultural and Intellectual History (New York: Palgrave Macmillan, 2013), 255–65; Boris Dubin, "Simvoly vozvrata vmesto simvolov peremen," *Pro et contra* 5, no. 53 (2011): 19.
45. Richard Sennett, *The Corrosion of Character: The Personal Consequences of Work in the New Capitalism* (New York: Norton, 1999), 52.
46. Sarah Banet-Weiser, *Authentic TM: Politics and Ambivalence in a Brand Culture*, Critical Cultural Communication (New York: New York University Press, 2012), 140.
47. Julie Hemment, *Youth Politics in Putin's Russia: Producing Patriots and Entrepreneurs* (Bloomington: Indiana University Press, 2015).
48. Apurva Sanghi and Shahid Yusuf, "Russia's Uphill Struggle with Innovation," *World Bank*, September 17, 2018, https://www.worldbank.org/en/news/opinion/2018/09/17/russias-uphill-struggle-with-innovation.
49. Julia Lerner and Claudia Zbenovich, "Adapting the Therapeutic Discourse to Post-Soviet Media Culture: The Case of Modnyi Prigovor," *Slavic Review* 72, no. 4 (2013): 828–49, https://doi.org/10/ggqz26; Tomas Matza, "'Good Individualism'? Psychology, Ethics, and Neoliberalism in Postsocialist Russia," *American Ethnologist* 39, no. 4 (November 2012): 804–18, https://doi.org/10/f4d9sm.
50. Angela McRobbie, *Be Creative: Making a Living in the New Culture Industries* (Cambridge: Polity Press, 2016), 74.
51. Joseph A. Schumpeter, *The Theory of Economic Development: An Inquiry into Profits, Capital, Credit, Interest, and the Business Cycle*, Social Science Classics Series (New Brunswick, NJ: Transaction Books, 1983) Chapter 2.
52. S. L. Borodikhina, "Poisk novogo soderzhaniia poniatiia 'aktivnaia zhiznennaia pozitsiia' v sovremennykh obshchestvenno-politicheskikh usloviiakh," *Vestnik TGPU/ National Research Tomsk Polytechnic University* 3, no. 156 (2015): 182–85.

53. Wendy Brown, *In the Ruins of Neoliberalism: The Rise of Antidemocratic Politics in the West* (New York: Columbia University Press, 2019), 20.
54. Olga Malinova, "Constructing the 'Usable Past': The Evolution of the Official Historical Narrative in Post-Soviet Russia," in *Cultural and Political Imaginaries in Putin's Russia*, ed. Niklas Bernsand and Barbara Törnquist-Plewa (Leiden: BRILL, 2018), 85–104; Mischa Gabowitsch, Cordula Gdaniec, and Ekaterina Makhotina, eds., *Kriegsgedenken als Event. Der 9. Mai 2015 im postsozialistischen Europa* (Paderborn: Schöningh, 2017); Lev Gudkov, "The Fetters of Victory: How the War Provides Russia with Its Identity," *Osteuropa/ Eurozine*, 2005, 1–14; Elizaveta Gaufman, *Security Threats and Public Perception: Digital Russia and the Ukraine Crisis*, New Security Challenges (London: Palgrave Macmillan, 2017).
55. Martin Müller, *Making Great Power Identities in Russia: An Ethnographic Discourse Analysis of Education at a Russian Elite University*, Forum Politische Geographie 4 (Berlin: Lit Verlag, 2009).
56. See also Mabel Berezin's argument that treating the aesthetics of fascist political ritual as a property of regimes problematically assumes, "first, that regimes have total power and elides the process of regime choice, and second, that publics passively receive regime messages." *Making the Fascist Self: The Political Culture of Interwar Italy*, The Wilder House Series in Politics, History, and Culture (Ithaca, NY: Cornell University Press, 1997), 246.
57. Sasse, *Der Krieg gegen die Ukraine*.
58. Marlies Glasius, "What Authoritarianism Is . . . and Is Not: A Practice Perspective," *International Affairs* 94, no. 3 (May 1, 2018): 527, https://doi.org/10/gdkww5.
59. Glasius, 526; Steven Levitsky and Lucan Way, "The New Competitive Authoritarianism," *Journal of Democracy* 31, no. 1 (2020): 51–65, https://doi.org/10/ghv2qn; James Richter, "The ministry of civil society? The public chambers in the regions," *Problems of Post-Communism* 56, no. 6 (2009): 7–20, https://doi.org/10/dh3n42.
60. Such new forms of public participation and their negative effects on democracy are also seen to be spreading in states considered liberal democracies: Caroline W. Lee, Michael McQuarrie, and Edward T. Walker, "Rising Participation and Declining Democracy," in *Democratizing Inequalities: Dilemmas of the New Public Participation*, ed. Caroline W. Lee, Michael McQuarrie, and Edward T. Walker (New York: NYU Press, 2015), 3–23.
61. Glasius, "What Authoritarianism Is . . . and Is Not," 524.
62. Greene and Robertson, *Putin v. the People*, 205.
63. Such as those cultural understandings informing the so-called Immortal Regiment movement in Russia: Mischa Gabowitsch, "Are Copycats Subversive? Strategy-31, the Russian Runs, the Immortal Regiment, and the Transformative Potential of Non-Hierarchical Movements," *Problems of Post-Communism* 64, no. 3–4 (2017): 10–14.
64. Valerie Sperling, *Sex, Politics, and Putin: Political Legitimacy in Russia*, Oxford Studies in Culture and Politics (New York: Oxford University Press, 2015).
65. This definition of "nonpolitical" follows John Street's argument that conceiving of all spheres of life as political just because they may have an impact on political process

blunts the analytical power of defining phenomena as political: John Street, *Music and Politics*, Polity Contemporary Political Communication Series (Cambridge: Polity, 2012), 8.
66. Margaret R. Somers and Gloria D. Gibson, "Reclaiming the Epistemological 'Other': Narrative and the Social Constitution of Identity," in *Social Theory and the Politics of Identity*, ed. Craig Calhoun (Oxford: Blackwell, 1994), 37–99; Francesca Polletta, "Politicizing Childhood: The 1980 Zurich Burns Movement," *Social Text*, no. 33 (1992): 82, https://doi.org/10/dc2x3t.
67. Francesca Polletta, "Storytelling in Social Movements," in *Culture, Social Movements, and Protest*, ed. Hank Johnston (Farnham: Ashgate, 2009), 33–54.
68. Thomas Luckmann, "Comments on Legitimation," *Current Sociology* 35, no. 2 (1987): 112, https://doi.org/10/bvv7gh.
69. Mabel Berezin, "Events as Templates of Possibility: An Analytic Typology of Political Facts," in *The Oxford Handbook of Cultural Sociology*, ed. Jeffrey C. Alexander, Ronald N. Jacobs, and Philip Smith (Oxford: Oxford University Press, 2013), 613–35.
70. Easton, "A Re-Assessment of the Concept of Political Support."
71. Regarding international factors for regime stability see Oisín Tansey, *The International Politics of Authoritarian Rule*, Oxford Studies in Democratization (Oxford: Oxford University Press, 2016).
72. Steffen Kailitz and Daniel Stockemer, "Regime Legitimation, Elite Cohesion and the Durability of Autocratic Regime Types," *International Political Science Review / Revue Internationale de Science Politique* 38, no. 3 (2017): 332–48, https://doi.org/10/ghw29m; Alexander Dukalskis and Johannes Gerschewski, "What Autocracies Say (and What Citizens Hear): Proposing Four Mechanisms of Autocratic Legitimation," *Contemporary Politics* 23, no. 3 (July 2017): 251–68, https://doi.org/10/gjmqwr.
73. Easton, "A Re-Assessment of the Concept of Political Support."
74. Gerschewski, "Legitimacy in Autocracies," 17.
75. Kurt Lewin and Ronald Lippitt, "An Experimental Approach to the Study of Autocracy and Democracy: A Preliminary Note," *Sociometry* 1, no. 3/4 (1938): 292–300, https://doi.org/10/c9p5vj. Lewin's studies are widely quoted in literature on "leadership styles" today. Focusing on the efficiency of different leadership styles, such studies tend to depoliticize Lewin's research, which was influenced by the authoritarian personality project. See Jeanette Ziehm, Gisela Trommsdorf, and Isabelle Albert, "Erziehungsstile," in *Dorsch—Lexikon Der Psychologie*, ed. Markus Antonius Wirtz (Bern: Hogrefe, 2014).
76. Philip G. Cerny, "In the Shadow of Ordoliberalism: The Paradox of Neoliberalism in the 21st Century," *European Review of International Studies* 3, no. 1 (2016): 91.
77. Mel van Elteren, "Cultural Globalization and Transnational Flows of Things American," in *The Systemic Dimension of Globalization*, ed. Piotr Pachura (London: InTechOpen, 2011), 150.
78. Cabanas and Illouz, *Manufacturing Happy Citizens*.
79. For an account of the influence of cultural globalization and transnational flows in the late 1990s and early 2000s see Hilary Pilkington et al., eds., *Looking West? Cultural Globalization and Russian Youth Cultures*, Post-Communist Cultural Studies Series (University Park: Pennsylvania State University Press, 2002).

80. Mabel Berezin, Emily Sandusky, and Thomas Davidson, "Culture in Politics and Politics in Culture: Institutions, Practices, and Boundaries," in *The New Handbook of Political Sociology*, ed. Cedric de Leon et al. (Cambridge: Cambridge University Press, 2020), 112.
81. Thomas Meaney, "The Swaddling Thesis," *London Review of Books*, March 6, 2014.
82. Greene and Robertson, *Putin v. the People*, 128–32.
83. Dietrich Geyer, "Ostpolitik und Geschichtsbewusstsein in Deutschland," *Vierteljahrsschrift für Zeitgeschichte* 34, no. 2 (1986): 159. Quoted passage was translated by the author.
84. Gwendolyn Sasse, *The Crimea Question: Identity, Transition, and Conflict*, Harvard Series in Ukrainian Studies (Cambridge: Distributed by Harvard University Press for the Harvard Ukrainian Research Institute, 2007), 15.
85. See Chris Hann, "Introduction: Postsocialism as a Topic of Anthropological Investigation. Farewell to the Socialist 'Other,'" in *Postsocialism Ideals, Ideologies, and Practices in Eurasia*, ed. Chris Hann (London: Routledge, 2002), 8.
86. Vladimir Gel'man, *Authoritarian Russia: Analyzing Post-Soviet Regime Changes*, Pittsburgh Series in Russian and East European Studies (Pittsburgh: University of Pittsburgh Press, 2015), 20–22. He appears to tar with the same brush Samuel Huntington's highly questionable and reductionist use of the culture concept in the *Clash of Civilizations* and Alena Ledeneva's highly reflective and elaborate use of the concept of culture. Alena Ledeneva, *Can Russia Modernise? Sistema, Power Networks and Informal Governance* (Cambridge: Cambridge University Press, 2013).
87. Mabel Berezin, "Sociology of Culture," in *International Encyclopedia of the Social & Behavioral Sciences*, ed. James D. Wright (Oxford: Elsevier, 2015), 618.
88. This is different from an understanding of an ideal as a tool of reasoning. For instance, the Weberian notion of ideal type does not entail a moral judgment that identifies what ought to be. Instead, ideal types are highly schematic representations of situations in a pure or extreme form that can facilitate scientific discovery.
89. Dennis Galvan, "Neotraditionalism," in *Encyclopedia of Governance*, ed. Mark Bevir, 2 vols. (Thousand Oaks, CA: SAGE Publications, 2007), 600–601, https://doi.org/g9rr.
90. Gavin O'Toole, "A New Nationalism for a New Era: The Political Ideology of Mexican Neoliberalism," *Bulletin of Latin American Research* 22, no. 3 (July 2003): 274, https://doi.org/10/bd3zkr.
91. Aldo Madariaga, *Neoliberal Resilience: Lessons in Democracy and Development from Latin America and Eastern Europe* (Princeton, NJ: Princeton University Press, 2020), 263; Katharina Bluhm and Mihai Varga, *New Conservatives in Russia and East Central Europe*, ed. Katharina Bluhm and Mihai Varga (New York: Routledge, 2019).
92. Kevork Oskanian, *Russian Exceptionalism between East and West: The Ambiguous Empire* (London: Palgrave Macmillan, 2021); Andrei Tsygankov, "Crafting the State-Civilization. Vladimir Putin's Turn to Distinct Values," *Problems of*

Post-Communism 63, no. 3 (2016): 146–58, https://doi.org/10/gd55k6; Aleksandr Verkhovskii and Emil Pain, "Civilizational Nationalism: The Russian Version of the 'Special Path,'" *Russian Politics and Law* 50, no. 5 (September 2012): 52–86, https://doi.org/10/gd53fk.

93. Rogers Brubaker, "Nationhood and the National Question in the Soviet Union and Post-Soviet Eurasia: An Institutionalist Account," *Theory and Society* 23, no. 1 (1994): 47–78; Francine Hirsch, *Empire of Nations: Ethnographic Knowledge and the Making of the Soviet Union*, Culture & Society after Socialism (Ithaca, NY: Cornell University Press, 2005); Yuri Slezkine, "The USSR as a Communal Apartment, or How a Socialist State Promoted Ethnic Particularism," *Slavic Review* 53, no. 2 (1994): 414, https://doi.org/10/d55pn5.

94. Olga Malinova, *Konstruirovanie smyslov. Issledovanie simvolicheskoi politiki v sovremennoi Rossii* (Moscow: INION RAN, 2013), 291–97; Alexander Lukin, *The Political Culture of the Russian "Democrats"* (Oxford: Oxford University Press, 2000), 289.

95. For a discussion of the ethnic and racializing overtones in the discourse of becoming a normal country see Nikolay Zakharov, *Race and Racism in Russia* (London: Palgrave Macmillan, 2015), 145.

96. Aleksandr Etkind, *Internal Colonization: Russia's Imperial Experience* (Cambridge: Polity Press, 2011); Bruce Grant, *The Captive and the Gift: Cultural Histories of Sovereignty in Russia and the Caucasus* (Ithaca: Cornell University Press, 2009).

97. A proponent of the indigenous concept is Vadim Volkov, "'Obshchestvennost': Russia's Lost Concept of Civil Society," in *Civil Society in the Baltic Sea Region*, ed. Norbert Götz and Jörg Hackmann (Aldershot: Ashgate, 2003), 63–74. For a critical appraisal of the thesis see Olga Malinova, "Obshchestvo, publika, obshchestvennost' v Rossii ser. XIX—nachala XX veka: Otrazhenie v poniatiiakh praktik publichnoi kommunikatsii i obshchestvennoi samodeiatel'nosti," in *"Poniatiia o Rossii': K istoricheskoi semantike imperskogo perioda*, ed. D. Sdvizhkova and I. Shirle (Moscow: Novoe Literaturnoe Obozrenie, 2012), 428–63.

98. Alexander von Schelting, *Russland und Europa im russischen Geschichtsdenken* (Bern: A. Francke Verlag, 1948).

99. Jutta Scherrer, "The 'Cultural/Civilizational Turn' in Post-Soviet Identity Building," in *Power and Legitimacy: Challenges from Russia*, ed. Per-Arne Bodin, Stefan Hedlund, and Elena Namli, Routledge Contemporary Russia and Eastern Europe Series 39 (London: Routledge, 2013), 152–68; Jutta Scherrer, *Kulturologie: Russland auf der Suche nach einer zivilisatorischen Identität*, Essener kulturwissenschaftliche Vorträge, Bd. 13 (Göttingen: Wallstein, 2003), 93–126.

100. Berezin, Sandusky, and Davidson, "Culture in Politics and Politics in Culture."

101. Quinn Slobodian, *Globalists: The End of Empire and the Birth of Neoliberalism* (Cambridge: Harvard University Press, 2018).

102. Brown, *In the Ruins of Neoliberalism*; Loïc Wacquant, "Three Steps to a Historical Anthropology of Actually Existing Neoliberalism," *Social Anthropology* 20, no. 1 (February 2012): 66–79, https://doi.org/10/fzv34p.

103. For an overview see James Ferguson, "The Uses of Neoliberalism," *Antipode* 41 (January 2010): 166–84, https://doi.org/10/dxvdbk.
104. Thomas Biebricher, "Einleitung: Neoliberalismus und Staat—ziemlich beste Feinde," in *Der Staat des Neoliberalismus*, ed. Thomas Biebricher (Baden-Baden: Nomos, 2016), 9–28.
105. See Philipp Cerny's writings on the competition state: "Competition State," in *Encyclopedia of Governance*, ed. Mark Bevir, 2 vols. (Thousand Oaks: SAGE Publications, 2007), 129. For more recent works, see Madariaga, *Neoliberal Resilience*; Slobodian, *Globalists*; Cornel Ban, *Ruling Ideas: How Global Neoliberalism Goes Local* (New York: Oxford University Press, 2016). After the financial and economic crises that started in 2007, more social scientists studied how states supported markets to survive. See for instance Colin Crouch, Donatella della Porta, and Wolfgang Streeck, "Democracy in Neoliberalism?," *Anthropological Theory* 16, no. 4 (December 2016): 497–512, https://doi.org/10/gdtnp6.
106. Brown, *Undoing the Demos*.
107. Katharyne Mitchell, *Making Workers: Radical Geographies of Education*, Radical Geography (London: Pluto Press, 2018).
108. Johanna Bockman, *Markets in the Name of Socialism: The Left-Wing Origins of Neoliberalism* (Stanford, CA: Stanford University Press, 2011), 6.
109. Aihwa Ong, *Neoliberalism as Exception: Mutations in Citizenship and Sovereignty* (Durham: Duke University Press, 2006); Stephen J. Collier, *Post-Soviet Social: Neoliberalism, Social Modernity, Biopolitics* (Princeton, NJ: Princeton University Press, 2011); Stephen J. Collier, "Neoliberalism as Big Leviathan, or . . .? A Response to Wacquant and Hilgers," *Social Anthropology* 20, no. 2 (May 2012): 186–95, https://doi.org/10/gdtnst; Peter Miller and Nikolas S. Rose, *Governing the Present: Administering Economic, Social and Personal Life* (Cambridge: Polity Press, 2009).
110. Margaret Wetherell, "Feeling Rules, Atmospheres and Affective Practice: Some Reflections on the Analysis of Emotional Episodes," in *Privilege, Agency and Affect*, ed. Claire Maxwell and Peter Aggleton (London: Palgrave Macmillan UK, 2013), 228. For a critical take on the use of assemblage concepts in case studies on neoliberalism see also Wacquant, "Three Steps to a Historical Anthropology of Actually Existing Neoliberalism."
111. Ulrich Bröckling, *The Entrepreneurial Self: Fabricating a New Type of Subject* (Los Angeles: Sage, 2016), 164.
112. Ban, *Ruling Ideas*, 3.
113. Madariaga, *Neoliberal Resilience*.
114. As frequently assumed in ethnographies on neoliberalism, for a critique see Ferguson, "The Uses of Neoliberalism."
115. Madariaga, *Neoliberal Resilience*; Ban, *Ruling Ideas*; Appel and Orenstein, *From Triumph to Crisis*.
116. Ban, *Ruling Ideas*.
117. Appel and Orenstein, *From Triumph to Crisis*.
118. Scheiring, *The Retreat of Liberal Democracy*.

119. This interpretation runs through the following books: Janine R. Wedel, *Collision and Collusion: The Strange Case of Western Aid to Eastern Europe; 1989—1998* (New York: St. Martin's Press, 2001); Hemment, *Youth Politics in Putin's Russia*.
120. For an example from the post-Soviet space see Lisa McIntosh Sundstrom, *Funding Civil Society: Foreign Assistance and NGO Development in Russia* (Stanford, CA: Stanford University Press, 2006), http://www.sup.org/books/title/?id=4828.
121. Aleksandr Bikbov, "Neo-Traditionalist Fits with Neo-Liberal Shifts in Russian Cultural Policy," in *Russia: Art Resistance and the Conservative-Authoritarian Zeitgeist*, ed. Lena Jonson and Andrei Erofeev (New York: Routledge, 2017), 65–83; Lerner and Zbenovich, "Adapting the Therapeutic Discourse to Post-Soviet Media Culture"; Matza, "'Good Individualism'?"; Katharina Klingseis, "The Power of Dress in Contemporary Russian Society: On Glamour Discourse and the Everyday Practice of Getting Dressed in Russian Cities," *Laboratorium: Russian Review of Social Research* 3, no. 1 (2011): 84–115; Sundstrom, *Funding Civil Society*.
122. Hae-Yung Song, *The State, Class and Developmentalism in South Korea: Development as Fetish* (London: Routledge, 2019), 75.
123. Song, *The State, Class and Developmentalism in South Korea*, 76–77.
124. Ian Bruff, "The Rise of Authoritarian Neoliberalism," *Rethinking Marxism* 26, no. 1 (January 2014): 113–29, https://doi.org/10/gdnb73; Adam Fabry and Sune Sandbeck, "Introduction to Special Issue on 'Authoritarian Neoliberalism,'" *Competition & Change* 23, no. 2 (April 2019): 109–15, https://doi.org/10/gm7ms5.
125. Hoffman, *Patriotic Professionalism in Urban China*; Hemment, *Youth Politics in Putin's Russia*.
126. Glasius, "What Authoritarianism Is ... and Is Not," 527.
127. Slobodian, *Globalists*.
128. Cerny, "In the Shadow of Ordoliberalism: The Paradox of Neoliberalism in the 21st Century."
129. Ralf Ptak, "Neoliberalism in Germany: Revisiting the Ordoliberal Foundations of the Social Market Economy," in *The Road from Mont Pèlerin: The Making of the Neoliberal Thought Collective*, ed. Philip Mirowski and Dieter Plehwe (Cambridge: Harvard University Press, 2009), 98–138.
130. Ralf Ptak, "Das Staatsverständnis im Ordoliberalismus. Eine theoriegeschichtliche Analyse mit aktuellem Ausblick," in *Der Staat des Neoliberalismus*, ed. Thomas Biebricher (Baden-Baden: Nomos, 2016), 45.
131. Ptak, "Das Staatsverständnis im Ordoliberalismus," 49.
132. Rüstow quoted in Ptak, "Neoliberalism in Germany," 111.
133. Philip Mirowski, "Postface: Defining Neoliberalism," in *The Road from Mont Pèlerin: The Making of the Neoliberal Thought Collective*, ed. Philip Mirowski and Dieter Plehwe (Cambridge: Harvard University Press, 2009), 417–55; Phillip Becher et al., "Ordoliberal White Democracy, Elitism, and the Demos: The Case of Wilhelm Röpke," *Democratic Theory* 8, no. 2 (December 1, 2021): 70–96, https://doi.org/10/gpn7h9.
134. Tim Christiaens, "The Entrepreneur of the Self beyond Foucault's Neoliberal Homo Oeconomicus," *European Journal of Social Theory* 23, no. 4 (July 25, 2019): 493–511,

https://doi.org/10/ghtzs7; Dieter Plehwe, "Schumpeter Revival?: How Neoliberals Revised the Image of the Entrepreneur," in *Nine Lives of Neoliberalism*, ed. Dieter Plehwe, Quinn Slobodian, and Philip Mirowski (London: Verso, 2020), 120–42.
135. Christiaens, "The Entrepreneur of the Self beyond Foucault's Neoliberal Homo Oeconomicus," 503.
136. Joseph A. Schumpeter, *Capitalism, Socialism and Democracy* (London: Routledge, 2005), 212.
137. Schumpeter, *Capitalism, Socialism and Democracy*, 212 footnote 8.
138. Similar sensitivities have shaped his economic and political theorizing, see Richard Swedberg, "Introduction," in *Capitalism, Socialism and Democracy*, by Joseph A. Schumpeter (London: Routledge, 2005), ix–xix.
139. Schumpeter, *Capitalism, Socialism and Democracy*, 214.
140. Dietrich Rueschemeyer, Evelyne Huber, and John D. Stephens, *Capitalist Development and Democracy* (Chicago: University of Chicago Press, 1992), 271.
141. For the US-American perspective on this race see Robert D. Atkinson and Stephen J. Ezell, *Innovation Economics: The Race for Global Advantage* (New Haven, CT: Yale University Press, 2012).
142. Neil R. Anderson and Rosina M. Gasteiger, "Innovation and Creativity in Organisations: Individual and Work Team Research Findings and Implications for Government Policy," in *Micro-Foundations for Innovation Policy*, ed. Bart Nooteboom and Erik Stam (Amsterdam: Amsterdam University Press, 2008), 249–72.
143. Lewin and Lippitt, "An Experimental Approach to the Study of Autocracy and Democracy: A Preliminary Note."
144. Marina Minor, "Wer motiviert wen, wozu und warum? Selbstbestimmtes Handeln und Motivation in Gamification und Nudging als Beispiele gegenwärtiger Motivationsforschung—Versuche einer Reinterpretation," in *Ask them Why: Ausgewählte Beiträge der Ferienuni Kritische Psychologie 2018*, ed. Nora Dietrich and Thomas Dohmen (Hamburg: Argument Verlag mit Ariadne, 2020), 63–82, https://www.kritische-psychologie.de/files/FKP-Spezial-2018-Minor.pdf; Ute Holzkamp-Osterkamp, *Grundlagen der psychologischen Motivationsforschung*, vol. 1, 2 vols., Texte zur kritischen Psychologie (Frankfurt: Campus Verlag, 1975); Lizzie Ward, "Caring for Ourselves?: Self-Care and Neoliberalism," in *Ethics of Care: Critical Advances in International Perspective*, ed. Marian Barnes et al. (Bristol: Policy, 2015), 45–56.
145. Sennett, *The Corrosion of Character*; Christian Meier, *Die Entstehung des Politischen bei den Griechen*, 6th ed. (Frankfurt am Main: Suhrkamp, 2011).
146. Charles Taylor, *The Ethics of Authenticity* (Cambridge: Harvard University Press, 1992), 74.
147. Taylor, *The Ethics of Authenticity*, 15.
148. Taylor, *The Ethics of Authenticity*, 77.
149. Some historians link the birth of politics in ancient times with the emergence of a can-do spirit (*Könnensbewusstsein*). Meier, *Die Entstehung des Politischen bei den Griechen*, 245.

150. Brown, *Undoing the Demos*, 222.
151. Olga Shevchenko, *Crisis and the Everyday in Postsocialist Moscow* (Bloomington: Indiana University Press, 2009), 150.
152. Anna Schwenck, "Performances of Closeness and the Staging of Resistance with Mainstream Musics. Analyzing the Symbolism of Pandemic Skeptical Protests," German Politics and Society 41, no. 2 (2023).
153. See for a similar argument the subchapter "Russian Eyes" in Greene and Robertson, *Putin v. the People*.
154. Greg Simons, "Putin's International Political Image," *Journal of Political Marketing* 18, no. 4 (October 2019): 307–29, https://doi.org/10/gjfg7z. On hypermasculinity see Elizabeth A. Wood, "Hypermasculinity as a Scenario of Power," *International Feminist Journal of Politics* 18, no. 3 (July 2, 2016): 329–50, https://doi.org/10/gnqkx8.
155. Jan-Werner Müller, "Moscow's Trojan Horse," August 6, 2014, https://www.foreignaffairs.com/articles/central-europe/2014-08-06/moscows-trojan-horse; János Mátyás Kovács and Balázs Trencsényi, "Conclusion: Hungary–Brave and New? Dissecting a Realistic Dystopia," in *Brave New Hungary: Mapping the "System of National Cooperation,"* ed. János Mátyás Kovács and Balázs Trencsényi (Lanham: Lexington Books, 2020), 379–427.
156. Kristina Stoeckl, "The Rise of the Russian Christian Right: The Case of the World Congress of Families," *Religion, State and Society* 48, no. 4 (August 2020): 223–38, https://doi.org/10/ghrpdg; Kristina Stoeckl and Kseniya Medvedeva, "Double Bind at the UN: Western Actors, Russia, and the Traditionalist Agenda," *Global Constitutionalism* 7, no. 3 (November 2018): 383–421, https://doi.org/10/gm7ms7; Katharina Bluhm and Mihai Varga, "Introduction: Toward a New Illiberal Conservatism in Russia and East Central Europe," in *New Conservatives in Russia and East Central Europe*, ed. Katharina Bluhm and Mihai Varga (New York: Routledge, 2019), 1–22.

Chapter 2

1. For a description of such tourist bases still operative in many countries once counted as allies or members of the Soviet Union, see Diane Koenker, *Club Red: Vacation Travel and the Soviet Dream* (Ithaca, NY: Cornell University Press, 2013).
2. I had been offered a free seat on a charter flight that was organized for teaching staff from Western Russia to fly to the Sakha Republic. See Appendix I for more details.
3. Anton Troianovski, "As Frozen Land Burns, Siberia Fears: 'If We Don't Have the Forest, We Don't Have Life,'" *The New York Times*, July 17, 2021, https://www.nytimes.com/2021/07/17/world/europe/siberia-fires.html.
4. "MAO DOL 'Usad'ba Buluus,'" Usad'ba Buluus Leisure Camp, accessed March 15, 2023, https://xn—90ausgb.xn—80aaa7bi1aw.xn—p1ai/.

5. "Photo 'Buluus'. Napravlenie 'Politika' (SakhaSeliger 2013)," Vkontakte [Russian Social Network] SakhaSeliger 2013, accessed February 22, 2023, https://vk.com/club5 0017940?z=photo-50017940_307631920%2Falbum-50017940_170272124%2Frev.
6. Monica Rüthers, "Picturing Soviet Childhood: Photo Albums of Pioneer Camps," *Jahrbücher für Geschichte Osteuropas* 67, no. 1 (2019): 81–82, https://doi.org/10/grrqzs.
7. Kristin Luker, *Salsa Dancing into the Social Sciences: Research in an Age of Info-Glut* (Cambridge, MA: Harvard University Press, 2008), 164.
8. Some professionally produced video clips to advertise *Biriusa* provide a good overview of this upbeat spirit: TIM "Biryusa". *Biriusa 2022 — Liubov' [Biriusa 2022 — Love]*. VK. September 28, 2022. 4:15. https://vk.com/video-10493768_456239529. TIM "Biryusa". *Biriusa Zhdet! [Biriusa Is Waiting!]*. VK. July 17, 2021. 0:15. https://vk.com/video-10493768_456239356.
9. Personal communication, Krasnoyarsk, July 2013.
10. My back-translation slightly differs from the original. See Lauren Effron, "Steve Jobs' Commencement Speech Talked About Death," *ABC News*, October 6, 2011, http://abcnews.go.com/blogs/technology/2011/10/steve-jobs-talked-about-death-in-2005-stanford-commencement-speech-2.
11. Jussi Lassila, *The Quest for an Ideal Youth in Putin's Russia: The Search for Distinctive Conformism in the Political Communication of Nashi, 2005-2009*, Soviet and Post-Soviet Politics and Society (Stuttgart: Ibidem-Verlag, 2014).
12. Ulrich Schmid, "Naši—Die Putin-Jugend: Sowjettradition und politische Konzeptkunst," *Osteuropa* 56, no. 5 (2006): 5–18.
13. Julie Hemment, "Soviet-Style Neoliberalism? Nashi, Youth Voluntarism, and the Restructuring of Social Welfare in Russia," *Problems of Post-Communism* 56, no. 6 (2009): 36–50, https://doi.org/10/d5gbxs.
14. "*V liubom proekte vazhneishim faktorom iavliaetsia vera v uspekh. Bez very uspekh nevozmozhen. Uil'iam Dzheims*" My back-translation: "The most important factor for every project [to succeed] is belief in success. Without belief success is impossible" (William James).
15. Arci is an acronym for *Associazione Ricreativa e Culturale Italiana*, an Italian civil society organization. See "Chi Siamo," Arci, accessed February 12, 2023, https://www.arci.it/chi-siamo/.
16. For a discussion of the popularity of such conspiratorial thought see Eliot Borenstein, *Plots against Russia: Conspiracy and Fantasy after Socialism* (Ithaca, NY: Cornell University Press, 2019).
17. On the Russian government's construction of a Pink Threat see Anna Schwenck, "Russian Politics of Radicalisation and Surveillance," in *Governing Youth Politics in the Age of Surveillance*, ed. Maria Grasso and Judith Bessant, The Criminalization of Political Dissent (London: Routledge, 2018), 168–82.
18. My fellow campers suggested that I dress up, like them, in the stereotypical way Native Americans have been dominantly represented in movies. I did so despite my reservations about the stereotyping. Withdrawing my participation or raising concerns seemed to me inadequate, given my status as a visitor from Western Europe and the Sakha Republic's inhabitants' own history of oppression and experiences of racism.

Chapter 3

1. Cornel Ban, *Ruling Ideas: How Global Neoliberalism Goes Local* (New York: Oxford University Press, 2016).
2. Monica Rüthers, "Picturing Soviet Childhood: Photo Albums of Pioneer Camps," *Jahrbücher für Geschichte Osteuropas* 67, no. 1 (2019): 66, https://doi.org/10/grrqzs. She highlights the importance of the camp *Artek* on Crimea, symbolizing like no other such a geography of a happy Soviet childhood and youth.
3. Diane Koenker, *Club Red: Vacation Travel and the Soviet Dream* (Ithaca, NY: Cornell University Press, 2013); Iuliia Skubytska, "It Takes a Union to Raise a Soviet: Children's Summer Camps as a Reflection of Late Soviet Society" (PhD diss., University of Pennsylvania, 2018), https://repository.upenn.edu/edissertations/2935.
4. Jochen Hellbeck, *Revolution on My Mind: Writing a Diary under Stalin* (Cambridge, MA: Harvard University Press, 2006).
5. 1991 draft program of the Communist party's Central Committee, entitled "Socialism, Democracy, Progress." Quoted in Graeme Gill, *Symbols and Legitimacy in Soviet Politics* (Cambridge: Cambridge University Press, 2011), 254.
6. Anna-Jutta Pietsch, "Self-Fulfillment Through Work: Working Conditions in Soviet Factories," in *Quality of Life in the Soviet Union*, ed. Horst Herlemann and Shaun Murphy (New York: Routledge, 2019).
7. Jon Elster, "Self-Realization in Work and Politics: The Marxist Conception of the Good Life," *Social Philosophy and Policy* 3, no. 2 (1986): 97, https://doi.org/10/b3k3jr.
8. Isaiah Berlin, *The Crooked Timber of Humanity: Chapters in the History of Ideas*, 2nd ed. (Princeton, NJ: Princeton University Press, 2013), 238.
9. A notable exception to this focus dominant in the literature is: Giorgio Comai, "Youth Camps in Post-Soviet Russia and the Northern Caucasus: The Cases of Seliger and Mashuk 2010," *Anthropology of East Europe Review* 30, no. 1 (2012): 184–212. Another exception, though downplaying *Nashi*'s authoritarianness to make an argument about neoliberalism, is Julie Julie Hemment, *Youth Politics in Putin's Russia: Producing Patriots and Entrepreneurs* (Bloomington: Indiana University Press, 2015).
10. Jussi Lassila, "From Failed Mobilization of Youth to Paternalistic Visualization of Putin: The Rocky Road of the Nashi Youth Movement," *Critique & Humanism* 46, no. 2 (2016): 33–50.
11. Valerie Bunce and Sharon L. Wolchik, *Defeating Authoritarian Leaders in Postcommunist Countries*, Cambridge Studies in Contentious Politics (Cambridge: Cambridge University Press, 2011); Michael Schwirtz, "Russia's Political Youths," *Demokratizatsiya: The Journal of Post-Soviet Democratization* 15, no. 1 (2007): 73–85.
12. For how this portrayal of an Orange Threat was—as early as 2004/ 2005—connected to allegations that the anti-Yanukovych protesters were corrupted by fascists or would be fascists themselves, see Anna Schwenck, "Russian Politics of Radicalisation and Surveillance," in *Governing Youth Politics in the Age of Surveillance*, ed. Maria Grasso

and Judith Bessant, *The Criminalization of Political Dissent* (London: Routledge, 2018), 171–72.
13. Also in 2005, the Public Chamber was founded—a public consultation body financed by the presidential administration with members largely appointed by Putin. In 2006, a first law restricting the practices of NGOs was introduced, a predecessor to the later "foreign agent law". See James Richter, "Integration from below?: The Disappointing Effort to Promote Civil Society in Russia," in *Russia and Globalization: Identity, Security, and Society in an Era of Change*, ed. Douglas W. Blum (Washington, DC: Woodrow Wilson Center Press; Johns Hopkins University Press, 2008), 181–203.
14. Lassila, "From Failed Mobilization of Youth to Paternalistic Visualization of Putin." For other government-sponsored youth organizations at *Seliger* in these early years see Elena Loskutova, *Iunaia politika. Istoriia molodezhnykh politicheskikh organizatsii sovremennoi Rossii* (Moscow: Tsentr "Panorama," 2008).
15. Ulrich Schmid, "Naši—Die Putin-Jugend: Sowjettradition und politische Konzeptkunst," *Osteuropa* 56, no. 5 (2006): 5–18.
16. See also Félix Krawatzek, *Youth in Regime Crisis: Comparative Perspectives from Russia to Weimar Germany*, Oxford Studies in Democratization (Oxford: Oxford University Press, 2018).
17. Evidence shows that many *Nashi* commissars became employees of the newly founded "State Committee of Youth Affairs," which was later transformed into *Rosmolodezh*. Roman Shleinov, "Kak Kreml' finansiruet svoe molodezhnoe dvizhenie," *Vedomosti*, November 29, 2010, http://www.vedomosti.ru/newspaper/articles/2010/11/29/dengi_nashih; Zinaida Burskaia, "Bezhim za toboi!," *Novaia Gazeta*, December 8, 2010, http://www.novayagazeta.ru/sports/483.html; Lenta.ru, "Interv'iu s glavoi Rosmolodezhi Vasiliem Iakemenko," January 17, 2012, https://lenta.ru/articles/2012/01/17/jakemenko/. See also Chapter 6.
18. There are no official figures on the total number of youth-leadership summer camps in today's Russia. The Russian Youth League (*Rossiisskii Soiuz Molodezhi*) states that in 2022 more than 20 000 young adults between 18 and 35 years participated in youth-leadership summer camps: "Rosmolodezh' zapuskaet Vserossiiskuiu forumnuiu kampaniiu 2022 goda," Rossiiskii Soiuz Molodezhi, March 29, 2022, https://ruy.ru/press/news/rosmolodezh-zapuskaet-vserossiyskuyu-forumnuyu-kampaniyu-2022-goda-/. I am grateful to Sima and Elena Renje for their kind support.
19. Sabrina Tavernise, "Russia Entrepreneurs Try the Business of Governing," *The New York Times*, February 11, 2001, https://www.nytimes.com/2001/02/11/world/russia-entrepreneurs-try-the-business-of-governing.html.
20. Wendy Brown, *Undoing the Demos: Neoliberalism's Stealth Revolution* (New York: Zone Books, 2015), 34.
21. Angela McRobbie, *Be Creative: Making a Living in the New Culture Industries* (Cambridge: Polity Press, 2016), 39.
22. Michel Foucault, *Discipline and Punish: The Birth of the Prison* (New York: Random House, 1977).
23. Amelia Horgan, *Lost in Work: Escaping Capitalism*, Outspoken by Pluto (London: Pluto Press, 2021).

24. Marlies Glasius, "What Authoritarianism Is . . . and Is Not: A Practice Perspective," *International Affairs* 94, no. 3 (May 1, 2018): 515-33, https://doi.org/10/gdkww5.
25. See for instance Stefan Niklas, "On the Reissue of The Authoritarian Personality," *Krisis | Journal for Contemporary Philosophy* 41, no. 1 (June 15, 2021): 202-9, https://doi.org/10/gm7nf2; Andreas Stahl et al., *Konformistische Rebellen: zur Aktualität des autoritären Charakters* (Berlin: Verbrecher Verlag, 2020); Wilhelm Heitmeyer, *Autoritäre Versuchungen*, 3rd ed. (Berlin: Suhrkamp, 2018).
26. Theodor W. Adorno et al., *The Authoritarian Personality*, Studies in Prejudice (New York: Harper & Row, 1950).
27. Kurt Lewin and Ronald Lippitt, "An Experimental Approach to the Study of Autocracy and Democracy: A Preliminary Note," *Sociometry* 1, no. 3/4 (1938): 292-300, https://doi.org/10/c9p5vj. Lewin's studies are widely quoted in literature on "leadership styles" today. Focusing on the efficiency of different leadership styles, such studies tend to depoliticize Lewin's research which was influenced by the authoritarian personality project. See Jeanette Ziehm, Gisela Trommsdorf, and Isabelle Albert, "Erziehungsstile," in *Dorsch—Lexikon Der Psychologie*, ed. Markus Antonius Wirtz (Bern: Hogrefe, 2014).
28. Kenny Cupers, "Governing through Nature: Camps and Youth Movements in Interwar Germany and the United States," *Cultural Geographies* 15, no. 2 (April 1, 2008): 186, https://doi.org/10/cdw6dm; John A. Williams, *Turning to Nature in Germany: Hiking, Nudism, and Conservation, 1900-1940* (Stanford: Stanford University Press, 2007); Eva Barlösius, Naturgemäße Lebensführung: Zur Geschichte der Lebensreform um die Jahrhundertwende (Frankfurt: Campus, 1997).
29. Abigail A. Van Slyck, *A Manufactured Wilderness: Summer Camps and the Shaping of American Youth, 1890-1960* (Minneapolis: University of Minnesota Press, 2006), 3-4.
30. Michael B. Smith, "'The Ego Ideal of the Good Camper' and the Nature of Summer Camp," *Environmental History* 11, no. 1 (2006): 73, https://doi.org/10/dw8zcd.
31. Although the Boy Scouts and the Girl Guides were founded around the same time, it was only in the 1920s that camping for girls and young women became established in the US. These camps, though promoting marriage and motherhood as life goals for women, engendered fears that women would leave their traditional roles due to the summer camp experience. Van Slyck, *Summer Camps and the Shaping of American Youth*, 10-11; Leslie Paris, *Children's Nature: The Rise of the American Summer Camp*, American History and Culture (New York: New York University Press, 2008), 19.
32. Paris, *Children's Nature*, 18; Cupers, "Governing through Nature."
33. Cupers, "Governing through Nature."
34. Van Slyck, *Summer Camps and the Shaping of American Youth*, 9.
35. Peter Kenez, *The Birth of the Propaganda State: Soviet Methods of Mass Mobilization, 1917-1929* (Cambridge: Cambridge University Press, 1985), 89. From about 1919 it was portrayed as an anti-Soviet instrument of the enemy, and it disappeared some years after the October Revolution.
36. Catriona Kelly, *Children's World: Growing up in Russia, 1890-1991* (New Haven, CT: Yale University Press, 2007), 545-46.

37. Kelly, *Children's World*, 546.
38. Kelly, *Children's World*, 546.
39. Kenez, *The Birth of the Propaganda State*, 191. During these years, only about 6 percent of the relevant age group participated in Young Pioneer organizations.
40. Kelly, *Children's World*, 548.
41. Kenez, *The Birth of the Propaganda State*, 193.
42. Skubytska, "It Takes A Union To Raise A Soviet: Children's Summer Camps As A Reflection Of Late Soviet Society," 67.
43. David L. Hoffmann, *Stalinist Values: The Cultural Norms of Soviet Modernity, 1917–1941* (Ithaca, NY: Cornell University Press, 2003), 51.
44. Concerns over cultured behavior spread after the Bolsheviks had secured their power position in 1921. Now that they were to control state and society, social disorder was no longer seen as conducive to the socialist cause, but as antithetical to the construction of an advanced socialist society. Anne E. Gorsuch, *Youth in Revolutionary Russia: Enthusiasts, Bohemians, Delinquents* (Bloomington: Indiana University Press, 2000), 91–92.
45. Hoffmann, *Stalinist Values*, 17.
46. Hoffmann, *Stalinist Values*, 60.
47. Koenker, *Club Red*, 6 & 256–57.
48. Koenker, *Club Red*, 57.
49. Koenker, *Club Red*, 45 & 221.
50. Koenker, 58.
51. Hellbeck, *Revolution on My Mind*, 21.
52. Hoffmann, *Stalinist Values*, 35–36.
53. As quoted in Hoffmann, 42.
54. Kelly, *Children's World*, 549.
55. Konstantin Zotov, *Pionerskii lager'—baza kul'turnogo i zdorovogo otdykha . . .*, 1935, Poster RU/SU 1818, 29 × 41 in. (73.7 × 104.1 cm), Hoover Institution, https://digital collections.hoover.org/objects/23413/pionerskii-lager—baza-kulturnogo-i-zdorov ogo-otdykha.
56. See also Skubytska, "It Takes A Union To Raise A Soviet: Children's Summer Camps As A Reflection Of Late Soviet Society."
57. Kelly, *Children's World*, 559. See also Koenker, *Club Red*, 36 & 204. See also endnote 39 of this chapter.
58. Kelly, *Children's World*, 549–59.
59. Rüthers, "Picturing Soviet Childhood"; Skubytska, "It Takes A Union To Raise A Soviet: Children's Summer Camps As A Reflection Of Late Soviet Society," 196–253.
60. Kelly, *Children's World*, 557–59. See also Aleksei V. Kudryashev, "The Dialectics of Everyday Life in Pioneer Camps: Romanticism and Regimen," *Russian Education & Society* 61, no. 5–6 (2019): 231–38, https://doi.org/10/gnjhps.
61. Quoted in Kudryashev, "The Dialectics of Everyday Life in Pioneer Camps," 236. The author does not state the source of the quoted primary document.
62. Gorsuch, *Youth in Revolutionary Russia*, 25.

63. In addition to academic literature such as: Skubytska, "It Takes A Union To Raise A Soviet: Children's Summer Camps As A Reflection Of Late Soviet Society"; Kudryashev, "The Dialectics of Everyday Life in Pioneer Camps"; Boris V. Kupriianov, "Soviet Adolescents' First Experiences of Romantic Feelings and Relationships at Pioneer Camps between the 1960s and 1980s," *Russian Education & Society* 61, no. 2–3 (2019): 125–38, https://doi.org/10/gnjhtj; Rüthers, "Picturing Soviet Childhood."
64. Kudryashev, "The Dialectics of Everyday Life in Pioneer Camps," 233.
65. Arun Kumar, "Welcome, Or No Trespassing [1964] Review—A Marvelous Soviet Camp Comedy," *High On Films* (blog), March 17, 2021, https://www.highonfilms.com/welcome-or-no-trespassing-1964-review/; Will Noah, "Elem Klimov's Boundary-Pushing Satires," *The Criterion Collection*, January 10, 2018, https://www.criterion.com/current/posts/5257-elem-klimovs-boundary-pushing-satires.
66. Noah, "Elem Klimov's Boundary-Pushing Satires."
67. See Aleksei Semenenko, "The Mystery of The Blue Cup," *Baltic Worlds* 9, no. 4 (2017): 43–51.
68. Kelly, *Children's World*, 554–55.
69. Documenting campers' weight gains was also practiced in US-American summer camps: Van Slyck, *Summer Camps and the Shaping of American Youth*, 104.
70. Mosfilm, "Dobro pozhalovat', ili postoronnim vkhod vospreshchen," 1964, *YouTube*, May 16, 2017, 1:10:12, https://www.youtube.com/watch?v=GX54eNpGYyM&feature=player_embedded.
71. Regarding authoritarian values such as these see Lewin and Lippitt, "An Experimental Approach to the Study of Autocracy and Democracy: A Preliminary Note"; Niklas, "On the Reissue of The Authoritarian Personality."
72. "A vy pomnite svoi pionerskie lageria," Strana Pensioneriia. Sotsial'naia set' Pensionerov, 2013, https://pensionerka.com/forum/thread1384-1.html.
73. Ol'ga Koval', "Mestnye i lagernye," *Obrazy detstva* (blog), February 23, 2014, http://obrazdetstva.ru/98-mestnye-i-lagernye.html#commen.
74. Nadezhda, "Sovetskie pionerskie lageria," *Obrazy detstva* (blog), May 24, 2011, http://obrazdetstva.ru/38-sovetskie-pionerskie-lagerya.html.
75. Kudryashev, "The Dialectics of Everyday Life in Pioneer Camps," 236.
76. Ekaterina Maslakova, "Upravlenie razvitiem detskogo turizma v novykh ekonomicheskikh usloviiakh khoziaistvovaniia. Avtoreferat" (Moscow: OUVPO "Gosudarstvennyi universitet upravleniia," 2009); I.E. Sadkova, "Problemy detsko-iunosheskogo turizma v sovremennoi Rossii," *Problemy sovremennoi ekonomiki* 2, no. 34 (2010), http://www.m-economy.ru/art.php?nArtId=3172.
77. M.A. Morozov, "Marketingovoe issledovanie rossiiskogo rynka detskogo turizma," HR-Portal, March 21, 2014, http://hr-portal.ru/article/marketingovoe-issledovanie-rossiyskogo-rynka-detskogo-turizma; Maslakova, "Upravlenie razvitiem detskogo turizma."
78. See Tomas Matza, "'Good Individualism'? Psychology, Ethics, and Neoliberalism in Postsocialist Russia," *American Ethnologist* 39, no. 4 (November 2012): 804–18, https://doi.org/10/f4d9sm; Ina Schröder, "Shaping Youth: Quest for Moral Education

in an Indigenous Community in Western Siberia" (PhD diss., Halle-Wittenberg, Martin-Luther-Universität, 2017).
79. Galina Stanislavovna Sukhoveiko, "Sotsial'no znachimye initsiativy v pionerskoi organizatsii kak sredstvo formirovaniia samodeiatel'nosti detei i podrostkov," Avtoreferat dissertatsii na soiskanie nauchnoi stepeni kandidata pedagogicheskikh nauk (Moscow: Vysshaia komsomol'skaia shkola pri TsK VLKSM, 1990).
80. Sukhoveiko, "Sotsial'no znachimye," 3.
81. They were jointly built by pioneers and members of the *Komsomol*. See Dmitrii V. Sutiagin, "Children's Railways of the Former USSR—Kratovo," 2012, http://www.dzd-ussr.ru/towns/kratovo/index-eng.html.
82. "Distsiplina—Letnii lager," MetodViki, Summercamp.ru—letnii lager, 2015, https://summercamp.ru/Дисциплинарные_принципы.
83. Detskii ozdorovitel'nyi lager' «Kratovo», *Pamiatka dlia roditelei otpravliaiushchikh detei v DOL «Kratovo»*, 2015, http://www.rzd.ru/ent/public/ru?STRUCTURE_ID=5185&layer_id=5554&id=3677#main.
84. Detskii ozdorovitel'nyi lager' «Kratovo», 2015; Maslakova, "Upravlenie razvitiem detskogo turizma." Maslakova mentions that missing safety precautions had been a problem at some children's' summer camps during the 1990s, though she does not provide details.
85. Aleksandr Bikbov, "Neo-Traditionalist Fits with Neo-Liberal Shifts in Russian Cultural Policy," in *Russia: Art Resistance and the Conservative-Authoritarian Zeitgeist*, ed. Lena Jonson and Andrei Erofeev (New York: Routledge, 2017), 79.
86. "Chto takoe chelovek goda," *Ekspert*, December 23, 2002, https://expert.ru/expert/2002/48/48ex-people_34982/.
87. As quoted in Alexei Yurchak, "Russian Neoliberal: The Entrepreneurial Ethic and the Spirit of 'True Careerism,'" *The Russian Review* 62, no. 1 (2003): 79, https://doi.org/10/bjf9hz.
88. Victoria E. Bonnell, "Winners and Losers in Russia's Economic Transition," in *Identities in Transition: Eastern Europe and Russia after the Collapse of Communism*, ed. Victoria E. Bonnell (Berkeley: Center for Slavic and East European Studies, 1996), 13–28.
89. Yurchak, "Russian Neoliberal," 79.
90. As quoted in Yurchak, 79.
91. Michael Burawoy, "Transition without Transformation: Russia's Involutionary Road to Capitalism," *East European Politics & Societies* 15, no. 2 (2001): 287.
92. N. V. Zubarevich and S. G. Safronov, "People and Money: Incomes, Consumption, and Financial Behavior of the Population of Russian Regions in 2000–2017," *Regional Research of Russia* 9, no. 4 (October 2019): 359–69, https://doi.org/10/gnbn29.
93. Rosmolodezh, "Molodezh' Rossii 2000-2025: Razvitie chelovecheskogo kapitala" (Federal Agency for Youth Affairs, 2013), 116 & 147, http://www.orthedu.ru/vstrechi/16649-molodezh-rossii-2000-2025.html.

94. Gulnaz Sharafutdinova, "Redistributing Sovereignty and Property under Putin: A View from Resource-Rich Republics of the Russian Federation," in *The Politics of Sub-National Authoritarianism in Russia*, ed. Cameron Ross and Vladimir Gel'man, Post-Soviet Politics (Farnham: Ashgate, 2010), 202.
95. Julia Ioffe, "The Master And Mikhail," *The New Yorker*, February 19, 2012, http://www.newyorker.com/magazine/2012/02/27/the-master-and-mikhail.
96. Sabrina Tavernise, "In a Russian Governor's Race, Elements of Farce," *The New York Times*, September 8, 2002, https://www.nytimes.com/2002/09/08/world/in-a-russian-governor-s-race-elements-of-farce.html.
97. Rostislav Turovsky, "The Influence of Russian Big Business on Regional Power: Models and Political Consequences," in *Politics in the Russian Regions*, ed. Graeme Gill (London: Palgrave Macmillan, 2007), 155.
98. Sharafutdinova, "Redistributing Sovereignty."
99. Richard Sakwa, *The Quality of Freedom: Khodorkovsky, Putin, and the Yukos Affair* (Oxford: Oxford University Press, 2009), 113.
100. Turovsky, "The Influence of Russian Big Business," 155.
101. Boris El'shin, "Boris Nemtsov obnaruzhil glavnoe preimushchestvo Krasnoiarskogo kraia," *Kommersant*, April 17, 2003; Mikhail Mishkin, "Aleksandr Khloponin zashchitil prezidentskie popravki ot somnenii v ikh demokratichnosti," *Kommersant*, September 22, 2004. See also Alla Barakhova, Il'ia Bulavinov, and Boris El'shin, "Vladimir Putin zanialsia naznacheniem gubernatorov," *Kommersant*, April 10, 2002, https://www.kommersant.ru/doc/344330.
102. Schmid, "Sowjettradition und politische Konzeptkunst."
103. Olga G. Gerasimova, *Ottepel', Zamarozki i studenty Moskovskogo Universiteta* (Moscow: AIRO-XXI, 2015), 242–66.
104. "Na ploshchadi Revoliutsii proshel parad kraevykh studencheskikh otriadov," *Newslab.ru*, July 1, 2005, http://newslab.ru/news/166349.
105. For photographs see: "KKSO. Krasnoyarsk (@kkso_krsk)," Instagram, accessed March 7, 2023, https://www.instagram.com/kkso_krsk/.
106. "Dve tysiachi krasnoiarskikh studentov uzhe podali zaiavki na vstuplenie v kraevoi studotriad," *Newslab.ru*, April 10, 2006, https://newslab.ru/news/187843.
107. "Dve tysiachi krasnoiarskikh studentov."
108. Daria Ivanovna Glazkova, Personal interview with organizer of "TIM Biriusa," interview by Anna Schwenck, August 8, 2014.
109. "Aleksandr Khloponin: Glavnoe—eto initsiativnost' molodykh," *Newslab.ru*, June 27, 2006, https://newslab.ru/news/195012.
110. Richard Sennett, *The Culture of the New Capitalism*, The Castle Lectures in Ethics, Politics, and Economics (New Haven, CT: Yale University Press, 2006), 97–98.
111. Daria Ivanovna Glazkova, Personal interview with organizer of "TIM Biriusa."
112. Daria Ivanovna Glazkova.
113. Aleksandr Aleksandrovich Abramovich, Personal interview with youth politician of the Krasnoyarsk Region, interview by Anna Schwenck, August 8, 2014.
114. Lisa M. Hoffman, *Patriotic Professionalism in Urban China: Fostering Talent*, Urban Life, Landscape, and Policy (Philadelphia: Temple University Press, 2010), 8–9.

115. Daria Ivanovna Glazkova, Personal interview with organizer of "TIM Biriusa."
116. Aleksandr Aleksandrovich Abramovich, Personal interview with youth politician of the Krasnoyarsk Region.
117. Vladimir Putin, "Zaiavlenie v sviazi s vneseniem na rassmotrenie Gosudarstvennoi Dumy zakonoproektov o gosudarstvennoi simvolike," Prezident Rossii, April 12, 2000, http://kremlin.ru/events/president/transcripts/21137.
118. Olga Malinova, "Russian Political Discourse in the 1990s: Crisis of Identity and Conflicting Pluralism of Ideas," in *Identities and Politics During the Putin Presidency: The Discursive Foundations of Russia's Stability*, ed. Philipp Casula and Jeronim Perovic, Soviet and Post-Soviet Politics and Society (Stuttgart: Ibidem-Verlag, 2009), 100.
119. Olga Malinova, *Aktual'noe proshloe: Simvolicheskaia politika vlastvuiushchei elity i dilemmy rossiiskoi identichnosti* (Moscow: ROSSPEN, 2015), 38.
120. Malinova, *Aktual'noe proshloe*, 168.
121. Ilya Kalinin, "Nostalgic Modernization: The Soviet Past as 'Historical Horizon,'" *Slavonica* 17, no. 2 (2011): 158, https://doi.org/10/bzc3b9; Ilya Kalinin, "Russian Culture as a Public Good, Private Property, National Value, and State Resource," Wissenschaftskolleg Berlin, November 10, 2021, https://www.wiko-berlin.de/fellows/akademisches-jahr/2021/kalinin-ilya. See also Malinova, *Aktual'noe proshloe*, 68.
122. Malinova, *Aktual'noe proshloe*, 30.
123. Boris Dubin, "Simvoly vozvrata vmesto simvolov peremen," *Pro et contra* 5, no. 53 (2011): 19.
124. V.A. Pristupko, *Studencheskie otriady: Istoricheskii opyt 1959–1990 godov* (Moscow: Moskovskii Gumanitarnii Universitet, 2008), 251.
125. Natalia Ermakova, "Kak krasnoiartsy 55 let igraiut v KVN: vspominaem samye uboinye shutki i vsekh zvezd," November 25, 2016, https://ngs24.ru/text/gorod/2016/11/25/50169501/.
126. Christine E. Evans, *Between Truth and Time: A History of Soviet Central Television*, Eurasia Past and Present (New Haven, CT: Yale University Press, 2016), 183–84.
127. Iuliia Shlenko, "Konstantin Gureev: «Za granitsei turistov pytaiutsia udivit' banal'nymi veshchami»," *Konkurent*, October 24, 2007, http://www.konkurent-krsk.ru/index.php?id=844.
128. Shlenko, "Konstantin Gureev."
129. Żaneta Goździk-Ormel, "Development and Implementation of Participation Projects at Local and Regional Level" (Strasbourg: Council of Europe, European Youth Centre, December 2006), 9–10, http://rm.coe.int/09000016806fcf6d. Interestingly, the source evidences that a representative of Krasnoyarsk state youth politics participated in a training course offered by the European Youth Centre Strasbourg in 2006.
130. Mariia Bozhovich, "«Nevazhno — uedut deti ili ostanutsia». Kak v taezhnom sele sozdali sovremennuiu shkolu," *Pravmir*, September 6, 2021, https://www.pravmir.ru/deti-rasskazyvali-vzroslym-chto-nuzhno-delat-kak-kraevoj-chinovnik-stal-direktorom-selskoj-shkoly/.

131. "Letom v Krasnoiarske nachnetsia stroitel'stvo tsentra ekstremal'nogo sporta," *Newslab.ru*, January 20, 2007, https://newslab.ru/news/211140.
132. Kira Sergeeva, "V «Sportekse» kalechat liudei i provodiat korporativy bankov," *Newslab.ru*, March 25, 2011, https://newslab.ru/article/371848.l-
133. Stefan Krätke, "'Creative Cities' and the Rise of the Dealer Class: A Critique of Richard Florida's Approach to Urban Theory," *International Journal of Urban and Regional Research* 34, no. 4 (2010): 835–53, https://doi.org/10/fd57dp; Luc Boltanski and Eve Chiapello, "The New Spirit of Capitalism," *International Journal of Politics, Culture, and Society* 18, no. 3–4 (December 7, 2006): 161–88, https://doi.org/10/d4r9qh.
134. Aleksandr Cherniavskii, "Sibirskuiu prokuraturu zainteresovali 'Antibiriusoi,'" *Nezavisimaia Gazeta*, January 7, 2011, http://www.ng.ru/regions/2011-07-01/5_antibirusa.html.
135. Aleksandr Aleksandrovich Abramovich, Personal interview with youth politician of the Krasnoyarsk Region.
136. Ekaterina Savina, "'Nashim' ustroili lagernuiu zhizn'. Molodezhnaia politika," *Kommersant*, July 24, 2006, http://www.kommersant.ru/doc/692203.
137. For characterizations of *Seliger* in these years see also "Putin's Patriotic Youth Camp," *TIME.Com*, July 25, 2007, https://web.archive.org/web/20210805150032/http://content.time.com/time/photogallery/0,29307,1646809,00.html; *Nashi*, 16:9, documentary (eye film institute, 2008), http://www.filmbank.nl/film/3895/; Loskutova, *Iunaia politika*, 367–68; Dmitrii Gromov, "Dvizhenie 'Nashi'. 2007 god.," in *Molodezhnye subkultury Moskvy* (Moscow: Institut Etnologii i Antropologii, Rossiiskaia Akademia Nauk, 2009), 115–72, http://evartist.narod.ru/text26/0013.htm; Ivo Mijnssen, *Back to Our Future! History, Modernity and Patriotism According to Nashi, 2005-2012*, The quest for an ideal youth in Putin's Russia, Soviet and Post-Soviet Politics and Society (Stuttgart: Ibidem-Verlag, 2012).
138. "V Krasnoiarske sostoialos' torzhestvennoe zakrytie Vserossiiskogo sleta studotriadov," *Newslab.ru*, September 10, 2007, http://newslab.ru/news/231661.
139. Cherniavskii, "Sibirskuiu prokuraturu zainteresovali 'Antibiriusoi.'"
140. Daria Ivanovna Glazkova, Personal interview with organizer of "TIM Biriusa." In 2013 the Young Guard was one out of 25 teams (*druzhiny*) present during the themed session "Volunteering and Civic Society."
141. Mischa Gabowitsch, *Protest in Putin's Russia* (Cambridge: Polity Press, 2016), 115.
142. Vladimir Gel'man, *Authoritarian Russia: Analyzing Post-Soviet Regime Changes*, Pittsburgh Series in Russian and East European Studies (Pittsburgh: University of Pittsburgh Press, 2015).
143. Bozhovich, "«Nevazhno — uedut deti ili ostanutsia»."
144. Douglas W. Blum, *National Identity and Globalization: Youth, State and Society in Post-Soviet Eurasia* (Cambridge: Cambridge University Press, 2007), 79.
145. Hemment, *Youth Politics in Putin's Russia*, 104–40.
146. Maya Atwal, "Investigating the Democratic Effects of State-Sponsored Youth Participation in Russia: Nashi and the Young Guard of United Russia" (PhD diss., Birmingham, University of Birmingham, 2011), 233, http://etheses.bham.ac.uk/2842/.

147. Andrei, Personal interview with "TIM Biriusa" camper, interview by Anna Schwenck, August 6, 2014.
148. "Khloponin rasskazal Putinu o krasnoiarskoi molodezhnoi politike," *Newslab.ru*, February 19, 2009, https://newslab.ru/news/279156.
149. Vladimir Kuz'min, "Prorvalis': Dmitrii Medvedev vruchil premii molodezhi," *Rossiiskaia Gazeta*, December 18, 2009.
150. Ellen Barry, "Blasts Could Derail Medvedev's Softer Tack in the Caucasus," *The New York Times*, March 30, 2010, https://www.nytimes.com/2010/03/31/world/europe/31moscow.html.
151. Musa Musaev, "Khloponin: molodezh' dolzhna svoimi initsiativami rasshiriat' doliu malogo biznesa v SKFO," *Kavkazskii Uzel*, February 16, 2011, https://www.kavkaz-uzel.media/articles/181184/; Aleksandra Larintseva, "'Kakie vy vse-taki vse russkie...' Polpred Aleksandr Khloponin poznakomilsia s kavkazskoi molodezh'iu," *Kommersant*, August 18, 2010, https://www.kommersant.ru/doc/1489167; Comai, "Youth Camps in Post-Soviet Russia and the Northern Caucasus."
152. Mariia Pliusnina, "Kak ANO 'Rossiia—strana vozmozhnostei,' sozdannaia ukazom Putina, potratit R3 mlrd subsidii," *Znak*, September 17, 2019, https://web.archive.org/web/20210413043148/https:/www.znak.com/2019-09-17/kak_ano_rossiya_strana_vozmozhnostey_sozdannaya_ukazom_putina_potratit_3_mlrd_subsidiy. The legal form in Russia is that of an "Autonomous Non-Commercial Organization" (*Avtonomnaia nekommercheskaia organizatsiia, ANO*).
153. Pliusnina, "Kak ANO 'Rossiia—strana vozmozhnostei.'"
154. Lisa M. Hoffman and Hope Reidun St. John, "'Doing Good': Affect, Neoliberalism, and Responsibilization Among Volunteers in China and the United States," in *Assembling Neoliberalism: Expertise, Practices, Subjects*, ed. Vaughan Higgins and Wendy Larner (New York: Palgrave Macmillan, 2017), 243–62; Tanja Petrovic, "Affective and Voluntary Labor in Post-Yugoslav Societies and the Politics of the Future" (Presentation, Council of European Studies Conference, Paris, July 10, 2015).
155. Humanitarian Research Lab, "Russia's Systematic Program for the Re-Education & Adoption of Ukraine's Children," Conflict Observatory Report (New Haven, CT: Yale School of Public Health, February 14, 2023), https://hub.conflictobservatory.org/portal/sharing/rest/content/items/97f919ccfe524d31a241b53ca44076b8/data.
156. Humanitarian Research Lab, "Russia's Systematic Program," 19.
157. Isobel Koshiw, "Weeks Turn to Months as Children Become Stuck at Camps in Crimea," *The Guardian*, December 27, 2022, https://www.theguardian.com/world/2022/dec/27/children-become-stuck-at-camps-in-crimea-ukraine-russia.
158. Humanitarian Research Lab, "Russia's Systematic Program for the Re-Education & Adoption of Ukraine's Children," 15.
159. Koshiw, "Weeks Turn to Months as Children Become Stuck at Camps in Crimea."
160. Koshiw, "Weeks Turn to Months as Children Become Stuck at Camps in Crimea."

Chapter 4

1. Leora Klapper and Georgios A. Panos, "Financial Literacy and Retirement Planning: The Russian Case," *Journal of Pension Economics and Finance* 10, no. 4 (2011): 599–618, https://doi.org/10/bbwc72.
2. UNESCO, "Participation in Education. Russian Federation. (Data for the Sustainable Development Goals)," Russian Federation, November 27, 2016, http://uis.unesco.org/en/country/ru?theme=education-and-literacy.
3. Sam Potolicchio, "Preparing Global Leaders Forum," 2021, http://www.sampotolicchio.com/pglf; Sam Potolicchio, "Global Governance and Leadership in Russia," 2021, http://www.sampotolicchio.com/ggl-russia.
4. Julia Smirnova, "Wo Russland dem Nachwuchs Patriotismus beibringt," *DIE WELT*, August 11, 2014, https://www.welt.de/politik/ausland/article131058670/Wo-junge-Russen-Patriotismus-mit-der-AK-47-lernen.html.
5. Aleksandr Verkhovskii and Emil Pain, "Civilizational Nationalism: The Russian Version of the 'Special Path,'" *Russian Politics and Law* 50, no. 5 (September 2012): 52–86, https://doi.org/10/gd53fk. Please note that "Alexander Verkhovsky" is the author's name according to a different style of transliteration.
6. Andrei Tsygankov, "Crafting the State-Civilization. Vladimir Putin's Turn to Distinct Values," *Problems of Post-Communism* 63, no. 3 (2016): 146–58, https://doi.org/10/gd55k6.
7. Mabel Berezin, *Making the Fascist Self: The Political Culture of Interwar Italy*, The Wilder House Series in Politics, History, and Culture (Ithaca, NY: Cornell University Press, 1997), 187.
8. Sally Falk Moore, "Political Meetings and the Simulation of Unanimity: Kilimanjaro 1973," in *Secular Ritual*, ed. Sally Falk Moore and Barbara G. Myerhoff (Assen: Van Gorcum, 1977), 152.
9. Graeme B. Robertson, *The Politics of Protest in Hybrid Regimes: Managing Dissent in Post-Communist Russia* (Cambridge: Cambridge University Press, 2011), 175.
10. As quoted in Eliot Borenstein, *Plots against Russia: Conspiracy and Fantasy after Socialism* (Ithaca, NY: Cornell University Press, 2019), 22.
11. Charles Taylor, *The Ethics of Authenticity* (Cambridge, MA: Harvard University Press, 1992), 18.
12. Berezin, *Making the Fascist Self*, 30.
13. Aleksei V. Kudryashev, "The Dialectics of Everyday Life in Pioneer Camps: Romanticism and Regimen," *Russian Education & Society* 61, nos. 5–6 (2019): 231–38, https://doi.org/10/gnjhps.
14. Tamir Sorek, *Palestinian Commemoration in Israel: Calendars, Monuments, and Martyrs*, Stanford Studies in Middle Eastern and Islamic Societies and Cultures (Stanford: Stanford University Press, 2015), 180.
15. Eva Barlösius, Naturgemäße Lebensführung: Zur Geschichte der Lebensreform um die Jahrhundertwende (Frankfurt: Campus, 1997); Michael B. Smith, "'The Ego Ideal of the Good Camper' and the Nature of Summer Camp," *Environmental*

History 11, no. 1 (2006): 70–101, https://doi.org/10/dw8zcd; Jürgen Schiedeck and Martin Stahlmann, "Totalizing of Experience: Educational Camps," in *Education and Fascism: Political Identity and Social Education in Nazi Germany*, ed. Heinz Sünker and Hans-Uwe Otto (London: Falmer Press, 1997), 54–80; Iuliia Skubytska, "It Takes A Union To Raise A Soviet: Children's Summer Camps As A Reflection Of Late Soviet Society" (PhD diss., University of Pennsylvania, 2018), https://repository.upenn.edu/edissertations/2935; Sorek, *Palestinian Commemoration in Israel*, 182.

16. Berezin, *Making the Fascist Self*, 35.
17. James C. Scott, *Domination and the Arts of Resistance: Hidden Transcripts* (New Haven, CT: Yale University Press, 1990), 90.
18. Sally Falk Moore and Barbara G. Myerhoff, "Introduction. Secular Ritual: Forms and Meanings," in *Secular Ritual*, ed. Sally Falk Moore and Barbara G. Myerhoff (Assen: Van Gorcum, 1977), 4; Berezin, *Making the Fascist Self*, 35.
19. Margaret Wetherell, "Feeling Rules, Atmospheres and Affective Practice: Some Reflections on the Analysis of Emotional Episodes," in *Privilege, Agency and Affect*, ed. Claire Maxwell and Peter Aggleton (London: Palgrave Macmillan UK, 2013), 232.
20. Mabel Berezin, "Events as Templates of Possibility: An Analytic Typology of Political Facts," in *The Oxford Handbook of Cultural Sociology*, ed. Jeffrey C. Alexander, Ronald N. Jacobs, and Philip Smith (Oxford: Oxford University Press, 2013), 627.
21. Moore and Myerhoff, "Secular Ritual: Forms and Meanings," 8.
22. Laura L. Adams, *The Spectacular State: Culture and National Identity in Uzbekistan* (Durham: Duke University Press, 2010), 70–71.
23. Artem Nikolaev Baranov, Personal interview with organizer of "SakhaSeliger," interview by Anna Schwenck, July 23, 2014.
24. They had qualified to attend *Seliger* through a competition called "Young Yakutia" (*Iakutiia Molodaia*) that was sponsored, among others, by *Rosmolodezh* and the "Foundation for National Perspectives" (*Natsional'nye Perspektivy*), which financed several of *Nashi*'s projects before the latter's liquidation. "Forum 'Iakutiia Molodaia-2010,'" Vkontakte [Russian Social Network] Forum "Iakutiia Molodaia 2010," accessed March 14, 2023, https://vk.com/club17915414.
25. Artem Nikolaev Baranov, Personal interview with organizer of "SakhaSeliger"; Lenta.ru notes that according to Belokonev's personal site, he had created the foundation already in 2003 and became its president: Lenta.ru, "Belokonev, Sergei," *Lenta.ru*, 2013, https://lenta.ru/lib/14160096/#35.
26. Evgeniia and Aleksandr, Group interview with participants of "SakhaSeliger," interview by Anna Schwenck, July 18, 2014.
27. Artem Nikolaev Baranov, Personal interview with organizer of "SakhaSeliger."
28. Such enormous differences are also characteristic for Russia on the whole: Natalia V. Zubarevich, "Four Russias: Human Potential and Social Differentiation of Russian Regions and Cities," in *Russia 2025: Scenarios for the Russian Future*, ed. Maria Lipman and Nikolay Petrov (London: Palgrave Macmillan, 2013), 67–85.
29. Stepan Petrovich Smirnov, Skype interview with teacher at "SakhaSeliger," interview by Anna Schwenck, June 6, 2014.

30. Sophia Kishkovsky, "Viktor Astafyev, Who Wrote of Rural Russia, Dies at 77," *The New York Times*, December 3, 2001, https://www.nytimes.com/2001/12/03/arts/viktor-astafyev-who-wrote-of-rural-russia-dies-at-77.html.
31. Liniia, Sud'by. *Life Line. Part 1*, 1989. Krasnoiarskaia Kinostudiia. YouTube. September 30, 2016. 13:33 https://www.youtube.com/watch?v=gNp4a80YKfU.
32. At SakhaSeliger similar slogans were printed on posters in 2013: "Youth + Initiative = Success", or imperatives of the kind "Dream! Act!" or "Awaken Your Talent!" as well as worldly wisdoms such as "The Great Is in the Small" (*Velikoe v malom*).
33. Daria Ivanovna Glazkova, Personal interview with organizer of "TIM Biriusa," interview by Anna Schwenck, August 8, 2014.
34. Maggie Wooll, "What Exactly Is Workforce Development?," September 14, 2021, https://www.betterup.com/blog/how-to-use-workforce-development-to-close-the-skills-gap.
35. Hermann Kocyba, "Aktivierung," in *Glossar der Gegenwart*, ed. Ulrich Bröckling, Susanne Krasmann, and Thomas Lemke (Frankfurt am Main: Suhrkamp, 2004), 17–22.
36. I adapted the English translation so that the number of syllables of the Russian original could be maintained.
37. Melanie Schiller, "Pop, Politik und Populismus als Massenkultur," in *Druckwellen: Eskalationskulturen und Kultureskalationen in Pop, Gesellschaft und Politik*, ed. Beate Flath et al. (Bielefeld: Universität Paderborn, 2022), 21–36, https://doi.org/10.14361/9783839453230-003.
38. Rosmolodezh, "Begi za mnoi," Power Point Presentation, author's archive, 2013.
39. Angela McRobbie, *The Aftermath of Feminism: Gender, Culture and Social Change* (London: SAGE Publications, 2009), 124–28.
40. Berezin, *Making the Fascist Self*, 30.
41. For some impressions see "V Iakutii nachal rabotu molodezhnyi forum 'SakhaSeliger' (foto)," *News.Ykt Novosti Iakutii*, July 22, 2013, https://news.ykt.ru/article/12529.
42. Nikita, Alla, and Nadezhda, Group interview with participants of "SakhaSeliger," interview by Anna Schwenck, July 23, 2014.
43. Émile Durkheim, *The Elementary Forms of Religious Life*, trans. Karen E. Fields (New York: Free Press, 1995), 217.
44. Maksim, Personal interview with participant of "SakhaSeliger," interview by Anna Schwenck, July 23, 2014.
45. Matsura, Denis. *My Biriusa 2013 [Song, Foam Party]*. Vkontakte [Russian Social Network]. VK. July 17, 2013. 1:37. https://vk.com/video/@biryusa_tim?z=video-10493768_165473850%2Fclub10493768%2Fpl_-10493768_-2.
46. Sevil Sönmez et al., "Bar Crawls, Foam Parties, and Clubbing Networks: Mapping the Risk Environment of a Mediterranean Nightlife Resort," *Tourism Management Perspectives* 8 (October 2013): 49–59, https://doi.org/10/gm7msx.
47. Sönmez et al.

48. Boris V. Kupriianov, "Soviet Adolescents' First Experiences of Romantic Feelings and Relationships at Pioneer Camps between the 1960s and 1980s," *Russian Education & Society* 61, no. 2–3 (2019): 125–38, https://doi.org/10/gnjhtj.
49. Valerie Sperling, *Sex, Politics, and Putin: Political Legitimacy in Russia*, Oxford Studies in Culture and Politics (New York: Oxford University Press, 2015), 152–54.
50. Pokinsokha, Daniil. *Biriusa Today. Smena "Grazhdanskoe obshchestvo" i "Dobrovol'chestvo". Den' tretii.* Youtube. Krasnoyarsk. July 15, 2013, 16:07. https://www.youtube.com/watch?time_continue=732&v=Kg79RGZqbrc.
51. Sébastien Tutenges, "Stirring up Effervescence: An Ethnographic Study of Youth at a Nightlife Resort," *Leisure Studies* 32, no. 3 (June 2013): 243, https://doi.org/10/fd26f5.
52. Tutenges, "Stirring up Effervescence," 239.
53. Oleg and Mitislav, Group interview with participants of "TIM Biriusa," interview by Anna Schwenck, August 8, 2014.
54. "Photo 'Zariadka'. SakhaSeliger 2013. 'Molodezh' Sela' 1 Chast'" [Youth of the Countryside. 1st Part]," Vkontakte [Russian Social Network] SakhaSeliger. Napravlenie Molodezh Sela, 2013, https://vk.com/photo-50581938_307628215.
55. Vlas, Personal interview with participant of "TIM Biriusa," interview by Anna Schwenck, August 12, 2014.
56. Mikhail, Personal interview with participant of "TIM Biriusa," interview by Anna Schwenck, August 8, 2014.
57. Alexei Yurchak, *Everything Was Forever, until It Was No More: The Last Soviet Generation* (Princeton, NJ: Princeton University Press, 2006), 144–51.
58. Lidiia and Vera, Group interview with participants of "SakhaSeliger," interview by Anna Schwenck, July 15, 2014.
59. See Yurchak, *Everything Was Forever*, 102–14.
60. Nikita, Alla, and Nadezhda, Group interview with participants of "SakhaSeliger."
61. Evgeniia and Aleksandr, Group interview with participants of "SakhaSeliger."
62. Igor, Personal interview with participant of "TIM Biriusa," interview by Anna Schwenck, August 7, 2014.
63. Margarita, Personal interview with participant of "TIM Biriusa," interview by Anna Schwenck, August 12, 2014.
64. Serafima, Personal interview with participant of "SakhaSeliger," interview by Anna Schwenck, July 24, 2014.
65. Lidiia and Vera, Group interview with participants of "SakhaSeliger."
66. Berezin, *Making the Fascist Self*, 168.
67. Natalia Kovalyova, "Power and Talk in Russian Political Culture," *Ohio Communication Journal* 56 (2018): 1–18.
68. Kovalyova, "Power and Talk in Russian Political Culture," 5–6.
69. Aleksei Ivanovich Orlov, Personal interview with staff member of "Rosmolodezh," interview by Anna Schwenck, June 4, 2014.
70. This difference is also highlighted in Julie Hemment, *Youth Politics in Putin's Russia: Producing Patriots and Entrepreneurs* (Bloomington: Indiana University Press, 2015), 106–7.

71. Egor, Elena, and Galina, Group interview with participants of "SakhaSeliger," interview by Anna Schwenck, July 22, 2014.
72. Igor, Personal interview with participant of "TIM Biriusa."
73. Such hierarchical relationships are prevalent at those higher education institutions that are not eligible for "international excellence" funding as is argued by Judith Marquand, *Democrats, Authoritarians and the Bologna Process. Universities in Germany, Russia, England and Wales* (Bingley: Emerald, 2018), 107 & 110. Hierarchical structures of authority might anchor more deeply in an institutional culture than Marquand's case study suggests: See Vasily Bushnev et al., "'Public' Sociology in Russia," trans. Mischa Gabowitsch, *Laboratorium: Russian Review of Social Research* 1 (2009): 205–7.
74. Aleksei Ivanovich Orlov, Personal interview with staff member of "Rosmolodezh."
75. Serafima, Personal interview with participant of "SakhaSeliger."
76. Mikhail, Personal interview with participant of "TIM Biriusa."
77. Biriusa Today. *Smena "Grazhdanskoe obshchestvo" i "Dobrovol'chestvo". Den' tretii.* (Krasnoyarsk, 2013), https://www.youtube.com/watch?time_continue=732&v=Kg79RGZqbrc.
78. Kirill Davydenko, "Masterskaia 'Sil'nye liudi,'" Facebook Masterskaia "Sil'nye liudi," 2018, https://www.facebook.com/Мастерская-Сильные-люди-211076542984449/.
79. Davydenko, "Masterskaia 'Sil'nye liudi.'"
80. Mariia Elina et al., "Analiticheskii otchet po rezul'tatam metodicheskogo (sotsiologicheskogo) soprovozhdeniia mezhregional'nogo molodezhnogo foruma 'Territoriia initsiativnoi molodezhi Biriusa-2013'" (Krasnoiarsk: Nauchno-issledovatel'skaia laboratoriia sotsiologii (Students and alumni of the Siberian Federal University), 2013). The polls were conducted and analyzed by a team of sociology students and alumni of the Siberian Federal University on behalf of the Krasnoyarsk state-funded autonomous institution (*gosudarstvennoe avtonomnoe ucherezhdenie*) Center of Youth Initiatives "Forum" (*Tsentr molodezhnykh initiativ "Forum"*) which organized *TIM Biriusa*. Not all participants got to know all trainers and lecturers, because trainings for different working groups took place simultaneously.
81. Oleg and Mitislav, Group interview with participants of "TIM Biriusa."
82. Stepan Petrovich Smirnov, Skype interview with teacher at "SakhaSeliger.".
83. George T. Doran, "There's a S.M.A.R.T. Way to Write Management's Goals and Objectives," *Management Review*, 1981.
84. A copy of the exercise book is in the author's archive.
85. Lidiia and Vera, Group interview with participants of "SakhaSeliger."
86. Sonja Luehrmann, *Secularism Soviet Style: Teaching Atheism and Religion in a Volga Republic*, New Anthropologies of Europe (Bloomington: Indiana University Press, 2011), 10.
87. Edgar Cabanas and Eva Illouz, *Manufacturing Happy Citizens: How the Science and Industry of Happiness Control Our Lives* (Cambridge: Polity Press, 2019).
88. Aleksandr Aleksandrovich Abramovich, Personal interview with youth politician of the Krasnoyarsk Region, interview by Anna Schwenck, August 8, 2014.

NOTES   253

89. Some neuro-psychological findings highlight the benefits of positive emotion for goal pursuit: Klaus Grawe, *Neuropsychotherapy: How the Neurosciences Inform Effective Psychotherapy* (New York: Routledge, 2007), 279 & 407.
90. Several recommendations and exercises seem to have been inspired by Stephen R. Covey, *The 7 Habits of Highly Effective People: Restoring the Character Ethic* (New York: Free Press, 1989). It is a bestselling business and self-help book.
91. Covey.
92. Kurt Lewin and Ronald Lippitt, "An Experimental Approach to the Study of Autocracy and Democracy: A Preliminary Note," *Sociometry* 1, no. 3/4 (1938): 292–300, https://doi.org/10/c9p5vj.
93. I am grateful to journalist Julia Smirnova for providing me with a scan of the exercise book.
94. TIM Biriusa, "Pamiatka uchastniku," 2013, Author's Archive; SakhaSeliger, "Pamiatka uchastniku foruma SakhaSeliger '13," 2013, Author's Archive.
95. Zinaida, Personal interview with participant of "TIM Biriusa," interview by Anna Schwenck, August 11, 2014.
96. Zinaida.
97. The rules of the team competition were all defined in an official statute, signed by the head of the forum's organizing body (*Polozhenie o provedenii olimpiady druzhin Mezhdunarodnogo molodezhnogo foruma "TIM Biriusa-2014"*). I saved this document, downloadable from the official *Biriusa* homepage, after youth political organizer Daria Glazkova expressed her pride in this novelty during our 2014 interview. Daria Ivanovna Glazkova, Personal interview with organizer of "TIM Biriusa."
98. Oleg Kharkhordin, *The Collective and the Individual in Russia: A Study of Practices*, Studies on the History of Society and Culture (Berkeley: University of California Press, 1999), 206.
99. Fedor, Personal interview with participant of "SakhaSeliger," interview by Anna Schwenck, July 19, 2014.
100. Zinaida, Personal interview with participant of "TIM Biriusa."
101. Arkadii and some of his friends, Group interview with "TIM Biriusa" campers, interview by Anna Schwenck, August 4, 2014.
102. Arkadii and some of his friends.
103. Ina Schröder, "Shaping Youth: Quest for Moral Education in an Indigenous Community in Western Siberia" (PhD diss., Halle-Wittenberg, Martin-Luther-Universität, 2017), 213.
104. Mikhail, Personal interview with participant of "TIM Biriusa."
105. Mikhail, Personal interview.
106. Mikhail, Personal interview.
107. Mikhail, Personal interview.
108. See also Schröder, "Shaping Youth."
109. Wendy Brown, *Undoing the Demos: Neoliberalism's Stealth Revolution* (New York: Zone Books, 2015), 35.
110. Vlas, Personal interview with participant of "TIM Biriusa."
111. Arkadii and some of his friends, Group interview with "TIM Biriusa" campers.

112. See Serguei Oushakine, *The Patriotism of Despair* (Ithaca, NY: Cornell University Press, 2009), 100–103.
113. Theroux, Marcel. *Death of a Nation 1/6*. YouTube April 23, 2006. 7:22. https://www.youtube.com/watch?v=J1OyIJtjdpo.
114. Olga Maiorova, *From the Shadow of Empire: Defining the Russian Nation through Cultural Mythology, 1855-1870* (Madison: University of Wisconsin Press, 2010), 32–33.
115. Berezin, *Making the Fascist Self*, 30.
116. Richard Jenkins, *Social Identity*, 3rd ed., Key Ideas (London: Routledge, 2008), 174.
117. Erving Goffman, *Asylums: Essays on the Social Situation of Mental Patients and Other Inmates* (New York: Anchor Books, Doubleday, 1961), 5–6. The comparison to Goffman's work has been made by Sorek, *Palestinian Commemoration in Israel*.
118. Berezin, *Making the Fascist Self*, 23.
119. I use "civic" to denote the collective, problem-solving orientation of a public activity that is carried out by "actors who pursue a good *they* [emphasis mine] define as relevant to some larger collectivity." Paul Lichterman, "Reinventing the Concept of Civic Culture," in *The Oxford Handbook of Cultural Sociology*, ed. Jeffrey C. Alexander, Ronald N. Jacobs, and Philip Smith (Oxford: Oxford University Press, 2013), 207. Thus, my use of civic does not imply that the action is democratic or leads to democratic change.
120. Caroline W. Lee, Michael McQuarrie, and Edward T. Walker, eds., *Democratizing Inequalities: Dilemmas of the New Public Participation* (New York: NYU Press, 2015).
121. As has been found for public spectacles in post-Soviet Uzbekistan, TV broadcasting plays a special role in spreading images of broad support to the regime: Adams, *The Spectacular State*, 3.
122. Egor, Elena, and Galina, Group interview with participants of "SakhaSeliger."
123. Arkadii and some of his friends, Group interview with "TIM Biriusa" campers.

Chapter 5

1. On such informal practices in business in Russia, see Alena Ledeneva, *How Russia Really Works: The Informal Practices That Shaped Post-Soviet Politics and Business* (Ithaca, NY: Cornell University Press, 2006).
2. Egor, Elena, and Galina, Group interview with participants of "SakhaSeliger," interview by Anna Schwenck, July 22, 2014.
3. Egor, Elena, and Galina, Group interview.
4. David Easton, "A Re-Assessment of the Concept of Political Support," *British Journal of Political Science* 5, no. 4 (1975): 436–37, https://doi.org/10/b5phsd.
5. Ledeneva, *How Russia Really Works*.
6. Easton, "A Re-Assessment of the Concept of Political Support," 436.
7. Easton, "A Re-Assessment of the Concept of Political Support," 436–37.

8. In both cases, the Soviet and the contemporary one, the literal translation would be "Youth Union" or "Union of Youth." I am using "Youth League" because it is the more common designation in the pertaining English-language literature.
9. Grzegorz Rossolinski-Liebe, *Stepan Bandera: The Life and Afterlife of a Ukrainian Nationalist: Fascism, Genocide, and Cult* (Stuttgart: Ibidem-Verlag, 2014), 148. See also Eliot Borenstein, *Plots against Russia: Conspiracy and Fantasy after Socialism* (Ithaca, NY: Cornell University Press, 2019), 216.
10. Aleksandr Bikbov, *Grammatika poriadka. Istoricheskaia sotsiologiia poniatii, kotorye meniaiut nashu real'nost'*, Seriia sotsial'naia teoriia (Moscow: Izdatel'skii dom Vysshei shkoly ekonomiki, 2014), 176.
11. Tatiana Zhurzhenko, "'Capital of Despair': Holodomor Memory and Political Conflicts in Kharkiv after the Orange Revolution," *East European Politics and Societies: And Cultures* 25, no. 3 (2011): 597–639, https://doi.org/10/fw8g9r; Andriy Portnov, "Memory Wars in Post-Soviet Ukraine (1991–2010)," in *Memory and Theory in Eastern Europe*, ed. Uilleam Blacker, Alexander Etkind, and Julie Fedor, Palgrave Studies in Cultural and Intellectual History (New York: Palgrave Macmillan, 2013), 233–54; Rossolinski-Liebe, *Stepan Bandera*, ch. 9; see also footnote 2037.
12. Anna Popova, "Nam partiia mat', rektorat nash otets. Pochemu v rossiiskikh vuzakh net studencheskogo samoupravleniia," *Lenta.ru*, November 18, 2013, https://lenta.ru/articles/2013/11/18/studsovet/; Akkreditatsiia v obrazovanii, "Artem Khromov o studencheskom samoupravlenii," *Akkreditatsiia v obrazovanii*, September 28, 2011, https://www.akvobr.ru/artem_hromov_o_samoupravlenii.html.
13. Natal'ia M. Beliaeva, "Evoliutsiia vzaimootnoshenii gosudarstva s molodezhnymi politicheskimi i obshchestvennymi organizatsiiami v sovremennoi Rossii" (Piatyi Vserossiiskii kongress politologov, Moscow, November 20, 2009), 6, http://www.civisbook.ru/files/File/Belyaeva.pdf.
14. V. V. Aliev and S. V. Lukov, "Gosudarstvennaia podderzhka molodezhnykh i detskikh obshchestvennykh ob"edinenii," in *Gosudarstvennaia molodezhnaia politika: Rossiiskaia i mirovaia praktika realizatsii v obshchestve innovatsionnogo potentsiala novykh pokolenii*, ed. Val. A. Lukov (Moscow: Izdatel'stvo Moskovskogo gumanitarnogo universiteta, 2013), 250–51.
15. Natal'ia M. Beliaeva, "Novyi vzgliad gosudarstva na molodezhnuiu politiku v Rossii v seredine 2010-kh godov," *Vestnik Permskogo universiteta: POLITOLOGIIA* 2 (2016): 9.
16. Hilary Pilkington, "'Vorkuta Is the Capital of the World': People, Place and the Everyday Production of the Local," *The Sociological Review* 60, no. 2 (May 2012): 278, https://doi.org/10/f33k7j; Tatjana Zimenkova, "Sharing Political Power or Caring for the Public Good? The Impact of Service Learning on Civic and Political Participation," in *Education for Civic and Political Participation: A Critical Approach*, ed. Reinhold Hedtke and Tatjana Zimenkova, Routledge Research in Education 92 (New York: Routledge, 2013), 178–79.
17. Alexander Libman and Vladimir Kozlov, "The Legacy of Compliant Activism in Autocracies: Post-Communist Experience," *Contemporary Politics* 23, no. 2 (April 3, 2017): 195–213, https://doi.org/10/gm7t62; Thomas Janoski, "The Dynamic

Processes of Volunteering in Civil Society: A Group and Multi-Level Approach," *Journal of Civil Society* 6, no. 2 (September 2010): 112, https://doi.org/10/b3trh4.

18. For an alternative conceptualization of indifference, see Vasilina Orlova, "Citizens of the Future: Infrastructures of Belonging in Post-Industrial Eastern Siberia" (PhD diss., University of Texas at Austin, 2021), 178–83, https://repositories.lib.utexas.edu/handle/2152/86732. The example Orlova raises on page 94 fully accords with the use of the term as I describe it.
19. As quoted in Nikolay Zakharov, *Race and Racism in Russia* (London: Palgrave Macmillan, 2015), 154.
20. Evgeniia and Aleksandr, Group interview with participants of "SakhaSeliger," interview by Anna Schwenck, July 18, 2014.
21. Igor, Personal interview with participant of "TIM Biriusa," interview by Anna Schwenck, August 7, 2014.
22. Liubov and Daria, Group interview with participants of "Sakha Seliger," interview by Anna Schwenck, July 22, 2014.
23. Liubov and Daria, Group interview.
24. See Peter Frase, "In Defense of Soviet Waiters. Sometimes Bad Service Is Class Struggle," *Jacobin*, June 2, 2013, http://jacobinmag.com/2013/02/soviet-waiters-emotional-labor-customer-service.
25. Liubov and Daria, Group interview.
26. Liudmila Khakhulina, "The Persistence of Mass Conceptions of Justice," *Sociological Research* 54, no. 2 (March 2015): 83, https://doi.org/10/gntgsj.
27. Frase, "In Defense of Soviet Waiters."
28. Fedor, Personal interview with participant of "SakhaSeliger," interview by Anna Schwenck, July 19, 2014.
29. Aleksei, Personal interview with participant of "SakhaSeliger," interview by Anna Schwenck, July 24, 2014.
30. Vlas, Personal interview with participant of "TIM Biriusa," interview by Anna Schwenck, August 12, 2014.
31. Vlas, Personal interview.
32. Alena Ledeneva, *Russia's Economy of Favours: Blat, Networking, and Informal Exchange*, Cambridge Russian, Soviet and Post-Soviet Studies 102 (Cambridge: Cambridge University Press, 1998), 115–21.
33. Vlas, Personal interview with participant of "TIM Biriusa."
34. Alena Ledeneva, *Can Russia Modernise? Sistema, Power Networks and Informal Governance* (Cambridge: Cambridge University Press, 2013).
35. Aleksei, Personal interview.
36. Aleksei, Personal interview.
37. Aleksei, Personal interview.
38. Meduza.io, "How to Steal 60 Million: Former Defense Ministry Official Gets 5-Year Sentence and Walks Free, 4 Months Later," *Meduza*, August 26, 2015, https://meduza.io/en/feature/2015/08/26/how-to-steal-60-million.
39. Arkadii and some of his friends, Group interview with "TIM Biriusa" campers, interview by Anna Schwenck, August 4, 2014.

40. Arkadii and some of his friends, Group interview.
41. Arkadii and some of his friends, Group interview. Denis knew that he joined an interview that was recorded and had consented to participate in it.
42. Maksim, Personal interview with participant of "Sakha Seliger," interview by Anna Schwenck, July 23, 2014.
43. Maksim, Personal interview.
44. Oleg and Mitislav, Group interview with participants of "TIM Biriusa," interview by Anna Schwenck, August 8, 2014.
45. Yuri Nikulin. *A Joke about Russian Character*. YouTube. July 13, 2017, at 1:25. https://www.youtube.com/watch?v=0_xVyEfSolc.
46. Evgeniia and Aleksandr, Group interview.
47. Already at the time the discussed war scenarios never involved the Ukrainian army, but were only imagined as a showdown between the two former Cold War great powers.
48. Félix Krawatzek and Nina Frieß, "A Foundation for Russia? Memories of World War II for Young Russians," *Nationalities Papers*, April 12, 2022, 1–21, https://doi.org/10/gpxp37; David L. Hoffmann, *The Memory of the Second World War in Soviet and Post-Soviet Russia* (London: Routledge, 2021).
49. Liubov and Daria, Group interview.
50. Lidiia and Vera, Group interview with participants of "Sakha Seliger," interview by Anna Schwenck, July 15, 2014.
51. See also Jussi Lassila and Anna Sanina, "Attitudes to Putin-Era Patriotism Amongst Russia's 'In Between' Generation," *Europe-Asia Studies* 74, no. 7 (2022): 1190–209, https://doi.org/10/grx8r8.
52. S. L. Borodikhina, "Poisk novogo soderzhaniia poniatiia 'aktivnaia zhiznennaia pozitsiia' v sovremennykh obshchestvenno-politicheskikh usloviiakh," *Vestnik TGPU/ National Research Tomsk Polytechnic University* 3, no. 156 (2015): 182–85.
53. Timur et al., Group interview with participants of "TIM Biriusa," interview by Anna Schwenck, August 7, 2014.
54. Fedor, Personal interview with participant of "SakhaSeliger."
55. See Michael Burawoy, "Transition without Transformation: Russia's Involutionary Road to Capitalism," *East European Politics & Societies* 15, no. 2 (2001): 269–90.
56. Igor, Personal interview with participant of "TIM Biriusa."
57. Igor, Personal interview.
58. Timur et al., Group interview with participants of "TIM Biriusa."
59. Timur et al., Group interview.
60. Olga Shevchenko, *Crisis and the Everyday in Postsocialist Moscow* (Bloomington: Indiana University Press, 2009).
61. Aleksei, Personal interview with participant of "SakhaSeliger."
62. Aleksei, Personal interview.
63. Nikita, Alla, and Nadezhda, Group interview with participants of "SakhaSeliger," interview by Anna Schwenck, July 23, 2014.
64. Egor, Elena, and Galina, Group interview with participants of "SakhaSeliger."
65. Timur et al., Group interview.

66. Serafima, Personal interview with participant of "SakhaSeliger," interview by Anna Schwenck, July 24, 2014.
67. Serafima, Personal interview.
68. James V. Wertsch, "Blank Spots in Collective Memory: A Case Study of Russia," *The ANNALS of the American Academy of Political and Social Science* 617, no. 1 (2008): 58–71, https://doi.org/10/cm8jx6.
69. Borenstein, *Plots against Russia*, 14.
70. Nikita, Alla, and Nadezhda, Group interview with participants of "SakhaSeliger."
71. Oleg and Mitislav, Group interview with participants of "TIM Biriusa."
72. Government officials frequently invoke this notion of a better life, interpreted as one of material well-being, see Zakharov, *Race and Racism in Russia*, 177.
73. Lidiia and Vera, Group interview with participants of "SakhaSeliger."
74. Volodia, Personal interview with participant of "TIM Biriusa," interview by Anna Schwenck, August 6, 2014.
75. Maksim, Personal interview with participant of "SakhaSeliger."
76. Margarita, Personal interview with participant of "TIM Biriusa," interview by Anna Schwenck, August 12, 2014.
77. Margarita, Personal interview.
78. Oleg and Mitislav, Group interview with participants of "TIM Biriusa."
79. Zinaida, Personal interview with participant of "TIM Biriusa," interview by Anna Schwenck, August 11, 2014.
80. Oleg and Mitislav, Group interview.
81. Oleg Kharkhordin, *The Collective and the Individual in Russia: A Study of Practices*, Studies on the History of Society and Culture (Berkeley: University of California Press, 1999), 205–6.
82. Catriona Kelly, *Children's World: Growing up in Russia, 1890–1991* (New Haven, CT: Yale University Press, 2007), 543.
83. Bikbov, *Grammatika poriadka*, 220.
84. Egor, Elena, and Galina, Group interview with participants of "SakhaSeliger."
85. I am grateful to sociologist Tatiana Golova for introducing me to the term *obshchestvennik* as a designation that is closer to the connotations of "activist" in English-speaking countries.
86. Iana, Personal interview with participant of "SakhaSeliger," interview by Anna Schwenck, July 21, 2014.
87. Anton, Personal interview with participant of "TIM Biriusa," interview by Anna Schwenck, August 12, 2014.
88. Anton, Personal interview.
89. On the use of Soviet pedagogic concepts in contemporary Russian state youth politics, see Jussi Lassila, *The Quest for an Ideal Youth in Putin's Russia: The Search for Distinctive Conformism in the Political Communication of Nashi, 2005–2009*, Soviet and Post-Soviet Politics and Society (Stuttgart: Ibidem-Verlag, 2014), 44.
90. Margarita, Personal interview.
91. Nikita, Alla, and Nadezhda, Group interview with participants of "SakhaSeliger."

92. Nikita, Alla, and Nadezhda, Group interview.
93. Evgeniia and Aleksandr, Group interview with participants of "SakhaSeliger."
94. Evgeniia and Aleksandr, Group interview.
95. Evgeniia and Aleksandr, Group interview.
96. Michael Urban, "The Politics of Identity in Russia's Postcommunist Transition: The Nation against Itself," *Slavic Review* 53, no. 3 (1994): 733–65, https://doi.org/10/bdnngs; Michael Urban, "Stages of Political Identity Formation in Late Soviet and Post-Soviet Russia," in *Identities in Transition: Eastern Europe and Russia after the Collapse of Communism*, ed. Victoria E. Bonnell (Berkeley: University of California, 1996), 141; Kathleen E. Smith, "Competing Myths of Political Legitimacy: August 1991 versus October 1993" (Washington, DC: The National Council for Eurasian and East European Research, April 14, 1997); Olga Malinova, "Russian Political Discourse in the 1990s: Crisis of Identity and Conflicting Pluralism of Ideas," in *Identities and Politics During the Putin Presidency: The Discursive Foundations of Russia's Stability*, ed. Philipp Casula and Jeronim Perovic, Soviet and Post-Soviet Politics and Society (Stuttgart: Ibidem-Verlag, 2009), 98.
97. Evgeniia and Aleksandr, Group interview.
98. See Anna Schwenck, "Performances of Closeness and the Staging of Resistance with Mainstream Musics. Analyzing the Symbolism of Pandemic Skeptical Protests," *German Politics and Society* 41, no. 2 (2023).
99. Nikita, Alla, and Nadezhda, Group interview.
100. Arkadii and some of his friends, Group interview with "TIM Biriusa" campers.
101. Bruce Grant, *The Captive and the Gift: Cultural Histories of Sovereignty in Russia and the Caucasus* (Ithaca, NY: Cornell University Press, 2009).
102. On the history of empowerment as a democratic approach in social work see Lizzie Ward, "Caring for Ourselves?: Self-Care and Neoliberalism," in *Ethics of Care: Critical Advances in International Perspective*, ed. Marian Barnes et al. (Bristol: Policy, 2015), 45–56.
103. For the US-American context, see Nina Eliasoph, "Spirals of Perpetual Potential: How Empowerment Project's Noble Mission Tangle in Everyday Interaction," in *Democratizing Inequalities: Dilemmas of the New Public Participation*, ed. Caroline W. Lee, Michael McQuarrie, and Edward T. Walker (New York: New York University Press, 2015), 165–86.
104. Lidiia and Vera, Group interview.
105. Mabel Berezin, *Illiberal Politics in Neoliberal Times: Culture, Security and Populism in the New Europe*, Cambridge Cultural Social Studies (Cambridge: Cambridge University Press, 2009), 219.
106. Dorottya Szikra, "Ideology or Pragmatism?: Interpreting Social Policy Change under the System of National Cooperation," in *Brave New Hungary: Mapping the "System of National Cooperation,"* ed. János Mátyás Kovács and Balázs Trencsényi (Lanham: Lexington Books, 2020), 236–38; Jelena Tošić and Andreas Streinzer, eds., *Ethnographies of Deservingness: Unpacking Ideologies of Distribution and Inequality*, EASA Series 45 (New York: Berghahn Books, 2022).

107. Andrew E. Kramer, "In Siberia, a 'Blood River' in a Dead Zone Twice the Size of Rhode Island," *The New York Times*, September 8, 2016, sec. World, https://www.nytimes.com/2016/09/09/world/europe/russia-red-river-siberia-norilsk-nickel.html.
108. Anton, Personal interview.
109. Libman and Kozlov, "The Legacy of Compliant Activism in Autocracies."
110. On government-critical activism in Norilsk see Anton Troianovski, "On 'Island' in Russian Arctic, Arrival of Fast Internet Shakes Political Calm," *The New York Times*, October 20, 2019, https://www.nytimes.com/2019/10/20/world/europe/russia-internet-norilsk-youtube-arctic.html.
111. Aleksei, Personal interview. It is most likely that he refers to Valentin Urusov, who received the international Arthur Svensson Prize for Trade Union Rights in 2013: Alexander Nurik, "Valentin Urusov—a Russian Trade Union Martyr," *Equal Times*, February 1, 2013, https://www.equaltimes.org/valentin-urusov-a-russian-trade.
112. Evgeniia and Aleksandr, Group interview.
113. Evgeniia and Aleksandr, Group interview.
114. Egor, Elena, and Galina, Group interview.
115. A similar observation has been made in Vasilina Orlova, "Affective Infrastructures of Immobility: Staying While Neighbors Are Leaving Rural Eastern Siberia," *Journal of Contemporary Ethnography* 5 (2022), https://doi.org/10/grzmb9.
116. Aleksei, Personal interview.
117. See also Orlova, "Affective Infrastructures of Immobility."
118. Personal communication with a participant of SakhaSeliger in 2013.
119. Timur et al., Group interview.
120. The saying is also highlighted as relevant in Orlova, "Affective Infrastructures of Immobility," 4.
121. Aleksei, Personal interview.
122. Aleksei, Personal interview.
123. Orlova, "Affective Infrastructures of Immobility."
124. Igor, Personal interview with participant of "TIM Biriusa."
125. Igor, Personal interview.
126. Nikita, Alla, and Nadezhda, Group interview.
127. Timur et al., Group interview.
128. See Zakharov, *Race and Racism in Russia*, 161.
129. Heike Becker, "I Write What I Like: Steve Biko's Legacy of Black Consciousness and Anti-Capitalism Revisited," *The Elephant*, August 27, 2021, https://www.theelephant.info/ideas/2021/08/27/i-write-what-i-like-steve-bikos-legacy-of-black-consciousness-and-anti-capitalism-revisited/.
130. Aleksei, Personal interview.
131. Oleg Vasil'evich Kozlov, Personal interview with teacher at "SakhaSeliger," interview by Anna Schwenck, July 23, 2014.
132. Author's observation at *SakhaSeliger* 2013.
133. Liubov' and Daria, Group interview.

134. Aleksandr Griboiedoff, *Gore Ot Ouma: A Comedy*, trans. Nicholas Benardaky (London: Simpkin, Marshall, & CO., 1825), 32.
135. Oleg Vasil'evich Kozlov, Personal interview.
136. Oleg Vasil'evich Kozlov, Personal interview.
137. Mikhail, Personal interview with participant of "TIM Biriusa," interview by Anna Schwenck, August 8, 2014.
138. Serafima, Personal interview.
139. Oleg and Mitislav, Group interview.
140. Natalia Donig, "Die Erfindung der 'sowjetischen Heimat': Zur Geschichte eines Ideologems," in *Heimat als Erfahrung und Entwurf*, ed. Natalia Donig, Silke Flegel, and Sarah Scholl-Schneider (Münster: Lit Verlag, 2009), 67–69.
141. Yuri Slezkine, "The USSR as a Communal Apartment, or How a Socialist State Promoted Ethnic Particularism," *Slavic Review* 53, no. 2 (1994): 420, https://doi.org/10/d55pn5.
142. Francine Hirsch, *Empire of Nations: Ethnographic Knowledge and the Making of the Soviet Union*, Culture & Society after Socialism (Ithaca: Cornell University Press, 2005), 14.
143. Rowenna Jane Baldwin, "Pereosmysliaia patrioticheskoe obrazovanie: keis-stadi v Sankt-Peterburge," in *S chego nachinaetsia rodina: Molodezh v labirintakh patriotizma*, ed. Elena Omelchenko and Hilary Pilkington (Ulianovsk: Izdatel'stvo Ulianovskogo Gosudarstvennogo Universiteta, 2012), 155; Anatoli Rapoport, "In Search of Identity: Competing Models in Russia's Civic Education," in *World Yearbook of Education 2011: Curriculum in Today's World: Configuring Knowledge, Identities, Work and Politics*, ed. Lyn Yates and Madeleine R. Grumet (London: Routledge, 2011), 200. On the idea of integrating identification with the federal state through local identification see Giorgio Comai, "Youth Camps in Post-Soviet Russia and the Northern Caucasus: The Cases of Seliger and Mashuk 2010," *Anthropology of East Europe Review* 30, no. 1 (2012): 206–10.
144. Liubov and Daria, Group interview.
145. Andrei Tsygankov, "Crafting the State-Civilization. Vladimir Putin's Turn to Distinct Values," *Problems of Post-Communism* 63, no. 3 (2016): 146–58, https://doi.org/10/gd55k6.
146. Maksim, Personal interview with participant of "SakhaSeliger."
147. Andrei, Personal interview with "TIM Biriusa" camper, interview by Anna Schwenck, August 6, 2014.
148. Andrei, Personal interview.
149. Ledeneva, *Russia's Economy of Favours*; Ledeneva, *Can Russia Modernise?*
150. Liubov and Daria, Group interview with participants of "SakhaSeliger."
151. Martin Müller, *Making Great Power Identities in Russia: An Ethnographic Discourse Analysis of Education at a Russian Elite University*, Forum Politische Geographie 4 (Berlin: Lit Verlag, 2009).
152. See also Hilary Pilkington, "'Vorkuta eto stolitsa mira': deterritorizatsiia, lokal'nost' i 'patriotizm,'" in *S chego nachinaetsia rodina: Molodezh v labirintakh patriotizma*,

ed. Elena Omelchenko and Hilary Pilkington (Ulianovsk: Izdatel'stvo Ulianovskogo Gosudarstvennogo Universiteta, 2012), 69–73.
153. See also Katharina Klingseis, "The Power of Dress in Contemporary Russian Society: On Glamour Discourse and the Everyday Practice of Getting Dressed in Russian Cities," *Laboratorium: Russian Review of Social Research* 3, no. 1 (2011): 91.
154. See also Bikbov, "Neo-Traditionalist Fits with Neo-Liberal Shifts in Russian Cultural Policy," 12.
155. On how rallying for community-level concerns might tend to fail confronting larger social ills see Elizabeth A. Bennett et al., "Disavowing Politics: Civic Engagement in an Era of Political Skepticism," *American Journal of Sociology* 119, no. 2 (September 2013): 520–21, https://doi.org/10/gmhmk8.

Chapter 6

1. An earlier version of this chapter has been published by *Europe-Asia Studies*: Anna Schwenck, "Russia's Vigilante YouTube Stars. Digital Entrepreneurship and Heroic Masculinity in the Service of Flexible Authoritarianism," *Europe-Asia Studies* 74, no. 7 (2022): 1166–89, https://doi.org/10/grzwh9.
2. Melanie Schiller, "Pop, Politik und Populismus als Massenkultur," in *Druckwellen: Eskalationskulturen und Kultureskalationen in Pop, Gesellschaft und Politik*, ed. Beate Flath et al. (Bielefeld: Universität Paderborn, 2022), 21–36, https://doi.org/10.14361/9783839453230-003.
3. Jussi Lassila, *The Quest for an Ideal Youth in Putin's Russia: The Search for Distinctive Conformism in the Political Communication of Nashi, 2005–2009*, Soviet and Post-Soviet Politics and Society (Stuttgart: Ibidem-Verlag, 2014).
4. Dennis Galvan, "Neotraditionalism," in *Encyclopedia of Governance*, ed. Mark Bevir, 2 vols. (Thousand Oaks, CA: SAGE Publications, 2007), 600–1, https://doi.org/g9rr.
5. My translation diverges from that of the vigilantes but is closer to the Russian meaning.
6. *Khrushi Protiv* (Piglets Versus) is another vigilante initiative developed within *Nashi* that relies on similar tools. Vigilantes wearing piglet costumes punish shop owners who allegedly sell expired products. Since the initiative is much less successful than Stop Rudeness and Lion Versus, I have not included it in this chapter. See also Rashid Gabdulhakov, "Media Control and Citizen-Critical Publics in Russia: Are Some 'Pigs' More Equal Than Others?" *Media and Communication* 9, no. 4 (October 21, 2021): 62–72, https://doi.org/10/gnms7d.
7. Theodor W. Adorno et al., *The Authoritarian Personality* (New York: Harper & Row, 1950), 228.
8. Marion Fourcade-Gourinchas, "State Metrology: The Rating of Sovereigns and the Judgment of Nations," in *The Many Hands of the State: Theorizing Political Authority and Social Control*, ed. Kimberly J. Morgan and Ann Shola Orloff (New York: Cambridge University Press, 2017), 103–27.

9. Melissa Aronczyk, *Branding the Nation: The Global Business of National Identity* (Oxford: Oxford University Press, 2013), 3.
10. Sarah Banet-Weiser, *Authentic TM: Politics and Ambivalence in a Brand Culture*, Critical Cultural Communication (New York: New York University Press, 2012), 4.
11. Schiller, "Pop, Politik und Populismus als Massenkultur."
12. Oliver Nachtwey and Maurits Heumann, "Regressive Rebellen und autoritäre Innovatoren: Typen des neuen Autoritarismus," in *Große Transformation? Zur Zukunft moderner Gesellschaften: Sonderband des Berliner Journals für Soziologie*, ed. Klaus Dörre et al. (Wiesbaden: Springer Fachmedien, 2019), 435–53.
13. Rashid Gabdulhakov, "Heroes or Hooligans? Media Portrayal of StopXam (Stop a Douchebag) Vigilantes in Russia," *Laboratorium: Russian Review of Social Research* 11 no. 3 (2019): 29, https://doi.org/10/ggpnjd.
14. Stuart Cunningham and David Craig, "Being 'Really Real' on YouTube: Authenticity, Community and Brand Culture in Social Media Entertainment," *Media International Australia* 164, no. 1 (August 2017): 71, https://doi.org/10/gddcwx.
15. Kirill Rukov and Ivan Chesnokov, "Junge Talente," trans. Anja Lutter, *DEKODER Journalismus aus Russland in deutscher Übersetzung*, November 17, 2015, https://www.dekoder.org/de/article/junge-talente.
16. Gabdulhakov, "Heroes or Hooligans?," 21.
17. See Oleg Nikolaevich Smolin, "Socioeconomics: Uniquely Russian Poverty" (Russian Social Forum, St. Petersburg, March 18, 2021), https://www.transform-network.net/en/blog/article/socioeconomics-uniquely-russian-poverty/.
18. I have added up estimates for the three Stop Rudeness YouTube channels on the platform Social Blade: "YouTube, Twitch, Twitter, & Instagram Statistics," Socialblade.com, accessed April 12, 2023, https://socialblade.com/.
19. *"Lev Protiv" otvetil za svoi reidy*, 2020, https://vk.com/wall-73013298_2071732?ysclid=lezi4y893k916124750. Milonov is widely known for drafting St. Petersburg's first homophobic law.
20. Stop a Douchebag, "Stop a Douchebag Is Creating Citizen Activism Videos," Patreon, December 4, 2021, https://www.patreon.com/stopadouchebag.
21. Gabdulhakov, "Heroes or Hooligans?" 21.
22. Eva Hartog, "A Kremlin Youth Movement Goes Rogue," *The Moscow Times*, April 8, 2016, http://themoscowtimes.com/articles/a-kremlin-youth-movement-goes-rogue-52435.
23. Gilles Favarel-Garrigues, "'Vigilante Shows' and Law Enforcement in Russia," *Europe-Asia Studies* 73, no. 1 (January 2021): 221–42, https://doi.org/10/gkcpqk; Gilles Favarel-Garrigues and Ioulia Shukan, "Perspectives on Post-Soviet Vigilantism. Introduction," *Laboratorium: Russian Review of Social Research*, no. 3 (2019): 4–15, https://doi.org/10/gm7mtm.
24. Julie Hemment, *Youth Politics in Putin's Russia: Producing Patriots and Entrepreneurs* (Bloomington: Indiana University Press, 2015), 104–40.
25. Roman Shleinov, "Kak Kreml' finansiruet svoe molodezhnoe dvizhenie," *Vedomosti*, November 29, 2010, http://www.vedomosti.ru/newspaper/articles/2010/11/29/

dengi_nashih; Zinaida Burskaia, "Bezhim za toboi!," *Novaia Gazeta*, December 8, 2010, http://www.novayagazeta.ru/sports/483.html; Lenta.ru, "Interv'iu s glavoi Rosmolodezhi Vasiliem Iakemenko," January 17, 2012, https://lenta.ru/articles/2012/01/17/jakemenko/.

26. Government of the Russian Federation, "Rasporiazhenie o rukovoditele federal'nogo agenstva po delam molodezhi," 971-p N § (2008), base.garant.ru/6390254/; Government of the Russian Federation, "Postanovlenie o federal'nom agenstve po delam molodezhi," 409 N § (2008).

27. Burskaia, "Bezhim za toboi!"; Shleinov, "Kak Kreml' finansiruet svoe molodezhnoe dvizhenie."

28. Press-sluzhba Lipetskogo oblastnogo Soveta deputatov, "Pervyi vypusk molodezhnoi shkoly biznesa," Lipetskii oblastnoi Sovet deputatov, April 27, 2007, https://lrnews.ru/news-1/3252-.html.

29. "Elena Bocherova: Ia vsegda zhelaiu molodezhi tol'ko odnogo: mechtat'," Vkontakte [Russian Social Network] Forum—ty predprinimatel', June 14, 2013, https://vk.com/wall-38780252?offset=380&w=wall-38780252_563%2Fall.

30. Liliia Varyukhina, Ivan Gorbunov, and Anna Kiseleva, "Dmitriy Chugunov: 'StopKham' — eto ne proyekt, eto spravedlivost'!," *Nasha Molodezh* (blog), February 29, 2016, http://nasha-molodezh.ru/society/dmitriy-chugunov-stopham-eto-ne-proekt-eto-spravedlivost.html.

31. *"Lev Protiv" otvetil za svoi reidy*; Rukov and Chesnokov, "Junge Talente."

32. Rukov and Chesnokov, "Junge Talente."

33. Samuel A. Greene, *Moscow in Movement: Power and Opposition in Putin's Russia* (Stanford: Stanford University Press, 2014), 198.

34. "Avtomobilisty Moskvy protestuiut protiv 'migalok,'" *BBC News Russia*, May 22, 2010, https://www.bbc.com/russian/russia/2010/05/100522_moscow_car_owners_demo.

35. Alfred B. Evans Jr., "Protests in Russia: The Example of the Blue Buckets Society," *Demokratizatsiya* 26, no. 1 (2018): 8.

36. *Russian Drivers Protest State Officials Using Blue Lights."Sinie Vederki" Slideshow.*, 2010, https://www.youtube.com/watch?v=VQ3suJLel74.

37. Alexander Libman and Vladimir Kozlov, "The Legacy of Compliant Activism in Autocracies: Post-Communist Experience," *Contemporary Politics* 23, no. 2 (April 3, 2017): 195–213, https://doi.org/10/gm7t62.

38. Aleksandr Bikbov, "Neo-Traditionalist Fits with Neo-Liberal Shifts in Russian Cultural Policy," in *Russia: Art Resistance and the Conservative-Authoritarian Zeitgeist*, ed. Lena Jonson and Andrei Erofeev (New York: Routledge, 2017), 81.

39. Dorottya Szikra, "Ideology or Pragmatism?: Interpreting Social Policy Change under the System of National Cooperation," in *Brave New Hungary: Mapping the "System of National Cooperation*," ed. János Mátyás Kovács and Balázs Trencsényi (Lanham: Lexington Books, 2020), 238.

40. Chugunov as cited in Hartog, "A Kremlin Youth Movement Goes Rogue."

41. Vadim Volkov, *Violent Entrepreneurs: The Use of Force in the Making of Russian Capitalism* (Ithaca, NY: Cornell University Press, 2002), 18.

42. Alena Ledeneva, *How Russia Really Works: The Informal Practices That Shaped Post-Soviet Politics and Business* (Ithaca, NY: Cornell University Press, 2006); Alena Ledeneva, *Can Russia Modernise? Sistema, Power Networks and Informal Governance* (Cambridge: Cambridge University Press, 2013); Alena V Ledeneva et al., eds., *The Global Encyclopaedia of Informality: Understanding Social and Cultural Complexity* (London: UCL Press, 2018).
43. Anthony Anemone, "About Killers, Freaks, and Real Men: The Vigilante Hero of Aleksei Balabanov's Films," in *Insiders and Outsiders in Russian Cinema*, ed. Stephen M. Norris and Zara M. Torlone (Indiana: Indiana University Press, 2008), 138.
44. Anemone, "About Killers, Freaks, and Real Men," 127.
45. Anemone, "About Killers, Freaks, and Real Men," 130.
46. Aleksandr Verkhovskii and Emil Pain, "Civilizational Nationalism: The Russian Version of the 'Special Path,'" *Russian Politics and Law* 50, no. 5 (September 2012): 52–86, https://doi.org/10/gd53fk; Andrei Tsygankov, "Crafting the State-Civilization. Vladimir Putin's Turn to Distinct Values," *Problems of Post-Communism* 63, no. 3 (2016): 146–58, https://doi.org/10/gd55k6.
47. Oleg Riabov and Tatiana Riabova, "The Remasculinization of Russia? Gender, Nationalism, and the Legitimation of Power under Vladimir Putin," *Problems of Post-Communism* 61, no. 2 (March 2014): 39, https://doi.org/10/gf9ps5.
48. Riabov and Riabova, "The Remasculinization of Russia?" 39.
49. Alec Luhn, "Russian Politician Condemns Eurovision as 'Europe-Wide Gay Parade'. St Petersburg Legislator Vitaly Milonov Proposes Boycott before Demanding Exclusion of Austrian Drag-Queen Contestant," *The Guardian*, April 30, 2014, http://www.theguardian.com/world/2014/apr/30/russia-boycott-eurovision-gay-parade.
50. Susan Larsen, "National Identity, Cultural Authority, and the Post-Soviet Blockbuster: Nikita Mikhalkov and Aleksei Balabanov," *Slavic Review* 62, no. 3 (2003): 508–11, https://doi.org/10/bxt598.
51. Elizabeth A. Wood, "Hypermasculinity as a Scenario of Power," *International Feminist Journal of Politics* 18, no. 3 (July 2, 2016): 329–50, https://doi.org/10/gnqkx8.
52. Valerie Sperling, *Sex, Politics, and Putin: Political Legitimacy in Russia*, Oxford Studies in Culture and Politics (New York: Oxford University Press, 2015), 77.
53. Birgit Sauer, "Neoliberalisierung von Staatlichkeit. Geschlechterkritische Überlegungen," in *Der Staat des Neoliberalismus*, ed. Thomas Biebricher (Baden-Baden: Nomos, 2016), 164.
54. Philip Auslander, "Musical Personae," *The Drama Review* 50, no. 1 (March 2006): 102, https://doi.org/10/dmfb56.
55. Philip Auslander, "Performance Analysis and Popular Music: A Manifesto," *Contemporary Theatre Review* 14, no. 1 (February 2004): 9, https://doi.org/10/frws2k.
56. Banet-Weiser, *Authentic TM*, 4.
57. Shensheng Wang, Scott O. Lilienfeld, and Philippe Rochat, "Schadenfreude Deconstructed and Reconstructed: A Tripartite Motivational Model," *New Ideas in Psychology* 52 (January 2019): 1–11, https://doi.org/10/ggspzx; Mina Cikara and Susan T. Fiske, "Stereotypes and Schadenfreude: Affective and Physiological Markers

of Pleasure at Outgroup Misfortunes," *Social Psychological and Personality Science* 3, no. 1 (January 2012): 63–71, https://doi.org/10/b3q522.
58. As cited in Christopher Brennan, "Controversial Activist 'Pigs' Confront Russian Shop Workers on Video over Expired Foods," *The Observers—France 24*, July 11, 2019, https://observers.france24.com/en/20190711-controversial-food-activist-pigs-confront-russian-shop-workers-video.
59. Birgit Sauer, "Restrukturierung von Männlichkeit: Staat und Geschlecht im Kontext von ökonomischer Globalisierung und Politischer Internationalisierung," in *In der Krise? Männlichkeiten im 21. Jahrhundert*, ed. Mechthild Bereswill and Anke Neuber, Forum Frauen- und Geschlechterforschung (Münster: Westfälisches Dampfboot, 2011), 97.
60. Sauer, "Restrukturierung von Männlichkeit," 97.
61. Jelena Tošić and Andreas Streinzer, eds., *Ethnographies of Deservingness: Unpacking Ideologies of Distribution and Inequality*, EASA Series 45 (New York: Berghahn Books, 2022)..
62. R. W. Connell, "Globalization, Imperialism, and Masculinities," in *Handbook of Studies on Men & Masculinities* (Thousand Oaks, CA: SAGE, 2005), 71–89.
63. Tanja Petrovic, "Affective and Voluntary Labor in Post-Yugoslav Societies and the Politics of the Future" (Presentation, Council of European Studies Conference, Paris, July 10, 2015).
64. Chris Moores, "Thatcher's Troops? Neighbourhood Watch Schemes and the Search for 'Ordinary' Thatcherism in 1980s Britain," *Contemporary British History* 31, no. 2 (April 2017): 232, https://doi.org/10/gnvk62; See also Joshua Reeves, "If You See Something, Say Something: Lateral Surveillance and the Uses of Responsibility," *Surveillance & Society* 10, no. 3/4 (December 2012): 235–48, https://doi.org/10/gf656m.
65. Gleb Tsipursky, "Public Discourse and Volunteer Militias in Post-Soviet Russia," in *Eastern European Youth Cultures in a Global Context*, ed. Matthias Schwartz and Heike Winkel (London: Palgrave Macmillan, 2016), 278–79.
66. Tsipursky, Public Discourse and Volunteer Militias in Post-Soviet Russia," 278.
67. In the first years after the revolutions similar patrols existed. Today's proponents however usually refer to the late Soviet period. For a more detailed account see Tsipursky.
68. Tsipursky, "Public Discourse and Volunteer Militias in Post-Soviet Russia," 273.
69. Juliane Fürst, *Stalin's Last Generation: Soviet Post-War Youth and the Emergence of Mature Socialism* (Oxford: Oxford University Press, 2010), 194.
70. Fürst, *Stalin's Last Generation*, 181.
71. Peter Meylakhs, "Drugs and Symbolic Pollution: The Work of Cultural Logic in the Russian Press," *Cultural Sociology* 3, no. 3 (November 2009): 377–95, https://doi.org/10/dbc5j9; John Charles Walker, *Learning to Labour in Post-Soviet Russia: Vocational Youth in Transition*, BASEES/Routledge Series on Russian and East European Studies (Milton Park: Routledge, 2011), 85; Hilary Pilkington, *Russia's Youth and Its Culture. A Nation's Constructors and Constructed* (London: Routledge, 1994),

175; Hilary Pilkington, ed., *Gender, Generation and Identity in Contemporary Russia* (London: Routledge, 1996), 241. Hilary Pilkington cautions that experimenting with drugs should be not only viewed in the context of impoverishment, but also attributed to a new freedom of expression in different youth cultural scenes at the time. My emphasis here lies on the moral panics vis-à-vis drug use fueled by conservative civil society groups in the late 1990s.
72. Olga Shevchenko, *Crisis and the Everyday in Postsocialist Moscow* (Bloomington: Indiana University Press, 2009).
73. Tsipursky, "Public Discourse and Volunteer Militias in Post-Soviet Russia," 274.
74. Viatcheslav Morozov, *Russia's Postcolonial Identity: A Subaltern Empire in a Eurocentric World* (Houndmills: Palgrave Macmillan, 2015), 163–64; Ellen Propper Mickiewicz, *No Illusions: The Voices of Russia's Future Leaders* (Oxford: Oxford University Press, 2014), 78–79; Valerie Sperling, "Pussy Riot's Real Crime Was Feminism," *OUPblog* (blog), February 5, 2015, http://blog.oup.com/2015/02/pussy-riot-politics-crime-feminism/.
75. Tsipursky, "Public Discourse and Volunteer Militias in Post-Soviet Russia," 277–78; Andrei Kozenko, "'Mestnye' diktuiut zakony rynkam. Podmoskovnaia molodezh' ustroila oblavu na migrantov," *Kommersant*, November 27, 2006, https://www.kommersant.ru/doc/725043; Daniil Turovskii, Ekaterina Savina, and Andrei Kozenko, "Vyselitel'naia programma prazdnika 'Molodaia gvardiia' i 'Mestnye' ob"edinilis' protiv migrantov," *Kommersant*, November 5, 2008, https://www.kommersant.ru/doc/1051988; Giorgio Comai, "Molodaya Gvardiya: The Young Guard of Russia's Elite" (Bologna: Portal on Central Eastern and Balkan Europe by IECOB & AIS, 2006), http://www.pecob.net/molodaya-gvardiya-young-guard-russia-elite-giorgio-comai; Anna Schwenck, "Antifaschistische Bewegung" als Selbstbezeichnung," *DEKODER*, January 6, 2016, https://www.dekoder.org/de/gnose/antifaschistische-bewegung-als-selbstbezeichnung.
76. See also Nikolay Zakharov, *Race and Racism in Russia* (London: Palgrave Macmillan, 2015), ch. 5. For *Mestnye*'s connections to the Militant Organization of Russian Nationalists BORN, responsible for a series of murders of people of non-Russian ethnicity, see the book by the journalists Grigorii Tumanov, Viacheslav Kozlov, and Elena Shmaraeva, *Likvidatsiia BORNa* (Moscow: Common Place, 2015), https://vk.com/common_place.
77. Kozenko, "'Mestnye' diktuiut zakony rynkam."
78. Favarel-Garrigues, "'Vigilante Shows.'"
79. Andrew Roth, "Russian Youth Group With a Mission: Sniffing Out Illegal Migrants," *The New York Times*, September 4, 2013, sec. World, https://www.nytimes.com/2013/09/04/world/europe/russian-youth-group-with-a-mission-sniffing-out-illegal-migrants.html.
80. Dar'ia Manina, "'Dogoniai, ubivai': za chto bande Tesaka vynosiat prigovor," *Komitet "Grazhdanskoe sodeistvie,"* June 28, 2017, https://refugee.ru/news/dogonyaj-ubivaj-za-chto-bande-tesaka-vynosyat-prigovor/.

81. Vladimir Todorov and Anton Bolotov, "Nezdorovyi obraz zhizni," *Lenta.ru*, February 13, 2017, https://lenta.ru/articles/2017/02/13/lionagainthumanrights/.
82. See for example *Lev protiv pedofilov. Korol' pedofilov. Okkupai Pedofiliai 19 vypusk*, 2017, https://www.youtube.com/watch?time_continue=17&v=PJotKYKIZsw. Accessed June 24, 2021—now removed by YouTube due to its violation of the platform's regulation.
83. Tass, "Lider dvizheniia po bor'be s pedofilami 'Kamen'' protiv' otpushchen pod podpisku o nevyezde. Andrei Makarov i ego pomoshchnik Mikhail Lazutin podozrevaiutsia v grabezhe," *TACC*, January 21, 2014, https://tass.ru/proisshestviya/902563; Todorov and Bolotov, "Nezdorovyi obraz zhizni."
84. Nikita Girin, "U podrostka sud korotkii," *Novaia Gazeta*, June 24, 2014, https://novayagazeta.ru/articles/2014/06/24/60085-u-podrostka-sud-korotkiy.
85. *Mikhail Lazutin—interv'yu dlya "Novoi gazety" Lev Protiv.*, 2019, https://www.youtube.com/watch?v=7y5LT-8XaOc. It is highly unlikely that Lazutin could overlook his colleague's convictions, as is shown by the Kamen' Protiv clips in which he also features (cf. "Kamen' Protiv: Novyi God 2014," Vkontakte [Russian Social Network] Kamen' protiv, 2014, https://vk.com/video/@restrukt_000.
86. *Lev Protiv—Skinkhedov Natsistov [Potasovka] Protiv Rasizma*, 2018, https://www.youtube.com/watch?v=wJJaD8966Pc. Some analysts believe that the fact that Lazutin himself has been the target of racist insults, him being often identified as a person from the Caucasus, would *testify* that he distanced himself from Neo-Nazi views (Gilles Favarel-Garrigues, "Criticism of Moral Policing in Russia: Controversies around Lev Protiv in Moscow," in *Violence and Trolling on Social Media: History, Affect, and Effects of Online Vitriol*, by Sara Polak and Daniel Trottier (Amsterdam: Amsterdam University Press, 2020), 33, https://books.openedition.org/obp/15542?lang=de.) However, comparative research on the far right shows that such seeming paradoxes between self-interest and ideological conviction occur regularly.
87. Marlène Laruelle, *Russian Nationalism: Imaginaries, Doctrines, and Political Battlefields*, vol. 61, Media, Culture and Social Change in Asia (Abingdon: Routledge, 2019).
88. Elena Omelchenko and Hilary Pilkington, eds., "Vmesto vvedeniia. Liubit', gorditsia, uezzhat'? Rossiiskaia molodezh v patrioticheskom labirinte," in *S chego nachinaetsia rodina: Molodezh v labirintakh patriotizma* (Ulianovsk: Izdatel'stvo Ulianovskogo Gosudarstvennogo Universiteta, 2012), 8.
89. Anna Schwenck, "Conservative National Narratives in Poland, Russia and Hungary," *Baltic Worlds* 2021, no. 3 (October 2021), http://balticworlds.com/conservative-national-narratives-in-poland-russia-and-hungary/.
90. James M. Jasper, *The Art of Moral Protest: Culture, Biography, and Creativity in Social Movements* (Chicago: University of Chicago Press, 1997), 237.
91. Francesca Polletta et al., "The Sociology of Storytelling," *Annual Review of Sociology* 37, no. 1 (August 2011): 99, https://doi.org/10/cpz9gf.
92. Polletta et al., 109.
93. James M. Jasper, Michael P Young, and Elke Zuern, *Public Characters: The Politics of Reputation and Blame* (Oxford: Oxford University Press, 2020), 3.

94. Wolfgang Brossat, "Heroismus," in *Politische Ikonographie: ein Handbuch. Bd. 1: Abdankung bis Huldigung*, ed. Uwe Fleckner, Martin Warnke, and Hendrik Ziegler (Munich: Beck, 2014).
95. Brossat.
96. Michele Rivkin-Fish, "Pronatalism, Gender Politics, and the Renewal of Family Support in Russia: Toward a Feminist Anthropology of 'Maternity Capital,'" *Slavic Review* 69 (October 1, 2010): 719, https://doi.org/10/gmjb82.
97. Sperling, *Sex, Politics, and Putin*, 36.
98. Riabov & Riabova quoted and translated in Sperling, 36.
99. Libman and Kozlov, "The Legacy of Compliant Activism in Autocracies," 197.
100. PASMI.RU, "Osnovatel' dvizheniia "StopKham' Dmitrii Chugunov: predlagali milliony, no reputatsiia dorozhe," May 23, 2016, https://pasmi.ru/archive/142529/.
101. Gabdulhakov, "Heroes or Hooligans?," 37. Rashid Gabdulhakov does interpret the quote as an indicator of regime opposition.
102. Putin quoted in Wood, "Hypermasculinity as a Scenario of Power," 8.
103. *StopKham—Bez Suda i Sledstviia / Extrajudicially*, 2014, https://www.youtube.com/watch?v=BoTTQ0snWZg.
104. Jason Bush, "Small Businesses Cower after Moscow's Night of Bulldozers," *Reuters*, February 17, 2016, https://www.reuters.com/article/us-russia-economy-bulldozers-idUSKCN0VQ1W5.
105. Dmitrii Florin, "FSRB vzryvaet Moskvu: v Moskve pod prikrytiem silovikov deistvuet gruppirovka po zakhvatu zemel'," *Novosti politicheskikh partii*, November 11, 2014, http://www.qwas.ru/russia/yabloko/FSRB-vzryvaet-Moskvu-v-Moskve-pod-prikrytiem-silovikov-deistvuet-gruppirovka-po-zahvatu-zemel/.
106. *SADB—Garage Wars*, 2016, https://www.youtube.com/watch?v=RmCMs4C9Hwk.
107. *StopKham—Bez Suda i Sledstviia / Extrajudicially*.
108. *Garage Wars*.
109. Jens Jäger, "Polizei," in *Politische Ikonographie: ein Handbuch. Bd. 2: Imperator bis Zwerg*, ed. Uwe Fleckner, Martin Warnke, and Hendrik Ziegler (Munich: Beck, 2014).
110. Anastasia Marchenko, "Nurgaliev pokazhet roliki 'Nashikh' vsem militsioneram strany. Ministr vnutrennikh del posetil forum 'Seliger-2010,'" *Moskovskii Komsomolets*, July 22, 2010, https://www.mk.ru/politics/article/2010/07/22/518303-nurgaliev-pokazhet-roliki-nashih-vsem-militsioneram-stranyi.html.
111. Wood, "Hypermasculinity as a Scenario of Power," 9.
112. *Lev Protiv—Kurenie i Rukoprikladstvo Politsii*, 2015, https://www.youtube.com/watch?v=1iKXacN0uCE.
113. Jäger, "Polizei" 254.
114. *Garage Wars*.
115. Lyubim Murzakov, "Mother Russia: kak prodavat' rodinu i ne krasnet'—Oftop na vc.ru," June 10, 2018, https://vc.ru/flood/39068-mother-russia-kak-prodavat-rodinu-i-ne-krasnet.
116. *Meeting Lev Lazutin (Lion Versus)*, 2016, https://www.youtube.com/watch?v=xdmOknVJ0T0. In late 2021 the video was removed from Leonov's channel. The channel still exists and is accessible under https://www.youtube.com/channel/UCOahMmtT3QW2Dba1muvjbhw

117. *Meeting Lev Lazutin (Lion Versus)*.
118. Jasper, Young, and Zuern, *Public Characters*, 165.
119. *Spasenie Kotenka Ot Smerti*, 2015, https://www.youtube.com/watch?v=D0uE XoL04OM.
120. Banet-Weiser, *Authentic TM*, 140.
121. *Meeting Lev Lazutin (Lion Versus)*.
122. Rosmolodezh Business. "Program: You Are an Entrepreneur." *VK*. August 21, 2018. https://vk.com/video-130482053_456239037.
123. *StopKham—Krasnogorskaia Niasha*, 2015, https://www.youtube.com/watch?v=53WbKPqgbdQ.
124. *SADB—Cutie Worldstar*, 2015, https://www.youtube.com/watch?v=OEWDt1XIsZg.
125. *StopKham-Zhenskii Top 10*, 2016, https://www.youtube.com/watch?v=vswPtRwxcA8.
126. *SADB—A Muscovite Born and Bred*, 2018, https://www.youtube.com/watch?v=5ABtIyi5RBY.
127. *StopKham—"Moskvichka v Tret'em Kolene,"* 2018, https://www.youtube.com/watch?v=WBcJxfB1hTU.
128. *StopKham—"Moskvichka v Tret'em Kolene."*
129. *StopKham—Semeinoe Obostrenie. Chast' 1*, 2018, https://www.youtube.com/watch?v=9_QAXp8ZFuQ; *StopKham—Semeinoe Obostrenie. Chast' 2. Prodolzhenie*, 2018, https://www.youtube.com/watch?v=Yf7k_rTHzRo.
130. *StopKham—Semeinoe Obostrenie. Chast' 2. Prodolzhenie*.
131. *SADB—Mama's Boy*, 2015, https://www.youtube.com/watch?v=rbjFv81l1qQ. To be sure, the targets of raids often use misogynistic language themselves. Female Stop Rudeness vigilantes, who actually never play a heroic role, are sometimes called "sluts" by female targets. Male vigilantes are often referred to as "faggots."
132. *Lev Protiv—Ia Koroleva*, 2020, https://www.youtube.com/watch?v=jlSH8hab4QI.
133. Jasper, Young, and Zuern, *Public Characters*, 3.
134. Jasper, Young, and Zuern, 244.
135. *Lev Protiv—Tolpa Bydla i VDV*, 2018, https://www.youtube.com/watch?v=5a9Au1F9bUY.
136. *Lev Protiv—Tolpa Bydla i VDV*, sec. 07:43-07:50.
137. *Lev Protiv—Bydlo Oret pro Ukrainu i Donbass v Tsentre Moskvy!*, 2022, https://www.youtube.com/watch?v=xfljKVKSatg.
138. *Meeting Lev Lazutin (Lion Versus)*.
139. On the question of visibility see Anna Schwenck, "Russian Politics of Radicalisation and Surveillance," in *Governing Youth Politics in the Age of Surveillance*, ed. Maria Grasso and Judith Bessant, The Criminalization of Political Dissent (London: Routledge, 2018), 168–82.
140. Gabdulhakov, "Heroes or Hooligans?" 31–35.
141. Sauer, "Neoliberalisierung von Staatlichkeit."
142. Wang, Lilienfeld, and Rochat, "Schadenfreude Deconstructed and Reconstructed."
143. Sauer, "Restrukturierung von Männlichkeit: Staat und Geschlecht im Kontext von ökonomischer Globalisierung und politischer Internationalisierung."

144. Richard Sennett, *The Corrosion of Character: The Personal Consequences of Work in the New Capitalism* (New York: Norton, 1999), 139.

Chapter 7

1. Philip G. Cerny, "In the Shadow of Ordoliberalism: The Paradox of Neoliberalism in the 21st Century," *European Review of International Studies* 3, no. 1 (2016): 91. For a similar argument in relation to Putinist youth politics see Julie Hemment, "Occupy Youth! State-Mobilized Movements in the Putin Era (or, What Was Nashi and What Comes Next?)," in *Ruling by Other Means: State-Mobilized Movements*, ed. Grzegorz Ekiert, Elizabeth J. Perry, and Xiaojun Yan, Cambridge Studies in Contentious Politics (Cambridge: Cambridge University Press, 2020), 185–88.
2. Ágnes Gagyi and Tamás Geröcs, "The Political Economy of Hungary's New 'Slave Law,'" *Lefteast*, January 1, 2019, https://lefteast.org/the-political-economy-of-hungarys-new-slave-law/. I am grateful to Émilia Barna and Ágnes Patakfalvi-Czirják for drawing my attention to these developments.
3. Cornel Ban, *Ruling Ideas: How Global Neoliberalism Goes Local* (New York: Oxford University Press, 2016).
4. Samuel A. Greene and Graeme B. Robertson, *Putin v. the People: The Perilous Politics of a Divided Russia* (New Haven, CT: Yale University Press, 2019), 205.
5. I am grateful to the Facebook user for allowing me to use her post. I did change the name.
6. Félix Krawatzek and Nina Frieß, "A Foundation for Russia? Memories of World War II for Young Russians," *Nationalities Papers*, April 12, 2022, 1–21, https://doi.org/10/gpxp37; Olga Malinova, "Constructing the 'Usable Past': The Evolution of the Official Historical Narrative in Post-Soviet Russia," in *Cultural and Political Imaginaries in Putin's Russia*, ed. Niklas Bernsand and Barbara Törnquist-Plewa (Leiden: BRILL, 2018), 85–104.
7. Aleksandr Bikbov, "Travma Neomerkantilizma i zadachi novoi kul'tury," in *Pered licom katastrofy: sbornik statej*, ed. Nikolaj Plotnikov, Philosophie: Forschung und Wissenschaft 57 (Münster: Lit Verlag, 2023), 61–72.
8. Dar'ia Vos'mukhina, "Ot Momenta Priniatiia Resheniia Do Polnogo Pereezda v Melitopol' Proshlo Desiat' Dnei," *Higher School of Economics News*, February 20, 2023, https://www.hse.ru/our/news/816076827.html.
9. Bikbov, "Travma Neomerkantilizma i zadachi novoi kul'tury."

Appendix I

1. Maya Atwal, "Evaluating Nashi's Sustainability: Autonomy, Agency and Activism," *Europe-Asia Studies* 61, no. 5 (2009): 743–58, https://doi.org/10/cvr6ts; Julie

Hemment, "Soviet-Style Neoliberalism? Nashi, Youth Voluntarism, and the Restructuring of Social Welfare in Russia," *Problems of Post-Communism* 56, no. 6 (2009): 36–50, https://doi.org/10/d5gbxs; Julie Hemment, "Nashi, Youth Voluntarism, and Potemkin NGOs: Making Sense of Civil Society in Post-Soviet Russia," *Slavic Review* 71, no. 2 (2012): 234–60, https://doi.org/10/gghw3r; Ivo Mijnssen, *Back to Our Future! History, Modernity and Patriotism According to Nashi, 2005-2012,* The quest for an ideal youth in Putin's Russia, Soviet and Post-Soviet Politics and Society (Stuttgart: Ibidem-Verlag, 2012).

2. Interviews with vigilante activists form the basis of a very insightful documentary: *Nashi byvshie "Nashi,"* Documentary, vol. 2, 2 vols., Chto znachit byt' molodym v sovremennoi Evrope (St. Petersburg: Center for Youth Studies at the National Research University Higher School of Economics, 2014), https://www.youtube.com/watch?v=lVjQDB_vBCo&t=29s; *Our former "Ours,"* 2014, https://www.youtube.com/watch?v=lVjQDB_vBCo. See also Chapter 6.

3. I discovered a scholarly article on the youth-leadership summer camp *Mashuk*, taking place in the Northern Caucasus, only much later: Giorgio Comai, "Youth Camps in Post-Soviet Russia and the Northern Caucasus: The Cases of Seliger and Mashuk 2010," *Anthropology of East Europe Review* 30, no. 1 (2012): 184–212.

4. I am very thankful to Silvia von Steinsdorff and the members of her research colloquium at the time for support and feedback. Without their encouragement I would not have applied for participation in youth-leadership summer camps after *Nashi*'s dissolution in spring 2013.

5. Mabel Berezin, *Illiberal Politics in Neoliberal Times: Culture, Security and Populism in the New Europe*, Cambridge Cultural Social Studies (Cambridge: Cambridge University Press, 2009), 10.

6. Compare Richard Swedberg's idea of separating a pre-study phase, that is a context of discovery, from a main study phase, which is ideally reserved for justifying an emerging theory: Richard Swedberg, "Theorizing in Sociology and Social Science: Turning to the Context of Discovery," *Theory and Society* 41, no. 1 (2012): 1–40, https://doi.org/10/bgjzdv.

7. Campers at federal youth-leadership summer camps such as *Seliger* come from all parts of Russia. In contrast, regional youth-leadership summer camps are mainly attended by young people from the republic or region. Though there are often delegations visiting from other regions or countries visiting regional camps, they make up only a minority of campers.

8. I am thankful to sociologist Alena Ledeneva for providing me with advice for regional comparisons in the Russian Federation.

9. Kristin Luker, *Salsa Dancing into the Social Sciences: Research in an Age of Info-Glut* (Cambridge: Harvard University Press, 2008), 147–48.

10. Luker, *Salsa Dancing into the Social Sciences,* 148.

11. A theme developed in a more journalistic manner in Joshua Yaffa, *Between Two Fires: Truth, Ambition, and Compromise in Putin's Russia*. (New York: Tim Duggan Books, 2020).

12. It was published in 2013 in issue 26 (965) on page 6. A copy of that issue of *Eder Saas* is in my personal archive.
13. Bronislaw Malinowski, *Argonauts of the Western Pacific: An Account of Native Enterprise and Adventure in the Archipelagoes of Melanesian New Guinea* (London: Routledge, 1922).
14. Kathy Charmaz, *Constructing Grounded Theory: A Practical Guide through Qualitative Analysis* (London: Sage, 2006), 21.
15. Barney Glaser, *Awareness of Dying* (Chicago: Aldine, 1965); Michael Burawoy, "The Extended Case Method," *Sociological Theory* 16, no. 1 (1998): 4–33, https://doi.org/10/fwpvgm; Loïc Wacquant, *Body & Soul: Notebooks of an Apprentice Boxer* (Oxford: Oxford University Press, 2004).
16. Charmaz, *Constructing Grounded Theory*, 2006, 22.
17. Hermann Kocyba, "Aktivierung," in *Glossar der Gegenwart*, ed. Ulrich Bröckling, Susanne Krasmann, and Thomas Lemke (Frankfurt am Main: Suhrkamp, 2004), 17–22.
18. The attribute "autonomous" denotes that the institution has a (relatively) independent administration, but is funded through the state budget. Thanks to Aleksandr for the explanation and the suggestions for translation.
19. Kathy Charmaz, *Constructing Grounded Theory: A Practical Guide through Qualitative Analysis* (London: Sage, 2006), 107.
20. James Mahoney and Gary Goertz, "A Tale of Two Cultures: Contrasting Quantitative and Qualitative Research," *Political Analysis* 14, no. 3 (July 1, 2006): 239, https://doi.org/10/d5fdwt.
21. Charmaz, *Constructing Grounded Theory*, 103.
22. Berezin, *Illiberal Politics in Neoliberal Times*, 10–11.
23. Barbara G. Myerhoff, *Number Our Days* (New York: Simon and Schuster, 1980), 26.
24. Myerhoff, *Number Our Days*, 29.
25. Charles C Ragin, *The Comparative Method: Moving beyond Qualitative and Quantitative Strategies* (Berkeley: University of California Press, 1987).
26. Given that my host university was in Moscow, I was registered there and had access to the local student home and to the library. While I would have liked to spend more time in the Sakha Republic and the Krasnoyarsk Region, these factors were the reason for my longer stay in the capital.
27. Luker, *Salsa Dancing into the Social Sciences*, 167.
28. Luker, *Salsa Dancing into the Social Sciences*, 167.
29. Robert Stuart Weiss, *Learning from Strangers: The Art and Method of Qualitative Interview Studies* (New York: Free Press, 1995), 48–49; Aglaja Przyborski and Monika Wohlrab-Sahr, *Qualitative Sozialforschung: Ein Arbeitsbuch*, 4th ed., Lehr- und Handbücher der Soziologie (München: Oldenbourg Verlag, 2014), 127.
30. Weiss, *Learning from Strangers*, 12.
31. Przyborski and Wohlrab-Sahr, *Qualitative Sozialforschung*, 126.
32. Weiss, *Learning from Strangers*, 48.
33. Olga Malinova, *Konstruirovanie smyslov. Issledovanie simvolicheskoi politiki v sovremennoi Rossii* (Moscow: INION RAN, 2013). I also relied on Philipp Casula,

> *Hegemonie und Populismus in Putins Russland: Eine Analyse des russischen politischen Diskurses* (Bielefeld: Transcript, 2012).

34. I am very thankful to Ivan Klimov for his support and for calling attention to the theme of "loyalty" and the role of volunteering in state youth political programs.
35. Kathleen Blee, *Inside Organized Racism: Women in the Hate Movement* (Berkeley: University of California Press, 2002), 11.
36. Luker, *Salsa Dancing into the Social Sciences*, 2008, 177.
37. Christian Fröhlich, "Interviewforschung im russischsprachigen Raum—ein Balanceakt zwischen methodologischen und feldspezifischen Ansprüchen," in *Qualitative Interviewforschung in und mit fremden Sprachen. Eine Einführung in Theorie und Praxis*, ed. Jan Kruse et al. (Weinheim: Beltz Juventa, 2012), 190–206.
38. Weiss, *Learning from Strangers*, 154.
39. Charmaz, *Constructing Grounded Theory*, 2006, 50–53.
40. Weiss, *Learning from Strangers*, 155.
41. Luker, *Salsa Dancing into the Social Sciences*, 2008, 201.
42. Charmaz, *Constructing Grounded Theory*, 2006, 55.
43. Luker, *Salsa Dancing into the Social Sciences*, 2008, 202.
44. Charmaz, *Constructing Grounded Theory*, 2006, 60.
45. I am very thankful to Elena for making the visit possible.

Appendix II

1. "Rosmolodezh' zapuskaet Vserossiiskuiu forumnuiu kampaniiu 2022 goda," *Rossiiskii Soiuz Molodezhi*, March 29, 2022, https://ruy.ru/press/news/rosmolodezh-zapuskaet-vserossiyskuyu-forumnuyu-kampaniyu-2022-goda-/. I am grateful to Sima and Elena Renje for their kind support.

Bibliography

Abrahams, Ray. "Some Thoughts on the Comparative Study of Vigilantism." In *Global Vigilantes*, edited by David Pratten and Atreyee Sen, 419–40. London: Hurst, 2007.
Adams, Laura L. *The Spectacular State: Culture and National Identity in Uzbekistan*. Durham, NC: Duke University Press, 2010.
Adorno, Theodor W., Else Frenkel-Brunswik, Daniel J. Levinson, and Nevitt Sanford. *The Authoritarian Personality*. Studies in Prejudice. New York: Harper & Row, 1950.
Akkreditatsiia v obrazovanii. "Artem Khromov o studencheskom samopravlenii." *Akkreditatsiia v obrazovanii*, September 28, 2011. http://www.akvobr.ru/artem_hromov_o_samoupravlenii.html.
Alexander, Jeffrey C. *Performance and Power*. Cambridge: Polity Press, 2011.
Allina-Pisano, Jessica. *The Post-Soviet Potemkin Village: Politics and Property Rights in the Black Earth*. Cambridge: Cambridge University Press, 2008.
Aliev, V. V., and S. V. Lukov. "Gosudarstvennaia podderzhka molodezhnykh i detskikh obshchestvennykh obedinenii." In *Gosudarstvennaia molodezhnaia politika: Rossiiskaia i mirovaia praktika realizatsii v obshchestve innovatsionnogo potentsiala novykh pokolenii*, edited by Val. A. Lukov, 247–54. Moscow: Izdatel'stvo Moskovskogo gumanitarnogo universiteta, 2013.
Anderson, Neil R., and Rosina M. Gasteiger. "Innovation and Creativity in Organisations: Individual and Work Team Research Findings and Implications for Government Policy." In *Micro-Foundations for Innovation Policy*, edited by Bart Nooteboom and Erik Stam, 249–72. Amsterdam: Amsterdam University Press, 2008.
Anemone, Anthony. "About Killers, Freaks, and Real Men: The Vigilante Hero of Aleksei Balabanov's Films." In *Insiders and Outsiders in Russian Cinema*, edited by Stephen M. Norris and Zara M. Torlone, 127–41. Bloomington: Indiana University Press, 2008.
Appel, Hilary, and Mitchell A. Orenstein. *From Triumph to Crisis: Neoliberal Economic Reform in Postcommunist Countries*. Cambridge: Cambridge University Press, 2018.
Arci. "Chi Siamo." Accessed February 12, 2023. https://www.arci.it/chi-siamo/.
Arendt, Hannah. *The Origins of Totalitarianism*. San Diego: Harcourt Brace Jovanovich, 1973.
Aronczyk, Melissa. *Branding the Nation: The Global Business of National Identity*. Oxford: Oxford University Press, 2013.
Atkinson, Robert D., and Stephen J. Ezell. *Innovation Economics: The Race for Global Advantage*. New Haven, CT: Yale University Press, 2012.
Atwal, Maya, and Edwin Bacon. "The Youth Movement Nashi: Contentious Politics, Civil Society, and Party Politics." *East European Politics* 28, no. 3 (June 2012): 256–66. https://doi.org/10/ggk5n9.
Atwal, Maya. "Evaluating Nashi's Sustainability: Autonomy, Agency and Activism." *Europe-Asia Studies* 61, no. 5 (2009): 743–58. https://doi.org/10/cvr6ts.

Atwal, Maya. "Investigating the Democratic Effects of State-Sponsored Youth Participation in Russia: Nashi and the Young Guard of United Russia." PhD diss., University of Birmingham, 2011. http://etheses.bham.ac.uk/2842/.

Auslander, Philip. "Musical Personae." *The Drama Review* 50, no. 1 (March 2006): 100–119. https://doi.org/10/dmfb56.

Auslander, Philip. "Performance Analysis and Popular Music: A Manifesto." *Contemporary Theatre Review* 14, no. 1 (February 2004): 1–13. https://doi.org/10/frws2k.

Baldwin, Rowenna Jane. "Pereosmysliaia patrioticheskoe obrazovanie: keis-stadi v Sankt-Peterburge." In *S chego nachinaetsia rodina: Molodezh v labirintakh patriotizma*, edited by Elena Omelchenko and Hilary Pilkington, 111–54. Ulianovsk: Izdatel'stvo Ulianovskogo Gosudarstvennogo Universiteta, 2012.

Baldwin, Rowenna Jane. "Rethinking Patriotic Education in the Russian Federation: Invitations to Belong to 'Imagined Communities': A Case Study of St. Petersburg." PhD diss., University of Warwick, 2011.

Balzer, Marjorie Mandelstam, and Uliana Alekseevna Vinokurova. "Nationalism, Interethnic Relations and Federalism: The Case of the Sakha Republic (Yakutia)." *Europe-Asia Studies* 48, no. 1 (January 1996): 101–20. https://doi.org/10.1080/09668139608412335.

Balzer, Marjorie Mandelstam. "A State within a State: The Sakha Republic (Yakutia)." In *Rediscovering Russia in Asia: Siberia and the Russian Far East*, edited by Stephen Kotkin and David Wolff, 139–59. Armonk, NY: M.E. Sharpe, 1995.

Balzer, Harley. "Managed Pluralism: Vladimir Putin's Emerging Regime." *Post-Soviet Affairs* 19, no. 3 (January 1, 2003): 189–227. https://doi.org/10/ftk423.

Ban, Cornel. *Ruling Ideas: How Global Neoliberalism Goes Local*. New York: Oxford University Press, 2016.

Banco, Erin, Garrett M. Graff, Lara Seligman, Nahal Toosi, and Alexander Ward. "'Something Was Badly Wrong': When Washington Realized Russia Was Actually Invading Ukraine. A First-Ever Oral History of How Top U.S. and Western Officials Saw the Warning Signs of a European Land War, Their Frantic Attempts to Stop It—and the Moment Putin Actually Crossed the Border." *POLITICO*, February 24, 2023, https://www.politico.com/news/magazine/2023/02/24/russia-ukraine-war-oral-history-00083757.

Banet-Weiser, Sarah. *Authentic TM: Politics and Ambivalence in a Brand Culture*. Critical Cultural Communication. New York: New York University Press, 2012.

Barakhova, Alla, Il'ia Bulavinov, and Boris El'shin. "Vladimir Putin zanialsia naznacheniem gubernatorov." *Kommersant*. April 10, 2002. https://www.kommersant.ru/doc/344330.

Barlösius, Eva. Naturgemäße Lebensführung: Zur Geschichte der Lebensreform um die Jahrhundertwende. Frankfurt: Campus, 1997.

Barker, Rodney S. *Political Legitimacy and the State*. Oxford: Oxford University Press, 1990.

Barna, Emília. "Managing the Eastern European Position in the Digital Era: Music Industry Showcase Events and Popular Music Export in Hungary." In *Eastern European Music Industries and Policies after the Fall of Communism*, edited by Patryk Galuszka, 138–152. London: Routledge, 2021.

Barry, Ellen. "Blasts Could Derail Medvedev's Softer Tack in the Caucasus." *The New York Times*, March 30, 2010. https://www.nytimes.com/2010/03/31/world/europe/31moscow.html.

BBC News Russia. "Avtomobilisty Moskvy protestuiut protiv 'migalok,'" May 22, 2010. https://www.bbc.com/russian/russia/2010/05/100522_moscow_car_owners_demo.

Becher, Phillip, Katrin Becker, Kevin Rösch, and Laura Seelig. "Ordoliberal White Democracy, Elitism, and the Demos: The Case of Wilhelm Röpke." *Democratic Theory* 8, no. 2 (December 1, 2021): 70–96. https://doi.org/10/gpn7h9.

Becker, Heike. "Ideas I Write What I Like: Steve Biko's Legacy of Black Consciousness and Anti-Capitalism Revisited." *The Elephant*, August 27, 2021. https://www.theelephant.info/ideas/2021/08/27/i-write-what-i-like-steve-bikos-legacy-of-black-consciousness-and-anti-capitalism-revisited/.

Becker, Howard S. "Problems of Inference and Proof in Participant Observation." *American Sociological Review* 23, no. 6 (1958): 652–60. https://doi.org/10/b3z42v.

Beliaeva, Natal'ia M. "Evoliutsiia vzaimootnoshenii gosudarstva s molodezhnymi politicheskimi i obshchestvennymi organizatsiiami v sovremennoi Rossii." Presented at the Piatyi Vserossiiskii kongress politologov, Moscow, November 20, 2009. http://www.civisbook.ru/files/File/Belyaeva.pdf.

Beliaeva, Natal'ia M. "Novyi vzgliad gosudarstva na molodezhnuiu politiku v Rossii v seredine 2010-kh godov." *Vestnik Permskogo universiteta. POLITOLOGIIA* 2 (2016): 5–18.

Bennett, Elizabeth A., Alissa Cordner, Peter Taylor Klein, Stephanie Savell, and Gianpaolo Baiocchi. "Disavowing Politics: Civic Engagement in an Era of Political Skepticism." *American Journal of Sociology* 119, no. 2 (September 2013): 518–48. https://doi.org/10/gmhmk8.

Berezin, Mabel. "Events as Templates of Possibility: An Analytic Typology of Political Facts." In *The Oxford Handbook of Cultural Sociology*, edited by Jeffrey C. Alexander, Ronald N. Jacobs, and Philip Smith, 613–35. Oxford: Oxford University Press, 2013.

Berezin, Mabel. *Illiberal Politics in Neoliberal Times: Culture, Security and Populism in the New Europe*. Cambridge Cultural Social Studies. Cambridge: Cambridge University Press, 2009.

Berezin, Mabel. *Making the Fascist Self: The Political Culture of Interwar Italy*. The Wilder House Series in Politics, History, and Culture. Ithaca, NY: Cornell University Press, 1997.

Berezin, Mabel. "Sociology of Culture." In *International Encyclopedia of the Social & Behavioral Sciences*, edited by James D. Wright, 617–21. Oxford: Elsevier, 2015.

Berezin, Mabel, Emily Sandusky, and Thomas Davidson. "Culture in Politics and Politics in Culture: Institutions, Practices, and Boundaries." In *The New Handbook of Political Sociology*, edited by Cedric de Leon, Isaac William Martin, Joya Misra, and Thomas Janoski, 102–31. Cambridge: Cambridge University Press, 2020.

Berlin, Isaiah. *The Crooked Timber of Humanity: Chapters in the History of Ideas*. 2nd ed. Princeton, NJ: Princeton University Press, 2013.

Biebricher, Thomas. "Einleitung: Neoliberalismus und Staat – ziemlich beste Feinde." In *Der Staat des Neoliberalismus*, edited by Thomas Biebricher, 9–28. Baden-Baden: Nomos, 2016.

Bikbov, Aleksandr. *Grammatika poriadka. Istoricheskaia sotsiologiia poniatii, kotorye meniaiut nashu real'nost'*. Seriia sotsial'naia teoriia. Moscow: Izdatel'skii dom Vysshei shkoly ekonomiki, 2014.

Bikbov, Aleksandr. "Neo-Traditionalist Fits with Neo-Liberal Shifts in Russian Cultural Policy." In *Russia: Art Resistance and the Conservative-Authoritarian Zeitgeist*, edited by Lena Jonson and Andrei Erofeev, 65–83. New York: Routledge, 2017.

Bikbov, Aleksandr. "Travma Neomerkantilizma i zadachi novoi kul'tury." In *Pered licom katastrofy: sbornik statej*, edited by Nikolaj Plotnikov, 61–72. Philosophie: Forschung und Wissenschaft 57. Münster: Lit Verlag, 2023.

Bikbov, Aleksandr, and Asia Leofreddi. "Inequalities and Resistance in Putin's Russia." *OBC Transeuropa*, November 15, 2022. https://www.balcanicaucaso.org/eng/Areas/Russia/Inequalities-and-resistance-in-Putin-s-Russia-221607.

Pokinsokha, Daniil. "Biriusa Today. Smena "Grazhdanskoe obshchestvo" i "Dobrovol'chestvo". Den' tretii." YouTube. Krasnoyarsk. July 15, 2013, 16:07. https://www.youtube.com/watch?time_continue=732&v=Kg79RGZqbrc.

Blee, Kathleen. *Inside Organized Racism: Women in the Hate Movement*. Berkeley: University of California Press, 2002.

Bluhm, Katharina, and Mihai Varga. "Introduction: Toward a New Illiberal Conservatism in Russia and East Central Europe." In *New Conservatives in Russia and East Central Europe*, edited by Katharina Bluhm and Mihai Varga, 1–22. New York: Routledge, 2019.

Bluhm, Katharina, and Mihai Varga. *New Conservatives in Russia and East Central Europe*, edited by Katharina Bluhm and Mihai Varga. New York: Routledge, 2019.

Blum, Douglas W. *National Identity and Globalization: Youth, State and Society in Post-Soviet Eurasia*. Cambridge: Cambridge University Press, 2007.

Bockman, Johanna. *Markets in the Name of Socialism: The Left-Wing Origins of Neoliberalism*. Stanford: Stanford University Press, 2011.

Boltanski, Luc, and Eve Chiapello. "The New Spirit of Capitalism." *International Journal of Politics, Culture, and Society* 18, no. 3–4 (December 2006): 161–88. https://doi.org/10/d4r9qh.

Boltanski, Luc, and Laurent Thévenot. *On Justification: Economies of Worth*. Princeton: Princeton University Press, 2006.

Bonnell, Victoria E. "Winners and Losers in Russia's Economic Transition." In *Identities in Transition: Eastern Europe and Russia after the Collapse of Communism*, edited by Victoria E. Bonnell, 13–28. Berkeley: Center for Slavic and East European Studies, University of California at Berkeley, 1996.

Borenstein, Eliot. *Plots against Russia: Conspiracy and Fantasy after Socialism*. Ithaca, NY: Cornell University Press, 2019.

Borodikhina, S. L. "Poisk novogo soderzhaniia poniatiia 'aktivnaia zhiznennaia pozitsiia' v sovremennykh obshchestvenno-politicheskikh usloviiakh." *Vestnik TGPU/ National Research Tomsk Polytechnic University* 3, no. 156 (2015): 182–85.

Bozhovich, Mariia. "«Nevazhno — uedut deti ili ostanutsia». Kak v taezhnom sele sozdali sovremennuiu shkolu." *Pravmir*, September 6, 2021. https://www.pravmir.ru/deti-rasskazyvali-vzroslym-chto-nuzhno-delat-kak-kraevoj-chinovnik-stal-direktorom-selskoj-shkoly/.

Brennan, Christopher. "Controversial Activist 'Pigs' Confront Russian Shop Workers on Video over Expired Foods." *The Observers - France 24*, July 11, 2019. https://observers.france24.com/en/20190711-controversial-food-activist-pigs-confront-russian-shop-workers-video.

Bröckling, Ulrich. *The Entrepreneurial Self: Fabricating a New Type of Subject*. Los Angeles: Sage, 2016.

Bröckling, Ulrich, Susanne Krasmann, and Thomas Lemke, eds. *Glossar der Gegenwart*. Frankfurt am Main: Suhrkamp, 2004.

Bronwen, Gora. "Kostya Tszyu to Russia without Love." *The Sunday Telegraph*. September 15, 2012. https://www.dailytelegraph.com.au/kostya-tszyu-to-russia-without-love/news-story/1b65655d3759e603045e35067e2e4dfa.

Brossat, Wolfgang. "Heroismus." In *Politische Ikonographie: ein Handbuch. Bd. 1: Abdankung bis Huldigung*, edited by Uwe Fleckner, Martin Warnke, and Hendrik Ziegler, 473–80. Munich: Beck, 2014.

Brown, Wendy. *In the Ruins of Neoliberalism: The Rise of Antidemocratic Politics in the West*. New York: Columbia University Press, 2019.

Brown, Wendy. "Neoliberalism's Frankenstein: Authoritarian Freedom in Twenty-First Century 'Democracies.'" In *Authoritarianism: Three Inquiries in Critical Theory*, edited by Wendy Brown, Max Pensky, and Peter Eli Gordon, 7–44. Chicago: University of Chicago Press, 2018.

Brown, Wendy. *Undoing the Demos: Neoliberalism's Stealth Revolution*. New York: Zone Books, 2015.

Brown, Wendy, Peter Eli Gordon, and Max Pensky. *Authoritarianism: Three Inquiries in Critical Theory*. Chicago: University of Chicago Press, 2018.

Brubaker, Rogers. "Nationhood and the National Question in the Soviet Union and Post-Soviet Eurasia: An Institutionalist Account." *Theory and Society* 23, no. 1 (1994): 47–78.

Brubaker, Rogers, and Frederick Cooper. "Beyond 'Identity.'" *Theory and Society* 29, no. 1 (2000): 1–47. https://doi.org/10.1023/a:1007068714468.

Bruff, Ian. "The Rise of Authoritarian Neoliberalism." *Rethinking Marxism* 26, no. 1 (January 2014): 113–29. https://doi.org/10/gdnb73.

Bunce, Valerie, and Sharon L. Wolchik. *Defeating Authoritarian Leaders in Postcommunist Countries*. Cambridge Studies in Contentious Politics. Cambridge: Cambridge University Press, 2011.

Burawoy, Michael. "The Extended Case Method." *Sociological Theory* 16, no. 1 (1998): 4–33. https://doi.org/10/fwpvgm.

Burawoy, Michael. "Transition without Transformation: Russia's Involutionary Road to Capitalism." *East European Politics & Societies* 15, no. 2 (2001): 269–90.

Burgess, Jean, and Joshua Green. *Youtube: Online Video and Participatory Culture*. 2nd ed. Digital Media and Society. Cambridge: Polity Press, 2018.

Burskaia, Zinaida. "Bezhim za toboi!" *Novaia Gazeta* 138. December 8, 2010. https://novayagazeta.ru/articles/2010/12/08/327-bezhim-za-toboy.

Bush, Jason. "Small Businesses Cower after Moscow's Night of Bulldozers." *Reuters*, February 17, 2016. https://www.reuters.com/article/us-russia-economy-bulldozers-idUSKCN0VQ1W5.

Bushnev, Vasily, Elena Moskovkina, Natalia Savelieva, and Oleg Zhuravlev. "'Public' Sociology in Russia." Translated by Mischa Gabowitsch. *Laboratorium: Russian Review of Social Research* 1 (2009): 205–7.

Buzogány, Aron, and Mihai Varga. "Against 'Post-Communism': The Conservative Dawn in Hungary." In *New Conservatives in Russia and East Central Europe*, edited by Katharina Bluhm and Mihai Varga, 70–91. New York: Routledge, 2019.

Cabanas, Edgar, and Eva Illouz. *Manufacturing Happy Citizens: How the Science and Industry of Happiness Control Our Lives*. Cambridge: Polity Press, 2019.

Cahen, Dava. *Nashi*. 16:9, Documentary. eye film institute, 2008. http://www.filmbank.nl/film/3895/.

Casula, Philipp. *Hegemonie und Populismus in Putins Russland: Eine Analyse des russischen politischen Diskurses*. Bielefeld: Transcript, 2012.

Cerny, Philip G. "Competition State." In *Encyclopedia of Governance*, edited by Mark Bevir, 129. Thousand Oaks: SAGE Publications, 2007.

Cerny, Philip G. "In the Shadow of Ordoliberalism: The Paradox of Neoliberalism in the 21st Century." *European Review of International Studies* 3, no. 1 (2016): 78–92.

Charmaz, Kathy. *Constructing Grounded Theory: A Practical Guide through Qualitative Analysis*. London: Sage, 2006.

Chatterje-Doody, Precious N, and Vera Tolz. "Regime Legitimation, Not Nation-Building: Media Commemoration of the 1917 Revolutions in Russia's Neo-Authoritarian State." *European Journal of Cultural Studies* 23, no. 3 (June 2020): 335–53. https://doi.org/10/gjhgc3.

Chebankova, Elena. *Civil Society in Putin's Russia*. London: Routledge, 2013.

Cherniavskii, Aleksandr. "Sibirskuiu prokuraturu zainteresovali 'Antibiriusoi.'" *Nezavisimaia Gazeta*, January 7, 2011. http://www.ng.ru/regions/2011-07-01/5_antibirusa.html.

Christiaens, Tim. "The Entrepreneur of the Self beyond Foucault's Neoliberal Homo Oeconomicus." *European Journal of Social Theory* 23, no. 4 (July 25, 2019): 493–511. https://doi.org/10/ghtzs7.

Cikara, Mina, and Susan T. Fiske. "Stereotypes and Schadenfreude: Affective and Physiological Markers of Pleasure at Outgroup Misfortunes." *Social Psychological and Personality Science* 3, no. 1 (January 2012): 63–71. https://doi.org/10/b3q522.

Collier, Stephen J. "Neoliberalism as Big Leviathan, or . . .? A Response to Wacquant and Hilgers." *Social Anthropology* 20, no. 2 (May 2012): 186–95. https://doi.org/10/gdtnst.

Collier, Stephen J. *Post-Soviet Social: Neoliberalism, Social Modernity, Biopolitics*. Princeton: Princeton University Press, 2011.

Comai, Giorgio. "Molodaya Gvardiya: The Young Guard of Russia's Elite." Bologna: Portal on Central Eastern and Balkan Europe by IECOB & AIS, 2006. http://www.pecob.net/molodaya-gvardiya-young-guard-russia-elite-giorgio-comai.

Comai, Giorgio. "Youth Camps in Post-Soviet Russia and the Northern Caucasus: The Cases of Seliger and Mashuk 2010." *Anthropology of East Europe Review* 30, no. 1 (2012): 184–212.

Confino, Alon. "Collective Memory and Cultural History: Problems of Method." *The American Historical Review* 102, no. 5 (1997): 1386–1403. https://doi.org/10.2307/2171069.

Connell, R. W. "Globalization, Imperialism, and Masculinities." In *Handbook of Studies on Men & Masculinities*, edited by Michael S. Kimmel and Jeff Hearn, 71–89. Thousand Oaks, CA: SAGE, 2005.

Connell, Tula. "Russian Unionist Wins Svensson Prize for Trade Union Rights." *Solidarity Center*, May 13, 2013. https://www.solidaritycenter.org/russian-unionist-wins-svensson-prize-for-trade-union-rights/.

Cooper, Melinda. *Family Values: Between Neoliberalism and the New Social Conservatism*. Near Futures. New York: Zone Books, 2017.

Covey, Stephen R. *The 7 Habits of Highly Effective People: Restoring the Character Ethic*. New York: Free Press, 1989.

Crouch, Colin, Donatella della Porta, and Wolfgang Streeck. "Democracy in Neoliberalism?" *Anthropological Theory* 16, no. 4 (December 2016): 497–512. https://doi.org/10/gdtnp6.

Cunningham, Stuart, and David Craig. "Being 'Really Real' on YouTube: Authenticity, Community and Brand Culture in Social Media Entertainment." *Media International Australia* 164, no. 1 (August 2017): 71–81. https://doi.org/10/gddcwx.

Cupers, Kenny. "Governing through Nature: Camps and Youth Movements in Interwar Germany and the United States." *Cultural Geographies* 15, no. 2 (April 2008): 173–205. https://doi.org/10/cdw6dm.

Daucé, Françoise. "The Duality of Coercion in Russia: Cracking down on 'Foreign Agents.'" *Demokratizatsiya: The Journal of Post-Soviet Democratization* 23, no. 1 (2015): 57–75.

Davydenko, Kirill. "Trening Tsentr 'Sil'nye liudi.'" Facebook Trening Tsentr "Sil'nye liudi," 2018. https://www.facebook.com/Мастерская-Сильные-люди-211076542984449/.

Detskii ozdorovitel'nyi lager' «Kratovo», Pamiatka dlia roditelei otpravliaiushchikh detei v DOL «Kratovo», 2015. http://www.rzd.ru/ent/public/ru?STRUCTURE_ID=5185&layer_id=5554&id=3677#main.

Dmitrieva, Alexandra, and Zhanna Kravchenko. "Unhealthy, Deviant and Criminal. Drug Control Policies in Russia." *Baltic Worlds* 9, no. 4 (2016): 12–22.

Donig, Natalia. "Die Erfindung der „sowjetischen Heimat". Zur Geschichte eines Ideologems." In *Heimat als Erfahrung und Entwurf*, edited by Natalia Donig, Silke Flegel, and Sarah Scholl-Schneider, 61–85. Münster: LIT Verlag, 2009.

Doran, George T. "There's a S.M.A.R.T. Way to Write Management's Goals and Objectives." *Management Review* 70 (1981): 35–36.

Douglas, Nadja. *Public Control of Armed Forces in the Russian Federation*. Cham: Palgrave Macmillan, 2017.

Dubin, Boris. "Simvoly vozvrata vmesto simvolov peremen." *Pro et contra* 5, no. 53 (2011): 6–22.

Dubina, Vera, and Alexandra Arkhipova. "'No Wobble': Silent Protest in Contemporary Russia." *Russian Analytical Digest. Hidden Resistance to the Russian-Ukrainian War Inside Russia* 291 (January 2023): 8–11. https://doi.org/10/grv897.

Dukalskis, Alexander, and Johannes Gerschewski. "What Autocracies Say (and What Citizens Hear): Proposing Four Mechanisms of Autocratic Legitimation." *Contemporary Politics* 23, no. 3 (July 2017): 251–68. https://doi.org/10/gjmqwr.

Durkheim, Émile. *The Elementary Forms of Religious Life*. Translated by Karen E. Fields. New York: Free Press, 1995.

Easton, David. "A Re-Assessment of the Concept of Political Support." *British Journal of Political Science* 5, no. 4 (1975): 435–57. https://doi.org/10/b5phsd.

Ebel, Francesca, and Mary Ilyushina. "Russians Abandon Wartime Russia in Historic Exodus." *Washington Post*, February 13, 2023. https://www.washingtonpost.com/world/2023/02/13/russia-diaspora-war-ukraine/.

Eder, Klaus. "The Making of a European Civil Society: 'Imagined', 'Practised' and 'Staged.'" *Policy and Society* 28, no. 1 (April 2009): 23–33. https://doi.org/10.1016/j.polsoc.2009.02.003.

Eder, Klaus. "Klassentheorie als Gesellschaftstheorie." In *Klassenlage, Lebensstil und kulturelle Praxis: Beiträge zur Auseinandersetzung mit Pierre Bourdieus Klassentheorie*, edited by Klaus Eder, 15–43. Frankfurt: Suhrkamp, 1989.

Effron, Lauren. "Steve Jobs' Commencement Speech Talked About Death." *ABC News*, October 6, 2011. http://abcnews.go.com/blogs/technology/2011/10/steve-jobs-talked-about-death-in-2005-stanford-commencement-speech-2.

Eisenstadt, Shmuel Noah. "Socialism and Tradition." In *Socialism and Tradition*, edited by Yael Azmon and Shmuel Noah Eisenstadt, 1–18. The Van Leer Jerusalem Foundation Series. Atlantic Highlands, NJ: Humanities Press, 1975.

Ekiert, Grzegorz, Elizabeth J. Perry, and Xiaojun Yan, eds. *Ruling by Other Means: State-Mobilized Movements*. Cambridge Studies in Contentious Politics. Cambridge: Cambridge University Press, 2020.

Ekspert. "Chto takoe chelovek goda," December 23, 2002. https://expert.ru/expert/2002/48/48ex-people_34982/.

"Elena Bocherova: Ia vsegda zhelaiu molodezhi tol'ko odnogo: mechtat'." Vkontakte [Russian Social Network] Forum - ty predprinimatel', June 14, 2013. https://vk.com/wall-38780252?offset=380&w=wall-38780252_563%2Fall.

Eliasoph, Nina. "Spirals of Perpetual Potential: How Empowerment Project's Noble Mission Tangle in Everyday Interaction." In *Democratizing Inequalities: Dilemmas of the New Public Participation*, edited by Caroline W. Lee, Michael McQuarrie, and Edward T. Walker, 165–86. New York: NYU Press, 2015.

Eliasoph, Nina, and Karine Clément. "Doing Comparative Ethnography in Vastly Different National Conditions: The Case of Local Grassroot Activism in Russia and the United States." *International Journal of Politics, Culture, and Society* 33, no. 2 (June 2020): 251–82. https://doi.org/10/gnm4th

Elina, Mariia, Anastasiia Butorina, Mariia Shvytkova, Aleksandra Perminova, Ol'ga Vasil'eva, and Dmitrii Chen. "Analiticheskii otchet po rezul'tatam metodicheskogo (sotsiologicheskogo) soprovozhdeniia mezhregional'nogo molodezhnogo foruma 'Territoriia initsiativnoi molodezhi Biriusa-2013.'" Krasnoiarsk: Nauchno-issledovatel'skaia laboratoriia sotsiologii (Students and alumni of the Siberian Federal University), 2013.

El'shin, Boris. "Boris Nemtsov obnaruzhil glavnoe preimushchestvo Krasnoiarskogo kraia." *Kommersant*. April 17, 2003.

Elster, Jon. "Self-Realization in Work and Politics: The Marxist Conception of the Good Life." *Social Philosophy and Policy* 3, no. 2 (1986): 97. https://doi.org/10/b3k3jr.

Elteren, Mel van. "Cultural Globalization and Transnational Flows of Things American." In *The Systemic Dimension of Globalization*, edited by Piotr Pachura, 149–72. London: InTechOpen, 2011.

Enroth, Henrik. "The Return of the Repressed: Populism and Democracy Revisited." *American Journal of Cultural Sociology* 8, no. 2 (August 2020): 246–62. https://doi.org/10/gjbrn2.

Ermakova, Natalia. "Kak krasnoiartsy 55 let igraiut v KVN: vspominaem samye uboinye shutki i vsekh zvezd," November 25, 2016. https://ngs24.ru/text/gorod/2016/11/25/50169501/.

Etkind, Aleksandr. *Internal Colonization: Russia's Imperial Experience*. Cambridge: Polity Press, 2011.

Reuters. "Kremlin: Many People in Russia Are Showing Themselves to Be Traitors." *Euronews*, March 18, 2022. https://www.euronews.com/2022/03/18/us-ukraine-crisis-kremlin-traitors.

Evans, Alfred B., Jr. "Protests in Russia: The Example of the Blue Buckets Society." *Demokratizatsiya* 26, no. 1 (2018): 3–24.

Evans, Christine E. *Between Truth and Time: A History of Soviet Central Television*. Eurasia Past and Present. New Haven, CT: Yale University Press, 2016.

Fabry, Adam. *The Political Economy of Hungary From State Capitalism to Authoritarian Neoliberalism*. London: Palgrave Macmillan, 2019. https://doi.org/10.1007/978-3-030-10594-5.

Fabry, Adam, and Sune Sandbeck. "Introduction to Special Issue on 'Authoritarian Neoliberalism.'" *Competition & Change* 23, no. 2 (April 2019): 109–15. https://doi.org/10/gm7ms5.

Fagerberg, Jan, Martin Srholec, and Bart Verspagen. "Innovation and Economic Development." In *Handbook of the Economics of Innovation. Vol. 2*, edited by Bronwyn H. Hall and Nathan Rosenberg, 833–72. Handbooks in Economics. Amsterdam: Elsevier, 2010.

Favarel-Garrigues, Gilles. "Criticism of Moral Policing in Russia: Controversies around Lev Protiv in Moscow." In *Violence and Trolling on Social Media: History, Affect, and Effects of Online Vitriol*, edited by Sara Polak and Daniel Trottier, 107–27. Amsterdam: Amsterdam University Press, 2020. https://books.openedition.org/obp/15542?lang=de.

Favarel-Garrigues, Gilles. "'Vigilante Shows' and Law Enforcement in Russia." *Europe-Asia Studies* 73, no. 1 (January 2021): 221–42. https://doi.org/10/gkcpqk.

Favarel-Garrigues, Gilles, and Ioulia Shukan. "Perspectives on Post-Soviet Vigilantism. Introduction." *Laboratorium: Russian Review of Social Research*, 11, no. 3 (2019): 4–15. https://doi.org/10/gm7mtm.

Ferguson, James. "The Uses of Neoliberalism." *Antipode* 41 (January 2010): 166–84. https://doi.org/10/dxvdbk.

Florin, Dmitrii. "FSRB vzryvaet Moskvu: v Moskve pod prikrytiem silovikov deistvuet gruppirovka po zakhvatu zemel.'" Novosti politicheskikh partii, November 11, 2014. http://www.qwas.ru/russia/yabloko/FSRB-vzryvaet-Moskvu-v-Moskve-pod-prikrytiem-silovikov-deistvuet-gruppirovka-po-zahvatu-zemel/.

Foucault, Michel. *Discipline and Punish: The Birth of the Prison*. New York: Random House, 1977.

Foucault, Michel. "Technologies of the Self". In *Technologies of the Self: A Seminar with Michel Foucault*, edited by Luther H. Martin, Huck Gutman, and Patrick H. Hutton, 16–49. Amherst: University of Massachusetts Press, 1988.

Fourcade-Gourinchas, Marion. "State Metrology: The Rating of Sovereigns and the Judgment of Nations." In *The Many Hands of the State: Theorizing Political Authority and Social Control*, edited by Kimberly J. Morgan and Ann Shola Orloff, 103–27. New York: Cambridge University Press, 2017.

Fourcade, Marion, and Kieran Healy. "Moral Views of Market Society." *Annual Review of Sociology* 33, no. 1 (August 2007): 285–311. https://doi.org/10/bg3h76.

Frantz, Erica, and Andrea Kendall-Taylor. "A Dictator's Toolkit: Understanding How Co-Optation Affects Repression in Autocracies." *Journal of Peace Research* 51, no. 3 (2014): 332–46. https://doi.org/10/f54qr6.

Frase, Peter. "In Defense of Soviet Waiters. Sometimes Bad Service Is Class Struggle." *Jacobin*, June 2, 2013. http://jacobinmag.com/2013/02/soviet-waiters-emotional-labor-customer-service.

Fröhlich, Christian. "Interviewforschung im russischsprachigen Raum – ein Balanceakt zwischen methodologischen und feldspezifischen Ansprüchen." In *Qualitative Interviewforschung in und mit fremden Sprachen. Eine Einführung in Theorie und Praxis*, edited by Jan Kruse, Stephanie Bethmann, Debora Niermann, and Christian Schmieder, 190–206. Weinheim: Beltz Juventa, 2012.

Fürst, Juliane. *Stalin's Last Generation: Soviet Post-War Youth and the Emergence of Mature Socialism*. Oxford: Oxford University Press, 2010.

Gabdulhakov, Rashid. "Citizen-Led Justice in Post-Communist Russia: From Comrades' Courts to Dotcomrade Vigilantism." *Surveillance & Society* 16, no. 3 (October 2018): 314–31. https://doi.org/10/ggpnxm.

Gabdulhakov, Rashid. "Heroes or Hooligans? Media Portrayal of StopXam (Stop a Douchebag) Vigilantes in Russia." *Laboratorium: Russian Review of Social Research*, 11, no. 3 (2019): 16–45. https://doi.org/10/ggpnjd.

Gabdulhakov, Rashid. "Media Control and Citizen-Critical Publics in Russia: Are Some 'Pigs' More Equal Than Others?" *Media and Communication* 9, no. 4 (October 2021): 62–72. https://doi.org/10/gnms7d.

Gabowitsch, Mischa. "Are Copycats Subversive? Strategy-31, the Russian Runs, the Immortal Regiment, and the Transformative Potential of Non-Hierarchical Movements." *Problems of Post-Communism* 64, no. 3–4 (2017): 33–51.

Gabowitsch, Mischa. *Protest in Putin's Russia*. Cambridge: Polity Press, 2016.

Gabowitsch, Mischa, Cordula Gdaniec, and Ekaterina Makhotina, eds. *Kriegsgedenken als Event. Der 9. Mai 2015 im postsozialistischen Europa*. Paderborn: Schöningh, 2017.

Gagyi, Ágnes, and Tamás Geröcs. "Reconfiguring Regimes of Capitalist Integration: Hungary Since the 1970s". In *The Political Economy of Eastern Europe 30 years into the 'Transition'*, edited by Ágnes Gagyi and Ondřej Slačálek, 115–131. International Political Economy Series. London: Palgrave Macmillan, 2022. https://doi.org/10.1007/978-3-030-78915-2_7.

Gagyi, Ágnes, and Tamás Geröcs. "The Political Economy of Hungary's New 'Slave Law.'" *Lefteast*, January 1, 2019. https://lefteast.org/the-political-economy-of-hungarys-new-slave-law/.

Galvan, Dennis. "Neotraditionalism." In *Encyclopedia of Governance*, edited by Mark Bevir, 600–601. Thousand Oaks: SAGE Publications, 2007. https://doi.org/g9rr.

Gaufman, Elizaveta. *Security Threats and Public Perception: Digital Russia and the Ukraine Crisis*. New Security Challenges. London: Palgrave Macmillan, 2017.

Geddes, Barbara. "Why Parties and Elections in Authoritarian Regimes?" *Annual Meeting of the American Political Science Association* 101 (January 2005): 456–71.

Gel'man, Vladimir. *Authoritarian Russia: Analyzing Post-Soviet Regime Changes*. Pittsburgh Series in Russian and East European Studies. Pittsburgh: University of Pittsburgh Press, 2015.

Gerasimova, Olga G. *Ottepel', Zamarozki i studenty Moskovskogo Universiteta*. Moscow: AIRO-XXI, 2015.

Gerschewski, Johannes. "Legitimacy in Autocracies: Oxymoron or Essential Feature?" *Perspectives on Politics* 16, no. 3 (2018): 652–65. https://doi.org/10/ggjpf4.

Gert, Bernard. "Loyalty and Morality." In *Loyalty*, edited by Sanford Levinson, Paul Woodruff, and Joel Parker, 3–21. New York: New York University Press, 2013.

Geyer, Dietrich. "Ostpolitik und Geschichtsbewusstsein in Deutschland." *Vierteljahrsschrift für Zeitgeschichte* 34, no. 2 (1986): 147–59.

Gill, Graeme. *Symbols and Legitimacy in Soviet Politics*. Cambridge: Cambridge University Press, 2011.

Girin, Nikita. "U podrostka sud korotkii." *Novaia Gazeta*, June 24, 2014. https://novayagazeta.ru/articles/2014/06/24/60085-u-podrostka-sud-korotkiy.

Gitelman, Zvi. "Comment on Prazauskas, Tishkov, and Yamskov." *Theory and Society* 20, no. 5 (1991): 701–4. https://doi.org/10/bvbt5b.

Glaser, Barney. *Awareness of Dying*. Chicago: Aldine, 1965.
Glasius, Marlies. "What Authoritarianism Is . . . and Is Not: A Practice Perspective." *International Affairs* 94, no. 3 (May 1, 2018): 515–33. https://doi.org/10/gdkww5.
Glasius, Marlies. *Authoritarian Practices in a Global Age*. Oxford: Oxford University Press, 2023.
Goffman, Erving. *Asylums: Essays on the Social Situation of Mental Patients and Other Inmates*. New York: Anchor Books, 1961.
Goffman, Erving. *Frame Analysis: An Essay on the Organization of Experience*. Boston: Northeastern University Press, 1986.
Goffman, Erving. *Stigma: Notes on the Management of Spoiled Identity*. Englewood Cliffs, NJ: Prentice-Hall, 1963.
Golova, Tatiana. "How Do Quite Ordinary People Support a Quite Ordinary Hybrid Regime, and Do They?" Presented at the 11th ECPR general Conference, Oslo, September 8, 2017.
Gorsuch, Anne E. *Youth in Revolutionary Russia: Enthusiasts, Bohemians, Delinquents*. Bloomington: Indiana University Press, 2000.
Goździk-Ormel, Żaneta. "Development and Implementation of Participation Projects at Local and Regional Level." Strasbourg: Council of Europe, European Youth Centre, December 2006. http://rm.coe.int/09000016806fcf6d.
Grant, Bruce. *In the Soviet House of Culture: A Century of Perestroikas*. Princeton, NJ: Princeton University Press, 1995.
Grant, Bruce. *The Captive and the Gift: Cultural Histories of Sovereignty in Russia and the Caucasus*. Ithaca, NY: Cornell University Press, 2009.
Grawe, Klaus. *Neuropsychotherapy: How the Neurosciences Inform Effective Psychotherapy*. New York: Routledge, 2007.
Greene, Samuel A. *Moscow in Movement: Power and Opposition in Putin's Russia*. Stanford, CA: Stanford University Press, 2014.
Greene, Samuel A., and Graeme B. Robertson. "State-Mobilized Movements after Annexation of Crimea: The Construction of Novorossiya." In *Ruling by Other Means: State-Mobilized Movements*, edited by Grzegorz Ekiert, Elizabeth J. Perry, and Xiaojun Yan, 193–216. Cambridge Studies in Contentious Politics. Cambridge: Cambridge University Press, 2020.
Greene, Samuel A., and Graeme B. Robertson. *Putin v. the People: The Perilous Politics of a Divided Russia*. New Haven, CT: Yale University Press, 2019.
Griboiedoff, Aleksandr. *Gore Ot Ouma. A Comedy*. Translated by Nicholas Benardaky. London: Simpkin, Marshall, & Co., 1825.
Gromov, Dmitrii. "Dvizhenie 'Nashi'. 2007 god." In *Molodezhnye subkultury Moskvy*, edited by Dmitrii Gromov and Marina Martynova, 115–72. Moscow: Institut Etnologii i Antropologii, Rossiiskaia Akademia Nauk, 2009. http://evartist.narod.ru/text26/0013.htm.
Gudkov, Lev. "The Fetters of Victory. How the War Provides Russia with Its Identity." *Osteuropa/ Eurozine* 4–6 (2005): 1–14. https://zeitschrift-osteuropa.de/hefte/international/eurozine-en/the-fetters-of-victory/
Hann, Chris. "Introduction: Postsocialism as a Topic of Anthropological Investigation. Farewell to the Socialist 'Other.'" In *Postsocialism Ideals, Ideologies, and Practices in Eurasia*, edited by Chris Hann, 1–12. London: Routledge, 2002.
Hartog, Eva. "A Kremlin Youth Movement Goes Rogue." *The Moscow Times*, April 8, 2016. http://themoscowtimes.com/articles/a-kremlin-youth-movement-goes-rogue-52435.

Harrison, Graham. *Developmentalism: The Normative and Transformative within Capitalism*. Critical Frontiers of Theory, Research, and Policy in International Development Studies. Oxford: Oxford University Press, 2020.

He, Baogang, and Mark E. Warren. "Authoritarian Deliberation: The Deliberative Turn in Chinese Political Development." *Perspectives on Politics* 9, no. 2 (2011): 269–89. https://doi.org/10/dnzffn.

Heitmeyer, Wilhelm. *Autoritäre Versuchungen*. 3rd ed. Berlin: Suhrkamp, 2018.

Hellbeck, Jochen. *Revolution on My Mind: Writing a Diary under Stalin*. Cambridge: Harvard University Press, 2006.

Hemment, Julie. "Nashi, Youth Voluntarism, and Potemkin NGOs: Making Sense of Civil Society in Post-Soviet Russia." *Slavic Review* 71, no. 2 (2012): 234–60. https://doi.org/10/gghw3r.

Hemment, Julie. "Occupy Youth! State-Mobilized Movements in the Putin Era (or, What Was Nashi and What Comes Next?)." In *Ruling by Other Means: State-Mobilized Movements*, edited by Grzegorz Ekiert, Elizabeth J. Perry, and Xiaojun Yan, 166–92. Cambridge Studies in Contentious Politics. Cambridge: Cambridge University Press, 2020.

Hemment, Julie. "Soviet-Style Neoliberalism? Nashi, Youth Voluntarism, and the Restructuring of Social Welfare in Russia." *Problems of Post-Communism* 56, no. 6 (2009): 36–50. https://doi.org/10/d5gbxs.

Hemment, Julie. *Youth Politics in Putin's Russia: Producing Patriots and Entrepreneurs*. Bloomington: Indiana University Press, 2015.

Hirsch, Francine. *Empire of Nations: Ethnographic Knowledge and the Making of the Soviet Union*. Culture & Society after Socialism. Ithaca, NY: Cornell University Press, 2005.

Hirschi, Caspar. "Die Organisation von Innovation - über die Geschichte einer Obsession." *Angewandte Chemie* 125, no. 52 (December 2013): 14118–22. https://doi.org/10/f2nd5r.

Hobsbawm, E. J. *Nations and Nationalism since 1780: Programme, Myth, Reality*. 2nd ed. Cambridge: Cambridge University Press, 1992.

Hoffman, Lisa M. *Patriotic Professionalism in Urban China: Fostering Talent*. Urban Life, Landscape, and Policy. Philadelphia: Temple University Press, 2010.

Hoffman, Lisa M., and Hope Reidun St. John. "'Doing Good': Affect, Neoliberalism, and Responsibilization Among Volunteers in China and the United States." In *Assembling Neoliberalism: Expertise, Practices, Subjects*, edited by Vaughan Higgins and Wendy Larner, 243–62. New York: Palgrave Macmillan, 2017.

Hoffmann, David L. *Stalinist Values: The Cultural Norms of Soviet Modernity, 1917–1941*. Ithaca, NY: Cornell University Press, 2003.

Hoffmann, David L. *The Memory of the Second World War in Soviet and Post-Soviet Russia*. London: Routledge, 2021.

Holzkamp-Osterkamp, Ute. *Grundlagen der psychologischen Motivationsforschung*. Vol. 1. 2 vols. Texte zur kritischen Psychologie. Frankfurt: Campus Verlag, 1975.

Honey, Larisa. "Self-Help Groups in Post-Soviet Moscow: Neoliberal Discourses of the Self and Their Social Critique." *Laboratorium: Russian Review of Social Research* 6, no. 1 (January 2014): 5–29.

Horgan, Amelia. *Lost in Work: Escaping Capitalism*. Outspoken by Pluto. London: Pluto Press, 2021.

Horvath, Robert. "Putin's 'Preventive Counter-Revolution': Post-Soviet Authoritarianism and the Spectre of Velvet Revolution." *Europe-Asia Studies* 63, no. 1 (2011): 1–25. https://doi.org/10/b2ph4c.

Humanitarian Research Lab. "Russia's Systematic Program for the Re-Education & Adoption of Ukraine's Children." Conflict Observatory Report. New Haven, CT: Yale School of Public Health, February 14, 2023. https://hub.conflictobservatory.org/portal/sharing/rest/content/items/97f919ccfe524d31a241b53ca44076b8/data.

Hutchings, Steven, and Joanna Szostek. "Dominant Narratives in Russian Political and Media Discourse during the Ukraine Crisis." In *Ukraine and Russia: People, Politics, Propaganda and Perspectives*, edited by Agnieszka Pikulicka-Wilczewska and Richard Sakwa, 173–85. Bristol: E-International Relations Publishing, 2016.

Instagram. "KKSO. Krasnoyarsk (@kkso_krsk)." Accessed March 7, 2023. https://www.instagram.com/kkso_krsk/.

Ioffe, Julia. "The Master And Mikhail." *The New Yorker*, February 19, 2012. http://www.newyorker.com/magazine/2012/02/27/the-master-and-mikhail.

Jäger, Jens. "Polizei." In *Politische Ikonographie: ein Handbuch. Bd. 2: Imperator bis Zwerg*, edited by Uwe Fleckner, Martin Warnke, and Hendrik Ziegler, 249–55. Munich: Beck, 2014.

James, William. *The Will to Believe, and Other Essays in Popular Philosophy*. Cambridge: Cambridge University Press, 1897.

Janoski, Thomas. "The Dynamic Processes of Volunteering in Civil Society: A Group and Multi-Level Approach." *Journal of Civil Society* 6, no. 2 (September 2010): 99–118. https://doi.org/10/b3trh4.

Jasper, James M. *The Art of Moral Protest: Culture, Biography, and Creativity in Social Movements*. Chicago: University of Chicago Press, 1997.

Jasper, James M., Michael P Young, and Elke Zuern. *Public Characters: The Politics of Reputation and Blame*. Oxford: Oxford University Press, 2020.

Jenkins, Richard. *Social Identity*. 3rd ed. Key Ideas. London: Routledge, 2008.

Jenkins, Richard. *Rethinking Ethnicity*. 2nd ed. Thousand Oaks, CA: Sage, 2008.

Johnston, Les. "What Is Vigilantism?" *The British Journal of Criminology* 36, no. 2 (1996): 220–36. https://doi.org/10/gkdzb4.

Joppke, Christian. *Neoliberal Nationalism: Immigration and the Rise of the Populist Right*. Cambridge: Cambridge University Press, 2021.

Kailitz, Steffen, and Daniel Stockemer. "Regime Legitimation, Elite Cohesion and the Durability of Autocratic Regime Types." *International Political Science Review / Revue Internationale de Science Politique* 38, no. 3 (2017): 332–48. https://doi.org/10/ghw29m.

Kailitz, Steffen, and Stefan Wurster. "Legitimationsstrategien von Autokratien: Eine Einführung." *Zeitschrift für Vergleichende Politikwissenschaft* 11, no. 2 (June 2017): 141–51. https://doi.org/10/gm7ms3.

Kalb, Don. "Afterword. Globalism and Postsocialist Prospects." In *Postsocialism. Ideals, Ideologies, and Practices in Eurasia*, by Chris Hann, 317–34. London: Routledge, 2002.

Kalb, Don. "Post-Socialist Contradictions: The Social Question in Central and Eastern Europe and the Making of the Illiberal Right." In *The Social Question in the Twenty-First Century: A Global View*, edited by Jan Breman, Kevan Harris, Ching Kwan Lee, and Marcel van der Linden, 208–26. Berkeley: University of California Press, 2019.

Kalinin, Ilya. "Nostalgic Modernization: The Soviet Past as 'Historical Horizon.'" *Slavonica* 17, no. 2 (2011): 156–66. https://doi.org/10/bzc3b9.

Kalinin, Ilya. "Russian Culture as a Public Good, Private Property, National Value, and State Resource." Wissenschaftskolleg Berlin, November 10, 2021. https://www.wiko-berlin.de/fellows/akademisches-jahr/2021/kalinin-ilya.

Kalinin, Ilya. "The Struggle for History: The Past as a Limited Resource." In *Memory and Theory in Eastern Europe*, edited by Uilleam Blacker, Alexander Etkind, and Julie Fedor, 255–65. Palgrave Studies in Cultural and Intellectual History. New York: Palgrave Macmillan, 2013.

Keller, Suzanne. *Beyond the Ruling Class: Strategic Elites in Modern Society*. New York: Random House, 1963.

Kelly, Catriona. *Children's World: Growing up in Russia, 1890-1991*. New Haven, CT: Yale University Press, 2007.

Kenez, Peter. *The Birth of the Propaganda State: Soviet Methods of Mass Mobilization, 1917-1929*. Cambridge: Cambridge University Press, 1985.

Khakhulina, Liudmila. "The Persistence of Mass Conceptions of Justice." *Sociological Research* 54, no. 2 (March 2015): 71–90. https://doi.org/10/gntgsj.

Kharkhordin, Oleg. *The Collective and the Individual in Russia: A Study of Practices*. Studies on the History of Society and Culture. Berkeley: University of California Press, 1999.

Kielmansegg, Peter Graf. "Legitimität als analytische Kategorie." *Politische Vierteljahresschrift* 12, no. 3 (1971): 367–401.

Kishkovsky, Sophia. "Viktor Astafyev, Who Wrote of Rural Russia, Dies at 77." *The New York Times*, December 3, 2001. https://www.nytimes.com/2001/12/03/arts/viktor-astafyev-who-wrote-of-rural-russia-dies-at-77.html.

Klapper, Leora, and Georgios A. Panos. "Financial Literacy and Retirement Planning: The Russian Case." *Journal of Pension Economics and Finance* 10, no. 4 (2011): 599–618. https://doi.org/10/bbwc72.

Kleinig, John. "Loyalty." In *Stanford Encyclopedia of Philosophy*, edited by Edward N. Zalta. Stanford: Metaphysics Research Lab, Stanford University, 2020. https://plato.stanford.edu/archives/win2020/entries/loyalty.

Klingseis, Katharina. "The Power of Dress in Contemporary Russian Society: On Glamour Discourse and the Everyday Practice of Getting Dressed in Russian Cities." *Laboratorium: Russian Review of Social Research* 3, no. 1 (2011): 84–115.

Kocyba, Hermann. "Aktivierung." In *Glossar der Gegenwart*, edited by Ulrich Bröckling, Susanne Krasmann, and Thomas Lemke, 17–22. Frankfurt am Main: Suhrkamp, 2004.

Koenker, Diane. *Club Red: Vacation Travel and the Soviet Dream*. Ithaca, NY: Cornell University Press, 2013.

Kolstø, Pål. "Is Imperialist Nationalism an Oxymoron?" *Nations and Nationalism* 25, no. 1 (2019): 18–44. https://doi.org/10/gm7t6r.

Koshiw, Isobel. "Weeks Turn to Months as Children Become Stuck at Camps in Crimea." *The Guardian*, December 27, 2022. https://www.theguardian.com/world/2022/dec/27/children-become-stuck-at-camps-in-crimea-ukraine-russia.

Kovács, János Mátyás, and Balázs Trencsényi. "Conclusion: Hungary–Brave and New? Dissecting a Realistic Dystopia." In *Brave New Hungary: Mapping the "System of National Cooperation,"* edited by János Mátyás Kovács and Balázs Trencsényi, 379–427. Lanham: Lexington Books, 2020.

Koval', Ol'ga. "Mestnye i lagernye." *Obrazy detstva* (blog), February 23, 2014. http://obrazdetstva.ru/98-mestnye-i-lagernye.html#commen.

Kovalyova, Natalia. "Power and Talk in Russian Political Culture." *Ohio Communication Journal* 56 (2018): 1–18.

Kozenko, Andrei. "'Mestnye' diktuiut zakony rynkam. Podmoskovnaia molodezh' ustroila oblavu na migrantov." *Kommersant*, November 27, 2006. https://www.kommersant.ru/doc/725043.

Kramer, Andrew E. "In Siberia, a 'Blood River' in a Dead Zone Twice the Size of Rhode Island." *The New York Times*, September 8, 2016. https://www.nytimes.com/2016/09/09/world/europe/russia-red-river-siberia-norilsk-nickel.html.

Krätke, Stefan. "'Creative Cities' and the Rise of the Dealer Class: A Critique of Richard Florida's Approach to Urban Theory." *International Journal of Urban and Regional Research* 34, no. 4 (2010): 835–53. https://doi.org/10/fd57dp.

Krawatzek, Félix. *Youth in Regime Crisis: Comparative Perspectives from Russia to Weimar Germany*. Oxford Studies in Democratization. Oxford: Oxford University Press, 2018.

Krawatzek, Félix, and Nina Frieß. "A Foundation for Russia? Memories of World War II for Young Russians." *Nationalities Papers*: 1–21. https://doi.org/10/gpxp37.

Krivonos, Daria. "Zhizn' posle 'Nashikh': Avtonomiia, loial'nost' i iskrennost' v molodezhnom dvizhenii Stal'." *Etnograficheskoe obozrenie* 1 (2015): 72–89.

Kudryashev, Aleksei V. "The Dialectics of Everyday Life in Pioneer Camps: Romanticism and Regimen." *Russian Education & Society* 61, no. 5–6 (2019): 231–38. https://doi.org/10/gnjhps.

Kulmala, Meri. "Russian State and Civil Society in Interaction: An Ethnographic Approach." *Laboratorium: Russian Review of Social Research* 3, no. 1 (2011): 51–83.

Kulmala, Meri. "The Social Mission of Out-of-School Education in the USSR: A Historical Reconstruction of a Soviet Megaproject." *Russian Education & Society* 59, no. 3–4 (2017): 195–205. https://doi.org/10/gnjhsx.

Kumar, Arun. "Welcome, Or No Trespassing [1964] Review – A Marvelous Soviet Camp Comedy." *High On Films* (blog), March 17, 2021. https://www.highonfilms.com/welcome-or-no-trespassing-1964-review/.

Kupriianov, Boris V. "Soviet Adolescents' First Experiences of Romantic Feelings and Relationships at Pioneer Camps between the 1960s and 1980s." *Russian Education & Society* 61, no. 2–3 (2019): 125–38. https://doi.org/10/gnjhtj.

Kuz'min, Vladimir. "Prorvalis'. Dmitrii Medvedev vruchil premii molodezhi." *Rossiiskaia Gazeta*, December 18, 2009.

Lamont, Michèle. "National Identity and National Boundary Patterns in France and the United States." *French Historical Studies* 19, no. 2 (1995): 349–65. https://doi.org/10/bcz299.

Lamont, Michèle, and Ann Swidler. "Methodological Pluralism and the Possibilities and Limits of Interviewing." *Qualitative Sociology* 37, no. 2 (June 2014): 153–71. https://doi.org/10/f52mmk.

Lapidus, Gail W. "The Structural Context of Soviet Ethno-Nationalism." *Theory and Society* 20, no. 5 (1991): 705–9. https://doi.org/10/dxbjhc.

Lapidus, Gail W. "The War in Chechnya as a Paradigm of Russian State-Building under Putin." *Post-Soviet Affairs* 20, no. 1 (2004): 10–19. https://doi.org/10.2747/1060-586x.20.1.1.

Larintseva, Aleksandra. "'Kakie vy vse-taki vse russkie...' Polpred Aleksandr Khloponin poznakomilsia s kavkazskoi molodezh'iu." *Kommersant*, August 18, 2010. https://www.kommersant.ru/doc/1489167.

Larsen, Susan. "National Identity, Cultural Authority, and the Post-Soviet Blockbuster: Nikita Mikhalkov and Aleksei Balabanov." *Slavic Review* 62, no. 3 (2003): 491–511. https://doi.org/10/bxt598.
Laruelle, Marlène. *Russian Nationalism: Imaginaries, Doctrines, and Political Battlefields.* Vol. 61. Media, Culture and Social Change in Asia. Abingdon: Routledge, 2019.
Laruelle, Marlène. *Russian Eurasianism: An Ideology of Empire.* Washington, DC: Woodrow Wilson Center Press, Johns Hopkins University Press, 2008.
Laruelle, Marlène, ed. *Eurasianism and the European Far Right: Reshaping the Europe-Russia Relationship.* Lanham, MA: Lexington Books, 2015.
Lassila, Jussi, and Anna Sanina. "Attitudes to Putin-Era Patriotism Amongst Russia's 'In Between' Generation." *Europe-Asia Studies* 74, no. 7 (2022): 1190–1209. https://doi.org/10/grx8r8.
Lassila, Jussi. "From Failed Mobilization of Youth to Paternalistic Visualization of Putin: The Rocky Road of the Nashi Youth Movement." *Critique & Humanism* 46, no. 2 (2016): 33–50.
Lassila, Jussi. "The Russian People's Front and Hybrid Governance Dilemma." In *Authoritarian Modernization in Russia: Ideas, Institutions, and Policies*, edited by Vladimir Gel'man, 95–112. Abingdon: Routledge, 2016.
Lassila, Jussi. *The Quest for an Ideal Youth in Putin's Russia: The Search for Distinctive Conformism in the Political Communication of Nashi, 2005-2009.* Soviet and Post-Soviet Politics and Society. Stuttgart: Ibidem-Verlag, 2014.
Lassila, Jussi, and Anna Sanina. "Attitudes to Putin-Era Patriotism Amongst Russia's 'In Between' Generation." *Europe-Asia Studies* 74, no. 7 (2022): 1190–1209. https://doi.org/10/grx8r8.
Ledeneva, Alena. *Can Russia Modernise? Sistema, Power Networks and Informal Governance.* Cambridge: Cambridge University Press, 2013.
Ledeneva, Alena. *How Russia Really Works: The Informal Practices That Shaped Post-Soviet Politics and Business.* Ithaca, NY: Cornell University Press, 2006.
Ledeneva, Alena. *Russia's Economy of Favours: Blat, Networking, and Informal Exchange.* Cambridge Russian, Soviet and Post-Soviet Studies 102. Cambridge: Cambridge University Press, 1998.
Ledeneva, Alena V, Anna L Bailey, Sheelagh Barron, Costanza Curro, and Elizabeth Teague, eds. *The Global Encyclopaedia of Informality: Understanding Social and Cultural Complexity.* London: UCL Press, 2018.
Lee, Caroline W., Michael McQuarrie, and Edward T. Walker, eds. *Democratizing Inequalities: Dilemmas of the New Public Participation.* New York: NYU Press, 2015.
Lee, Caroline W., Michael McQuarrie, and Edward T. Walker. "Rising Participation and Declining Democracy." In *Democratizing Inequalities: Dilemmas of the New Public Participation*, edited by Caroline W. Lee, Michael McQuarrie, and Edward T. Walker, 3–23. New York: NYU Press, 2015.
Lenta.ru. "Belokonev, Sergei." *Lenta.ru.* 2013. https://lenta.ru/lib/14160096/#35.
Lenta.ru. "Interv'iu s glavoi Rosmolodezhi Vasiliem Iakemenko," January 17, 2012. https://lenta.ru/articles/2012/01/17/jakemenko/.
Lenta.ru. "Rossiia — strana vozmozhnostei. Kak prezidentskaia platforma zapuskaet novye sotsial'nye lifty," December 29, 2022. https://lenta.ru/articles/2022/12/29/platform/.
Leonov, Artem. "Meeting Lev Lazutin (Lion Versus)." YouTube. November 14, 2016. 10.45. https://www.youtube.com/watch?v=xdmOknVJ0T0.

Lerner, Julia, and Claudia Zbenovich. "Adapting the Therapeutic Discourse to Post-Soviet Media Culture: The Case of Modnyi Prigovor." *Slavic Review* 72, no. 4 (2013): 828–49. https://doi.org/10/ggqz26.
Lev Protiv. "Bydlo Oret pro Ukrainu i Donbass v Tsentre Moskvy!" YouTube. March 25, 2022. 10:46. https://www.youtube.com/watch?v=xfljKVKSatg.
Lev Protiv. "Ia Koroleva. " YouTube. March 13, 2020. 7:04. https://www.youtube.com/watch?v=jlSH8hab4QI.
Lev Protiv. "Kurenie i Rukoprikladstvo Politsii." YouTube. January 29, 2015. 17:30. https://www.youtube.com/watch?v=1iKXacN0uCE.
Lev Protiv. "Skinkhedov Natsistov [Potasovka] Protiv Rasizma." YouTube. November 24, 2018. 13:27. https://www.youtube.com/watch?v=wJJaD8966Pc.
Lev Protiv. "*Tolpa Bydla i VDV.*" YouTube. October 20, 2018. 13:25. https://www.youtube.com/watch?v=5a9Au1F9bUY.
Lev Protiv. ""Lev Protiv" otvetil za svoi reidy." VK. July 23, 2020. 55:09. https://vk.com/wall-73013298_2071732?ysclid=lezi4y893k916124750.
Lev Protiv. "Lev protiv pedofilov. Korol' pedofilov. Okkupai Pedofiliai 19 vypusk." YouTube. March 8, 2017. 15:03. https://www.youtube.com/watch?time_continue=17&v=PJotKYKIZsw.
Lev Protiv, "Spasenie Kotenka Ot Smerti." September 30, 2015. 5:34. https://www.youtube.com/watch?v=D0uEXoL04OM.
Levinson, Aleksei. "O molodezhi staroi i novoi." *Vedomosti*. May 22, 2017. https://www.vedomosti.ru/opinion/columns/2017/05/23/690975-molodezhi.
Levitsky, Steven, and Lucan Way. "The New Competitive Authoritarianism." *Journal of Democracy* 31, no. 1 (2020): 51–65. https://doi.org/10/ghv2qn.
Lewin, Kurt, and Ronald Lippitt. "An Experimental Approach to the Study of Autocracy and Democracy: A Preliminary Note." *Sociometry* 1, no. 3/4 (1938): 292–300. https://doi.org/10/c9p5vj.
Libman, Alexander, and Vladimir Kozlov. "The Legacy of Compliant Activism in Autocracies: Post-Communist Experience." *Contemporary Politics* 23, no. 2 (April 2017): 195–213. https://doi.org/10/gm7t62.
Lichterman, Paul. "Reinventing the Concept of Civic Culture." In *The Oxford Handbook of Cultural Sociology*, edited by Jeffrey C. Alexander, Ronald N. Jacobs, and Philip Smith, 207–31. Oxford: Oxford University Press, 2013.
Lichterman, Paul. "Self-Help Reading as a Thin Culture." *Media, Culture & Society* 14, no. 3 (July 1992): 421–47. https://doi.org/10/bz4x7v.
Lichterman, Paul, and Nina Eliasoph. "Civic Action." *American Journal of Sociology* 120, no. 3 (2014): 798–863. https://doi.org/10/f643x9.
Liniia, Sud'by. "Life Line. Part 1", 1989. Krasnoiarskaia Kinostudiia. YouTube. September 30, 2016. 13:33. https://www.youtube.com/watch?v=gNp4a80YKfU.
Loskutova, Elena. *Iunaia politika. Istoriia molodezhnykh politicheskikh organizatsii sovremennoi Rossii*. Moscow: Tsentr "Panorama", 2008.
Luckmann, Thomas. "Comments on Legitimation." *Current Sociology* 35, no. 2 (1987): 109–17. https://doi.org/10/bvv7gh.
Luehrmann, Sonja. *Secularism Soviet Style: Teaching Atheism and Religion in a Volga Republic*. New Anthropologies of Europe. Bloomington: Indiana University Press, 2011.
Luhmann, Niklas. *Legitimation durch Verfahren*. Frankfurt am Main: Suhrkamp, 2013.
Luhn, Alec. "Russian Politician Condemns Eurovision as 'Europe-Wide Gay Parade'. St Petersburg Legislator Vitaly Milonov Proposes Boycott before Demanding Exclusion

of Austrian Drag-Queen Contestant." *The Guardian*. April 30, 2014, http://www.theg uardian.com/world/2014/apr/30/russia-boycott-eurovision-gay-parade.

Luker, Kristin. *Salsa Dancing into the Social Sciences: Research in an Age of Info-Glut*. Cambridge: Harvard University Press, 2008.

Lukin, Alexander. *The Political Culture of the Russian "Democrats."* Oxford: Oxford University Press, 2000.

Madariaga, Aldo. *Neoliberal Resilience: Lessons in Democracy and Development from Latin America and Eastern Europe*. Princeton: Princeton University Press, 2020.

Magaril, Sergei. "Edinoderzhavie Putina: Itogi i 'perspektivy.'" *Svobodnaia mysl'* 12 (2011): 31–44.

Mahoney, James, and Gary Goertz. "A Tale of Two Cultures: Contrasting Quantitative and Qualitative Research." *Political Analysis* 14, no. 3 (July 2006): 227–49. https://doi.org/10/d5fdwt.

Maiorova, Olga. *From the Shadow of Empire: Defining the Russian Nation through Cultural Mythology, 1855-1870*. Madison: University of Wisconsin Press, 2010.

Malinova, Olga. *Aktual'noe proshloe: Simvolicheskaia politika vlastvuiushchei elity i dilemmy rossiiskoi identichnosti*. Moscow: ROSSPEN, 2015.

Malinova, Olga. "Constructing the 'Usable Past': The Evolution of the Official Historical Narrative in Post-Soviet Russia." In *Cultural and Political Imaginaries in Putin's Russia*, edited by Niklas Bernsand and Barbara Törnquist-Plewa, 85–104. Leiden: BRILL, 2018.

Malinova, Olga. *Konstruirovanie smyslov. Issledovanie simvolicheskoi politiki v sovremennoi Rossii*. Moscow: INION RAN, 2013.

Malinova, Olga. "Obshchestvo, publika, obshchestvennost' v Rossii ser. XIX - nachala XX veka: Otrazhenie v poniatiiakh praktik publichnoi kommunikatsii i obshchestvennoi samodeiatel'nosti." In *"Poniatiia o Rossii": K istoricheskoi semantike imperskogo perioda*, edited by D. Sdvizhkova and I. Shirle, 428–63. Moscow: Novoe Literaturnoe Obozrenie, 2012.

Malinova, Olga. "Russian Political Discourse in the 1990s: Crisis of Identity and Conflicting Pluralism of Ideas." In *Identities and Politics During the Putin Presidency: The Discursive Foundations of Russia's Stability*, edited by Philipp Casula and Jeronim Perovic, 94–111. Soviet and Post-Soviet Politics and Society. Stuttgart: Ibidem-Verlag, 2009.

Malinowski, Bronislaw. *Argonauts of the Western Pacific: An Account of Native Enterprise and Adventure in the Archipelagoes of Melanesian New Guinea*. London: Routledge, 1922.

Manina, Dar'ia. "'Dogoniai, ubivai': za chto bande Tesaka vynosiat prigovor." *Komitet "Grazhdanskoe sodeistvie,"* June 28, 2017. https://refugee.ru/news/dogonyaj-ubivaj-za-chto-bande-tesaka-vynosyat-prigovor/.

Mann, Michael. *Fascists*. Cambridge: Cambridge University Press, 2004.

Marchenko, Anastasia. "Nurgaliev pokazhet roliki 'Nashikh' vsem militsioneram strany. Ministr vnutrennikh del posetil forum 'Seliger-2010.'" *Moskovskii Komsomolets*, July 22, 2010. https://www.mk.ru/politics/article/2010/07/22/518303-nurgaliev-pokazhet-roliki-nashih-vsem-militsioneram-stranyi.html.

Marquand, Judith. *Democrats, Authoritarians and the Bologna Process. Universities in Germany, Russia, England and Wales*. Bingley: Emerald, 2018.

Maslakova, Ekaterina. "Upravlenie razvitiem detskogo turizma v novykh ekonomicheskikh usloviiakh khoziaistvovaniia. Avtoreferat". Moscow: OUVPO "Gosudarstvennyi universitet upravleniia", 2009.

Matsura, Denis. "My Biriusa 2013 [Song, Foam Party]". Vkontakte [Russian Social Network]. July 17, 2013. 1:37. https://vk.com/video/@biryusa_tim?z=video-1049376 8_165473850%2Fclub10493768%2Fpl_-10493768_-2.

Matveev, Ilya. "Russia, Inc." *OpenDemocracy*, March 16, 2016. https://www.opendemocracy.net/en/odr/russia-inc/.

Matza, Tomas. "'Good Individualism'? Psychology, Ethics, and Neoliberalism in Postsocialist Russia." *American Ethnologist* 39, no. 4 (November 2012): 804–18. https://doi.org/10/f4d9sm.

McGuigan, Jim. *Neoliberal Culture*. London: Palgrave Macmillan, 2016.

McRobbie, Angela. *Be Creative: Making a Living in the New Culture Industries*. Cambridge: Polity Press, 2016.

McRobbie, Angela. *The Aftermath of Feminism: Gender, Culture and Social Change*. London: SAGE Publications, 2009.

Meaney, Thomas. "The Swaddling Thesis." *London Review of Books*, March 6, 2014.

Meduza.io. "How to Steal 60 Million: Former Defense Ministry Official Gets 5-Year Sentence and Walks Free, 4 Months Later." *Meduza*, August 26, 2015. https://meduza.io/en/feature/2015/08/26/how-to-steal-60-million.

Medvedev, Sergei. "Strakh kak dukhovnaia skrepa." *Colta.ru*, May 28, 2015. http://www.colta.ru/articles/society/7474.

Meier, Christian. *Die Entstehung des Politischen bei den Griechen*. 6th ed. Frankfurt am Main: Suhrkamp, 2011.

Meylakhs, Peter. "Drugs and Symbolic Pollution: The Work of Cultural Logic in the Russian Press." *Cultural Sociology* 3, no. 3 (November 2009): 377–95. https://doi.org/10/dbc5j9.

Mickiewicz, Ellen Propper. *No Illusions: The Voices of Russia's Future Leaders*. Oxford: Oxford University Press, 2014.

Mijnssen, Ivo. *Back to Our Future! History, Modernity and Patriotism According to Nashi, 2005-2012. The quest for an ideal youth in Putin's Russia*. Soviet and Post-Soviet Politics and Society. Stuttgart: Ibidem-Verlag, 2012.

Mikhail Lazutin. "interv'yu dlya "Novoi gazety" Lev Protiv." YouTube. June 7, 2019. 48:31. https://www.youtube.com/watch?v=7y5LT-8XaOc.

Miller, Peter, and Nikolas S. Rose. *Governing the Present: Administering Economic, Social and Personal Life*. Cambridge: Polity Press, 2009.

Minor, Marina. "Wer motiviert wen, wozu und warum? Selbstbestimmtes Handeln und Motivation in Gamification und Nudging als Beispiele gegenwärtiger Motivationsforschung – Versuche einer Reinterpretation." In *»ask them why« Ausgewählte Beiträge der Ferienuni Kritische Psychologie 2018*, edited by Nora Dietrich and Thomas Dohmen, 63–82. Hamburg: Argument Verlag mit Ariadne, 2020. https://www.kritische-psychologie.de/files/FKP-Spezial-2018-Minor.pdf.

Mirowski, Philip. "Postface: Defining Neoliberalism." In *The Road from Mont Pèlerin: The Making of the Neoliberal Thought Collective*, edited by Philip Mirowski and Dieter Plehwe, 417–55. Cambridge, MA: Harvard University Press, 2009.

Mishkin, Mikhail. "Aleksandr Khloponin zashchitil prezidentskie popravki ot somnenii v ikh demokratichnosti." *Kommersant*. September 22, 2004.

Mitchell, Katharyne. *Making Workers: Radical Geographies of Education*. Radical Geography. London: Pluto Press, 2018.

Moore, Sally Falk. "Political Meetings and the Simulation of Unanimity: Kilimanjaro 1973." In *Secular Ritual*, edited by Sally Falk Moore and Barbara G. Myerhoff, 151–72. Assen: Van Gorcum, 1977.

Moore, Sally Falk, and Barbara G. Myerhoff, "Introduction. Secular Ritual: Forms and Meanings." In *Secular Ritual*, edited by Sally Falk Moore and Barbara G. Myerhoff, 3–24. Assen: Van Gorcum, 1977.

Moores, Chris. "Thatcher's Troops? Neighbourhood Watch Schemes and the Search for 'Ordinary' Thatcherism in 1980s Britain." *Contemporary British History* 31, no. 2 (April 2017): 230–55. https://doi.org/10/gnvk62.

Morozov, M. A. "Marketingovoe issledovanie rossiiskogo rynka detskogo turizma." HR-Portal, March 21, 2014. http://hr-portal.ru/article/marketingovoe-issledovanie-ross iyskogo-rynka-detskogo-turizma.

Morozov, Viatcheslav. *Russia's Postcolonial Identity: A Subaltern Empire in a Eurocentric World*. Houndmills: Palgrave Macmillan, 2015.

Mosfilm. "Dobro pozhalovat', ili postoronnim vkhod vospreshchen." 1964. YouTube. May 16, 2017. 1:10:12. https://www.youtube.com/watch?v=GX54eNpGYyM&feature=play er_embedded.

Müller, Jan-Werner. "Moscow's Trojan Horse," August 6, 2014. https://www.foreignaffa irs.com/articles/central-europe/2014-08-06/moscows-trojan-horse.

Müller, Martin. *Making Great Power Identities in Russia: An Ethnographic Discourse Analysis of Education at a Russian Elite University*. Forum Politische Geographie 4. Berlin: Lit Verlag, 2009.

Murzakov, Lyubim. "Mother Russia: kak prodavat' rodinu i ne krasnet' — Oftop na vc.ru," June 10, 2018. https://vc.ru/flood/39068-mother-russia-kak-prodavat-rodinu-i-ne krasnet.

Musaev, Musa. "Khloponin: molodezh' dolzhna svoimi initsiativami rasshiriat' doliu malogo biznesa v SKFO." *Kavkazskii Uzel*, February 16, 2011. https://www.kavkaz-uzel.media/articles/181184/.

Myerhoff, Barbara G. *Number Our Days*. New York: Simon and Schuster, 1980.

Nachtwey, Oliver, and Maurits Heumann. "Regressive Rebellen und autoritäre Innovatoren: Typen des neuen Autoritarismus." In *Große Transformation? Zur Zukunft moderner Gesellschaften: Sonderband des Berliner Journals für Soziologie*, edited by Klaus Dörre, Hartmut Rosa, Karina Becker, Sophie Bose, and Benjamin Seyd, 435–53. Wiesbaden: Springer Fachmedien, 2019.

Nadezhda. "Sovetskie pionerskie lageria." *Obrazy detstva* (blog), May 24, 2011. http://obrazdetstva.ru/38-sovetskie-pionerskie-lagerya.html.

Nechepurenko, Ivan, and Anton Troianovski. "Mass Beatings and Detentions in Belarus as President Clings to Power." *The New York Times*, August 13, 2020. https://www.nyti mes.com/2020/08/13/world/europe/beatings-detentions-belarus-lukashenko.html.

Newslab.ru. "Aleksandr Khloponin: Glavnoe – eto initsiativnost' molodykh," June 27, 2006. https://newslab.ru/news/195012.

Newslab.ru. "Dve tysiachi krasnoiarskikh studentov uzhe podali zaiavki na vstuplenie v kraevoi studotriad," April 10, 2006. https://newslab.ru/news/187843.

Newslab.ru. "Khloponin rasskazal Putinu o krasnoiarskoi molodezhnoi politike," February 19, 2009. https://newslab.ru/news/279156.

Newslab.ru. "Letom v Krasnoiarske nachnetsia stroitel'stvo tsentra ekstremal'nogo sporta," January 20, 2007. https://newslab.ru/news/211140.

Newslab.ru. "Na ploshchadi Revoliutsii proshel parad kraevykh studencheskikh otriadov," July 1, 2005. http://newslab.ru/news/166349.
Newslab.ru. "V Krasnoiarske sostoialos' torzhestvennoe zakrytie Vserossiiskogo sleta studotriadov," September 10, 2007. http://newslab.ru/news/231661.
NewsYkt. "V Iakutii nachal rabotu molodezhnyi forum 'SakhaSeliger' (foto)." *News.Ykt Novosti Iakutii*, July 22, 2013. https://news.ykt.ru/article/12529.
Niklas, Stefan. "On the Reissue of The Authoritarian Personality." *Krisis | Journal for Contemporary Philosophy* 41, no. 1 (June 2021): 202–9. https://doi.org/10/gm7nf2.
Nikulin, Yuri. "A Joke about Russian Character." YouTube. July 13, 2017. 1:25. https://www.youtube.com/watch?v=0_xVyEfSolc.
Noah, Will. "Elem Klimov's Boundary-Pushing Satires." *The Criterion Collection*, January 10, 2018. https://www.criterion.com/current/posts/5257-elem-klimovs-boundary-pushing-satires.
Nurik, Alexander. "Valentin Urusov – a Russian Trade Union Martyr." *Equal Times*, February 1, 2013. https://www.equaltimes.org/valentin-urusov-a-russian-trade.
Obshchestvennyi Verdikt. "«Lev protiv»." Accessed January 27, 2022. http://vigilant.myverdict.org/files/lion.
Omelchenko, Elena, ed. *Youth in Putin's Russia*. Cham: Palgrave Macmillan, 2021.
Omelchenko, Elena, and Hilary Pilkington, eds. "Vmesto vvedeniia. Liubit', gorditsia, uezzhat'? Rossiiskaia molodezh v patrioticheskom labirinte." In *S chego nachinaetsia rodina: Molodezh v labirintakh patriotizma*, 5–30. Ulianovsk: Izdatel'stvo Ulianovskogo Gosudarstvennogo Universiteta, 2012.
Omel'chenko, Dmitrii. "Nashi byvshie "Nashi."" Documentary. Vol. 2. 2 vols. Chto znachit byt' molodym v sovremennoi Evrope. St. Petersburg: Center for Youth Studies at the National Research University Higher School of Economics. YouTube. May 6, 2014. 53:43. https://www.youtube.com/watch?v=lVjQDB_vBCo&t=29s.
Omel'chenko, Dimitrii. "Our former "Ours"." YouTube. May 6, 2014. 53:43. https://www.youtube.com/watch?v=lVjQDB_vBCo.
Ong, Aihwa. *Neoliberalism as Exception: Mutations in Citizenship and Sovereignty*. Durham: Duke University Press, 2006.
Orlova, Vasilina. "Affective Infrastructures of Immobility: Staying While Neighbors Are Leaving Rural Eastern Siberia." *Journal of Contemporary Ethnography*, 2022, 1–27. https://doi.org/10/grzmb9.
Orlova, Vasilina. "Citizens of the Future: Infrastructures of Belonging in Post-Industrial Eastern Siberia," PhD diss., University of Texas. May 8, 2021. https://doi.org/10/grzmb4.
Oskanian, Kevork. *Russian Exceptionalism between East and West: The Ambiguous Empire*. London: Palgrave Macmillan, 2021.
O'Toole, Gavin. "A New Nationalism for a New Era: The Political Ideology of Mexican Neoliberalism." *Bulletin of Latin American Research* 22, no. 3 (July 2003): 269–90. https://doi.org/10/bd3zkr.
Oushakine, Serguei. *The Patriotism of Despair*. Ithaca, NY: Cornell University Press, 2009.
Paris, Leslie. *Children's Nature: The Rise of the American Summer Camp*. American History and Culture. New York: New York University Press, 2008.
PASMI.RU. "Osnovatel' dvizheniia "StopKham' Dmitrii Chugunov: predlagali milliony, no reputatsiia dorozhe," May 23, 2016. https://pasmi.ru/archive/142529/.
Patreon/ Stop a Douchebag. "Stop a Douchebag Is Creating Citizen Activism Videos." Patreon, December 4, 2021. https://www.patreon.com/stopadouchebag.

Pepinsky, Thomas. "Authoritarian Innovations: Theoretical Foundations and Practical Implications." *Democratization* 27, no. 6 (August 2020): 1092–1101. https://doi.org/10/gk4g4d.

Petrovic, Tanja. "Affective and Voluntary Labor in Post-Yugoslav Societies and the Politics of the Future." Presentation presented at the Council of European Studies Conference, Paris, July 10, 2015.

Pickel, Gert. "Die kulturelle Verankerung von Autokratien—Bestandserhalt durch ideologische Legitimationsstrategien und ökonomische Legitimität oder Demokratisierung?" In *Autokratien im Vergleich*, edited by Steffen Kailitz and Patrick Köllner, 181–209. Baden-Baden: Nomos, 2013.

Pietsch, Anna-Jutta. "Self-Fulfillment Through Work: Working Conditions in Soviet Factories." In *Quality of Life in the Soviet Union*, edited by Horst Herlemann and Shaun Murphy. Routledge, 2019, 117–132.

Pilkington, Hilary, ed. *Gender, Generation and Identity in Contemporary Russia*. London: Routledge, 1996.

Pilkington, Hilary. *Russia's Youth and Its Culture. A Nation's Constructors and Constructed*. London: Routledge, 1994.

Pilkington, Hilary. "'Vorkuta eto stolitsa mira': deterritorizatsiia, lokal'nost' i 'patriotizm.'" In *S chego nachinaetsia rodina: Molodezh v labirintakh patriotizma*, edited by Elena Omelchenko and Hilary Pilkington, 31–84. Ulianovsk: Izdatel'stvo Ulianovskogo Gosudarstvennogo Universiteta, 2012.

Pilkington, Hilary. "'Vorkuta Is the Capital of the World': People, Place and the Everyday Production of the Local." *The Sociological Review* 60, no. 2 (May 2012): 267–91. https://doi.org/10/f33k7j.

Pilkington, Hilary, Elena Omelchenko, Moya Flynn, and Uliana Bliudina, eds. *Looking West? Cultural Globalization and Russian Youth Cultures*. Post-Communist Cultural Studies Series. Pennsylvania: Pennsylvania State University Press, 2002.

Plehwe, Dieter, "Schumpeter Revival?: How Neoliberals Revised the Image of the Entrepreneur." In *Nine Lives of Neoliberalism*, edited by Dieter, Plehwe, Quinn Slobodian, and Philip Mirowski, 120–42. London: Verso, 2020.

Pliusnina, Mariia. "V Rossii rastet armiia volonterov — pri finansovoi podderzhke administratsii prezidenta." *Znak*, December 12, 2019. https://lyubimiigorod.ru/ekb/news/3081462.

Pliusnina, Mariia. "Kak ANO 'Rossiia - strana vozmozhnostei,' sozdannaia ukazom Putina, potratit R3 mlrd subsidii." *Znak*, September 17, 2019. https://web.archive.org/web/20210413043148/https:/www.znak.com/2019-09-17/kak_ano_rossiya_strana_vozmozhnostey_sozdannaya_ukazom_putina_potratit_3_mlrd_subsidiy.

Polletta, Francesca. "Politicizing Childhood: The 1980 Zurich Burns Movement." *Social Text*, no. 33 (1992): 82. https://doi.org/10/dc2x3t.

Polletta, Francesca. "Storytelling in Social Movements." In *Culture, Social Movements, and Protest*, edited by Hank Johnston, 33–54. Farnham: Ashgate, 2009.

Polletta, Francesca, Pang Ching Bobby Chen, Beth Gharrity Gardner, and Alice Motes. "The Sociology of Storytelling." *Annual Review of Sociology* 37, no. 1 (August 2011): 109–30. https://doi.org/10/cpz9gf.

Popova, Anna. "Nam partiia mat', rektorat nash otets. Pochemu v rossiiskikh vuzakh net studencheskogo samoupravleniia." *Lenta.ru*, November 18, 2013. https://lenta.ru/articles/2013/11/18/studsovet/.

Portnov, Andriy. "Memory Wars in Post-Soviet Ukraine (1991–2010)." In *Memory and Theory in Eastern Europe*, edited by Uilleam Blacker, Alexander Etkind, and Julie Fedor, 233–54. Palgrave Studies in Cultural and Intellectual History. New York: Palgrave Macmillan, 2013.

Postanovlenie Pravitel'stva RF o federal'nom agentstve po delam molodezhi [Regulation of the Government of the Russian Federation on the Federal Agency for Youth Affairs], Sobranie Zakonodatel'stva Rossiiskoi Federatsii [SZ RF] [Russian Federation Collection of Legislation] 2008, No. 45, Item 5490, https://base.garant.ru/193353/. Today the Agency is subordinated to the Federal Ministry of Education.

Potolicchio, Sam. "Global Governance and Leadership in Russia," 2021. http://www.sampotolicchio.com/ggl-russia.

Potolicchio, Sam. "Preparing Global Leaders Forum," 2021. http://www.sampotolicchio.com/pglf.

Press-sluzhba Lipetskogo oblastnogo Soveta deputatov. "Pervyi vypusk molodezhnoi shkoly biznesa." Lipetskii oblastnoi Sovet deputatov, April 27, 2007. https://lrnews.ru/news-1/3252-.html.

Pristupko, V. A. *Studencheskie otriady: Istoricheskii opyt 1959-1990 godov*. Moscow: Moskovskii Gumanitarnii Universitet, 2008.

Przyborski, Aglaja, and Monika Wohlrab-Sahr. *Qualitative Sozialforschung: Ein Arbeitsbuch*. 4th ed. Lehr- und Handbücher der Soziologie. Munich: Oldenbourg Verlag, 2014.

Ptak, Ralf. "Das Staatsverständnis im Ordoliberalismus. Eine theoriegeschichtliche Analyse mit aktuellem Ausblick." In *Der Staat des Neoliberalismus*, edited by Thomas Biebricher, 29–74. Baden-Baden: Nomos, 2016.

Ptak, Ralf. "Neoliberalism in Germany: Revisiting the Ordoliberal Foundations of the Social Market Economy." In *The Road from Mont Pèlerin: The Making of the Neoliberal Thought Collective*, edited by Philip Mirowski and Dieter Plehwe, 98–138. Cambridge: Harvard University Press, 2009.

Putin, Vladimir. "Zaiavlenie v sviazi s vneseniem na rassmotrenie Gosudarstvennoi Dumy zakonoproektov o gosudarstvennoi simvolike." Prezident Rossii, April 12, 2000. http://kremlin.ru/events/president/transcripts/21137.

Ragin, Charles C. *The Comparative Method: Moving beyond Qualitative and Quantitative Strategies*. Berkeley: University of California Press, 1987.

Rapoport, Anatoli. "In Search of Identity: Competing Models in Russia's Civic Education." In *World Yearbook of Education 2011: Curriculum in Today's World: Configuring Knowledge, Identities, Work and Politics*, edited by Lyn Yates and Madeleine R. Grumet, 195–209. London: Routledge, 2011.

Rasporiazhenie Pravitel'stva RF o rukovoditele Federal'nogo agentstva po delam molodezhi [Resolution of the Government of the Russian Federation on the Federal Agency for Youth Affairs], Sobranie Zakonodatel'stva Rossiiskoi Federatsii [SZ RF] [Russian Federation Collection of Legislation] 2008, No. 28, Item 3404, base.garant.ru/6390254/.

Reeves, Joshua. "If You See Something, Say Something: Lateral Surveillance and the Uses of Responsibility." *Surveillance & Society* 10, nos. 3/4 (December 2012): 235–48. https://doi.org/10/gf656m.

Reznikova, Olga. "'Ordinary People' and Fascism: A Conjunctural Perspective on (Pre) War Russia." *Global Labour Journal* 13, no. 3 (September 2022): 345–352. https://doi.org/10/grv898.

Reznikova, Olga. *Wut Der Fernfahrer. Ethnografie Eines Sozialen Protests*. Campus Verlag, 2023.

Riabov, Oleg, and Tatiana Riabova. "The Remasculinization of Russia? Gender, Nationalism, and the Legitimation of Power under Vladimir Putin." *Problems of Post-Communism* 61, no. 2 (March 2014): 23–35. https://doi.org/10/gf9ps5.

Richter, James. "Integration from Below?: The Disappointing Effort to Promote Civil Society in Russia." In *Russia and Globalization: Identity, Security, and Society in an Era of Change*, edited by Douglas W. Blum, 181–203. Washington: Woodrow Wilson Center Press; Johns Hopkins University Press, 2008.

Richter, James. "The Ministry of Civil Society? The Public Chambers in the Regions." *Problems of Post-Communism* 56, no. 6 (2009): 7–20. https://doi.org/10/dh3n42.

Ries, Nancy. *Russian Talk: Culture and Conversation during Perestroika*. Ithaca, NY: Cornell University Press, 1997.

Rivkin-Fish, Michele. "Pronatalism, Gender Politics, and the Renewal of Family Support in Russia: Toward a Feminist Anthropology of 'Maternity Capital.'" *Slavic Review* 69 (October 2010): 701–24. https://doi.org/10/gmjb82.

Robertson, Graeme B. *The Politics of Protest in Hybrid Regimes: Managing Dissent in Post-Communist Russia*. Cambridge: Cambridge University Press, 2011.

Rosmolodezh. "'Molodezh' Rossii 2000–2025: Razvitie chelovecheskogo kapitala." Federal Agency for Youth Affairs, 2013. http://www.orthedu.ru/vstrechi/16649-molodezh-rossii-2000-2025.html.

Rosmolodezh Business. Program. "You Are an Entrepreneur". VK. August 21, 2018. 0:55. https://vk.com/video-130482053_456239037.

Rossiiskii Soiuz Molodezhi. "Rosmolodezh' zapuskaet Vserossiiskuiu forumnuiu kampaniiu 2022 goda," March 29, 2022. https://ruy.ru/press/news/rosmolodezh-zapuskaet-vserossiyskuyu-forumnuyu-kampaniyu-2022-goda-/.

Rossolinski-Liebe, Grzegorz. *Stepan Bandera: The Life and Afterlife of a Ukrainian Nationalist: Fascism, Genocide, and Cult*. Stuttgart: Ibidem-Verlag, 2014.

Roth, Andrew. "Russian Youth Group With a Mission: Sniffing Out Illegal Migrants." *The New York Times*, September 4, 2013. https://www.nytimes.com/2013/09/04/world/europe/russian-youth-group-with-a-mission-sniffing-out-illegal-migrants.html.

Rothschild, Joseph. "Observations on Political Legitimacy in Contemporary Europe." *Political Science Quarterly* 92, no. 3 (1977): 487–501. https://doi.org/10/fgdx5r.

Rueschemeyer, Dietrich, Evelyne Huber, and John D. Stephens. *Capitalist Development and Democracy*. Chicago: University of Chicago Press, 1992.

Rukov, Kirill, and Ivan Chesnokov. "Junge Talente." Translated by Anja Lutter. *DEKODER Journalismus aus Russland in deutscher Übersetzung*, November 17, 2015. https://www.dekoder.org/de/article/junge-talente.

SlideShowNews. "*Russian Drivers Protest State Officials Using Blue Lights.'Sinie Vederki' Slideshow*". YouTube. April 20, 2010. 1:32. https://www.youtube.com/watch?v=VQ3suJLel74.

Rüthers, Monica. "Picturing Soviet Childhood: Photo Albums of Pioneer Camps." *Jahrbücher für Geschichte Osteuropas* 67, no. 1 (2019): 65. https://doi.org/10/grrqzs.

SADB. "A Muscovite Born and Bred." YouTube. May 15, 2018. 12:49. https://www.youtube.com/watch?v=5ABtIyi5RBY.

SADB. "Cutie Worldstar." YouTube. July 6, 2015. 6:10. https://www.youtube.com/watch?v=OEWDt1XIsZg.

SADB. "Garage Wars." YouTube. November 24, 2016. 10:49. https://www.youtube.com/watch?v=RmCMs4C9Hwk.
SADB. "Mama's Boy." YouTube. January 15, 2015. 5:40. https://www.youtube.com/watch?v=rbjFv81l1qQ.
Sadkova, I. E. "Problemy detsko-iunosheskogo turizma v sovremennoi Rossii." *Problemy sovremennoi ekonomiki* 2, no. 34 (2010). http://www.m-economy.ru/art.php?nArtId=3172.
SakhaSeliger. "Pamiatka uchastniku foruma SakhaSeliger '13," 2013. Author's Archive.
Sakwa, Richard. *The Putin Paradox*. London: Bloomsbury Publishing, 2020.
Sakwa, Richard. *The Quality of Freedom: Khodorkovsky, Putin, and the Yukos Affair*. Oxford: Oxford University Press, 2009.
Sanghi, Apurva, and Shahid Yusuf. "Russia's Uphill Struggle with Innovation." *World Bank*, September 17, 2018. https://www.worldbank.org/en/news/opinion/2018/09/17/russias-uphill-struggle-with-innovation.
Sasse, Gwendolyn. *Der Krieg gegen die Ukraine: Hintergründe, Ereignisse, Folgen*. Originalausgabe. Munich: Beck, 2022.
Sasse, Gwendolyn. *The Crimea Question: Identity, Transition, and Conflict*. Harvard Series in Ukrainian Studies. Cambridge: Distributed by Harvard University Press for the Harvard Ukrainian Research Institute, 2007.
Sauer, Birgit. "Neoliberalisierung von Staatlichkeit. Geschlechterkritische Überlegungen." In *Der Staat des Neoliberalismus*, edited by Thomas Biebricher, 153–82. Baden-Baden: Nomos, 2016.
Sauer, Birgit. "Restrukturierung von Männlichkeit: Staat und Geschlecht im Kontext von ökonomischer Globalisierung und politischer Internationalisierung." In *In der Krise? Männlichkeiten im 21. Jahrhundert*, edited by Mechthild Bereswill and Anke Neuber, 80–103. Forum Frauen- und Geschlechterforschung. Münster: Westfälisches Dampfboot, 2011.
Savina, Ekaterina. "'Nashim' ustroili lagernuiu zhizn'. Molodezhnaia politika." *Kommersant*, July 24, 2006. http://www.kommersant.ru/doc/692203.
Schatzberg, Michael G. *Political Legitimacy in Middle Africa: Father, Family, Food*. Bloomington: Indiana University Press, 2001.
Scheiring, Gábor. *The Retreat of Liberal Democracy:Authoritarian Capitalism and the Accumulative State in Hungary*. London: Palgrave Macmillan, 2020.
Schelting, Alexander von. *Russland und Europa im russischen Geschichtsdenken*. Bern: A. Francke Verlag, 1948.
Scherrer, Jutta. *Kulturologie: Russland auf der Suche nach einer zivilisatorischen Identität*. Essener kulturwissenschaftliche Vorträge, Bd. 13. Göttingen: Wallstein, 2003.
Scherrer, Jutta. "The 'Cultural/Civilizational Turn' in Post-Soviet Identity Building." In *Power and Legitimacy: Challenges from Russia*, edited by Per-Arne Bodin, Stefan Hedlund, and Elena Namli, 152–68. Routledge Contemporary Russia and Eastern Europe Series 39. London: Routledge, 2013.
Schiedeck, Jürgen, and Martin Stahlmann. "Totalizing of Experience: Educational Camps." In *Education and Fascism: Political Identity and Social Education in Nazi Germany*, edited by Heinz Sünker and Hans-Uwe Otto, 54–80. London: Falmer Press, 1997.
Schiller, Melanie. "Pop, Politik und Populismus als Massenkultur." In *Druckwellen: Eskalationskulturen und Kultureskalationen in Pop, Gesellschaft und Politik*, edited by Beate Flath, Ina Heinrich, Christoph Jacke, Heinrich Klingmann, and

Maryam Momen Pour Tafreshi, 21–36. Bielefeld: Universität Paderborn, 2022. https://doi.org/10.14361/9783839453230-003.

Schmid, Ulrich. "Naši – Die Putin-Jugend: Sowjettradition und politische Konzeptkunst." *Osteuropa* 56, no. 5 (2006): 5–18.

Schröder, Ina. "Ethnic Summer Camps for Children and Youth in the Khanty-Mansi Autonomous District Iugra." *Sibirica* 11, no. 1 (May 2012): 43–69. https://doi.org/10/gm7vbs.

Schröder, Ina. "Shaping Youth: Quest for Moral Education in an Indigenous Community in Western Siberia." PhD diss., Martin-Luther-Universität, 2017.

Schumpeter, Joseph A. *Capitalism, Socialism and Democracy.* London: Routledge, 2005.

Schumpeter, Joseph A. *The Theory of Economic Development: An Inquiry into Profits, Capital, Credit, Interest, and the Business Cycle.* Social Science Classics Series. New Brunswick: Transaction Books, 1983.

Schwenck, Anna. "Antifaschistische Bewegung" als Selbstbezeichnung." *DEKODER*, January 6, 2016. https://www.dekoder.org/de/gnose/antifaschistische-bewegung-als-selbstbezeichnung.

Schwenck, Anna. "Conservative National Narratives in Poland, Russia and Hungary." *Baltic Worlds* 2021, 3 (October 2021): 76–80. http://balticworlds.com/conservative-national-narratives-in-poland-russia-and-hungary/.

Schwenck, Anna. "Legitimacy in an Authoritarian Polity: Government-Sponsored Summer Camps and Youth Participation in Russia." PhD diss., Humboldt-Universität zu Berlin, 2018.

Schwenck, Anna. "Performances Of Closeness and the Staging of Resistance with Mainstream Musics. Analyzing the Symbolism of Pandemic Skeptical Protests." *German Politics and Society* 41, no. 2 (2023): 35–60. https://doi.org/10.3167/gps.2023.410203.

Schwenck, Anna. "Russian Politics of Radicalisation and Surveillance." In *Governing Youth Politics in the Age of Surveillance*, edited by Maria Grasso and Judith Bessant, 168–82. The Criminalization of Political Dissent. London: Routledge, 2018.

Schwenck, Anna. "Russia's Vigilante YouTube Stars. Digital Entrepreneurship and Heroic Masculinity in the Service of Flexible Authoritarianism." *Europe-Asia Studies* 74, no. 7 (2022): 1166–89. https://doi.org/10/grzwh9.

Schwenck, Anna. "Staatliche Jugendpolitik in Russland zwischen regierungstreuem Protest und konservativer Erneuerung." *Russland-Analysen*, 341 (January 2017): 2. https://doi.org/10/gnqkzb.

Schwirtz, Michael. "Russia's Political Youths." *Demokratizatsiya: The Journal of Post-Soviet Democratization* 15, no. 1 (2007): 73–85.

Scott, James C. *Domination and the Arts of Resistance: Hidden Transcripts.* New Haven, CT: Yale University Press, 1990.

Semenenko, Aleksei. "The Mystery of The Blue Cup." *Baltic Worlds* 9, no. 4 (2017): 43–51.

Sennett, Richard. *The Corrosion of Character: The Personal Consequences of Work in the New Capitalism.* New York: Norton, 1999.

Sennett, Richard. *The Culture of the New Capitalism.* The Castle Lectures in Ethics, Politics, and Economics. New Haven, CT: Yale University Press, 2006.

Sergeeva, Kira. "V «Sportekse» kalechat liudei i provodiat korporativy bankov." *Newslab.ru*, March 25, 2011. https://newslab.ru/article/371848.

Sharafutdinova, Gulnaz. "Redistributing Sovereignty and Property under Putin: A View from Resource-Rich Republics of the Russian Federation." In *The Politics of Sub-National*

Authoritarianism in Russia, edited by Cameron Ross and Vladimir Gel'man, 191–210. Post-Soviet Politics. Farnham: Ashgate, 2010.

Shevchenko, Olga. *Crisis and the Everyday in Postsocialist Moscow*. Bloomington: Indiana University Press, 2009.

Shleinov, Roman. "Kak Kreml' finansiruet svoe molodezhnoe dvizhenie." *Vedomosti*, November 29, 2010. http://www.vedomosti.ru/newspaper/articles/2010/11/29/dengi_nashih.

Shlenko, Iuliia. "Konstantin Gureev: «Za granitsei turistov pytaiutsia udivit' banal'nymi veshchami»." *Konkurent*. October 24, 2007. http://www.konkurent-krsk.ru/index.php?id=844.

Simons, Greg. "Putin's International Political Image." *Journal of Political Marketing* 18, no. 4 (October 2019): 307–29. https://doi.org/10/gjfg7z.

Skubytska, Iuliia. "It Takes A Union To Raise A Soviet: Children's Summer Camps As A Reflection Of Late Soviet Society." PhD diss., University of Pennsylvania, 2018. https://repository.upenn.edu/edissertations/2935.

Slezkine, Yuri. "The USSR as a Communal Apartment, or How a Socialist State Promoted Ethnic Particularism." *Slavic Review* 53, no. 2 (1994): 414. https://doi.org/10/d55pn5.

Slobodian, Quinn. *Globalists: The End of Empire and the Birth of Neoliberalism*. Cambridge: Harvard University Press, 2018.

Smirnova, Julia. "Wo Russland dem Nachwuchs Patriotismus beibringt." *DIE WELT*, August 11, 2014. https://www.welt.de/politik/ausland/article131058670/Wo-junge-Russen-Patriotismus-mit-der-AK-47-lernen.html.

Smith, Kathleen E. "Competing Myths of Political Legitimacy: August 1991 versus October 1993." Washington: The National Council for Eurasian and East European Research, April 14, 1997.

Smith, Michael B. "'The Ego Ideal of the Good Camper' and the Nature of Summer Camp." *Environmental History* 11, no. 1 (2006): 70–101. https://doi.org/10/dw8zcd.

Smolin, Oleg Nikolaevich. "Socioeconomics: Uniquely Russian Poverty." Presented at the Russian Social Forum, St. Petersburg, March 18, 2021. https://www.transform-network.net/en/blog/article/socioeconomics-uniquely-russian-poverty/.

Socialblade.com. "YouTube, Twitch, Twitter, & Instagram Statistics." Accessed April 12, 2022. https://socialblade.com/.

Somers, Margaret R., and Gloria D. Gibson. "Reclaiming the Epistemological 'Other': Narrative and the Social Constitution of Identity." In *Social Theory and the Politics of Identity*, edited by Craig Calhoun, 37–99. Oxford: Blackwell, 1994.

Somers, Margaret R. "Let Them Eat Social Capital: Socializing the Market versus Marketizing the Social." *Thesis Eleven* 81, no. 1 (May 2005): 5–19. https://doi.org/10/c2prqs.

Somers, Margaret R. "Narrating and Naturalizing Civil Society and Citizenship Theory: The Place of Political Culture and the Public Sphere." *Sociological Theory* 13, no. 3 (November 1995): 229–74. https://doi.org/10/d56p74.

Song, Hae-Yung. *The State, Class and Developmentalism in South Korea: Development as Fetish*. London: Routledge, 2019.

Sönmez, Sevil, Yorghos Apostolopoulos, Antonis Theocharous, and Kelley Massengale. "Bar Crawls, Foam Parties, and Clubbing Networks: Mapping the Risk Environment of a Mediterranean Nightlife Resort." *Tourism Management Perspectives* 8 (October 2013): 49–59. https://doi.org/10/gm7msx.

Sorek, Tamir. *Palestinian Commemoration in Israel: Calendars, Monuments, and Martyrs*. Stanford Studies in Middle Eastern and Islamic Societies and Cultures. Stanford: Stanford University Press, 2015.

Sperling, Valerie. "Pussy Riot's Real Crime Was Feminism." *OUPblog* (blog), February 5, 2015. http://blog.oup.com/2015/02/pussy-riot-politics-crime-feminism/.

Sperling, Valerie. "Nashi Devushki: Gender and Political Youth Activism in Putin's and Medvedev's Russia." *Post-Soviet Affairs* 28, no. 2 (2012): 232–61. https://doi.org/10/f3x7cn.

Sperling, Valerie. *Sex, Politics, and Putin: Political Legitimacy in Russia*. Oxford Studies in Culture and Politics. New York: Oxford University Press, 2015.

Stahl, Andreas, Kathrin Henkelmann, Christian Jäckel, Niklas Wünsch, and Benedikt Zopes. *Konformistische Rebellen: zur Aktualität des autoritären Charakters*. Berlin: Verbrecher Verlag, 2020.

Stoeckl, Kristina. "The Rise of the Russian Christian Right: The Case of the World Congress of Families." *Religion, State and Society* 48, no. 4 (August 2020): 223–38. https://doi.org/10/ghrpdg.

Stoeckl, Kristina, and Kseniya Medvedeva. "Double Bind at the UN: Western Actors, Russia, and the Traditionalist Agenda." *Global Constitutionalism* 7, no. 3 (November 2018): 383–421. https://doi.org/10/gm7ms7.

StopKham. "Bez Suda i Sledstviia / Extrajudicially." YouTube. November 6, 2014. 8:04. https://www.youtube.com/watch?v=BoTTQ0snWZg.

StopKham. "Krasnogorskaia Niasha." YouTube. June 30, 2015. 6:10. https://www.youtube.com/watch?v=53WbKPqgbdQ.

StopKham. "'Moskvichka v Tret'em Kolene'." YouTube. May 3, 2018. 13:09. https://www.youtube.com/watch?v=WBcJxfB1hTU.

StopKham. "Semeinoe Obostrenie. Chast' 1." YouTube. April 10, 2018. 14:29. https://www.youtube.com/watch?v=9_QAXp8ZFuQ.

StopKham. "Semeinoe Obostrenie. Chast' 2. Prodolzhenie." YouTube. April 23, 2018. 9:40. https://www.youtube.com/watch?v=Yf7k_rTHzRo.

StopKham. "Zhenskii Top 10." YouTube. October, 6 2016. 16:07. https://www.youtube.com/watch?v=vswPtRwxcA8.

Strana Pensioneriia. Sotsial'naia set' Pensionerov. "A vy pomnite svoi pionerskie lageria," 2013. https://pensionerka.com/forum/thread1384-1.html.

Straßenberger, Grit. "Autorität: Herrschaft ohne Zwang - Anerkennung ohne Deliberation." *Authority: To Rule without Constraint-Recognition without Deliberation* 23, no. 3/4 (2013): 493–509.

Street, John. *Music and Politics*. Polity Contemporary Political Communication Series. Cambridge: Polity, 2012.

Sukhoveiko, Galina Stanislavovna. "Sotsial'no znachimye initsiativy v pionerskoi organizatsii kak sredstvo formirovaniia samodeiatel'nosti detei i podrostkov." Avtoreferat dissertatsii na soiskanie nauchnoi stepeni kandidata pedagogicheskikh nauk. Moscow: Vysshaia komsomol'skaia shkola pri TsK VLKSM, 1990.

Summercamp.ru – letnii lager. "Distsiplina – Letnii lager'." MetodViki, 2015. https://summercamp.ru/Дисциплинарные_принципы.

Sundstrom, Lisa McIntosh. *Funding Civil Society: Foreign Assistance and NGO Development in Russia*. Stanford: Stanford University Press, 2006. http://www.sup.org/books/title/?id=4828.

Sutiagin, Dmitrii V. "Children's Railways of the Former USSR – Kratovo," 2012. http://www.dzd-ussr.ru/towns/kratovo/index-eng.html.

Svolik, Milan W. *The Politics of Authoritarian Rule*. Cambridge Studies in Comparative Politics. Cambridge: Cambridge University Press, 2012.

Swedberg, Richard. "Introduction." In *Capitalism, Socialism and Democracy* by Joseph A. Schumpeter, ix–xix. London: Routledge, 2005.

Swedberg, Richard. "Theorizing in Sociology and Social Science: Turning to the Context of Discovery." *Theory and Society* 41, no. 1 (2012): 1–40. https://doi.org/10/bgjzdv.

Swedberg, Richard, and Ola Agevall. "Legitimacy." In *The Max Weber Dictionary: Key Words and Central Concepts*, edited by Richard Swedberg and Ola Agevall, 189–91. Stanford: Stanford Social Sciences, an imprint of Stanford University Press, 2016.

Szikra, Dorottya. "Ideology or Pragmatism?: Interpreting Social Policy Change under the System of National Cooperation." In *Brave New Hungary: Mapping the "System of National Cooperation,"* edited by János Mátyás Kovács and Balázs Trencsényi, 225–42. Lanham: Lexington Books, 2020.

Tansel, Cemal Burak. "Authoritarian Neoliberalism and Democratic Backsliding in Turkey: Beyond the Narratives of Progress." *South European Society and Politics* 23, no. 2 (April 2018): 197–217. https://doi.org/10/gf68m9.

Tansey, Oisín. *The International Politics of Authoritarian Rule*. Oxford Studies in Democratization. Oxford: Oxford University Press, 2016.

Tass. "Lider dvizheniia po bor'be s pedofilami 'Kamen' protiv' otpushchen pod podpisku o nevyezde. Andrei Makarov i ego pomoshchnik Mikhail Lazutin podozrevaiutsia v grabezhe." *TACC*, January 21, 2014. https://tass.ru/proisshestviya/902563.

Tavernise, Sabrina. "In a Russian Governor's Race, Elements of Farce." *The New York Times*, September 8, 2002. https://www.nytimes.com/2002/09/08/world/in-a-russian-governor-s-race-elements-of-farce.html.

Tavernise, Sabrina. "Russia Entrepreneurs Try the Business of Governing." *The New York Times*, February 11, 2001. https://www.nytimes.com/2001/02/11/world/russia-entrepreneurs-try-the-business-of-governing.html.

Taylor, Charles. *The Ethics of Authenticity*. Cambridge: Harvard University Press, 1992.

Tarasov, Aleksandr. "Nasazhdenie imperskogo natsionalizma i klerikalizma sredi molodezhi." *POLIT.RU*, February 16, 2014. http://m.polit.ru/article/2014/02/16/ideologia/.

Theroux, Marcel. "Death of a Nation 1/6." YouTube April 23, 2006. 7:22. https://www.youtube.com/watch?v=J1OyIJtjdpo.

TIM Biriusa. "Pamiatka uchastniku," 2013. Author's Archive.

TIM "Biryusa". "Biriusa 2022 — Liubov' [Biriusa 2022 — Love]." VK. September 28, 2022. 4:15. https://vk.com/video-10493768_456239529.

TIM "Biryusa". "Biriusa Zhdet! [Biriusa Is Waiting!]." VK. July 17, 2021. 0:15. https://vk.com/video-10493768_456239356.

TIME.com. "Putin's Patriotic Youth Camp," July 25, 2007. https://web.archive.org/web/20210805150032/http://content.time.com/time/photogallery/0,29307,1646809,00.html.

Todorov, Vladimir, and Anton Bolotov. "Nezdorovyi obraz zhizni." *Lenta.ru*, February 13, 2017. https://lenta.ru/articles/2017/02/13/lionagainthumanrights/.

Tošić, Jelena, and Andreas Streinzer, eds. *Ethnographies of Deservingness: Unpacking Ideologies of Distribution and Inequality*. EASA Series 45. New York: Berghahn Books, 2022.

Troianovski, Anton. "As Frozen Land Burns, Siberia Fears: 'If We Don't Have the Forest, We Don't Have Life.'" *The New York Times*, July 17, 2021. https://www.nytimes.com/2021/07/17/world/europe/siberia-fires.html.

Troianovski, Anton. "On 'Island' in Russian Arctic, Arrival of Fast Internet Shakes Political Calm." *The New York Times*, October 20, 2019. https://www.nytimes.com/2019/10/20/world/europe/russia-internet-norilsk-youtube-arctic.html.

Tsipursky, Gleb. "Public Discourse and Volunteer Militias in Post-Soviet Russia." In *Eastern European Youth Cultures in a Global Context*, edited by Matthias Schwartz and Heike Winkel, 271–92. London: Palgrave Macmillan, 2016.

Tsygankov, Andrei. "Crafting the State-Civilization. Vladimir Putin's Turn to Distinct Values." *Problems of Post-Communism* 63, no. 3 (2016): 146–58. https://doi.org/10/gd55k6.

Tumanov, Grigorii, Viacheslav Kozlov, and Elena Shmaraeva. *Likvidatsiia BORNa*. Moscow: Common Place, 2015. https://vk.com/common_place.

Turovskii, Daniil, Ekaterina Savina, and Andrei Kozenko. "Vyselitel'naia programma prazdnika 'Molodaia gvardiia' i 'Mestnye' ob"edinilis' protiv migrantov." *Kommersant*, November 5, 2008. https://www.kommersant.ru/doc/1051988.

Turovsky, Rostislav. "The Influence of Russian Big Business on Regional Power: Models and Political Consequences." In *Politics in the Russian Regions*, edited by Graeme Gill, 138–60. London: Palgrave Macmillan, 2007.

Tutenges, Sébastien. "Stirring up Effervescence: An Ethnographic Study of Youth at a Nightlife Resort." *Leisure Studies* 32, no. 3 (June 2013): 233–48. https://doi.org/10/fd26f5.

Tyler, Tom R. "Psychological Perspectives on Legitimacy and Legitimation." *Annual Review of Psychology* 57, no. 1 (2006): 375–400.

UNESCO. "Participation in Education. Russian Federation. (Data for the Sustainable Development Goals)." Russian Federation, November 27, 2016. http://uis.unesco.org/en/country/ru?theme=education-and-literacy.

Urban, Michael. "Stages of Political Identity Formation in Late Soviet and Post-Soviet Russia." In *Identities in Transition: Eastern Europe and Russia after the Collapse of Communism*, edited by Victoria E. Bonnell, 140–54. Berkeley: University of California, 1996.

Urban, Michael. "The Politics of Identity in Russia's Postcommunist Transition: The Nation against Itself." *Slavic Review* 53, no. 3 (1994): 733–65. https://doi.org/10/bdnngs.

Usad'ba Buluus Leisure Camp. "MAO DOL 'Usad'ba Buluus.'" Accessed March 15, 2023. https://xn--90ausgb.xn--80aaa7bi1aw.xn--p1ai/.

Van Slyck, Abigail A. *A Manufactured Wilderness: Summer Camps and the Shaping of American Youth, 1890–1960*. Minneapolis: University of Minnesota Press, 2006.

Varyukhina, Liliia, Ivan Gorbunov, and Anna Kiseleva. "Dmitriy Chugunov: 'StopKham'— eto ne proekt, eto spravedlivost'!" *Nasha Molodezh* (blog), February 29, 2016. http://nasha-molodezh.ru/society/dmitriy-chugunov-stopham-eto-ne-proekt-eto-spravedlivost.html.

Verkhovskii, Aleksandr, and Emil Pain. "Civilizational Nationalism: The Russian Version of the 'Special Path.'" *Russian Politics and Law* 50, no. 5 (September 2012): 52–86. https://doi.org/10/gd53fk.

Vkontakte [Russian Social Network] Forum "Iakutiia Molodaia 2010." "Forum 'Iakutiia Molodaia-2010.'" Accessed March 14, 2023. https://vk.com/club17915414.

Vkontakte [Russian Social Network] Kamen' protiv™. "Kamen' Protiv: Novyi God 2014," 2014. https://vk.com/video/@restrukt_000.

Vkontakte [Russian Social Network] SakhaSeliger 2013. "Photo 'Buluus'. Napravlenie 'Politika' (SakhaSeliger 2013)." Accessed February 22, 2023. https://vk.com/club50017940?z=photo-50017940_307631920%2Falbum-50017940_170272124%2Frev.

Vkontakte [Russian Social Network] SakhaSeliger. Napravlenie Molodezh Sela. "Photo 'Zariadka'. SakhaSeliger 2013. 'Molodezh' Sela' 1 Chast' [Youth of the Countryside. 1st Part]," 2013. https://vk.com/photo-50581938_307628215.

Vlasova, Mariia. "Aleksandr Khloponin poBALoval «prodvinutuiu» molodezh'." *Kommersant*. November 30, 2004. https://www.kommersant.ru/doc/529118.

Volkov, Vadim. "'Obshchestvennost': Russia's Lost Concept of Civil Society." In *Civil Society in the Baltic Sea Region*, edited by Norbert Götz and Jörg Hackmann, 63–74. Aldershot: Ashgate, 2003.

Volkov, Vadim. *Violent Entrepreneurs: The Use of Force in the Making of Russian Capitalism*. Ithaca, NY: Cornell University Press, 2002.

Vos'mukhina, Dar'ia. "Ot Momenta Priniatiia Resheniia Do Polnogo Pereezda v Melitopol' Proshlo Desiat' Dnei." *Higher School of Economics News*, February 20, 2023. https://www.hse.ru/our/news/816076827.html.

Wacquant, Loïc. *Body & Soul: Notebooks of an Apprentice Boxer*. Oxford: Oxford University Press, 2004.

Wacquant, Loïc. "Three Steps to a Historical Anthropology of Actually Existing Neoliberalism." *Social Anthropology* 20, no. 1 (February 2012): 66–79. https://doi.org/10/fzv34p.

Walker, John Charles. *Learning to Labour in Post-Soviet Russia: Vocational Youth in Transition*. BASEES/Routledge Series on Russian and East European Studies. Milton Park: Routledge, 2011.

Wang, Shensheng, Scott O. Lilienfeld, and Philippe Rochat. "Schadenfreude Deconstructed and Reconstructed: A Tripartite Motivational Model." *New Ideas in Psychology* 52 (January 2019): 1–11. https://doi.org/10/ggspzx.

Ward, Lizzie. "Caring for Ourselves?: Self-Care and Neoliberalism." In *Ethics of Care: Critical Advances in International Perspective*, edited by Marian Barnes, Tula Brannelly, Lizzie Ward, and Nicki Ward, 45–56. Bristol: Policy, 2015.

Wedel, Janine R. *Collision and Collusion: The Strange Case of Western Aid to Eastern Europe: 1989–1998*. New York: St. Martin's Press, 2001.

Weiss, Robert Stuart. *Learning from Strangers: The Art and Method of Qualitative Interview Studies*. New York: Free Press, 1995.

Wertsch, James V. "Blank Spots in Collective Memory: A Case Study of Russia." *The ANNALS of the American Academy of Political and Social Science* 617, no. 1 (2008): 58–71. https://doi.org/10/cm8jx6.

Wetherell, Margaret. "Feeling Rules, Atmospheres and Affective Practice: Some Reflections on the Analysis of Emotional Episodes." In *Privilege, Agency and Affect*, edited by Claire Maxwell and Peter Aggleton, 221–39. London: Palgrave Macmillan UK, 2013.

Williams, John A. *Turning to Nature in Germany: Hiking, Nudism, and Conservation, 1900-1940*. Stanford: Stanford University Press, 2007.

Wood, Elizabeth A. "Hypermasculinity as a Scenario of Power." *International Feminist Journal of Politics* 18, no. 3 (July 2016): 329–50. https://doi.org/10/gnqkx8.

Wooll, Maggie. "What Exactly Is Workforce Development?," September 14, 2021. https://www.betterup.com/blog/how-to-use-workforce-development-to-close-the-skills-gap.

Yaffa, Joshua. *Between Two Fires: Truth, Ambition, and Compromise in Putin's Russia*. 1st ed. New York: Tim Duggan Books, 2020.

Yurchak, Alexei. *Everything Was Forever, until It Was No More: The Last Soviet Generation*. Princeton: Princeton University Press, 2006.

Yurchak, Alexei. "Russian Neoliberal: The Entrepreneurial Ethic and the Spirit of 'True Careerism.'" *The Russian Review* 62, no. 1 (2003): 72–90. https://doi.org/10/bjf9hz.

Yusupova, Guzel. "Silence Matters: Self-Censorship and War in Russia." *PONARS Policy Memo*, January 19, 2023. https://www.ponarseurasia.org/silence-matters-self-censorship-and-war-in-russia/.

Zakharov, Nikolay. *Race and Racism in Russia*. London: Palgrave Macmillan, 2015.

Zhang, Li, and Aihwa Ong, eds. *Privatizing China: Socialism from Afar*. Ithaca, NY: Cornell University Press, 2008.

Ziehm, Jeanette, Gisela Trommsdorf, and Isabelle Albert. "Erziehungsstile." In *Dorsch – Lexikon Der Psychologie*, edited by Markus Antonius Wirtz, 529. Bern: Hogrefe, 2014.

Zimenkova, Tatjana. "Sharing Political Power or Caring for the Public Good?: The Impact of Service Learning on Civic and Political Participation." In *Education for Civic and Political Participation: A Critical Approach*, edited by Reinhold Hedtke and Tatjana Zimenkova, 171–88. Routledge Research in Education 92. New York: Routledge, 2013.

Zhurzhenko, Tatiana. "'Capital of Despair': Holodomor Memory and Political Conflicts in Kharkiv after the Orange Revolution." *East European Politics and Societies And Cultures* 25, no. 3 (2011): 597–639. https://doi.org/10/fw8g9r.

Zotov, Konstantin. Pionerskii lager'—baza kul'turnogo i zdorovogo otdykha ..., 1935, Poster RU/SU 1818, 29 x 41 in. (73.7 x 104.1 cm), Hoover Institution. https://digitalcollections.hoover.org/objects/23413/pionerskii-lager--baza-kulturnogo-i-zdorovogo-otdykha.

Zubarevich, N. V., and S. G. Safronov. "People and Money: Incomes, Consumption, and Financial Behavior of the Population of Russian Regions in 2000–2017." *Regional Research of Russia* 9, no. 4 (October 2019): 359–69. https://doi.org/10/gnbn29.

Zubarevich, Natalia V. "Four Russias: Human Potential and Social Differentiation of Russian Regions and Cities." In *Russia 2025: Scenarios for the Russian Future*, edited by Maria Lipman and Nikolay Petrov, 67–85. London: Palgrave Macmillan, 2013.

Zuev, Denis. "The Russian March: Investigating the Symbolic Dimension of Political Performance in Modern Russia." *Europe-Asia Studies* 65, no. 1 (2013): 102–26. https://doi.org/10/gm7mtc.

Index

For the benefit of digital users, indexed terms that span two pages (e.g., 52–53) may, on occasion, appear on only one of those pages.

activation, 83, 203. *See also* individual initiative
active:
    disposition towards life (*aktivnaia zhiznennaia pozitsiia*), 11, 127, 132, 135
    society, 123
    way of life, 137. *See also* healthy lifestyle
activism, 36, 41, 61
    and cultured behavior, 170–71, 192
    and patriotism, 132–38, 156–57, 192
    changing meanings of, 135–38
    compliant, 116, 165
    small, small-scale, 2, 116, 145, 192
    Soviet form of, 137–38
    systemic limits of compliant, 138–45
    youth activism, 169, 173, 199–201
activists, active people, active youth, 11, 63, 65, 80, 83, 89–90, 102, 107, 109, 111, 114, 134–36, 165, 185. *See also* individual initiative
campers' definition of, 135
Afanas'ev, Vasilii, 93, 140–41
Alibasov, Bari, 93–95
ALROSA, Diamonds Russia-Sakha, 57, 144
ambitions, 113, 142, 155, 165, 192, 202
ambitious youth, 1–2, 9, 12, 14, 146, 160
Anemone, Anthony, 166
Anti-*Biriusa,* Territory of Civic Activists (*Territoria grazhdanskikh aktivistov*), 65
apolitical, 37, 114–15
Arci, 36, 237 n15
army:
    sacrifice for, 5
    serving, 154, 178–179

Artek, summer camp, 42, 216, 220
Astafyev, Viktor, 78
attachment. *See* place, unconditional love for
authoritarianism:
    classic, 6
    flexible. *See* flexible authoritarianism
    subjective side of, 44–45
authoritarian:
    Erziehungsstil, 45, 50–52, 55, 67, 84, 95, 100–103, 108–9
    pedagogical style. *See* Erziehungsstil
    personality, 16, 45
    practices, 6, 12–13, 22, 37, 110, 112, 122, 158, 189–90
    social foothold, 191
    states, 3, 6, 12, 22, 26, 108, 110, 160, 170
    values, 12, 23–24, 45, 99, 189
Autonomous Soviet Socialist Republic (ASSR), 137–38

backwardness, characterizing, 116–31
Baden-Powell, Robert, 46
Balabanov, Alexei, 166
Ban, Cornel, 41
Banet-Weiser, Sarah, 160
Bei-sich-selbst-seyn, 42. *See also* self-fulfillment and self-realization
Beliaeva, Natal'ia, 116
beliefs, unquestioned, taken-for-granted, 6, 13, 20–21, 24, 41, 114, 172, 189, 193
Berezin, Mabel, 73, 75, 107
Biriusa Today, daily news format at youth-leadership camp, 6, 80, 88

308 INDEX

Biriusa, youth-leadership summer camp, 64
  ethical considerations of participation, 200–203
  foam party (*pennaia vecherinka*), 87
  funding, 75–77
  Intelligence Place, cafe, 79
  IT-center (*IT-tsentr*), 80
  location of, 77–78
  nomenclature of, 79
  symbolic scenery of, 77–85
  taking photographs at, 80
Biriusintsy, 31–34, 36–38, 79–80, 82–83, 87–88
Blee, Kathleen, 212
Blue Buckets Society, 164
Bocherova, Elena, 163
Bockman, Johanna, 20
Bodrenkova, Galina, 93
Bikbov, Aleksandr, 19–22
Borenstein, Elliott, 131
Borisov, Yegor Afanasyevich, 75, 92
Boy Scouts, 46
brain drain, 5, 73. *See also* emigration
branding, 7, 80, 160, 168
Bröckling, Ulrich, 21
Brother crime movies, 166–68
Brown, Wendy, 2
Buluus, summer leisure camp, 29

calisthenics (*zariadka*), 89, 100
can-do spirit, 26, 32, 69, 82, 85, 141, 189, 194, 235 n149
Career (*Kar'era*), magazine, 57
Cerny, Philip, 15
character work, creating suspense through, 181–85
China, 7, 17, 61, 105, 149, 188
Chugunov, Dmitry, 162–63, 166, 174–77
civic:
  defining, 254 n119
  life, government-sponsored, 70, 107, 163, 189–91
civilization, term, 18, 167
  Russian, 104
  Siberian-Russian, Oswald Spengler, 105, 154
  state, 73, 105
  uniqueness, 167

civilizational nationalism, 72, 171–72, 195
co-creators of government-sponsored civic life, 107, 163, 190
Cold War, 16, 36–37, 108, 257 n47
common good, 110, 118, 124, 126–27, 146, 157, 180
Communist Party of the Russian Federation (*KPRF*), 65, 123, 205–6
community of feeling, 85–92
competition, 4, 20, 57, 157–55
  as trait of transnational business masculinity, 169
  at youth-leadership summer camps, 85, 89, 100–101, 193–94
  at summer camps for children and pioneer camps, 48–49, 51–52, 54
  -based system not existent in Russia (campers' narratives), 122–23
  global, 15, 17, 60
  grant/project funding, 70, 107
  human beings as subjects of, 11
  state (Philip Cerny), 15
Connell, R. W., 169
conservative, 23, 111
  civil society groups, 170, 267 n71
  elite networks, 27
  future, 17, 159
  morals, 159, 161–65, 167, 171–73
conspiracy stories, 211
creators (*sozdateli*), 105
criticism towards Russian state in campers' narratives, 11, 110–12, 122, 156, 192–93
Crimea, annexing, 117, 167
cultural:
  form, 6, 13, 41–42, 62, 67–68, 70, 189, 204, 209
  sociology, 17
  understandings, 3, 12–15, 18, 116
cultural insider, support of, 205–7
Culture and Personality project, 16
culturedness (*kul'turnost'*), 47–50, 104, 108. *See also* cultured behavior
cultured behavior, 50, 60, 136, 137, 170, 192, 241 n44

Davydenko, Kirill, 95–96
dehumanization, 186–87
Dell, Michael, 79

democracy:
  in campers' narratives, 111–12, 133, 141
  and neoliberalism, 23–27, 189
  and Russia, 106, 118, 129–30
democratic:
  change, 25, 26, 254 n119
  consequences, 25
  Erziehungsstil, 25. *See also*
    Erziehungsstil
  group atmospheres, 25, 45, 99
  ideal, 26, 190, 195
development:
  affirming, as a value in and of itself, 114
  economic, 4, 10, 23–24, 35, 44, 75, 99, 114, 117–18, 157, 188
  local, 1, 64, 70, 131, 135
  national, 6, 56, 60, 134, 156
  self-development, 2, 9, 13, 42–43, 87, 109, 134–38, 141, 149–50, 157, 192, 203, 213
Diamonds Russia-Sakha (*ALROSA*), 57, 144
diaperology, 16
Direct Line with Vladimir Putin, 92
Discipline and Punish (Foucault), 45
dorogi I duraki, 119–20. *See also* proverbs
Durkheim, Emile, 87

Easton, David, 14, 112
economic growth, 4, 5, 7, 10, 14, 21, 64, 159, 189
  globally circulating images of, 15–19
egoism, 126–29, 131–32, 155–56. *See also* individualism
Ekspert (magazine), 56
Elster, Jon, 42
emigration, 10, 73, 113, 145–52
Emotional Bank Account, 98
empirical research, 197–99
  ethical considerations, 200–203
  gaining entrée, 198–200
  initial sampling, 198–200
  participation, 203–4
  semistructured interviews, 207–8
  theoretical sampling, 205–7
engineering the soul, 20
entrepreneurial:
  literacy, 70, 106–9, 190
  patriot, 73–74
  spirit, 56
  start-up culture, 28–40, 192
  success, 20, 165
  type, heroic, 10–11
entrepreneurs (*predprinimateli*),
  entrepreneurial individuals, 15, 105, 189. *See also* vigilante–entrepreneurs
entrepreneurship, 20, 23, 41, 75, 163, 173, 203
Erziehungsstil:
  and group atmospheres, 45
  and culturedness, 104
  and dialogical teaching atmospheres at camp, 108
  and summer camp tradition, 108
  authoritarian, 45, 50–52, 55, 67, 84, 95, 99–104, 108–9
  democratic, 24
  dominant at camp, 92, 95, 100–104
  in campers' narratives, 99, 100–104, 109
ethno-cultural groups (*natsional'nosti*), 48, 105. *See also* nationality
European Union-Ukraine Association Agreement, 72

Federal Agency for Youth Affairs. *See* Rosmolodezh
females, villainizing. *See* women, villainizing
Fidesz, political party, 27
financial literacy, 70
first-hand story, 28
flexibilization, 191
flexible:
  capitalism (Richard Sennett), 60, 186
  demands of the market, 159
  labor policy, 8
flexible authoritarianism:
  and innovation-based economic growth, 3, 15–19
  and possibilities for self-realization, 4
  and self-fulfillment, 26, 42
  and social media brands, 173
  beyond Russia, 6–9, 17, 165, 167, 186–87
  campers' acceptance of, 110–12, 158, 193
  defining, 6–8, 188
  enforcing/stabilizing, 6, 30, 96, 161, 162, 185–87

flexible authoritarianism (*cont.*)
  in comparison to "authoritarian neoliberalism," 22
  in Russia, 5, 17, 66, 108, 159–60
  individualist quests for change and, 110–112, 155–158
  invested with emotional significance, 69–70, 71–75
  legitimacy and, 26, 41, 43, 55, 71–75, 155, 160, 165–72, 185–87
  life under, 4, 69, 106, 161, 164–65
  and social policies, 142, 165
flexibility:
  defining, 9
  as economic imperative, 7, 12, 22
  institutions promoting, 21
  lack of, 9
  legitimating authoritarian practices, 13
  as mindset/technique, 9–12
  and patriotism, 154–55
  praise of, 9
  in Russia, 55
fostering national cultures (*nasazhdat' national'nuiu kul'turu*), 153
Foucault, Michel, 44–45
"Foundation for National Perspectives" (*Natsional'nye Perspektivy*), 75
Fourcade-Gourinchas, Marion, 160
Frast, rapper, 178
FSB, Russia's Federal Security Service, 39

Gabdulhakov, Rashid, 161
Gaidar, Arkadi, 50
Gayropa, Putinist neologism, 167
gde rodilsia, tam I prigodilsia, 147–50. *See also* proverbs
Gel'man, Vladimir, 17
gender norms, 26, 167–68, 183
Geyer, Dietrich, 16
Glasius, Marlies, 12–13
Gorer, Geoffrey, 16
goskontrakty, 163
government-sponsored civic life. *See* civic
Government-sponsored summer camps, *see* youth-leadership summer camps
grants, 4, 38, 63, 66, 73, 161–62, 164, 175, 190–91
  competition. *See* competition
  governing through project, 104, 106
  writing, 69, 73, 106
Great Patriotic War, 11, 130, 193. *See also* war
Green Party. *See* Yabloko
Greene, Samuel A., 13, 191
Gryboedov, Alexander, 151
Gureev, Konstantin, 63

health certificates (*spravki*), 28, 55, 85
healthy lifestyle, *zdorovyi obraz zhizni* (*ZOZh*), 84, 96, 136, 137, 142–144
Heidegger, Martin, 18
Hellbeck, Jochen, 42
hero, heroism, 80–81, 131, 156, 165–66, 169, 175, 180, 185
  heroic masculinity. *See* masculinity
  traditional/classic heroism, 173, 180
  vigilante hero, 166–68, 184. *See also* Brother crime movies
Higher Komsomol School, 53
Hirsch, Francine, 153
historical periods, connected to legitimation of Putinism, 18, 118, 209
Hitlerjugend, 74
Hitler, Adolf, 23
homo faber, 25
hooliganism, as opposed to culturedness, 130, 170, 190
hooray-patriotism (*ura-patriotizm*), 10
human capital, 5, 10–11, 20, 57, 70
Hungary, as example for flexible authoritarianism, xi, 6–7, 17, 21, 27, 165, 188–89
Huntington, Samuel, 18
hypermasculinity. *See* masculinity

ID badge (*beidchik*), 30, 100–104, 211. *See also* youth-leadership summer camps
ideals, informing flexible authoritarianism:
  defining, 17–18
  neoliberal modernization, 5, 19–20, 25–26, 96, 159, 190–91
  neotraditional, 18, 96, 106–8, 110–12, 127, 161, 172, 188, 190, 194, 204
image/brand (*imidzh/brend*), 56. *See also* branding

imperial nationalism, 188, 195. *See also* civilizational nationalism
indifference as character trait, 110, 117, 118, 124–31, 154, 155–57, 161, 185, 214
individualist quests for change, 2, 192
  and striving for development, 155–58
  as arising from coexistence of criticism and loyalty, 110–16
  as precondition of being active/patriotic, 131–38
  characterization of backwardness, informing, 116–31
  systemic limits of, 138–45
individual:
  gain, 180
  initiative, 42, 48, 55, 83, 114, 133, 141. *See also* patriotism, activists
  pursuit of happiness, 157
  shortcomings of fellow citizens, 2, 138
  success, 2–3, 6, 157
individualism:
  modern (Charles Taylor), 25–26
  in campers' narratives, 121, 128, 174. *See also* egoism
  in Soviet times, 45
Industri Energi, 144
initiative. *See* individual initiative
innovator-person (*chelovek- innovator*), 61
Inochkin, Kostia, 50–51
innovation, 15, 23–24
  -based economic growth, 4–5, 24, 188, 195
  in youth politics, 60, 65, 72, 75, 77, 98, 203–4
inspiration (*vdokhnovenie*), 9, 11
International Association of Economic and Social Councils and Similar Institutions (AICESIS), 215
interview narratives, 208
interviewees, recruiting, 208–10
interviews:
  analysis of, 213–15
  building rapport, 212–13
  in numbers, 210–12
  participant observations, 215–16
  recruiting interviewees, 208–10
  structuring, 207–8

It's Bigger than Hip-Hop (song), 92

James, William, 35
Jobs, Steve, 79

Kamen' Protiv (Rock Versus), 171
Kamenka, 38
Kelly, Catriona, 47
Khloponin, Aleksandr, 44, 56, 58, 128, 191
  Lion Versus (*Lev Protiv*), 159–61, 191
  Stop Rudeness (*StopKham*), 107, 119, 159–66, 190
Khrushchev, Nikita, 50
Kirensky, Leonid, 35, 78
KKSO, Krasnoyarsk Region's Student Brigades (*Krasnoyarskie Kraevye Stroitel'nye Otryady*), 59, 64. *See also* student brigades
Klimov, Elem, 50
Klub veselykh i nakhodchivykh. *See* KVN
Komsomol, 60, 114, 126, 170. *See also* Soviet Youth League
Komsomoltsy (members of today's Leninist Communist Youth League), 114–15, 123, 128, 130, 141, 155
Kozlov, Oleg Vasil'evich, 151
Krasnoyarsk Region, Central Siberia, 38, 44, 56–60, 62, 66, 90–91, 95, 111, 115–17, 119, 122, 125, 129, 146–48, 152–54, 191, 210–11, 215
Krasnoyarsk Region's Student Brigades (*Krasnoyarskie Kraevye Stroitel'nye Otryady*). *See* KKSO
Kupriyanov, Boris, 88
KVN, "Club of the Merry and the Sharp-Witted" (*Klub veselykh i nakhodchivykh*), 54, 62, 64

law-and-order initiatives, 159, 161, 169–70. *See also* Lion Versus, Restrukt, Stop Rudeness, vigilante entrepreneurs
lawlessness, theme, 130, 163–66, 173–76
Lazutin, Mikhail, 162, 171–72, 176, 178–79, 184. *See also* Lion Versus
idti v nogu so vremenem, 132–34. *See also* proverbs
Lebed, Aleksandr, 58
Lebensreform, movement, 74

legitimacy, political, 3, 6, 75. *See also* loyalty, legitimation
  as opposed to loyalty, 14
legitimation, 73,168. *See also* legitimacy, loyalty
  and cultural understandings, 12–15
  defining, 3
  flexible authoritarian ideals central for, 17. *See also* ideals
  sources of, 13–14, 41–42, 168, 189
Leninist Communist Youth League of the Russian Federation (*Leninskii kommunisticheskii soiuz molodezhi Rossisskoi Federatsii, LKSM RF*), 114, 205
Leonov, Artiom, 176–81
Lev Protiv Pedofilov (Lion Versus Pedophiles), 171
Lev Protiv. See Lion Versus
Lewin, Kurt, 45
LGBTQI, 37–38, 104, 188
Libman, Alexander, 116
Lion Versus (*Lev Protiv*), 159–61, 190
literacy, entrepreneurial. *See* entrepreneurial literacy
Lomonosov, Mikhail, 78
Lord of the Rings, The, 139–40
loyalty, 1, 4–7, 14, 25, 41, 58, 69, 75, 112–13, 116, 160, 162. *See also* individualist quests
Luehrmann, Sonja, 98
Lukashenko, Aleksandr, 3
Luker, Kristin, 200–203

Maidan Revolution, 108, 167
Makarenko, Anton, 48
Makarov, Andrei, 171
manager of managers (*nachal'nik nachal'nikov*), 139–40
managers becoming governors, 56–59
Martsinkevich, Maxim, 171
Marxism, 42
masculinity:
  crisis of, 169, 173–74, 186
  heroic, 168–69, 185–87
  hypermasculinity, 168
  neoliberal, 169
  performing, 165–72, 185–87
material well-being (*zhit' luchshe*), 132, 154, 192
McRobbie, Angela, 44, 85
Mead, Margaret, 16
meaning-making, 13–14. *See also* cultural understandings
Medvedev, Dmitry, 62
Memorial, organization, 114
Menzel, Jiří, 50
Mestnye (the Locals), 171–72
migalki, 164. *See also* Blue Buckets Society
militaristic:
  daily regime at camp, 109
  educational measures and symbolism, 46–47
  installations at *Seliger,* 64
Milonov, Vitali, 162
modernization, 5, 10, 15, 17, 20, 25–26, 57, 67, 79, 96, 107–8, 148, 155, 159, 188, 190–92, 194. *See also* neoliberal modernization ideals
mokhnataia lapa, 121–24. *See also* proverbs
Molodaia Gvardiia (Young Guard of United Russia), youth organization, 171
Moore, Sally, 73
moral:
  diagnosis of social wrongs, 3, 110, 128, 150, 158, 160, 185–87
  education in Soviet times, 47
  force of modernity, 25–26
  panic, 170
  society, longing for/building, 156, 160
Moscow, 1
Mosfilm, 50
motherland
  big, 153–54
  small, *malaia Rodina,* 153
  sense of, 152–55
Movement Against Illegal Immigration (*Dvizhenie protiv nelegal'noi immigratsii*), 171
multinational:
  constitutive people, 18, 72, 167
  country, 117
  history of the country and region, 145
  Yakutia, 150

INDEX 313

muzhik, 174, 178, 190
Myerhoff, Barbara, 206

Nashi, government-sponsored youth group, 34–35, 43, 163–65
narratives. *See also* story/stories
 governmental, regarding Russo-Ukrainian war, 5, 67–68, 114, 193
 legitimating flexible authoritarianism in Russia, 5, 11, 14, 67–68, 110, 114, 118, 129, 131, 158, 192–93
 legitimation, 13
 nineties (1990s), dominant narrative, 129–31, 131
 Russia as hero, 131
nationality, *natsional'nost'*, *natsional'nosti*, 1, 30, 33, 35, 78, 153, 209
neformaly, 63
Nemov, Alexei, 162
neo-Foucauldians, 19–20
neoliberal:
 governmentality, 20, 204
 masculinity, 169
 mindset, 20
 modernization ideals. *See* ideals
 reforms, 19, 21, 56
 repurposing, 42
 techniques, 7, 22, 25, 191
neoliberalism. *See also* flexible capitalism
 and authoritarianism, 22–27
 and democracy, 22–27
 as ideal mode of modernization (myth), 15
 conceptualizing, 20–21
 as a force from outside, legitimating authoritarian practices, 21–22
 economic growth and, 15–19
 neo-Foucauldian, 19–20
 state and, 19–22
 subjective side of, 44–45
neotraditional:
 ideals. *See* ideals
 morals, 165–66
 policies, 188, 215
 values, 22, 95, 99, 198
neotraditionalism, 17, 69
new heroic character, styling of, 173–81
New Soviet Person, 42, 47

nichego ne znaiu, moia khata s kraiu, 124–31. *See also* proverbs
Nikolaev, Mikhail Efimovich, 129
Nikulin, Yuri, 125
non-governmental organizations (NGOs), 69
nonheterosexual intimate relationships, 37–38
Norilsk Nickel, company, 44, 56–57, 58, 128
Norilsk, Krasnoyarsk Region, 142
Northern Caucasus Federal District, Russia, 66
nuzhnye liudi, 121–24. *See also* proverbs

obshchenie (conversation), term, 90
oprichnik, term, 179
Orange Revolution, 34, 43, 72
Orange Threat, 43, 238 n12
Orbán, Viktor, 7, 27
Orlenok, 50
Orlov, Aleksei Ivanovich, 93–94
"Our Army," youth political project, 75

Pain, Emil, 72
Papp, Anatoly, 169
patriotism. *See also* unconditional love for place
 altruistic, 156
 and career-advancement, 85, 157
 and development, 157
 and emigration, 148
 as being active, 157, 164, 192
 heroic, 10, 159
 hooray-, 10, 192
 local, 154
 Russian, 105, 203
 striving for, 5, 155–58
patriot, of the country, 146
persona, concept, 168–69
personal development. *See* self-improvement training
Peter the Great, 133
Piglets Versus (*Khrushi Protiv*), 119
pioneer camps. *See* summer camps for children
pioneer camps, *Erziehungsstil* at, 49–55
pioneers. *See* Young Pioneers

place, unconditional love for, 146–47. *See also* patriotism
gde rodilsia, tam i prigodilsia, 147–50
vezde khorosho gde nas net, 150–55
plot, creating suspense through, 181–85
political legitimacy. *See* legitimacy
political spectacle, summer camp as, 73–75. *See also* political ritual
political support, 72–74, 105, 158, 193. *See also* legitimacy; loyalty
popification, creating suspense through, 181–85
Potanin, Vladimir, 58
potential strategic elites, 4–7, 22, 26, 69, 191
    ambitious youth, 1–2, 9, 13, 14, 146, 160
    up-and-coming youth, 5, 25, 191
Potolicchio, Sam, 71
power vertical, 129–30
presidential grants, 175
project, 10, 35, 63, 66, 92, 107, 140–42, 145
    conveyor (*proektnyi konveier*), 104
    and federal youth politics, 58, 70, 75–76, 116, 162–63, 177, 190, 197–98. *See also* vigilante projects
    ideas conceived/realized by campers, 33–34, 38, 97, 104, 109, 111, 141, 145, 158, 192, 199, 209
    management training, 9, 32, 35, 69, 73, 93–100, 106, 109, 203, 213. *See also* youth-leadership summer camps
    and regional youth politics, 35, 58, 62, 64, 66, 82
    thinking in (*proektnoe myshlenie*), 97
    vigilante. *See* vigilante projects
Prokhorov, Mikhail, 58
proverbs:
    dorogi i duraki, 119–20
    gde rodilsia, tam i prigodilsia, 147–50
    Idti v nogu so vremenem, 132–34
    mokhnataia lapa, 122–23
    nichego ne znaiu, moia khata s kraiu, 124–31
    nuzhnye liudi, 121–24
    rodina tam, gde my v teple, 154
    spustia rukava, 118–21
    vezde khorosho gde nas net, 150–55
Ptak, Ralf, 23

Public Chamber, public consultation body, 162, 215
Public Verdict, organization, 169
Pushkin, Alexander, 105
Pussy Riot, 37
Putin, Vladimir, 2–3, 5, 7, 58, 64, 66, 73, 122–23, 129, 162, 167
Putinism, 8, 13, 27, 43, 58, 62, 67, 72, 78, 100, 123, 154, 159–60 , 172, 197, 209

racism, 111, 144–145, 149, 152, 171, 214
reform pedagogy, 46
regime, underlying order of political (and economic) life
    authoritarian, 14, 112
    defining, 1, 4
    flexible authoritarian, 6, 14, 41, 75, 110–112, 158, 161, 165, 167, 169, 191, 193
    legitimation of, 6, 12–14, 41, 69, 73–75, 191, 193, 203
    neoliberal (Richard Sennett), 186–87
    opposition, 176
    staging support for, 69, 108, 159–61
    stability, 14
regime change, 4
register mechanism, 115–16
Reichskanzler, 23
reinvigorating Soviet youth engagement, 59–65. *See also* youth engagement
Representation of the Sakha Republic in Moscow, 215
Republic of Sakha (Yakutia), 1, 28, 71, 76, 125–26, 150, 199, 202, 215, 249 n24
Restrukt, 171
Riabov, Oleg, 167, 174
Riabova, Tatiana, 167, 174
ritual, political, 73–75. *See also* political spectacle
Robertson, Graeme B., 13, 191
rodina tam, gde my v teple, 154. *See also* proverbs
Rosmolodezh, Federal Agency for Youth Affairs, 5, 38, 43, 75–76, 93, 94, 151, 163
Rossiia Molodaia (Young Russia), youth organization, 171
"Run After Me" (*Begi za mnoi*), youth political project, 136

INDEX   315

Russia:
    backwardness in campers' narratives, 116–18
    "Great Russian national character," 16
    as hero in public stories and government-promoted narratives, 131, 156
    immigration threat and, 105
    invading Ukraine, 188–89, 191
    lawlessness as theme in, 166
    1990s dominant narrative, 129–31. See also nineties
    striving for development/patriotism in, 155–58
"Russia and the Contemporary World" (Rossiia i sovremennyi mir), textbook, 99, 105
"Russia— Country of Possibilities" (Rossiia— strana vozmozhnostei), NGO, 66
russkii, term, 153
Rüstow, Alexander, 23

Sakha Ministry for Youth and Family Policy, 29
Sakha Republic, 29–30, 38, 57, 75, 77, 87, 91, 111, 113, 116–18, 120–22, 127, 129–30, 145, 149–53
SakhaSeliger, youth-leadership summer camp, 28, 64, 131. See also *Sinergiia Severa* (Synergy of the North)
    arriving at, 29–31
    design of, 31–33
    ethical considerations of participation, 200–203
    founding of, 72
    history of, 75–77
    rustic setup at, 38–40
Sakwa, Richard, 8
Sauer, Birgit, 169
Savina, Ekaterina, 64
Schröder, Ina, 102
Schumpeter, Joseph, 10, 23–24, 189
Scott, James C., 74
self:
    -development, in campers' narratives, 2, 9, 13, 42–43, 87, 109, 110–58
    -fashioning, 173–81
    -fulfillment. See also self-realization
    -improvement, 20, 25, 32, 35, 42, 70, 93–100. See also neoliberal techniques
    -realization, 26, 42, 63, 113, 156. See also *Bei-sich-selbst-seyn*
Seliger, youth-leadership summer camp, 30, 34–36, 43, 65, 75, 200
Sennett, Richard, 9, 25, 186
Sinergiia Severa (Synergy of the North), youth-leadership summer camp, 215. See also SakhaSeliger
skauty, 46
Slobodian, Quinn, 23
Slyck, Abigail van, 46
Snowden, Edward, 36–38
Sobyanin, Sergey, 117
Sochi Olympics, 122
"Social Activity" (*sotsial'naia aktivnost'*), government-sponsored volunteer program, 66
social change. See also individualist quests for change
    apolitical understanding of, 114
    democratic, 26
    large-scale, 133
    prospects of, 11, 136
social media entertainment, 161, 168, 173, 186, 190
soft skills, 36, 48, 60, 69, 97, 204
Song, Hae-Yung, 22
South Korea, 22
Sovereign Democracy, ridiculed, 123–24
Soviet:
    traditions in service of flexible authoritarianism, 41–44
    nationality politics, 30
    summer camp tradition, 45–55
    youth engagement, 56–65, 71
Soviet Union, 16, 30, 34, 42, 46, 53, 59, 60–62, 128, 131, 188
Soviet Youth League *Komsomol*, 60, 114, 126, 170. See also Komsomol
Spengler, Oswald, 18, 105
Sperling, Valerie, 168
spy rumors at camp, 33–38
Sporteks (the Center for Extreme Sports), 34–35, 77
state, neoliberalism and, 19–22

state funding of youth-leadership summer camps, limits of, 161–65
state youth politics:
  federal, 66
  Krasnoyarsk, 58
  Putinist, 43, 67, 84
  regional youth politics as inspiration for, 43–44, 65–68
  Russian, 34, 185, 197
  Soviet, 65
  standard narrative of evolution of, 65–68
Stepanenko, Viktor, 105–6, 131, 167
Stop Rudeness (StopKham), 107, 119, 159–62, 190
  origins of, 165–66
  state funding, 161–65
story/stories:
  brand defined as, 160
  career/success, 112–13, 140–41
  first-hand, 28
  global story of modernity, 79
  governmentally-enforced, 114, 172, 185
  moral, 185
  of indifference to warfare, 126
  public/collective, 13, 18, 53, 114, 118, 123, 129–30, 151
  regarding Russia, 11, 78, 104, 131, 156
  of Russia's former wars, 11
  of "self-change, redemption and personal triumph," 3
  told in/through videoclips, 165, 172
storytelling, 13, 93, 95, 182–85
strategic elites, 6–8. See also potential strategic elites
"Strong People" (Sil'nye liudi), personal development business, 95, 96
student brigades (studencheskie stroitel'nye/ trudovye otriady), 58–65, 115, 190–91. See also KKSO
success, circulating images of, 15–19
Sukhoveiko, Galina, 53
summer camps. See youth-leadership summer camps and summer camps for children
summer camps for children (ozdorovitel'nye detskie lageria), 49–55, 89–90, 100, 209
  competition at. See competition
  culturedness and, 47–49
  dominant Erziehungsstil at, 49–55
  as form of education, 45–46
  political character of Soviet, 49
  Soviet tradition of. See Soviet summer camp tradition
  Young Pioneers, 47–49
symbolic scenery, at youth-leadership summer camp, 77–85
Szikra, Dorottya, 166

Tavrida, youth-leadership summer camp, 107
Taylor, Charles, 25–26
"Territory of Thoughts" (Territoriia Smyslov), youth-leadership summer camp, 107
"Territory of Youth Taking Initiative." See Biriusa, camp
theoretical sampling, 205–7
time management (taimmenedzhment), 59
To the Slanderers of Russia (Pushkin), 105
Toynbee, Arnold J., 18
tradition, defining, 42. See also Soviet summer camp tradition
transnational:
  audiences of vigilante brands, 168–69
  business/self-help culture, 10, 15
  elite networks, conservative, 27
  ideals, informing flexible authoritarianism, 17. See also ideals
  flows and cultural understandings, 15–20
  power of authoritarian governments, 7
  rise of authoritarianism, 13
  salience of heroic/business masculinity, 168–169
troops (otriady), 50
Tsarist Russia, 45–46
Tsipursky, Gleb, 170
Tszyu, Kostya, 149
Tuimaada, airport, 29

Ukraine, 5–8, 188–89, 191
unconditional love. See place, unconditional love for
underresourced groups, non-solidarity with, 141–42

understandings, cultural, 3, 12–15, 18, 116. *See also* beliefs, unquestioned
university jingle, 80–85. *See also Biriusa*, camp
up-and-coming youth, 5, 25, 191. *See also* potential strategic elites
Urban, Michael, 140
Usad'ba Buluus, 29–30

Verkhovsky, Alexander, 72
vezde khorosho gde nas net, 151–55. *See also proverbs*
vigilante:
  -entrepreneurs, 159, 165–66, 168
  analyzing videos of, 172–73
  brands, 168, 172–73, 185–87. *See also* law-and-order initiatives
  heroic, 181, 190
  projects, 171. *See also* law-and-order initiatives, vigilante brands
vigilantism. *See also* law-and-order initiatives
  digital in Russia, 171
Volkov, Vadim, 166
volunteer patrols, 170. *See also* Soviet youth engagement

war:
  and egoism in campers' narratives, 126–28
  and emigration, 5
  Cold. *See* Cold War
  critic of, 78
  economy, 5, 195
  fear of, in 2014, 117, 126, 212
  Great Patriotic, 11, 130, 193. *See also* Great Patriotic War
  in memory politics, 126
  joke regarding, 125, 156
  on Ukraine, 8, 12, 13, 22, 27, 67, 188, 193, 257 n47
  veterans, 50, 59, 176
"We Are *Biriusa*" (*My Biriusa*), song, 87
"We are Multinational Russians" (*My Rossiiane*), lecture, 72, 111
Weber, Max, 3
Welcome, or No Trespassing (film), 49–55
Wetherell, Margaret, 20, 74

willpower, 142–43
women, villainizing, 181–85
Wood, Elizabeth, 168, 175

Yabloko, Green party, 38, 114
Yakutsk, 1, 28–30, 132, 202
Year of Youth, 66
Yeltsin, Boris, 61, 170
"You Are an Entrepreneur," youth political program, 180
Young Active Citizens Award, 63
Young Pioneers, 47–49, 60, 74
Young South (*Iug molodoi*), youth-leadership summer camp, 5–6
Youth Educational Forums. *See* youth-leadership summer camps
youth, young adults:
  ambitious. *See* potential strategic elites
  up-and-coming. *See* potential strategic elites
youth engagement. *See also* activism, activists
  entrepreneurial spirit and, 56
  reinvigorating Soviet, 59–65
"Youth of Russia 2000–2025," report, 57
Youth School for Entrepreneurship (*Molodezhnaia shkola predprinimatel'stva*), 163
youth-leadership summer camps, 38, 76, 110, 197
  activism at, 136–37
  as political spectacle, 73–75
  authoritarian *Erziehungsstil* at, 92–106
  average peers at, 91
  Biriusa, youth-leadership summer camp. *See Biriusa*
  community of feeling at, 85–92
  competitions at. *See* competition
  consequences of participation in, 203–4
  education at, 81–82, 92–93
  ethical considerations of participation, 200–203
  ID badge (*beidchik*) at, 30, 100–104, 211. *See also* ID badge
  overt political appeals to campers at, 104–6
  participant observations at, 215–16
  project management training at. *See* project management training

youth-leadership summer camps (*cont.*)
  SakhaSeliger. *See SakhaSeliger* and *Sinergiia Severa* (Synergy of the North)
  self-improvement training, 93–100
  Seliger, youth-leadership summer camp. *See Seliger*
  selecting campers for, 70–71
  show at, 85–92
  soft techniques at, 104–6
  spy-rumors at, 33–38
  symbolic scenery, 77–85
  teaching entrepreneurial literacy, 106–9
  "Territory of Thoughts" (*Territoriia Smyslov*), youth-leadership summer camp. *See* "Territory of Thoughts"
  TIM Biriusa. *See Biriusa*
  VIP guests at, 38–39, 69, 71, 91–92, 113, 140–41
  Young South (*Iug molodoi*), 5–6
  Tavrida, youth-leadership summer camp. *See Tavrida*
  typical organizations campers were involved in, 114–16, 203
YouTube, analyzing videos from, 172–73

Zhukov, Aleksandr, 64
Zuern, Elke, 172

The manufacturer's authorised representative in the EU for product safety is Oxford
University Press España S.A. of El Parque Empresarial San Fernando de Henares,
Avenida de Castilla, 2 – 28830 Madrid (www.oup.es/en or product.safety@oup.com).
OUP España S.A. also acts as importer into Spain of products made by the manufacturer.

Printed in the USA/Agawam, MA
August 8, 2025

891696.007